FINCH, BLOODY FINCH

Also by Elaine Dundy

The Dud Avocado
The Old Man and Me
The Injured Party

Finch, Bloody Finch

A BIOGRAPHY OF PETER FINCH

Elaine Dundy

LONDON
MICHAEL JOSEPH

First Published in Great Britain by
Michael Joseph Ltd
44 Bedford Square
London WC1
1980

ISBN 0 7181 1904 5

Printed by Hollen Street Press, Slough
and bound by Redwood Burn Ltd. Trowbridge and Esher.

Author's Note

I have selected for use the adjective "bloody" in my title as the word best able to intensify such various meanings to the description of my Subject as unequivocally, utterly, essentially, irresistibly, hilariously, sanguinely, pathetically, tragically and monstrously. The reader may decide which meaning to apply when in the text.

Contents

List of Illustrations

Acknowledgements

To acknowledge my debt to everyone (both the living and the dead) who helped me in the preparation of this biography would be rather like rewriting the index. I would, however, especially like to thank the people of Australia who during my five-month stay in their country responded so enthusiastically to my appeals on Radio, TV and in the Press for information on Peter Finch's early years. Of them I would like to single out John Carter, Paul Brickhill, Marie Amos (Gillespie), Ralph Peterson, Redmond Phillips and Enid Lorimer for their invaluable assistance.

I also owe a great debt of gratitude to Tamara Finch for giving me access to and permission to use her private papers and letters pertaining to Peter Finch and for our many discussions which followed. I wish to thank Bryan Ingle Finch for permission to print parts of letters from his father George Ingle Finch to his mother Gladys Ingle Finch.

To Rosemary Harris, Tony Britton, Diana Quiseekay, Olive Harding, Alan White, B.R. Whiting, Jill Bennett and Mike Maslansky, again my heartfelt thanks; as well as to the incomparable Joan St George Saunders for her wisdom, knowledge and laughter, to my amiable assistant Fiona Lindsay for her nimble-footed assistance, and finally to Tessa Welborn for instructing me in the little-known facts about the manners and *mores* of Jamaica.

I would also like to express my appreciation for the excellent and perceptive articles about Peter Finch written by Roderick Mann, Douglas Keay, the late George Johnston and to Anne Edwards for her fine biography of Vivien Leigh.

The author and publishers would like to thank George Allen & Unwin Ltd. for permission to quote an extract from *My Mother Who Fathered Me: Study of the Family in Three Selected Communities in Jamaica* by Edith Clarke.

Introduction

The astounding story of Peter Finch which began even before his birth is, to put it politely, unbelievable, and I spent a good half year staring at the facts in front of me, unable to believe them. Frankly they struck me as impossible. It was only when I came across the following sentence of P. G. Wodehouse "Never confuse the unusual with the impossible", that I saw the light. Peter Finch's life was unusual, yes. But it was not impossible. How could it have been? He lived it.

Peter Finch was a fine actor, touching genius I believe in certain performances. But that he was able to leave any mark on the world at all after a childhood and adolescence composed mainly of abandonment, chaos and cruelty is, perhaps, an even more impressive achievement.

By the time Peter was six years old, he had passed through the hands of three very different women and had lived in two very different countries. By the age of ten he was to pass through many more people's hands and bring the total up to four very different countries: England, France, India and Australia.

I met Peter Finch many times in the fifties. We both lived in London and frequented the same theatrical clubs, hang-outs and restaurants and attended the same theatrical parties. But it was not till 5 April 1958 that Peter came startlingly into my focus. It was Easter Sunday — the day of the first Aldermaston March to Ban the Bomb.

It was not exactly pouring with rain that day. The weather was more what the Irish call "soft", that is, wet and uncomfortable. I was trudging along with a group of friends on the march when suddenly I was hailed by someone who struck me as looking like the happiest man I had ever seen. I cannot remember ever having seen a smile so wide and welcoming, a face so overjoyed and excited. It took me a moment to realise that this jubilant figure ecstatically greeting me was Peter Finch. By that time in his career, in the words of his friend the novelist George Johnston, Finch's "young-old eroded face with the sharp deep-set eyes and gaunt cheekbones, the big sensual mouth and the spiky tangle of hair had long become a regular presence on the news-stands." To me he looked, standing there in the drizzle, wearing an old raincoat, a white shirt without a tie, a sports jacket, grey flannel trousers and loafers, like the handsomest postgraduate student at Princeton. No. He looked like I'd always wished F. Scott Fitzgerald had looked.

I introduced him to my friends, some of whom he already knew, and we all marched on. But with a difference. His happiness was contagious. He had changed the whole mood of our group (Doris Lessing? Tom Maschler? Clancy Sigal? Arnold Wesker?) from being slightly grim and a little earnest to being fun and funny.

I remember at the time my surprise that he was there at all. One expected the Redgraves of course and Peggy Ashcroft et al., full force — but Peter Finch? Somehow I would not have thought (if I'd ever taken time to think) that he would have put himself on the line about banning the bomb.

"What are you so happy about in this weather?" I remember asking Peter.

"Two things make me happier than anything in the world — " he replied, "a cause I believe in and walking."

Later that evening we were all drying out at my flat. He was sitting on the floor, I remember, perhaps that is why he seemed so young, and I was sitting in the chair next to him. We were talking about ideas, ideals and religions. I remember remarking how interesting I thought it was that Buddhism seemed to be getting such a grip on this generation.

"Ah, Buddhism," Peter said. "I know all about Buddhism. I was a Buddhist monk once."

I stared at him in disbelief. "You were?"

"I was about nine years old. My grandmother had very advanced ideas. She put me in a Buddhist monastery in India for a couple of years. She thought it would be good for me."

Looking down at the F. Scott Fitzgerald of my imagination, I was as filled with indignation as if he had told me his grandmother had sold him into slavery to satisfy some arcane whim of hers. My face must have registered my horror for Peter said quickly, "It was very interesting, you know. I really liked it.''

''But how did you escape? I mean — ?''

''The British authorities got wind of it and came and took me away.''

Peter looked very young sitting on the floor, but his face wore an expression that was completely unfathomable to me. For a moment. Then I understood. I let out a gasp. ''You would have liked to have *stayed* there!'' I said incredulously.

''Yes. I would have liked to have stayed there,'' he said. ''I'm still a Buddhist, you know.''

I felt a frisson. I had such an eerie feeling about Peter at that moment. And I think that even if I'd known then what I do now about the truth of his Buddhist experience I would still have had that eerie feeling. It stays with me still, my belief that part of him wanted to be a Buddhist monk; that motives of behaviour you look for in people in order to understand them better — ambition, the desire for success, the drive for money, status, possessions, power — never carried the same weight with him that they do for other people; that, in fact, perhaps the only two words that had any relevance for him were ''love'' and ''hurt''.

After Aldermaston we knew each other better; saw each other more. And with the shock of his unexpected death in 1977 many memories of him came flooding back to me. One was Peter arguing late into the night with a Catholic priest and saying ''I think a man dying on a cross is a ghastly symbol for a religion. And I think a man sitting under a bo tree and becoming enlightened is a beautiful one.'' Another was Peter just returned from Russia in the summer of 1961 where he had gone to collect his award for the Best Actor at the Moscow Film Festival for *The Trials of Oscar Wilde*. He was in a state of wild euphoria about Russia though I couldn't seem to pin him down to telling me exactly why.

Finally he said, ''Well, they pay *you* for interviews.''

''Ah,'' I said, ''money.''

''No,'' he corrected me, ''respect.''

Perhaps my most vivid memory of Peter Finch is due to the fact that it so directly concerned me. Yet realising now that his behaviour towards me on that day was typical of his behaviour in general on a film set, I feel it is worth setting down.

It was in 1962 and Peter was filming *In the Cool of the Day* in England with Jane Fonda. Meade Roberts, the screenwriter, rang me to say he had written a tiny part for a young writer at a cocktail party who, determined to get published, corners Peter (playing an important publisher) and gushes five lines of dialogue at him. Roberts thought it would be fun for me to play the role since I had once been an actress and was now a writer. I was reluctant; I hadn't acted for years and I was in the middle of a novel. But it was only one day's work, he argued, and he could get me a lot of money for it. Finally I agreed.

About a week later, script in hand and feeling rather tense, I went to the film studio and arrived on a set which consisted of two large rooms filled with a lot of dress extras. The Literary Scene. What I was about to do, as every actor knows, is not easy. In short, I had to wait while Peter, as guest of honour, entered first the large room, traversed it graciously greeting various extras, then entered the second room with more of the same. Only when he got within striking distance, was I to collar him and gush out my lines. When the time came I gushed out less than a third of them because my mind had gone completely blank.

They did the shot again. Enter Peter into the first room graciously greeting. Enter Peter into the second room with more of the same. Now was my turn and this time *nothing* came out. They did the shot again. And again. And again. Peter was standing in front of me (Take 10? Take 11?). He paused. Finally he said, gently puzzled, "Elaine, what is the matter with you?"

What was the matter with me? I was getting something wrong on every take and I was never going to get it right. I was going to be fired; good. But Meade Roberts was probably also going to be fired for giving me the part. And all those dress extras were going to be fired because the scene couldn't be shot. And then the director would have to be fired too and that meant that Peter would never be able to complete the film.

What was the matter with me? "I don't know, Peter," I said, "but I am *hysterical!*"

Peter looked around at the crew, at the extras now draped limply around the furniture. "Well," he said, "this isn't much of a party." And he went and ordered two cases of champagne. We all sat around drinking it. And we all became very happy. Now it was a party! And when we went back to work I got my lines right on the very next take.

I remember thinking at the time, you don't have to be a bull-fighter or a deep-sea fisherman to exhibit grace under pressure. Peter, by his graceful gesture, had saved my face and saved the day.

Peter Finch sustained himself through life by laughter and drink. But he sustained himself also by a faith that was both spiritual and philosophical and, more than anything, by his capacity for understanding and for love which produced in the actor a very rare and special communication with audiences.

Rosemary Harris discussing Peter Finch said: "Peter didn't act his parts. He *understood* them. He understood their love and their pain and it was *his* love and *his* pain." Then she paused for a moment and wondered aloud: "Where did the pain come from? I never found out."

Perhaps ultimately what I have been trying to uncover in this biography is what had happened in Peter's life that made it so necessary for him to communicate his love and pain as an actor to an audience.

Rather than keeping footnotes and source references separate from the text I have tried to include them in it whenever possible.

I was singularly fortunate in finding that as people warmed to the subject of Peter Finch, their description of events and their ramifications in his life took the form of remembered conversations with him. Very occasionally I have given myself a biographer's prerogative, as it were, to put a conversation Peter held with an intimate, unobtrusively into his thoughts, thus avoiding too many "As he later said to so-and-so".

Some of the events in Peter's jumbled and tumbled childhood which he himself remembered, or remembered people around him talking about at the time, go back as far as when he was six years old. As far back as six — but no further.

Let us then begin at that point.

Part One

CHAPTER 1

Laura's Legacy

Six-year-old Peter George Ingle Finch, living in the picturesque old village of Vaucresson on the outskirts of Paris, was an extraordinary child. He knew he was because his grandmother Laura always told him so. She told him he was clairvoyant, and that he had psychic powers though he couldn't quite understand what she meant. And then there was his gift of mimicry. He would suddenly imitate people — anyone who came to the house, his Uncle Antoine playing the piano, his Aunt Dorothy who was a nurse. It was eerie, it was so exact it was as if he were a medium and the voices were being transmitted through him.

Peter was extraordinary. He was also beautiful with blond curls, blue eyes, a seraphic smile and shapely hands and feet. He grew up a beautiful young man and an extraordinarily handsome older man. It was to be a mixed blessing.

Peter knew he was extraordinary because he had no mother or father, and everyone had a mother or father unless they were dead. But Peter's parents were not dead. They were Elsewhere. That was why he was living in France with grandmother Laura.

It began with Laura. Peter Finch's life revolves around his grandmother from Orange, Australia. Tall, brilliant, graceful and strong of will, at the age of thirty-five she had finally prevailed upon her elderly, indulgent husband, Charles Finch, to take her and their three children on a Grand Tour of Europe.

First, they visited their Finch connections in England of whom Charles was inordinately proud. The family seat of these Finches was Little Shelford in Cambridgeshire. The first Finch to come up in the world (and be rich enough to have a monument erected to him when he died) was William Finch, born in 1667. His son, also William Finch, a very successful merchant, did him one better and purchased the Manor of Little Shelford. Now that they were landed gentry their daughter Elizabeth married a wealthy neighbour, William Ingle. The Ingles then inherited Little Shelford and called themselves Finch Ingle. The son, William Finch Ingle, a bit of an upper-class dandy, went to Harrow and Oxford, was granted arms, bought two other estates, Swaton Prior and Sybille Hedding, and changed his name (mysteriously) to Finch Finch (or sometimes, ffinch ffinch).

The next William Finch Finch produced a son called Henry who went into the Church and became the Rector of Little Shelford. His eldest son, Charles Wray Finch, was born in 1808 and went into the army. As a Captain in the 17th Regiment of Foot, he and his other two brothers went off to Australia in the 1830s in search of adventure, land, and possibly escape from the Rectory. Charles Wray Finch flourished in Australia: he married one of the daughters of the scandalous Irish reprobate, Henry Croasdale Wilson, who was the first Police Magistrate in Australia, and amassed some 10,000 acres in Wellington, N.S.W., which he called Nubrygn Station. He also became Speaker of the House of Parliament in Sydney. He and his wife had nine children. The fourth was a son, Charles Edward Finch (born 1843). At the time he asked the radiant twenty-year-old Laura Isobel Black to be his wife, he was a respected and respectable widower who had been first a Land Surveyor and then Chairman of the Land Board in Orange, N.S.W. He was twenty-four years older than she but he adored her. As for Laura Black (born 1867) of Scots descent, her family's fortunes had fluctuated sharply. Her father, Philip Barton Black, had come to Australia from outside Glasgow, prospered, married an Australian-born woman, Catherine Cox, and owned a station "Clermont" in Queensland. However, by 1870, the Blacks appear to have lost their money and their station and had gone to live in Orange.

Although in later life, Laura was to say that she had been "sold" to Charles to pay off a debt of her father's, she dutifully married him and dutifully gave him three children, one after another, a year apart, beginning in 1888: George, Dorothy and Maxwell (after a Scottish connection of whom she was particularly proud).

After visiting England, the Finches cruised the Mediterranean, stopping at all the European capitals, always staying at the best hotels. Laura had met Nellie Melba, the Australian diva, and worshipped her, and she always carried with her a finely wrought silver box given to Charles by his grandfather, Henry Croasdale Wilson, which contained a piece of Melba toast. Upon arrival at each grand hotel, Laura would immediately enter the kitchen, open the silver box and say to the chef, "I wish to have my toast done like this."

Charles was delighted to see Laura flowering under the stimulus of Europe. She had been so distant, so withdrawn during the past year, absorbed only in her religious and philosophical books which he felt were giving her strange and unhealthy notions. Though a proper Victorian who didn't approve of women gallivanting around the world, he was, nevertheless, a kindly, fair-minded man. He understood how hard it was for her with her quick, eternally searching mind and her dreams and her youth, to live day after day in the spartan frontierism of the district of Orange or even in Sydney, though they had a fine house there in Greenwich Point, which he called Nubrygn after his father's station in Wellington. Besides, he had always promised her a trip abroad as soon as he could take the time off from his work.

Meanwhile Laura, blossoming, was undergoing many changes and arriving at many determinations as they travelled around Europe. And these determinations all rolled into one single huge one in the heady atmosphere of Paris: she was not going back to Australia. First, there were her children to consider. They must have their horizons widened too; they must be educated abroad — especially George, her eldest, who even at an early age was showing unmistakable signs of becoming a scientific genius in spite of his passion for scrambling up every mountain in sight. In England, he had insisted on and succeeded in climbing Beachy Head, difficult even for a grown-up. He was destined to rise above the crowd. Then, too, she had always been musical: she played the harp and had a pleasant singing voice. In Paris, she could have her voice properly trained! And she loved painting.

Paris in 1902 was the centre of art, of culture, of the intellect — and this was vital. In 1894, when Laura was twenty-seven, she had heard the great Theosophist Leader, Annie Besant, lecture on the doctrine of Theosophy, at the Sydney Opera House. She had preached about universal brotherhood, about a society without distinction of race, creed, caste, colour or sex. She had talked of the importance for everyone to study *comparative* religion, philosophy and science, of the need to investigate the unexplained laws of nature and the powers latent in man — the powers latent in man *and* the powers latent in women, Annie Besant had emphasised, for she was the world's great leader of women's rights. She was a powerful, spellbinding speaker, so powerful that Laura couldn't take her eyes off her, though at the end she lowered them and whispered, "I agree with every word you said." She had heard her rallying call.

In Paris, as they were entertained at parties and Embassies, Laura saw how much a woman was admired there not only for her looks but for her brains: admired and attended to and *talked* to. Men didn't talk to women in Australia, and certainly not in public. Fair-haired, blue-eyed Laura with her serene, perfectly-cut features and stately carriage, was gratified. Paris was heady stuff indeed.

At Laura's insistence, the Finches and their entourage were installed in luxurious apartments at No. 1 Rue Michelet, an imposing mansion overlooking the Jardin de Luxembourg. They were now the Ingle Finches, Laura having put back the family name, though reversed the order. A double-barrelled name might not go down well in Australia but in Europe it was very *à la mode*. Charles indulged her.

A year later, Charles decided enough was enough and the time had come for them to go back to Australia. He was nearly sixty, an internationally known authority on land law but out of place in Laura's salon of Bohemians in Paris. He had to go back to work; the Land Board in Southern Australia was waiting for him.

Laura refused to leave. George was astounding his tutor with his brilliance, and he was studying for the École de Médecin at the Sorbonne from where he would embark on an illustrious career. Dorothy and Max were doing well also, happy in their lessons and stimulated by Paris. It was out of the question to deny them this opportunity which, if not taken, they would all regret for the rest of their lives. If Charles had to go back, very well, then he should go and they would follow him at some later date. As he knew, she had many friends in Parisian artistic circles, some stemming from her involvement in the Theosophy Movement which was burgeoning in Paris. Also there was another man she loved. A painter called Konstant.

So Charles went back to Australia alone and he never again saw Laura, George or Max. Brokenhearted though he was, he continued to support Laura for the rest of his life and to pay for his children's education and upkeep. But he never again spoke her name.

The Ingle Finches never seemed to suffer any feelings of disloca-tion from Australia while they were in Paris. They very quickly became internationals in this international city. In 1904 after Charles had left, Laura gave birth to another son named Antoine

Konstant Finch. She was a will-o-the-wisp, swathed in tulle but with a will of iron. Strictly, she supervised her children's studies and strictly, she supervised their meals. If they didn't eat their porridge for breakfast, it would be served again for lunch, and if not eaten then, it would be served again for dinner — it would be served again until they did eat it. Cold, lumpy, glutinous porridge — George never forgot it. In his later years, whenever he had a stomach complaint, he would grumble "cold porridge". If Laura was strict about her children's activities, she was no less strict about her own. She flung herself into studies of ancient religions especially those of the mystical East.

Mainly through the work of Madame Blavatsky, who had founded the Theosophical Society, the wisdom of the East was attracting widespread interest in the West for the first time. The theosophists were also much concerned with spiritualism and the occult. It was a curious phenomenon of the Age of Science and Invention, this interest in the paranatural. Even a supreme rationalist like Arthur Conan Doyle — or so one would have supposed from his creation of that master of logic, Sherlock Holmes — became totally enmeshed in spiritualism, and such eminent scientists as Lumière, Sir Oliver Lodge and Professor Charles Richet were equally excited. As for theosophy, George Bernard Shaw, Thomas Edison, Yeats, Havelock Ellis, Rabindranath Tagore, Krishna Menon, Maeterlinck, Rudolf Steiner and Gandhi were some of those who had been either influenced or involved in it at one time or another. All the important and fashionable people of the day were dabbling in the new thought and the occult. Enthusiastically, Laura began participating in various psychical experiments. She translated learned papers on the subject from French and German. She began writing articles for a magazine called *Annals of Psychical Research* and eventually became its editor for four years. She and Queen Marie of Romania together wrote several tracts.

Young George Ingle Finch was violently opposed to his mother's activities. He had grown into a tall, exceedingly handsome, charming young man, with a hot temper and a mind of his own. His mother's salon bored and irritated him. He thought she should be back in Australia looking after his father. As for her theosophists and spiritualists, he could only think of one word: charlatans! How Laura must have struggled for the soul of her best loved child, using all of her not inconsiderable powers of persuasion to get him to see the light. She failed. George was always immune to persuasion. One man in Laura's entourage, however, whom he did respect was Sir Oliver Lodge. At the Sorbonne, he had found his interest in medicine shifting to physical chemistry and it was to Sir Oliver that he went to seek advice. He wished to go into the field of chemistry: should he go to Cambridge and back to his English ancestors, in Little Shelford, which was just outside Cambridge? Sir Oliver strongly advised him to go to Zurich. Only there would he get what he wanted.

At nineteen, George went to the University of Zurich. Happily away from his mother's attempts at domination, he paused by one curious wayside. He studied piano with the Maestro Schnabel for a year. At the end of it, he said to Schnabel, "Tell me truthfully, how good am I?" "You are first-rate second-rate," said Schnabel. "I thought so," said George and left the piano for ever.

In everything else that he attempted in Zurich, he was first-rate first-rate. He excelled in his studies and he was the gold medallist in science for his year. Summer and winter he indulged his passion for climbing mountains. His exploits in the Alps were legendary. Count Aldo Bonocossa, a well-known Italian climber, has written of that time: "The recognised No. One mountaineer and most outstanding personality by far was George Ingle Finch."

In 1912, he elected to embark on an academic career and went to England as a demonstrator at the Imperial College of London where he remained on and off for the rest of his life. The college was most understanding about giving him leave to climb his mountains.

With the advent of World War I, George promptly joined the Royal Field Artillery and later, the Royal Artillery O/D as an officer. He was stationed in Portsmouth, awaiting orders to go overseas when abruptly, and without warning to either of his parents, he married Betty Fisher.

Alicia Gladys "Betty" Fisher, George's wife, was petite and svelte and assured, with ash blond hair, a short straight nose and wide-set china-blue eyes that stared at men unblinkingly. Betty looked as if she would say the first thing that popped into her head — and do it. High-spirited, gay and prankish, she was *dangerously* pretty. And if she was considered by some of the more stiff-necked to be, well, a bit fast — that was neither here nor there. And there was another side to her: she could extend a comforting hand of friendship and sympathy. Lieutenant Fred Powys Sketchley, when fighting in

Gallipoli in 1915, added a codicil to his will referring to her as "the dearest and truest friend a man ever had, Gladys 'Betty' Fisher" and appointing her as sole guardian of one of his children if anything happened to his wife.

Betty Staveley-Hill (as she is now), Peter Finch's mother, says, "I never really had a home as a child. My father died when I was nine, my mother married again and I was brought up by an uncle." Betty Fisher was born in November 1893, in a house called Rose Hill, in Marple, Chester, outside Manchester. The family roots were in the north of England. In Birmingham, a surgeon's daughter married a yeoman and their child, Frederick Fisher, an estate agent, made a killing in real estate which he extended up to Manchester. Frederick Fisher settled in Manchester, died a millionaire and left several children. One of these, also named Frederick Fisher, of chronically poor health, married a girl called Alicia Gladys Bentley. When Alicia gave birth to a daughter, she also named her Alicia Gladys. They called her "Betty". They moved southwards probably for reasons of Frederick's health, visiting health spas until he died in 1910, at the age of forty. Betty's mother settled in London, married a stockbroker, Conran Smith, and went to live with him at 63 Broadhurst Gardens in Hampstead. It would have seemed logical for her daughter, Betty, to live with them but this was not to happen. For some reason Betty was installed at the home of her uncle, Henry William Wilson, who lived with his family at 2 Fellowes Road, near the Conran Smiths.

In those days, Keith Prowse was the leading theatrical ticket agency in London, and every two weeks or so, Uncle Henry would receive their lists of opening nights to choose from. The many opening nights he took Betty to were great occasions for her. The glamour of such nights in 1913 — the women in their velvet cloaks, their low-cut gowns, their shining hair, their glittering jewels against a background of handsome men in black and white evening clothes — thrilled Betty as did the deep baroque crimson and gold of the theatre. The rise of the curtain, the stage lights brightly flooding the romantic plays of the era, all made Betty tingle with excitement as she sat in the stalls wearing the most beautiful dress she owned. And it was not lost upon her that entering or leaving the theatre, she was making the men around her tingle with excitement as well.

To her relatives' disapproval, Betty yearned to go on the stage. Like them, she had heard stories of actresses' romantic excesses, though perhaps this only made her yearn all the more. She spent long hours poring over photographs of her favourite actors and actresses in the glossy illustrated magazines. When either her uncle or her aunt caught her at this, the magazines were swiftly confiscated. Betty was sent away to Paris, as young ladies were in those days, to spend a year with a French family and be "finished". She came back from France stage-struck as ever.

At a party in London, she met a theatrical agent who arranged for her to go to his office to discuss what he could do for her. The next day, gorgeously dressed, Betty started out of the house to keep her appointment — only to be intercepted by her relatives.

"I was thwarted," says Betty today of the incident. And then, "So I got married." Why? "I don't know. I guess I was the marrying kind."

George met Betty sometime early in 1915 at an officers' dance in Portsmouth. She had been summering nearby on the Isle of Wight. On 15 June 1915, George Ingle Finch married Alicia Gladys Fisher. George's address was No Man's Land, which meant of course the fighting front. Two sisters, Molly Campbell and Mrs Phyllis Sketchley, Fred Powys Sketchley's wife, were witnesses to the ceremony.

George and Betty were magnetized towards each other by their shared good looks, their youthful exuberance, their dash and charm and doubtless above all, by the circumstances of the Great War. But that was all they shared. Betty was unpredictable, volatile, capricious. Except for that one year in France, she had never been out of England in her life yet she had been born sophisticated. George, for all his travels and adventures, was not. Underneath George's charm was a profoundly serious man. They were to prove tragically ill-matched.

The awareness of their error seems to have been borne upon them at an early stage in their marriage. On their honeymoon in London, George felt Betty was "flirting rather heavily with other men" and remonstrated with her. Betty shrugged it off.

On 20 June, five days after the wedding, George wrote to his father in Australia from Clarence Barracks in Portsmouth. His tone was strangely flat and subdued for the occasion:

My dear Father,
I have some quite startling news for you — I was married last week quietly by special licence to Miss Fisher to whom I have been

engaged but a comparatively short time. We spent our honeymoon — three days was all I could get — in London. My wife is staying at Southsea (a suburb of Portsmouth) and will remain there till I get my marching orders which I hope will not be long now ...

George eventually went to war. He had what a certain type of Englishman still calls a "good war" that is, a bad one. In Egypt, he contracted a serious case of cerebral malaria which was to recur for several years. He spent time in France and in Salonica where he was awarded the M.B.E. and was mentioned in despatches. Because of his scientific training, he was assigned the dangerous job of dismantling bombs. One of them blew up in his face, miraculously not disfiguring him but weakening one of his eyes so that later in life he wore a monocle.

George obtained his first leave and arrived home to England at the end of January in 1917. Peter had been born in a nursing home at 67 Cromwell Road, London, on 28 September 1916 although curiously, his birth had not yet been registered. George himself registered Peter on 5 February 1917, as Frederick (for Betty's father) George (for himself) Peter Ingle Finch. His leave over at the end of February, George returned to France, having written to his mother on 8 February: "Betty and my son was born on the 28th of September last. His name is Peter. He is a splendid boy and you will be awfully proud of him." There is one thing very strange about the letter: the notepaper on which it was written is bordered in black.

On returning to England in September 1918, having been invalided out of Salonica, George felt he had enough proof to instigate divorce proceedings against Betty for adultery.

One may judge the pitch of his fury by what follows in a letter written to his mother in November:

I told Betty that I intended taking proceedings. She fell in quite merrily with the idea until her hearing that it would naturally involve losing all touch with my son. She grovelled. Well she may continue to do so ...

George was as stone. Betty was not fit to raise the child. That was that. "I cannot take Peter away from her yet," he writes. "That worries me for he is over two years old and active in his mind and body beyond his years."

Both Betty Staveley-Hill and her friend Molly Campbell

(Poynder) corroborate that Peter was "nipped away" by George, while playing in the garden, some time in 1919. Molly remembers that the house was in Broadstairs. Certainly, the records show that Betty was moving around a great deal at that time, from Southsea to Hazelmere to Maidenhead to Lewes, probably to avoid just such a possibility.

Peter's long odyssey had begun.

George's sister, Dorothy, had become a nurse during the war. She had lost her fiancé and deciding that she would never marry, agreed to look after Peter temporarily. She continued nursing, however, taking the little three-year-old with her to wherever she found work in England. According to her records, she and Peter moved from Wiltshire to Devonshire to London to France and back again, and finally, back again to France. Incredibly, the constantly moving scenery of people and places does not seem to have outwardly affected Peter's cheerful disposition or his outgoing nature or his sunny charm.

It was as if the child knew even at an early age that his survival was dependent upon the kindness of strangers. And as if the gods, foretelling this, had showered upon him their golden gifts in order to make his extraordinary survival possible. Or it could have been that, in the accepting way that children have, the child Peter simply assumed that all children lived the way he did.

His grandmother Laura was on Betty's side and to George's intense annoyance seems to have insisted that he return Peter to Betty. George, with mounting irritation, refused.

On 15 May 1919, from the Isle of Wight, Betty wrote Laura a most dignified and moving letter. Laura had sent Betty photographs of Peter which Betty was thanking her for, describing them as a "pleasure and a pain". She "worships her son" she said, "every moment of his small life." If George could find satisfaction in the knowledge that he broke her heart when he took Peter, he was welcome to it. She went on to say that of Peter she did not think more than she could help — that way lay madness. But still there were times when the longing to have him was well-nigh more than she could bear. She ended by hoping that Laura would not think she was seeking sympathy. She asserted emphatically that *she could and would rebuild* her own life, and that she had the one priceless possession in loyal friends. Finally she said that she hoped Laura would believe she was sorry to be the indirect cause of sorrow in Laura's life.

George divorced Betty on grounds of adultery on 15 March 1920. The divorce was uncontested. The co-respondent was Major Wentworth Edward Dallas Campbell, an Indian Army Officer in the Poona Horse Regiment, and the brother of Molly Campbell and Phyllis Powys Sketchley. George received custody of the child Peter Ingle Finch. In 1922 Campbell married Betty and took her to India, first to the Province of Jamkhandi and then to Sagar where, as an expert horseman, he was made Chief Instructor of Equitation.

In 1922, George Ingle Finch rose higher above the crowd than anyone had ever done on foot. With the Leigh Mallory Everest Expedition, he led a party consisting of the Ghurka Tejbir and Captain Geoffrey Bruce, both inexperienced climbers, to within half a mile of the summit. George was the first to insist on the use of oxygen in climbing Everest at a time when both its efficacy and its sportsmanship were seriously doubted. Before his party descended, he left behind four oxygen tanks as a landmark for further explorers.

CHAPTER 2

The Boy Buddhist of Adyar

Though Peter had already visited his grandmother in Vaucresson for some happy months when he was three years old, according to Dorothy's records, he and Dorothy did not settle down there until 20 March 1923 when he was six.

Peter was ecstatic. The lovely old village of Vaucresson was on the banks of the Seine. Built on hills, its large villas of white and pinkish-brown stone all had balconies, tiled roofs and were surrounded by crumbling old walls trailing ivy. There were hedges and cypress trees, early lilacs bloomed, the gardens were beautiful and many of them had greenhouses full of exotic plants.

"Peterkin, how you've *grown*!" exclaimed the tall graceful Laura, all wisps of tulle, as she stooped to embrace him at the door of her house the Villa La Fleurette. They went inside. There Peter met his Uncle Antoine again, now studying to be a concert pianist, and a kindly, humorous man, the eminent Nobel Prize winner, Charles Richet (a dear friend of his grandmother). They talked in French among themselves which he didn't understand but the sounds of which fascinated him, and they always spoke English when talking to him. Peter hoped that this time he was going to stay. He stared in fascination at his grandmother. He knew that Dorothy loved him very much, looked after him well whenever she could find the time but instinctively, he found Laura more interesting. When the time came for him to go to bed, it was to Laura he turned. Laura took him upstairs, bathed him, tucked him in to his clean little white bed and talked to him of all the lovely things they were going to do the next day.

"Goodnight, Peterkin," she whispered as she glided out of the room, softly closing the door.

Alone, Peter lay on his bed in the dark and began to do something he had been doing for quite a while now though he couldn't recall exactly when it had started. Peter had invented a way of keeping people with him. For as long as he could remember, the people around him had kept changing. One day they would be with him and the next they would be gone. And so he had discovered that if he *talked in their voices* he could keep them with him. When he talked *like* them they were here when he wanted them. He could call them back at any time and they didn't go away. They stayed with him as long as he liked, until he fell asleep ... his grandmother ... Dorothy ... And as for Professor Richet and his Uncle Antoine, he simply duplicated the sounds they made and he was talking French. Laura drifted by his door to check that he was sleeping. She paused outside, listening in dumbfounded amazement. She sought Dorothy.

"Oh, yes," said Dorothy. "He always does that at night. Children often talk to themselves, don't they?"

But Laura, the Great Encourager, was never one to allow people's gifts to go unheralded or unexploited. She had already produced one great mountaineer who was on his way to becoming a great scientist, and one budding concert pianist. And now, a ... but what was the exact nature of darling Peterkin's gift?

Vaucresson in the twenties was a community of *avant-garde* artists, poets, painters, musicians and intellectuals. In her salon, Laura did not hesitate to urge Peter, who was at first shy then eager, to show off his talent for mimicry to her guests who reacted with astonishment, delight and applause.

There was a little girl who lived across the street in a house much bigger than the others. To Peter, it seemed like a castle and she a princess. She also possessed perhaps the most romantic thing in the world that a child could have — a tree house. She and Peter spent long hours playing in it. She wanted to play "Mothers and Fathers" — Peter wanted to play "Heroes and Heroines". "Where's your mother? Where's your father?" the little girl would ask. Peter would repeat what Laura told him "My mother got married again and went away. My father is in India climbing mountains. Let's play 'Heroes and Heroines'. I'll climb up a dangerous mountain ... "

"And I'll be the princess on top of it."

"And I'll rescue you."

Peter was in love with her. Her memory stayed with him all his life. When he became Australia's leading actor, he wrote to her and told her about himself. She replied to his letter, telling him that she, too, had become an actress and had changed her name to the exotic Cimestre de Monterai.

In Vaucresson, Peter had his princess, his dog, his bicycle and a beautiful garden. He loved working in the garden with the gardener, learning to grow plants and flowers, a knowledge he was to retain all his life. For two years he was content.

Looking back on this period, Peter remembers Laura thus: "Tall and elegant, flitting from room to room, with long slender fingers that played the harp most beautifully, she taught me to explore the frontiers of experience. She encouraged me to explore new places, to meet new people. I was a ready pupil."

It is ironic that Laura who had struggled so unsuccessfully with George's immortal soul should have found such ready access to Peter's.

"And then, quite inexplicably, for no logical reason, my grandmother suddenly took me off to India," is the way Peter often described what happened to him next. And so, indeed, it must have seemed to the nine-year-old.

Many things had been going on inside Laura during this time and they were oddly connected to what was happening around her. Dadaism had hit Bohemian Paris like an explosion, to be followed by the even more eruptive Surrealism. These new movements forced people to become aware of the deep regions of the unconscious. To be in touch with the unconscious was to be in touch with the universe; new frontiers of experience were being explored. To Laura these movements seemed to provide further justification for her belief in spiritualism, the psychic and theosophy and more what she felt to be the very heart of theosophical teachings: Buddhism.

For two years, Peter had been content but Laura had not. The child certainly had extraordinary powers, of that she was sure. She had been convinced he was a medium and had taken him to many seances but nothing had happened. He had merely seemed frightened at the time, though cheerfully he imitated everyone's voices after they came home. Perhaps he wasn't a medium but he had such a spiritual quality that perhaps he would be a teacher. What he needed was the chance for further spiritual development — in India.

In December 1925, at its Indian Headquarters in Adyar outside Madras, the Theosophical Society had its Golden Jubilee to celebrate the founding of theosophy in 1875 by Madame Blavatsky. Annie Besant, its President, was to preside over the celebrations and Krishnamurti, the young prophet, was to be introduced with all the fanfare attendant on a new Messiah. Delegates from all over the world would be there. It was only natural that Laura, a lifelong theosophist, should be determined to attend this very special triumphant celebration in India and to study Buddhism at first hand, at the same time giving her grandson, Peter, the opportunity for spiritual enlightenment. It is also logical to assume that Peter was excited at the prospect of India. "I was a ready pupil," he said of his grandmother's teachings and he added, "for I was a born roamer."

Thus the young boy and his grandmother set off for India in September 1925. Though he didn't know it, it was the last time Peter was to see Europe for twenty-three years.

Other children would have been desperately sad to leave a dog, a bicycle, and above all, a princess but they would not have had Peter's extraordinary background. He had learned something in his short life, an invaluable lesson that was to guide him always. He had learned to keep his eyes only on what was in front of him, and India was in front of him.

It is not clear where Dorothy was at this point, whether she accompanied them to Bombay and then continued on to Australia or whether she had already left for Australia. She seems to have become a shadowy figure in Peter's life at this time, blotted out by the more vivid presence of Laura.

At any rate, when they docked in Bombay, the young boy and his grandmother made their way alone through India and down to Ceylon. Ceylon is a Buddhist stronghold and it is probably there that Peter first saw Buddhist children of his age solemnly having their heads shaved and saffron robes draped around them as they went through the ceremony of becoming apprentice priests. Clearly, both Laura and Peter were profoundly affected by the sight.

One of the books that Laura carried with her everywhere that was in fact her little Bible, was a pamphlet called *At the Feet of the Master* written by Krishnamurti when he was only thirteen. The teachings contained in it were "given to him by his Master in preparing him for initiation", writes Annie Besant in the preface, implying that Krishnamurti received them in some mediumistic fashion. It is a document revered to this day by his followers. That an adolescent Indian boy of thirteen and one who didn't know much English could convey such sentiments with such simple piety made it all the more wonderful. An Englishman, R. Balfour Clarke, who had been Krishnamurti's tutor at the time, vouched for its authenticity.

Krishnamurti had been discovered bathing in the River Adyar and taken away from his Brahmin parents at an early age by Annie Besant and Charles Leadbeater, another prominent theosophist, who supervised his education, "protected him from injurious thought forms" and groomed him to become the Lord Maitreya, the new spiritual leader. The similarities between Krishnamurti and Peter must have occurred to both Laura and her grandson. Both were orphaned children of living parents. Was not Peter with his spiritual seeking very like Krishnamurti at his age?

Now, in December, as the young boy and his grandmother left Ceylon to make their pilgrimage to Adyar, they had added to their retinue an elderly Buddhist priest carrying an umbrella.

In Southern India, it was summer. Golden sunshine glistened off the white marble-columned temples of the Theosophy Centre on the banks of the river Adyar across from Madras. The sky was turquoise blue. There were avenues of mahogany trees, a feathery canopy of casuarinas and the mysterious gloom of spreading banyans.

Annie Besant, aged seventy-nine, presided over the festivities. This highly complex woman who had in turn embraced atheism, socialism and theosophy was a figure of remarkable achievement. Almost single-handed, she had brought about the Home Rule Movement for India and coined the phrase *India is the wage slave of the Empire*. Though a woman and English, she had been elected the First President of the National Congress of India. Now, in her old age, she was installed in Adyar as an idol, a total goddess. Everyone called her Mother.

Annie presided over the festivities but she gave the star part to her young protégé, Krishnamurti, now aged thirty. One day she gathered the delegates together and announced that the Christ, Lord Maitreya, had chosen that occasion to mark his acceptance of his chosen vehicle, and taking possession of Krishnamurti, would speak through his lips.

Here is her account of what followed:

Pulsing with waves of exquisite color, a pillar of golden mist vested Krishnamurti's body. Overhead shone great globes of light too dazzling to look upon. He stood on a dais under the banyan tree. An audience of three thousand delegates sat on the ground at his feet.

Krishnamurti finally spoke: "We are all expecting Him. He comes to those who want, who desire, who long ... ''

There was a pause and then, according to Mrs Besant, another voice rang out of Krishnamurti's being — a voice not heard on earth for two thousand years. Some saw a great light, some saw Christ himself and all heard the voice: ''*I* come to those who want sympathy, who want happiness, who are longing to be released. *I* come to reform and not to tear down, not to destroy but to build.''

Not everyone gathered at his feet saw the dazzling emanations from Krishnamurti and the great light — only the Chosen. Was young Peter, sitting entranced between his grandmother and the elderly Buddhist priest, one of them?

In later years, Peter was never to get right what happened next. In fact he got it completely wrong, he turned it upside down. According to his grown-up recollections (which differed as he told them from person to person and from day to day) his grandmother then left him, abandoned him, or put him in a Buddhist monastery — or apprenticed him to a Buddhist priest, and his incarceration lasted for either three days, three weeks, one year or two years. What actually happened, in fact, is in some ways stranger and certainly more revealing of Peter's essential character.

Captain Richard Balfour Clarke is ninety-two years old — the same Balfour Clarke who was Krishnamurti's tutor. He is a spry, active man still living in Adyar. He remembers: ''I met a nine or ten-year-old 'Peter Pan' boy — Peter Finch — son of Captain Ingle Finch — with his grandmother, Mrs L. Ingle Finch in 1925. Mrs Finch was temporarily a resident at the international headquarters of the Theosophical Society in Adyar. Peter was quite beautiful, his hands and feet included, spoke English and French, was clairvoyant in a natural and childlike way and to our delight did not realize that he could see what most of us could not.

''One day, Laura Finch came to me in tears saying she had lost Peter *for three days*. I searched the estate and found Peter in a dimly-lit room in an old house which still stands today; his golden halo of curls were gone, his head shaved, he wore a yellow robe, one shoulder bare and he held a grass fan in one hand. I said 'Peter' and he replied 'Halloo' and I told him of his grandmother's sorrow. He said 'I am a Chela now.' I saluted a harmless-looking Buddhist monk who smiled and raised no objection when I took Peter's hand and led him out of the room and delivered him to his grandmother at a bungalow called, as it is still called, 'Sevashrama'.

''There was no Buddhist monastery and the monk was only a temporary visitor at the Convention and I did not meet him again or try to find out how Peter had met him.''

In the uproar that followed, it is perhaps natural that the child Peter might forget that these events were largely of his own making. Laura had certainly prepared the ground but from the evidence, the completed fact of his conversion, the shaven head and the robes, were Peter's very own idea.

A lost impressionable child in the strangest and most mysterious of lands, India, seated at the feet of Krishnamurti, is suddenly seized in a moment of daring surrender by the inexplicable need to be possessed. By whom? Krishnamurti? The Lord Maitreya? Buddhism? A child of nine is a soaring spiritual vessel. Was there also a small secret hope that perhaps he too was destined to become a leader? Peter, in that moment, decided to become a Buddhist. It was a decision he was never to revoke. Throughout his life he was to remain more faithful to certain Buddhist vows than even he understood.

Enid Lorimer was an actress, a writer and a teacher, and is now ninety years old. A former theosophist, she was also in Adyar in 1925 as part of a delegation from Australia. She says, ''I first saw Peter in December 1925. I was at the Theosophical Headquarters at Adyar celebrating the fiftieth anniversary of the Society. I was walking in the compound when my companion and I saw a small group of people across the pool, among them a Buddhist priest in a yellow robe, an elderly white woman and a small boy dressed also in a yellow robe. That same day, a friend, Captain 'Dicky' Clarke, was telling me about this little boy. He said he was worried about this very bright little *English* boy as he put it being 'lugged all over the world by his apparently slightly dotty grandmother'.''

Captain Clarke was more than just ''worried''. Peter, though he had been brought back once to his grandmother, now had it firmly in his mind that he was a boy Buddhist. He had got hold of a begging bowl and he was running wild all over the place. Laura was no longer able to control him.

The theosophists were on the whole a tolerant lot. But they were not so tolerant that they allowed a little upper-class English boy with his head shaven, wearing saffron robes to run around with a begging bowl. Its members were mainly wealthy, respectable and white, with a smattering of Dutch and English aristocracy and some high caste Indians. Furthermore, they had suffered a few nasty scandals involving some of their leaders and the Press was always looking forward to another juicy one. There was also the whole disapproving British Raj community just across the river in Madras. The story of this English child gone native had all the makings of an international scandal. This Peter Pan, this Boy Buddhist of Adyar, was coming dangerously close to upstaging Krishnamurti and Annie Besant.

Captain Clarke took steps. He went to the great Annie Besant and the great Annie Besant sent for Laura.

What happened at this holy or unholy meeting between Laura and her ancient idol has never been revealed, but it must have been very different from what Laura had dreamed all her life. One can imagine what must have transpired: Mrs Besant excoriating, Laura hanging her head in shame. According to Enid, Mrs Besant told Laura in no uncertain terms that "she wasn't fit to be trusted with that child". She also elicited from her the fact that Peter's closest relatives, Laura's daughter, Dorothy, and Laura's husband, Charles, were living in Sydney, Australia. This presented a solution. The Theosophical Society had its headquarters in Sydney at The Manor in Mosman, a suburb and there was a school attached to it. Peter could be sent there and meanwhile his Sydney relatives would be contacted.

Some time soon after their meeting, Laura, (presumably in chagrin and under the powerful banishing eye of Mrs Besant) seems to have drifted away up to Darjeeling to continue following her star.

In later years, Peter was to refer to his grandmother as *"avant-garde"* or "very *avant-garde*" or "eccentric" or "very eccentric". One never sensed him avoiding the word "nuts" in any way. Was she? Certainly, she seems perfectly sane when she writes to Peter for the first time thirteen years later on the 10 June 1938, from Windsor Cottage, Happy Valley Estate, Darjeeling, saying "Remember your grandmother of thirteen years ago", and how happy she is that Peter has bravely succeeded in finding a "foothold on the slippery path of life" through his own "happy nature and intelligence". According to Peter, she died in Darjeeling writing pamphlets for Gandhi.

Rukmini Devi Arundale was an Indian girl of high caste still in her teens. She had dazzled and shocked India as a dancer (it was simply not done for Brahmins to become dancers) and then married an Englishman, George Arundale, an educator with a high position in theosophist circles. Rukmini's beauty was both awesome and oddly familiar; she was the ideal fairy princess. Her dark burnished hair flowed around her shoulders framing the childish flower-like face with its large clear lustrous eyes. Her sari seemed continually to be rippling in the wind whether she was in motion or still.

Rukmini recalls: "It was in the year 1925 when the Theosophical Society was celebrating its Golden Jubilee ... Peter Finch was a little boy, extremely attractive to look at but with a shaven head and yellow robes. I found him wandering about in the Theosophical Society's estate, meeting everybody and becoming a favorite of all the delegates. But I was feeling worried about the fact that he seemed to have no parents or elders with him. I chatted with him many times and asked him what had happened to him and what his name was. He said, 'I am a Buddhist Bhikshu. I came to India from Ceylon along with my grandmother who has left me saying "Many here will look after you." ' I was rather surprised and asked him 'Have you no guardian or someone to take care of you?'

"He said 'I have none.' My mother was a most loving motherly person. When she heard about this little boy, she said 'Please bring him immediately to our house.' So he came there and was a constant visitor to our house."

According to Enid, Annie Besant had asked Captain Clarke to try to take care of Peter while inquiries were made about his family, and the next time she saw Peter, "he had been outfitted in a cut-down white suit and a huge topee on his poor little bald head, much too large for him and I can see him now, a small thin little creature peering up at me like a frightened bird but with such bright and intelligent eyes. Inquiries brought to light an elderly grandfather with a daughter living in Sydney and it was decided that Peter should be brought back in Captain Clarke's charge till they were found."

C. W. Leadbeater who presided over The Manor was to take Peter with him on the same ship as the delegates (which included Rukmini and Enid) when they sailed to Sydney. But somehow, on account of some mysterious confusion or change of plans, they sailed without him and Peter made his voyage alone.

Captain Clarke continues: "Very soon after my arrival at The Manor, Mosman, in Sydney, a phone call informed me that the Captain of a ship from India had a small boy, Peter Finch, on board as a first-class passenger. He was to be handed over to an aunt (Dorothy) who was Matron in a big nursing institution in Sydney, or, if she could not take him, he was to be handed over to me with a letter explaining that twelve pounds was a first monthly payment of ten pounds per month in future (which, by the way, never came). I went down to the ship and saw a letter from Peter's aunt in which she explained the impossibility of accepting Peter. I signed for him and we installed him as a member of the Manor family under Mr Leadbeater.''

A small boy, Peter Finch, on board as a first-class passenger for how many weeks? Alone. Going where? To whom? He tried to see what was in front of him. But what was in front of him now? A vast threatening sea. Peter remembered that voyage accurately. He recalled many years later that in the Great Australian Bight, the ship ran into a raging storm.

In Adyar, before they left for Sydney and The Manor, Captain Clarke had applied to Enid for help. He had discovered that Peter, though nine years of age, could *neither read nor write English*! And he told her, ''If I send him to an ordinary public school, the kids will give him hell and I can't afford a private school or a tutor — will you take him on?'' Enid said she would.

The Manor in Mosman is a huge Victorian building overlooking Sydney harbour, dark red brick with white trim, with Victorian porches and verandahs. It was here that C. W. Leadbeater, an old Oxonian, formerly an English vicar, now a self-styled Bishop, had embraced the trappings and rituals of the Catholic Church without the hellfire and brimstone, and founded the Liberal Catholic Church. ''Liberal'' seems to be the operative word for his methods and his choice of curriculum. He persisted for instance, in the face of scandal, in teaching the young boys to masturbate. In February 1926 when Peter arrived, the mixed community of children and adults staying at The Manor were being given courses in Esperanto (world language), Astrology, Art, the reading of the Bhagavad Gita and Meditation. In other words, ideas, ideas, ideas were buzzing around The Manor like flies. But first, Peter had to learn to read and write English.

''And so'', says Enid, ''I came to teach Peter his first writing and reading lessons. He couldn't have been brighter, quicker. As to his future interest in the classics — I think I may have been the first person from whom he heard Shakespeare and other poets. At the time when he came to The Manor and I was giving him lessons, there was a group of young people also living at The Manor. We used, very often, a little knot of us, to wander out into the bush and I would read Shakespeare to them, tell them stories and sing to them.

Peter was always in the little group, saying very little, watching everything. And more than once, I heard him from my room, which opened on to the verandah, giving a most life-like imitation of me to the other children, never unkindly, there was never a trace of malice in that boy, but with a terrific sense of fun and a flawless ear.''

Enid taught him to read and write. She taught him the beauty of Shakespeare and poetry transmitted through her beautiful voice. But neither she nor anyone else would ever be able to teach him to spell. English spelling, with its freakish borrowings from Latin, French and German, was too much for his rational child's mind. Hence his lifelong phonetically correct, but misspelled ''noncence'', ''shaperone'', ''ciciatrist'', ''cinserity'' and, that triumph of reason over tradition: ''koka kola''. Peter's ear was flawless but his eye wandered.

And then there were Rukmini's memories: ''I lived in Australia with Dr Arundale, my husband, at The Manor in Mosman, off and on for nearly six years. Every single day Peter used to spend hours with me. He and another little boy called Arthur were always following me around because I was fond of them and they were fond of me. Peter used to say 'My father and mother have disowned me. I have only a brilliant uncle who is a pianist. I come from a very good family on the English side but I also have Russian relatives.' (A nice Parisian touch.) Peter used to say 'I have no father or mother. You are my mother.' I was very happy to be with him and he used to recite poems to me. He told me he could write poems also but I never heard any of them.

''Later on, his grandfather came. He was very much displeased to see Peter mixing with theosophists such as ourselves. One day, Peter came to me crying and said, 'I have to leave you because my grandfather does not want me to be here.' Later on, once in a while, I met him on the ferry and I was surprised to find he had developed an Australian accent. When I told him he had become an Australian, he said 'I can become anything.' We all enjoyed Peter's remarks. I think he had always a disappointment in his heart because his family would have nothing to do with him. He told me once that he never missed his family because he had found me!! It was really a very charming thing for a little boy to say and I can never forget it ... ''

One evening in London many years later in the early fifties, Rukmini was attending a theatre with a friend. ''Somehow the movements of the lips of the main actor and gestures of his hands appeared rather familiar. I told my friend 'He sounds and looks familiar to me.' I looked at the programme and saw the name — Peter Finch. I requested my friend to go to his dressing-room and ask him whether he remembered an Indian lady in Australia. Immediately, Peter Finch jumped up and said 'It must be Rukmini, I want to see her immediately.' So I went to see him and he was so thrilled to see me that he put his arms around me and would not let me go for some time.''

Curiously, it seems to have taken Peter's grandfather, Charles, almost a year to decide that he was "very much displeased" at finding Peter among the theosophists, that "he was very much opposed to theosophy as a 'doctrine of the devil' '' and to come to The Manor "with Government authority to remove Peter from our care" (Captain Clarke). And perhaps it was fortunate that Charles in his wrath did not descend immediately to snatch Peter from the theosophists' evil clutches.

For the young people at The Manor put on theatricals, pageants, masques. The Manor even had its own radio station, a powerful transmitter having been installed there in 1923 by one of the members. They broadcasted music, theosophical talks, playlets and poetry readings. Exciting strangers, Romanians, Italian Royalty, Swedes and Indians were always visiting. Peter, every now and then, referred to "my year with the Buddhist monks as the most thrilling of my life". Perhaps it was. But in fact it was spent with the theoso-phists — with Enid — learning to read and writes English, dis-covering Shakespeare, and with Rukmini, whom the young Peter loved passionately.

There is one more event that took place while Peter was at The Manor, which seems to prove conclusively how committed he was to the theosophists. On 10 October 1926, when he was ten years old, according to Church Registry records, Peter Finch, ever the eager acolyte, was baptised and confirmed in the Liberal Catholic Church of St Albans in Regent Street, in Sydney.

Just as it is not physically possible to force a nine-year-old boy to have his head shaved, so it is emotionally impossible to force a ten-year-old to go through two church ceremonies against his will. Peter yearned to belong. He had progressed from the peasant's smock and wooden shoes of a French child to the saffron robes and shaved head of a Buddhist Bhikshu to the sailor suit of a proper English boy in a theosophy centre in just two years.

Why was he not crazed by this chaos?

Change, says the Buddha. Life is change. Don't cling. And the theosophist creed is that all religions are basically the same.

Now the Finches were closing in. What had taken them so long was that none of the family really wanted the child. Charles was by this time an eighty-seven-year-old invalid. He lived in his house, Land House, in Richard Street in Greenwich Point, with his sister Kate, aged seventy-six. Next door lived brother Edward and his unmarried daughter, aged forty. Peter's grandfather had retired in 1918 and was living only on his pension, half of which he sent regularly to Laura. As he had also spent a considerable amount of money on his children's expensive education, he had very little left to support himself and Kate.

The elderly Charles was frankly appalled at the idea of having a young child living with him so a family conference was called. A cousin living in Brisbane, with daughters Cynthia and Marcia, was approached but she refused. And Dorothy, of course, had earlier stated her position.

While the family was thus pondering Peter's fate, Charles was galvanized into action by a letter he received from his son, George, on 16 March 1927.

> I enclose herewith the Power of Attorney for you to obtain custody of Peter. I was most distressed to hear that my mother had sent him to a theosophical school. Had I known she intended doing that I should not have given her control of the boy. She knows or should know quite well that I completely abominate anything to do with spiritualism, theosophy or any other form of charlatanism.

A solution was therefore reached but though well-meaning, it was desperate — and catastrophic.

CHAPTER 3

Pidgifif and the Dark Days

Peter was taken from The Manor and thrust into the house of the relatives who lived next door to his grandfather in Greenwich Point. He was put in to the charge of his elderly Uncle Edward who was to die two years later and his daughter, Peter's cousin, whom he always called his aunt. But not only was she *not* his aunt, she was not really even his cousin but, more distantly, his second cousin.

Peter's Uncle Edward was a remote man; he did not like fuss of any kind and kept well out of the way of domestic upheavals. His aunt was forty years old, had never married, had no children of her own and was therefore unused to them. Now, suddenly, it was borne upon her that it was her inescapable Victorian duty to become, in her middle age, the mother of an unknown, distantly related boy, and a problem child. She had every right to be seething with resentment at this new and heavy burden.

Looking back, Peter was to remember his grandfather lovingly, lyrically — he even named his son Charles after him. He was often to tell friends that his grandfather ''came over to India to get him'' (at an invalided eighty-seven?), but his story was mostly that directly he docked in Sydney, he was driven straight to his grandfather's house in Greenwich Point where a spry, old gentleman emerged. ''Hello, my boy, you look as if you could do with a meal, etc. etc.''

Certainly, some sort of rescuing action by his grandfather is implied here. As Peter tells it, he lived in bliss with his grandfather and Aunt Kate until his grandfather died when he was twelve. In fact, Peter went straight to his aunt's house next door and his grandfather didn't die until five years later, of senile debility. It was his Uncle Edward who died when Peter was twelve.

There must have been so much emotional anguish and confusion in Peter's young mind at this final move that he was never able to get it straightened out. For instance, he was never, ever to mention The

Manor nor the happy year he spent there.

This can perhaps be explained by Charles Finch's direct and George Ingle Finch's distant disapproval of the theosophist-devils-and-charlatans who were, after all, responsible for Laura's ruin. Nor were the other Finch relatives less disapproving. It must have been deeply impressed upon the young boy that he had done something shameful, disgraceful, never-to-be-mentioned — in short, a Finch secret.

Cousin Cynthia remembers her "Uncle Charlie" as "a very strict man, unapproachable, with a mass of white beard which terrified me as one who was smothered in it on being kissed" but adds, "he must have been kinder than I thought to be kissing a little girl." Most surely, Peter's grandfather was a very strict elderly man but he was also, and most importantly, the first *male* relative that Peter had met. In the rapidly worsening situation in which Peter found himself next door, it was to his grandfather that he increasingly went for security, respite and love. There was no doubt that Charles loved Peter in his Finch way, and that he felt strongly that "the boy never had a chance". He gave him penknives from his vast collection when Peter came visiting and encouraged him to read the bound volumes of books in his study.

Peter loved hearing stories of his grandfather's adventures land-surveying, and later appreciated his concern for trying to make a "man out of the boy", encouraging him to swim and play sports. Between Peter and Peter's aunt he was, perhaps, a buffer state. However, he would say sternly "Stop *acting*, Peter — you're always acting!" And he thrashed Peter when he came upon him going through the family papers, trying to find out *who* he was, and *what* had happened. But Peter, as Captain Clarke has said, "Saw what most of us could not" and he saw Charles' love and pain — this old-fashioned man deserted in his old age not only by Laura but by his children — a man so old-fashioned that he still kept chamber-pots on the sideboard in the dining-room though the custom, thanks to the progress in plumbing, had been abandoned in the early 1800s. And has there ever been a case of a child *not* loving a grandparent?

So Peter stayed with his grandfather for as many hours as possible though the time always came for him to leave his grandfather's house and go next door where he lived.

Because Peter was not her natural son, his aunt could not be relaxed about bringing him up and was overly concerned about disciplining every aspect of his behaviour. She was always trying to do what she felt was "the right thing by him" but she did not conceal her bitterness at the extra work he was making. Her solution was to make him do not only the extra but pretty much all the menial work.

When Captain Clarke visited Peter some months after he had been installed in the Finch's modest suburban home, he noted that Peter had settled down and was attending a government school. But, unable to conceal his deep dismay, he remarked that "Peter had deteriorated, having acquired an Australian accent, and grimy nails ... "

When Rukmini teased Peter on the ferry saying that he had become an Australian, Peter had replied, "I can become anything." It was easy for the protean child to become an Australian but it was not so easy for him to become a victim of tyranny.

As he was growing up at Greenwich Point from 1927 to 1931, that is from ten years of age to fifteen, Peter's character was beginning to take shape. Rebellion and its handmaiden, mockery, our strongest weapon against authority and oppression, became his vigilant companions. Waves of rebellion pounded inside him and he dealt with them in the only way possible for a small frightened boy. At home, he withdrew or rather was panicked into silence and self-absorption. Any utterance might cause a row or a beating. By day, his companions were imaginary people and his aunt's terrier with whom he constantly walked and talked. By night, his dreams were filled with the heroes and heroines of his tree house days in Vaucresson with his princess.

Peter was becoming a liar. He lied out of fear of getting caught and the consequences at home. And he lied because he didn't know what the truth *was*, so that when his classmates asked him, he'd have to invent it. The proud Finches could and did recite the family tree by heart but as to why he wasn't living with his father, who and where his mother was and what had happened to his grandmother — they were don't-mention secrets. "My name is *Peter George Frederick Ingle Finch*," he would say firmly. In fact he gave his list of names so often that his schoolmates called him "Pidgifif" which he liked very much. Pidgifif. That was all he actually knew about himself. The rest he'd have to spin out of dreams.

He also lied because he was never believed when he told the truth. To his new schoolmates, all that Indian Buddhist stuff was a lot of codswallop ... They thought he was just crackers the way he built up stories about all those imaginary people — Royalty and Lords and

Ladies, and claimed to have met them personally (which of course he had done as they were part of the constant flow of visitors at The Manor). No, one couldn't always believe what Peter said.

But the final reason why Peter lied — why all children lie at one time or another — is probably the most important one. He lied to feel opaque, to stop feeling so constantly nakedly transparent, so invaded, so threatened by the omnipotent, omniscient adults. Lying for this reason, it could be argued, is an important part of growing up. But Peter never got out of the habit.

At the beginning of Peter's first year at Greenwich Public School, what his classmates saw was a smallish tawny-haired boy of ten who was quiet, grubby, lonely and always late in the morning. What none of them knew was that he had to do all the washing up and housework before he left, and had to walk a mile to the school. And for being late, he was frequently caned by the headmaster. However, the mysterious new boy perked up as the term went on and revealed his natural and extraordinary talents.

This shy, well-mannered, courteous, amiable boy, this "very quiet bloke" says classmate John Carter, "was able to vomit at will. For a small fee, he would vomit on the floor of the lunch-room for those of his classmates who wanted a half day off from school. They'd claim sickness and, after cleaning up the mess, would be permitted to go home."

It is a fitting metaphor for such a rending actor as Peter was to become: spilling his guts on the screen for a small fee so that the audience can take half a day off.

John Carter also remembers that Peter displayed at times the welts of beatings he got from his aunt. "He told me he got one every day — for being a 'bad boy' and in case he was 'bad' during school."

In Sydney, in the twenties, corporal punishment was an accepted way of disciplining children. Up to a point. But other classmates as well as John tell too many stories of Peter's regular beatings (his aunt used a riding crop) for it not to be unequivocally clear that what was going on in the house where Peter lived was child abuse.

Moreover there was a very serious incident of a knife wound. Peter's Army Service Book (1945) records a "wide linear scar on left leg" as a distinguishing mark. This wide linear scar that ran from knee to thigh up the outer side of his left leg was probably inflicted before he was fourteen as his schoolmates only noticed it after then when he went swimming with them. It may have caused him to favour his right leg very slightly for the rest of his life as can be discerned on the screen.

The neighbours heard Peter crying and screaming; they knew he was unloved, unwanted and ill-treated. Why didn't they do something about it? The naiveté of this question can only make anyone who has been ill-treated as a child, smile. Why didn't they do something about it? Because it was none of their business.

A little girl, Muriel Farr, who lived two doors away, used to watch Peter. She wondered about this quiet boy who rarely played games with his peers, even though the playground was directly across the street from his home. His one pleasure in his spare time, she noticed, was to take his dog for long lonely walks and she often wondered what occupied his mind — he always looked so withdrawn. "His home life did not appear to be very cheerful. He was kept in his place by a woman we were told was his aunt."

But one night, at a local meeting, she witnessed a scene she can never forget:

"There was an election in the offing and in those days, the political candidates hired halls in which to air their views and claims for the party to be re-elected. Poor Peter was dragged along, unwillingly we thought at first. But he sat there as one entranced, taking in every word and gesture of the speaker, the Honourable William Morris Hughes, M.P. and sometime Prime Minister. My group was more interested in Peter than the speaker.

"Peter's expression changed in tune with Billy Hughes. His hand on the aisle near us and out of sight of his adult bodyguard, waved gently, pleadingly, clenched, unclenched, pointed, drew circles in the air, spread itself open palms up, closed, in fact, made all the movements a speaker of the day would use.

"Going home we discussed Peter's total absorption. My mother said 'Peter was taking all that in and storing it up. I would not be surprised if some day he becomes an actor.' "

The isolated unhappy adolescent dreams. He dreams and dreams and can then mourn his way into a dangerously catatonic state, unless he's one of the lucky ones like Peter Finch. Of the golden gifts showered upon Peter at birth and one that cannot be "unlearned" since it cannot be learned — was an active response to life.

A restless, energetic boy, he always connected, always made contact. And the only way he could do so, since he had to go straight home from school every afternoon to do his chores, and wasn't allowed to play cricket or football or box (Jack Dempsey was the school hero at the time) on that playing-field across the street from home, was to do what he could do best. He became an entertainer. "I was regarded as the comic of the class," Peter said. But he was more than that. Ingenious, enthusiastic, enterprising, with a theatrical know-how that came straight from heaven, he organised the other boys into putting on skits for the school's amusement with himself, quite naturally, in the leading roles.

"Most vividly, I remember his skit on Hamlet when he was in his last year (twelve years old) of primary school" says John Carter. "Written, produced, dressed and taking the title role, etc. etc. etc. So good the Headmaster had him perform it to each of the three senior classes. Most of us then had never heard of Hamlet. It was a riot."

"I think I must have been Peter's first leading lady," says Keith Gill, also referring back to primary school days. Keith had played Lady Macbeth to Peter's Macbeth. He wore one of his mother's nightgowns, tied with a green sash and the ghost chased them both around the classroom.

But at North Sydney Intermediate High, where Peter spent his years from thirteen to fifteen, Geoffrey Bower shared a double desk with him and found him a mystery — moody, aloof and remote. He was never friendly with anyone, never had any of the boys over to his house, they weren't even sure with whom or where he lived. The Maths teacher, Mr Harris, couldn't stand him but Mrs Conybeare, the English teacher, had a great liking for him. And in her class where she had them all act out Shakespearean parts, Peter was the best. In fact, he was the best in the whole school. Geoffrey's favourite performance which he still remembers was Peter as Shylock: a fawning cringing creature. Peter could recite passage after passage of Shakespeare, Latin and French by heart. But Geoffrey's opinion of him was that he resented discipline and was frequently and defiantly late for school (after he'd first finished up all his morning chores and caught the ferry to school). Scholastically, he stayed firmly in the lower half of the class.

Peter ran away at least twice, Geoffrey recalls, each time for about two or three weeks. Once he went to Queensland which was about six hundred miles away; the police eventually brought him back.

It was the sameness, the same dreary everyday sameness that was driving Peter wild. Sundays were the worst. Every Sunday, one thing followed the next with grim regularity: church, chores and the family gathering for high tea. Sometimes Uncle Jack would be there, though he tried to keep away as much as possible; always Aunt Kate, now eighty, and Aunt Dorothy who had reluctantly taken leave from the hospital and was doing her duty looking after her aged senile father, and — very rarely — Peter's spirited contemporary cousin, Cynthia, and her two sisters, down from Queensland for a holiday in Sydney. Cynthia remembers the oppressive discipline on those occasions when the young children's table manners were under constant scrutiny and correction.

"We don't do that in the house of Vere de Vere" was the perpetual reprimand until one day Cynthia cried out in exasperation, "I don't believe there *is* a house of Vere de Vere!"

To Peter, the endurance of those interminable high teas every Sunday was the nadir of his existence. Here was the enemy gathered full force, closing in on him, locking him out from the rest of the world and freedom. Zombies, he called them privately in his mocking effort to distance himself from the horrors of reality: "Zombs!"

Some memories can never heal. Years later, living happily at the Cross, making a name for himself as a leading actor and free swinging soul, he would have to say to friends, "Stay with me today. I can't talk. I've got a touch of the Zombs." And he would sit in his room silently all day while in his head the Zombs pursued him relentlessly like the furies.

At thirteen, Peter read a great deal. He read the romances of Dumas and Hugo, but mostly he read Dickens. He must have been the only boy in Sydney — perhaps the only boy in the world — for whom the bizarre adventures of Pip, Oliver Twist, David Copperfield and Little Nell were simply straight everyday factual accounts.

Australia in the early thirties was in the grip of the Depression. It was the greatest disaster Australia had ever known and like England in its finest hour, it was to bring forth all the resilience, fortitude and fellow feeling of the people. Peter longed to be part of it. Many of his former classmates had of necessity left school as early as aged thirteen to get work of one kind or another to help out their families. And ironically, Peter was still "privileged" to remain in High School at great sacrifice to all — and was hating every moment of it. He yearned to hit the road, to go bush. The pull of elsewhere was always strong in Peter and coupled with the examples provided by Dickens, it was finally overpowering.

The phrase "to run away" is of course misleading, for one is running towards something by the same token. Therefore it is interesting to speculate what Peter was running towards when he ran off to Queensland. Foremost, one gathers, was the consideration of running towards some place far enough away so as not to be caught. And at the back of his mind there might have been the thought that if things got really rough, he could contact his sympathetic cousin, Cynthia, who lived in Brisbane, Queensland.

Three things sustained him in the following wearisome years. One was young Mrs Conybeare, the attractive English teacher whom the boys adored. All Peter's classmates agree that Mrs Conybeare with her help and encouragement was a strong influence on his future development.

Years later, in 1956, when he was in Australia shooting *The Shiralee*, Mrs Conybeare recalls that she unexpectedly received a phone call from him. "We had a very friendly conversation and at the end, Peter said, 'I've always loved you. You know I've always loved you, don't you?' " Mrs Conybeare laughed. She was not unused to telephone calls from old pupils who report that immediately after the initial salutation, she would guess accurately, "Let me see, that must be so and so."

To his great joy, Peter was allowed to join the 2nd Greenwich Patrol of Boy Scouts. The boy who could "become anything" from an English baby to a French boy to a Boy Buddhist to a liberal Catholic theosophist had now become an Australian Boy Scout.

As might be expected, Peter briskly set about organising the Boy Scout troop to form his own acting company. He could tie knots, stalk, tell yarns around the campfire, learn bushcraft and first aid as well as any of them but acting was his heart and soul and his need. Luckily, Peter's need meshed with that of the Boy Scouts. They needed a hall for their meetings and in order to get it they had to raise money. One of the important ways they did it was by the shows Peter organised for which they charged admission. They were elaborate affairs with make-up, scenery and costumes. Charles Butler, the Patrol Leader, says, "They were really something to see. Because of Peter they were much talked about and two hundred people sat eagerly in the audience at every performance."

Paul Brickhill remembers a play which he performed with Peter for the Boy Scouts' fund-raising drive. Written, produced etc. by Peter, it was called *The Tragedy of the Romanoffs*. Peter played the last tragic Romanoff wearing Paul's swimming medal around his neck and Paul, his fellow artist, was, as he remembers, some sort of old family retainer whose task it was to shuffle back and forth in the background while an endless discussion was conducted between Peter and a boy seated opposite him. Today Paul judges that it was perhaps "a bit over the heads of the audience".

There was never any question, however, that Peter was the star attraction of these shows. Even the hand-written handbills always gave Peter top billing. Although at home Peter wouldn't, couldn't, *never* did anything right, he basked in the gratitude of the Boy Scouts for almost single-handedly raising the money for their hall and in the admiration of the public.

"Of all the people I knew who were at school with Peter," says John Carter, "I could not name one who was a close friend of his. I do not recall him having joined in the cricket, football, gymnastic or swimming-club activities of that era."

Peter had no friends at school. But one boy of his age who lived on the same street about seventy-five yards away and went to a different school not only noticed what a rough time Peter was having but attempted to do something about it. Paul Brickhill was Peter's first mate. Mateship is a concept of friendship exclusive to men, peculiar to Australian culture. It is probably of Irish or English working-class origin, going back to the days of the early Australian convicts banding together against their oppressive governors; it implies a common background and, to an unstated degree, a guarantee of uncritical, supportive, encouraging solidarity.

Peter Finch and Paul Brickhill were mates.

Paul was determined to rescue Peter — to get him out playing with the other boys. One afternoon he went over to his mate's house. As they were talking in the garden, the aunt yelled out the window, "Peter, go find my teeth." Paul remembers with horror how Peter without a word went about looking for them with a kind of ghastly *practicality*. When he found the false teeth, he merely picked them up and handed them to her. Paul adds: "He had a tough time. No one ever knew how bad it was. He was a skivvy, a servant — washing, cleaning, sweeping, scrubbing, making beds, working in the garden; he was rarely allowed out."

On the rare occasions when he was let out, Paul admired his guts. Once they nearly drowned together in a leaky canoe and were rescued just in time by a passing boat. "Peter always had a lucky star over him," Paul says. They both did. On one occasion Peter got into a fight with an older and bigger boy. Paul remembers Peter fighting gamely on and refusing to quit, covered in blood. It ended in a draw.

One day, Peter went over to Paul's house. "I'm not allowed to see you any more," he said. They looked at each other. "You're a very bad influence on me," he added. But of course they continued seeing each other — it was easy. By now, Peter had had long and expert training in the art of deception.

Fifteen was graduation age at the North Sydney Intermediate High School. It is doubtful that Peter actually graduated. "He never passed an exam in his life," says classmate Moran Callaghan. "I don't think he ever took one. To get out of a Latin exam he tripped over his leg, rubbed sand on his knee to make it red, convinced the doctor he'd broken his leg and was out of school in a splint for a fortnight." "I looked in his science note-book once," said David Lowe. "It was just full of caricatures of people."

In 1931, in the depth of the Depression, Peter left school. The Finches were at that time mostly banking people and his cousin Cynthia thinks that for one awful moment they actually put Peter into a job at a bank. If this is true, one can only guess what would have transpired.

Norman Johnson, an editor on the *Sun*, Sydney's leading newspaper, lived near Peter. What he had observed was a good-looking fine-featured fifteen-year-old, bright, imaginative, highly strung yet with the gentle irresistible appeal of an orphan. He told Peter (after talking to the aunt) that he would take him on as a copy boy at the *Sun*. Peter couldn't believe his luck. Infinite possibilities danced before him. The chance of Sydney. Once there, installed as a copy boy at the *Sun*, there would be the chance to audition at various theatres, followed by the immediate prospect of succeeding brilliantly in leading roles. The critics' approbation ... his name in lights ... Sydney at his feet ... the world at his feet ... the chance to escape from the Zombs. He might not be confident of anything else but his school days and Boy Scout days had made him supremely confident of his talent.

It was Peter and Paul in the leaky canoe all over again, just about to drown and rescued at the last moment. Both their lucky stars were shining upon them. Paul had also quit school, was fed up, his family had been wiped out by the Depression, he needed a job and didn't know what he could do. Peter asked Johnson to hire Paul as a copy boy too. Johnson refused. Peter, persuasive, prevailed. "If it hadn't been for Peter making Johnson hire me on the newspaper," says Paul Brickhill (who wrote *The Dambusters, The Great Escape* and *Reach for the Sky*), "I would never have become a newspaper man or a writer. I owe Peter a lot."

Peter and Paul set off bright and early every morning to board the Greenwich Point ferry and fantasised their way across the water to the city. Peter was going to be an actor and Paul a pilot. Their favourite fantasy was the one in which Peter unexpectedly receives a cable from London. An emergency! He must replace the actor in the leading role of a new play about to open! Peter is the only person in the world able to fill the role! He must arrive immediately! He will have to fly! And Paul of course is the only pilot in the world able to fly him!

They both had their wishes granted. Paul became a fighter pilot; in World War II. He flew forty missions and then "got careless" and crashed. But his lucky star was shining; he came out alive.

Peter's lucky star shone too. In the seventies, at a low point in his career, he became a last-minute replacement for the leading role in a film and was perhaps the only person in the world able to fill it. The film was *Sunday, Bloody Sunday*.

However, at the *Sun* newspaper offices in 1932, when they were sixteen, things were a little different. Protégés of their benevolent neighbour, Norman Johnson, Peter and Paul were not just relegated to the copy boy bench but assigned to particular journalists. Over the next year, it became evident that Paul was on his way to becoming a top newspaperman and Peter was on his way to being fired.

CHAPTER 4

Wild at the Cross

Peter should have been content in the newspaper world. True, he had only partially escaped the Zombs but if he could save his money (he was earning one pound a week) and show his stuff — he was an excellent cartoonist and very interested in writing — perhaps he could become a cadet, the next step up, and finally a newspaperman, an ambition which struck him as most worthy. He would then be financially solvent and the break from Greenwich Point would be easy. It might take time but he was only sixteen. He had time. But he had other inclinations.

More than a decade later, when Peter Finch was running the Mercury Theatre Acting School, he always told his students, "The only acceptable answer to 'Why do you want to be an actor?' is 'I can't help it!' "

Every day at lunchtime, Peter would entertain the copy boys. David Dixon, then a fellow copy boy, remembers how they all used to stand outside the newspaper building while Peter from across the street would yell out "Hitler!", run around the block and reappear impersonating Hitler. Then he would call out "Napoleon!" run around the block again and so forth. Little cameos for lunch. David also remembers that Peter's performance as the Hunchback of Notre Dame for the benefit of the editorial room was not much appreciated there. The story of his life that Peter was giving out at the time was that he had been brought up by a friendly Bengal tiger in the Indian jungle until the authorities found him and sent him to Australia.

One Friday afternoon, Peter seized the hat and walking stick of Sir Hugh Denison, Director of the *Sun*, from outside his office, went downstairs to the machine room, stood up on the table and gave, to the workers' amusement and amazement, a perfect imitation of Denison — his voice, his bearing, his manner of spitting sideways into a corner. Peter raised all their wages, gave them vacations and offered some bawdy suggestions as to how they should spend them. In the middle of his harangue he became aware that the crowd was melting. Sir Hugh had walked in.

"Boy, do you work here?" he barked.

"Yes, sir," said Peter.

"Well you don't any more!"

But Peter turned up bright and cheery on the next Monday morning. His protector, Norman Johnson, had intervened.

Peter was the special copy boy assigned to the eccentric George "Doggie" Marks who covered the Supreme Court for the *Sun* wearing a straw boater, winter or summer, and squeaky elastic-sided boots.

Even at the Supreme Court with this god-given opportunity to familiarize himself with the technique of on-the-spot reporting of important legal issues and rulings, Peter's real vocation gave him no rest. Ignoring the issues, he concentrated instead on the performances. Twenty years later, he still remembered them.

"I doubt whether I have ever seen such acting even in the years since, as the performances put on by those Sydney Judges and Counsel," said Peter. "I still think, for instance, of Boyce and Dovey and Windeyer as actors of the highest order. Dovey playing Iago to Windeyer's Othello is still a dream fantasy which fills me with the most exquisite pleasure." In the future, Peter was to say over and over again that he was a "frustrated journalist". Is this the dream fantasy of a frustrated *journalist*?

He was always missing on Wednesday afternoon. It turned out that he had found an acting school in Mosman that he was attending when he should have been going around to the police stations finding out if there had been any rapes, murders, fires or suicides. When he had applied to the newspaper for permission, it had been refused. He went anyway.

Being a copy boy was beginning to interfere seriously with his fantasies. Even sitting around the room with the other copy boys and hearing the sound "Boy!" and seeing a finger pointed at him, which meant having to race from a reporter to a sub-editor and back again, was a disagreeable interruption.

An actor is not an actor without an audience. But neither is he an actor without a theatre. Peter set about correcting this unhappy situation with all his might and main and need.

Except for touring productions, most professional theatre in Sydney had been closed down by the Depression and filming had been suspended while people waited to see if talkies were going to make it. Peter and Paul had long arguments about it on the Greenwich Point ferry. Peter definitely didn't think they were going to make it. That left the amateur societies and club socials. These were usually held on Sunday nights when aspiring young artists would perform for free for the sheer love of it.

Lorna Sisca was nineteen when she first saw Peter performing at one of these socials. He'd managed to get hold of a top hat and white tie and tails, and was singing *Champagne Charlie is my name* (Champagne drinking is my game) and dancing to it. Lorna was entranced. "He was so much better than all the rest. So much more professional." Afterwards she introduced herself to Peter and complimented him. They began seeing each other. "It was a very innocent relationship," says Lorna. "It never went beyond the hand-holding stage." They met every morning at the coffee-house at Repin's in King Street where they would sit holding hands while everyone around the table put the world to rights. Peter gave her a flower every morning when they met. During the daffodil season, he would say — "Please wear that suit tomorrow morning again because my daffodil will look so well with it."

Lorna came from a very happy family and he loved her home, especially her mother, and he would often say to Lorna, "I'm sorry I can't take you to my home too. I never take anybody." She saw that he was desperately unhappy there.

"He was a skinny young man with adolescent skin, always wearing the same heather-mix suit, but he was so *sure* of himself, so charming, so warm, so caring. He flowed out to anyone interested in him so that it was a compensatory act. His burning ambition to act seemed to be almost a spiritual one.

"Just to see him walking down King Street was a treat, holding himself so beautifully as if he were walking into life, as though he were going to buy the pavement."

Peter found another amateur group in the city in Kent Street, not too far away from the office, called The New Sydney Repertory Company; it was run in conjunction with an acting school by an old English actor, Scott Alexander. Its ambitious programme was to put on a different play every week. One production was *Caprice*, a play that the Lunts had done on Broadway with enormous success. There was a large part for a young man and Alexander, upon seeing

Peter, promptly gave it to him. Hugh Carlson in the company remembers that Peter always had a great deal of trouble getting to evening rehearsals because he had to climb out of a back window of his house.

At sixteen years of age, Peter made his Sydney début (after climbing out the back window and climbing in again later) with The New Sydney Repertory Company in *Caprice* in a part that fitted him like a glove. It was that of a passionate, poetic, idealistic sixteen-year-old who meets his father for the first time and falls in love with his mistress.

Meanwhile, his situation at home was untenable. He was virtually playing hide-and-seek dodging in and out of the house, his only aim to avoid confrontation with his aunt (and his Aunt Dorothy as well who was now siding against him). And the intolerable grimness of life at Greenwich Point was exacerbated by the fact that Peter, at last, had discovered his true spiritual home.

"Kings Cross is a wonderful place. Nothing since then, London, Paris, Hollywood or New York has been quite as wonderful — and although I lived always on the edge of destitution, I had never been happier in my life," said Peter in an interview with George Johnston in 1954. To the vaulting young troubadour about to invent his own song, his first scent of Bohemia is always the sweetest.

In the thirties, Kings Cross, an oasis high up in Sydney, was to that city what the Left Bank was to Paris. When Peter first saw it, it was what writers, painters, actors, eccentrics, con-men, criminals, madams and prostitutes alike all called home.

Today, Darlinghurst Road, from which the other streets of the Cross stem, looks gaudy without being sinister, sleazy but safe. The plane trees are still there on this boulevard as are the restaurants, coffee-houses, milk bars, chemists, brothels and prostitutes (substantially multiplied in numbers), and the winding streets still lead to a dazzling view of the harbour with its shimmering lights at night and its boats bobbing gently up and down as if asleep. But even if one manages to blot out the strip shows, the adult bookshops, the porn flicks and the neon and manages to conjure up the sidewalk cafés and other more pleasing architecture, the vital cast of characters that surrounded Peter who would eventually become first-rate poets, painters, writers and actors, have now all departed. And so has the atmosphere of a small Bohemian village, warm and matey, where everybody knew everybody else and no one seemed to work and no one seemed to worry and every morning people wandered down the street to buy their bottle of milk and box of cornflakes for breakfast.

Peter felt the Cross right down to his toes — being there provided a relief so intense that it felt like excitement. As Rukmini had observed him at nine years old wandering about the Theosophical Society's estate in India "meeting everybody and becoming a favorite of all the delegates", so now he wandered among the denizens of the Cross and did the same thing. There among the other rebels, he was at last able to throw off the oppressive mantle of Finch disapproval.

Peter had found Enid Lorimer again. Just before he was removed from The Manor in 1927, Enid had left to go to England. When she returned to Sydney five years later she formed an acting group called The Studio Theatre. Peter promptly joined it.

Enid says: "When I came back in 1932, I met Peter again. By this time he had found a job as copy boy for a newspaper and was most unhappy at home." She had met the aunts, they struck her as dull and middle class and "at no time, I imagine, people of other than narrow interests and totally incapable of dealing with a high-spirited emotionally unstable, mentally quite brilliant boy. And I must say that while I so much saw Peter's point of view, I couldn't help feeling a bit sorry for the unhappy hens who were trying to keep this duck from water. The aunts, poor dears, came to see me; but even if I hadn't faithfully promised not to tell them where he was, I couldn't see that it would be a good idea for them to try and get him back. He was over the legal age. I told them nothing." Peter's gratitude to Enid was boundless. For the rest of his life whenever they met he would embrace her saying "Ah, here she is, my deliverer from my aunts!"

The aunts were determined to prevent Peter from enjoying the evils and insecurities of the big city because he was a Finch — respectability and security were the names of the Finch game. In this way one might say, Peter's upbringing had been a resounding failure, for he would neither know nor want respectability or security for the rest of his life.

Peter had run away from Greenwich Point for the last time and Norman Johnson at the *Sun*, having heard what happened, found himself caught in the cross-fire. The worry of Peter — his all but invisible copy boy — was bad enough without the worry of his neighbours, the aunts, constantly pressuring him for the boy's return. At any rate he called Peter into his office and delivered his ultimatum. "Either you make up your mind to return home or you lose your job here."

This was a blow to Peter. He'd counted on his one pound a week salary from the newspaper to keep him going. Since he'd run away he'd spent his nights sleeping in the bandstand in Hyde Park. But he had not been alone. Many others in those days of rampant poverty were sleeping in the park. Thirty years later, Peter said of the period: "I've lived with men who've touched bottom and it was then I learned something of the essentials of what makes a human being."

"Either you make up your mind to return home or —"said Johnson.

Peter didn't pause to consider the alternative.

"Sack me," he said.

"Now please, Peter," Johnson temporized. "You're making this very hard for me."

"I'll make it easier," said Peter. He approached Johnson's desk, grabbed the water pitcher and emptied it over Johnson's head.

Peter was sacked. Peter was exultant. Peter was free.

"That took guts," said Paul when Peter told him. "Now what're you going to do?"

"I'm going to the Cross," said Peter happily and took off ...

Peter found himself quickly accepted by the inhabitants of the Cross, especially by those in the Arabian House coffee lounge where the intellectuals gathered. They found this skinny young would-be actor with his beautiful aesthetic face and his ribald sense of humour vastly entertaining. His gift of mimicry was developing into a style the writer Alex Macdonald was to call "berserk idiocy". They were also amenable to letting him scrounge the odd cup of coffee and to loan him the use of their attic, their sofa or their floor for a night's sleep.

Some had other ideas. As Peter and Paul sat over their coffee, Peter told Paul about a suave, sophisticated, amusing older man of twenty-five, whom he had met at the Cross. This man had offered to put Peter up. "I'm going to be kept! I'm going to be kept!" Peter crowed. Paul said nothing. Mates do not censure.

Two weeks later, over coffee again, Peter said to Paul, "It's not working. I'm moving out. I've found a room for five shillings a week only I don't have five shillings."

Paul, by then a cadet on the newspaper, was able to give him the necessary five shillings for a while.

In Sydney the queues for the dole stretched for hundreds of yards. The classified advertisement pages of the Sydney *Morning Herald* were pasted up outside the Salvation Army shelters with never less than two hundred youngsters queued up for any of the occasional jobs that were advertised. Peter developed an intimate knowledge of the dole and doss-houses.

Of this knowledge, he said later to George Johnston: "It was a wonderful experience. It gave me a tremendous affection for my fellow human beings. We were all pretty close to starvation and there didn't seem to be much future but everybody was always good-natured and they would go out of their way to be nice to each other. You never saw anything vicious or rotten."

Early on, when he didn't have money for rent, Peter slept in a Salvation Army shelter or went back to Hyde Park. He got jobs of sorts: he sold artificial flowers; he "borrowed" an old bicycle and worked as a taxi boy at Taylor Square; he tramped from door to door selling subscriptions to a magazine that turned out to be non-existent; he was a waiter at the Hotel Astra at Bondi Beach near Sydney.

At the Cross, the favorite tipple was a rough, dry potent sherry known as "plonk" or "nellie" which sold for two shillings a quart bottle. At seventeen, Peter was learning to drink — or, rather, he was failing to learn to drink. He never learned in the sense of being able to hold his liquor. He had no head for it. It only took a little to make him high and only a little more to make him drunk. Nevertheless, he was drinking. With the zeal of a disciple, he threw himself into it as he threw himself into everything. Peter never knew when to stop, nor did he waste any time starting. Especially not on a Saturday night at the Cross.

Jon Rose, in his book *At the Cross*, has left a living account of those nights through which we can trace Peter's somewhat dishevelled behaviour.

As soon as Saturday was born the Cross did herself proud. Everyone was out shopping like mad, the bars were full, and to walk down the street empty-handed seemed almost indecent. Saturdays always worked themselves up into an enormous climax of parties. Saturday night was party night. No matter how little money anyone had, they were either going to or giving a party. Only the lonely or the non-Crossites were abroad Saturday night. That is, until at least two a.m. when the other Cross rule came into force. It was to buy one's Sunday papers from one of the two little men who sold them down near its Film House. These one bought from two a.m. onwards and it seemed to me that one bought the papers in two ways only. Either you arrived "high" and with people from a party or you drifted through the heat of the night in your pyjamas.

This procedure was nearly sacred, the hot pie man, the old woman with the hot dogs and the newspaper men seemed almost to enforce it. And often a crazy and sometimes sad scene it was. People fighting after a party, couples saying long intense good-byes. Or someone having to leave a group which had within it the person they desired but for various reasons couldn't have ... The Crossites on the whole were the sharpest, maddest, cruellest and warmest people in the world.

Peter became a scrounge. He was the first to admit it and the last to think it wrong or degrading. Perhaps he was simply carrying his begging bowl around with him again. In Buddhist terms, begging monks are not considered the lowest rank of humanity but rather the highest, for it is in their power to grant that holiest of all blessings, the opportunity to bestow charity.

This could explain why the Buddhists at the Cross (in the unlikely event that there were any) were not driven to intolerance by Peter's incessant scrounging. But the non-Buddhists of the Community, who after all were in the majority, tolerated it also, if only just. They tolerated it because it was soon proven to them that if what was theirs was Peter's, what was Peter's was theirs.

He was a mooch, an opportunist and a free-loader, undoubtedly, but he gave away his money as soon as he got it, when his opportunities came he shared them, and he always sang for his suppers. There seems to be a certain amount of evidence that he stole for them as well.

Peter's main activity at the time consisted of getting invited to parties. Once inside, the course was strictly laid out: a bee-line to the kitchen to eat his way, hopefully, through the next two days and then into the main room where the party was going on. Starting quietly in a corner he would begin one of his brilliant "turns" — (a homosexual camel searching through the desert for another homo-sexual camel; and a man with a desperate hangover, frantically struggling to get out the magic words "Brandy, lime and soda" that will save his life, to the bartender, were two favourites) — and as the group around him grew larger and the laughter more hilarious, he would be induced to stand up in the centre of the room and to continue with two or three (or four if pressed) more of his acts. If, as Jon Rose says, the Crossites were the sharpest, cruellest, maddest people in the world, it must have been a tribute to Peter's genius rather than to Crossite benevolence that when the skinny young scarecrow stood up to perform, they didn't just tell him to sit down and shut up.

It was at one of these parties that Peter met Donald Friend. Today one of Australia's best-known painters, Donald at eighteen was a flamboyant, witty young man who believed as fiercely in his talent as Peter did in his. Peter had been thrown out of his lodgings and had no money. Donald lived in a ten-shillings-a-week attic in Rockwall Crescent off Macleay Street at the Cross. Peter moved in with him after they left the party. Their quarters were cramped and sordid with sloping walls, a penny-in-the-slot bath and constant nightmarish explosions from the gas heater on the floor below. "Peter's dramatization of our situation made even the worst parts funny," says Donald. "We lived largely on his wits." Peter would persuade the doorman of some gangsters' bottle club to let them in. Once in, he'd persuade the boss to give them a meal in exchange for a floor show in which Donald played Peter's stooge. At parties in the Maccabean Hall where underworld characters celebrated birthdays and other occasions, Peter also entertained, stubbornly insisting on including in his act at least one of his favourite speeches from Shakespeare which provoked great rage from the spivs and touts in the audience but always melted the golden hearts of the gangland madams.

Peter and Donald didn't share the attic for long. A crisis arose. Specifically, a matter of unpaid rent forced them to a serious assessment of their situation and they decided to "hump their blueys".

In nineteenth-century parlance, to "hump your bluey" meant to shoulder the bundle containing your worldly belongings and go out pleasuring. In the thirties, it meant to shoulder your bundle (your swag) and try to find work in the outback. But for Peter and Donald, the first definition was more precise.

It was not an original idea. The youth of Australia was on the move and the movement was away from the unemployment of the cities into the outback or up the coast. By the thousands they rode the rattlers, i.e., jumped a freight train. Often they got caught, spent the night in jail and were off again next morning.

There was something called the single man's dole, an effort on the government's part to keep the unemployed moving until they found work. Every Wednesday, at the police station of each town, you collected a coupon worth eight shillings to trade in at a food store. Eight shillings would purchase scraggy meat, sugar and tea. Cigarettes were tuppence and beer threepence. But it was only possible to collect this dole if you were twenty-two miles from where you received it last.

Depression babies have been labelled the "unfortunate generation" but perhaps in hindsight they might be called the fortunate ones. Exposed early to the basic hardships of survival, they were, it could be argued, more fit to deal with the rest of their lives than the subsequently more gently reared ones. These young Australian swagmen probably met with a lot more manly adventure than any Hemingway hero.

Donald pawned a valuable book and together he and Peter set forth. "Peter's concept of a vagabond's life had about it something of a strolling player," says Donald "and as we travelled, he continually chanted a jingle which he imbued with such mystical meaningfulness that I still remember it after forty years:

I eat my peas with honey
I've done it all my life
It makes the peas taste funny
But it keeps them on the knife

"For a while we camped outside Katoomba in an empty cottage in the Blue Mountains — bitterly cold. We lived on a terrible diet: oatmeal porridge, dates and vegetables pinched from a paddock. Going into the village, Peter was a White Russian polo player, a sort of orphan of the Revolution. He had a pair of boots which by some sleight of imagination became a complete Cossack costume, and he spoke no more than six words of English. My own part allowed me a few words more. I was a faithful serf who had helped him escape the Bolsheviks — so that as hoboes we had a certain outlandish *chic* which served better than a knock at the back door to ask a kind lady for a hand-out. But such masquerades were only for what we thought of as the bourgeoisie, never for authentic hoboes."

Eventually, Donald went back to Sydney and, for a few months, Peter bummed around on his own. He was not sorry to be alone, though with a nature like his that had become so dependent on other people, he might wonder that this was so. Peter called this time the most valuable philosophical period of his life. "To be a hobo was to be dead bottom and I felt there was a certain beauty and logic in being beyond the pale of respectability. It was so much better than being half-way down and having to keep up appearances."

The child who could "become anything" from a Boy Buddhist to a Boy Scout had now become a swaggie, a hobo, a bum. His soul rejoiced.

The Aboriginal of Australia, in the wisdom and poetry of his five thousand-year-old civilization, says: "When the pressures of the immediate world become so strong they take you away from your dreaming then you must go on walkabout and learn to live with the land and from the land and know you are a part of the life force which began before you began and began before time began and will continue after you and when you can do that it brings you back to your cycle of dreaming."

Peter went on walkabout. The ribbon of the road stretched out in front of him as he walked down it into the most valuable philosophical period of his life. He dropped the masquerade and abandoned the strolling player. Disembarrassed of ambition he felt a freedom different from the freedom of the Cross which entailed being an entertainer, a house pet. Disembarrassed of his gnawing, driving ambition to become world famous overnight he felt himself gliding, coasting, rolling down the road, getting a hitch, stopping off wherever there was work. At night he slept under the open skies, under the dog star and the brilliant Southern Cross.

Peter became a roustabout, a jackaroo, a farm labourer. He did odd jobs, he fed the livestock, he mended fences, looked after cows. He chopped wood and ring-barked. If he arrived at a property where there were sheep to herd, which meant you had to be able to ride a horse, he could do that too. As can be seen in his films, he was a superb horseman, a natural horseman, he rode like a stylish centaur. To him horses were people and he talked to them as if they were. And yet his only knowledge of them had been gleaned from two or three holidays spent as a boy with his cousin Cynthia and her twin sisters at "Wanna Wanna", a property in Queanbeyan run by his cousin Florrie Powell, a brisk energetic woman whom he liked, and her husband Alex. There Peter's greatest joy had been to ride the horses.

It was on the road that Peter finally grew up. He grew up with the discovery that he was able to take care of himself, by himself. Whether consciously or unconsciously he would always associate his growing up with the knowledge and love of poverty. This became as important to the structure of his future life as his embracing of Buddhism at the age of nine.

His heart, always quick to burst into love, now burst into song and it was certainly here on the road that inspiration for what was to become his poem *Tell Them* was born. It begins:

Tell them in the old worlds,
How we can love
Not the greensward
Underfoot,
But the basalt boulder,
White quartz,
River stones
Deep amber, crevassed clay —
No Roman edifice
No piles Baroque
Or Byzantine
But the gutted woolshed
Leaning charred
Against the wind
Rust-red and grey

Tell them how we can love
The blue hills haze
The eucalyptus scent
In smoke wisps
And the slow-winged ibis
Dripping downwards
At the Sun ...

In time Peter, back in his cycle of dreaming, returned to Sydney, took a room at Mrs Eva Hourigan's in Brougham Street and began looking for work in his chosen profession.

Doris Fitton's famous Independent Theatre, a highly professional amateur company (everyone got paid but the actors) was then housed in the Savoy Theatre in Sydney. "There is not one member of our profession in Australia, whether still here or overseas who is not indebted to the Independent," says Enid Lorimer.

However, Peter's connection with the Independent was minimal and indeed only notable for a very small part in Elmer Rice's *Counsellor-at-Law* (first produced at the Plymouth Theatre, New York 1931) in November 1934 when he was eighteen. The novelist

Sumner Locke Elliott, then a precocious sixteen-year-old actor-playwright, describes the impact Peter made on him: "I was playing the office boy and Peter an Italian bootblack in *Counsellor-at-Law*. He had five lines, I think. I watched him at rehearsals. I'd never seen him before and he was *electric*. I mean absolutely more brilliant than anybody in the entire cast put together and more brilliant than anyone we'd ever seen. He was rather grubby, looked as if he needed a bath, in shabby clothes and we didn't know where he lived or anything about him. But through the grubbiness, this marvellous thing shone out of him — this brilliance just shone. Offstage I remember he was always sneaking around trying to get someone to buy him a free cup of coffee."

Actually, Peter had seven lines not five and they were mostly "Yes, boss", "Sure, boss", "Yes, sure, boss", "All right, goodbye, boss", spoken while kneeling at the boss's feet shining his shoes. But the scene he was in was one of the most telling of the play, for Elmer Rice very cleverly juxtaposed three characters: the Counsellor-at-Law (one of Paul Muni's great parts), a fashionable divorce-murder corporation lawyer who has worked his way up from a poor Lower Eastside Jewish background, a Communist of the same background but a generation younger, and the bootblack. As the two protagonists begin their angry confrontation, the lawyer suddenly notices that the bootblack, the capitalist slave, is listening and dismisses him. But as the boy goes, for a moment the audience goes with him and wonders what will eventually become of him. Will he become a capitalist like the lawyer? A Communist? Or will he remain a bootblack all his life?

Peter, elated by the praise conferred on him by Doris Fitton and the experienced actors in the company, was now truly deep into his dream cycle.

At this time Mary Wallace was a servant in the house of Dr Skipton and on her day off, the doctor's young son John (who also worked at the Independent) once took his friend Peter home for lunch. Mary explained that she was off-duty but if they promised not to sit and talk over the meal she would rustle up a salad for them.

"While the two young men ate, I showered and dressed and then began to clear away and do the dishes. The visitor helped, shook the cloth and as I washed the dishes, he dried them — and talked! He was with Doris Fitton's Independent Theatre, but watch him hit Hollywood! His name would be in lights, he'd have a Hollywood starlet on each arm etc. etc. I told him to get the dishes dried, look at the time, but he rattled on about being a star one day. As I flew to catch my tram he called out 'Mary, watch for my name, it's Finch, Peter Finch' and I called out 'Good luck Peter and thank you for helping with the dishes.' "

"After *Counsellor-at-Law*," says Sumner Locke Elliott, "I was putting on a play I'd written called *The Café at the Corner*. It had only two characters. I, for some reason, was playing an eighty-year-old man and I cast Peter for the other one. He showed up for two rehearsals and then just disappeared. But what really annoyed me was that he turned up on the night of the performance and had the temerity to stand up and *wave* at me at the curtain! Then he just disappeared again."

Peter's disappearance might have been due to an embarrassment of theatrical engagements, for soon after completing the *Counsellor-at-Law* run at the Independent, he finally turned professional. As straight man to a Jewish-American comic called Bert le Blanc, he was earning thirty shillings a week.

Peter's official story to the press as to how it happened goes like this:

"One day as I was standing in the dole queue, I was advised by a fellow-unemployed to seek out work in the theatre because of what he called 'that bloody toffee voice of yours'. A comedian was in need of a straight man at the Maccabean Hall on Darlinghurst Road."

Now follows a bit of totally improbable dialogue dredged up from Peter's memory:

"But I don't know anything about playing straight man," Peter pointed out.

"That's all right," the man said. "You've got a toffee voice and that's what's wanted!"

"Unconvinced but willing to try anything, I went for the audition," continues Peter, endeavouring to leave the impression of strolling off at a leisurely pace in the direction of the Maccabean Hall. In fact the real Peter must have removed himself from that queue with the speed of frenzied lightning.

And then: "*To my astonishment I got the job. I'd never thought of being an actor, I'd had no training,*" he concludes.

It is this statement, which he repeated so many times to the press that it has become the official story, that has misled the world into assuming that Peter backed into acting wholly by accident.

On the surface it would seem that Peter was merely obeying the cardinal rule of his profession: Make it look easy. But it was feelings not facts that mattered with Peter, and this utterance sprang from certain insecurities that haunted him all his life and were based on what he felt was a lack of formal acting training.

"There is nothing so secure as *no*-talent," Orson Welles has said and Peter was too talented ever to be secure. Six years later, as Australia's foremost radio star, Peter was discovered sitting on the steps of the broadcasting building holding himself tight to keep from shaking before going on radio. "I'm only a beginner," he explained to a friend who expressed concern. "I've had no training. I get up to the microphone and something inside me comes down and something comes out and that's all I know. But I live in fear that one day it's not going to come out." And when he stated that he had never thought of being an actor he may have been stating the truth that it is far easier for a beginner to think of himself as a star than as a professional actor.

So Peter's baptism of fire as a professional was as a straight man back at the rowdy Maccabean Hall. Bert, according to Peter, was fast and unpredictable. He had sixty fixed comic routines and he would change any of them right in the middle when he wasn't getting laughs. "You had to think fast," said Peter. "He taught me a lot."

They were quite a team those two. Peter long, slim and elegant (in stage clothes infinitely more dapper than his own) and Bert short, round and vulgar. Peter toffee-voiced; Bert vehemently non-toffee-voiced.

Peter's head was always in the clouds and his feet were always in the mud. From the exaltation of his sky thoughts he could plunge to earth and splash happily about in the mud without the slightest twinge of conscience. He was a romantic.

Down where Darlinghurst Road meets William Street at the Cross was a section known as the Dirty Half Mile where the brothels flourished. The two rival houses there were run by Tilly and Kate. Peter had first met Kate at the Maccabean Hall with Donald. They had become friendly and would join each other for cups of coffee whenever they met at the Cross, exchanging gossip and confidences. Kate told Peter about her son, who thought she was his aunt and went to an exclusive boarding school. She told him how when her boy grew up he was going to marry a decent girl and she was going to give him a real white wedding in a church with flowers. Peter told her about his father who was a no-hoper and his mother who was a

French opera singer and how he'd lived in India in a Buddhist monastery until his father's sister came and brought him over to Australia. And he told her he was planning to go to Hollywood at the first chance he got and that he was going to be a big star, just you watch.

They both believed each other. Kate assured Peter she would "watch" but one day as she was listening to his voice it gave her an idea. She loved poetry, particularly Walt Whitman. Would Peter come over some night and read *Leaves of Grass* to her? She'd pay him, of course.

So Peter went to the brothel and read the inspiriting stanzas of *Leaves of Grass* to Kate while the girls of the establishment drifted in and out of the parlour often stopping to listen. After two or three poetry sessions it became clear to Kate from the way Peter was looking at the girls that he would prefer to be paid in some way other than money.

Peter's first sexual experiences with women were probably with the girls in the brothel. As an eighteen-year-old he would naturally have had a strong sexual drive but what was perhaps remarkable was that he equated it with love. Cruelly denied parental love as a child he would not be denied sexual love as an adult. The girls, alone with him, were first amazed and then delighted with the virile young man. Very soon he was on their free list.

Poetry and sex seem to have become inextricably meshed in his psyche forever. The common joke about him for many years in England was that you never knew when Peter took a girl to bed whether he was going to make love to her or sit up all night reading poetry to her.

The prostitutes were very fond of show people. Instinctively they felt they were in the same business — entertaining the customers; and they both kept the same hours. The prostitutes were making a lot of money and for Peter and another mate of his, a handsome young actor, they always picked up the tab when they went to the after-hours clubs like the Fifty-Fifty and The Four Hundred. Peter was raising his own kind of hell long before he met Errol Flynn.

Peter's strong erotic allegiance to prostitutes lasted all his life. In London, years later, successful and with money in the bank, Peter felt that now it was his place to return the compliment of the free list. One prostitute to whom he offered thirty pounds (over half his salary) for being his mistress turned him down explaining that she could earn that much in a night. To another, he paid a large sum so she wouldn't have to work that night. At one time he was so well known among the prostitutes in London that a fellow Australian told him "Whenever I say I'm an Australian, they ask me if I know Peter Finch," to which Peter replied "I've been hearing good things about you, my boy."

The prostitutes were grateful for Peter's ribald sense of humour. It helped them over some rough spots. This ribald streak of his had manifested itself early. At ten he'd had the classroom in an uproar with his portrayal of an ancient crone attempting to suckle a baby. At fifteen, at a High School prize-giving, Peter first performed Richard III and then went into a couple of skits of such a *risqué* nature that the Headmaster left and his more worldly deputy compèred the balance of the programme. During the war, a fellow soldier remembers being invited with Peter to a very grand house in Adelaide where, after dinner, Peter launched into a story so obscene and explicit that the soldier devoutly wished himself back in the barracks. This indiscriminate ribaldry was a lifetime blind spot in a man who was otherwise so sensitive to situations, so aware of appropriate behaviour, and it became very much part of the "Peter doesn't give a damn" legend.

At the same time that Peter was frequenting Kate's he was being painted as a saint. Virgil Lo Schiavo, an artist who specialised in religious murals, had been captivated by Peter's gaunt aesthetic face and was using him as a model for a fresco. In exchange for Peter's sittings, he gave him spaghetti meals and fencing lessons. Peter, Virgil and his younger sister, Iole, would sit around Virgil's studio which was an abandoned chapel arguing about religion. Peter always ended his side of the discussion with "If I can't make it as an actor, I'm going to become a Buddhist monk."

Eventually the variety show closed and Peter was out of work again. It was always a trying time for everyone at the Cross when Peter was out of work and especially for the landladies. He had left Brougham Street and lived in and out of Wylde Street, Victoria Street, Orwell Street, Elizabeth Bay Road and Macleay Street in the space of two months. He had become expert at the "moonlight flit" having done his basic training climbing in and out of his aunt's windows at Greenwich Point. He would cadge two bob from someone and sit in the cinema all day studying the actors, saying to people "I'm going to be up there too." Close to starvation, he would munch carrots from a bag saying cheerfully, "They're very sex-making, you know." The more bleak the actual reality, the more real his dreams became to him. As long as there was enough cheap sherry to dull his hunger pains he could keep going.

Everyone at the Cross heaved a sigh of relief when Peter passed his audition at the ABC and was offered a small part in the radio serial *Khyber Pass*. And everyone was in a flap again when he announced that he wouldn't get it unless he had a dinner jacket.

The ABC, Australia's official broadcasting station, modelled itself closely on its austere English parent, the BBC. One of the rules was that since by tradition all gentlemen wore dinner jackets after seven in the evening, the actors would be obliged to do so as well and never mind that no one saw them except the boys in the control booth. A man sitting on a tram at six p.m. in evening clothes was always correctly identified as an ABC actor.

The Dinner Jacket: The acquiring of it, the hiring of it, the borrowing of it, the pawning of it, the reclaiming of it, was a leitmotiv that ran all through Peter's radio days and left him with an enduring hatred of that article of clothing for the rest of his life. A young woman called Helen McPherson procured him his first one and Peter donning it slipped smoothly from straight man to a low comic into a young subaltern fighting intractable tribes over the Khyber Pass.

CHAPTER 5

The Making of an Actor

In his small role in the *Khyber Pass* radio serial, Peter made an impression on ABC directors but radio made no impression on him; it was good for a couple of meals but standing in front of a microphone and reading a script was not his idea of acting. When the job was over he disappeared.

Peter had heard that a play was going on tour. It was an American comedy of the genre that used to be called zany, with the giveaway title *So This is Hollywood*. The star was an American comedian, Bobby Capron, and the producer was J. C. Williamson. When Peter won the juvenile lead, he was elated. He would have at least six months' work on stage.

Peter strode into rehearsals, ready to excel. He was in a first-rate production with first-rate actors and a real live star. And it was still a month before he turned nineteen. He was not so far behind in his schedule.

During rehearsals Peter became profoundly disillusioned with himself: he was terrible. He was awkward, clumsy, wooden — and everyone knew it.

Bobby Capron spotted what the trouble was, and generously took Peter in hand. Capron explained to him that there was more to acting than inspiration and that there are more pitfalls in playing contemporary comedy than in playing Shakespeare. He began showing Peter how to do all the difficult, essential, simple things in stagecraft: how to pick up a telephone, light a cigarette, walk across the stage.

This was all new air for Peter, and just what he needed to know. Avidly he began rehearsing in his room for long hours; he opened and shut doors, made entrances and exits, poured out drinks and handed them around the way Capron had shown him. Peter was finding out that the hardest lesson a natural instinctive actor has to learn is to wed technique with feeling. "I will go to my grave trying to do so," said Peter when he was a star, "but I think I have narrowed the gap slightly."

Before they left for their opening date in Melbourne the cast, unable to bear Peter's threadbare clothes, got together and bought him some new ones. He had to borrow a suitcase.

Three weeks after the Melbourne opening Bobby Capron, his little terrier dog, an actress and Peter were enjoying a day's outing on the banks of the river Yarra. Suddenly Bobby realized that his dog had disappeared. From the riverbank he saw the dog in the water, desperately trying to scramble back on to land. He jumped in. Both Capron and the dog were immediately swirled away with the current. Peter jumped in after them and managed to save the dog, but the actor drowned in a flooded mining tunnel.

The newspapers made much of the tragic event and Peter's part in it. He received a scroll of commendation from the Royal Humane Society and a letter of appreciation from the American Consul. When the play re-opened with a new star, Peter received a standing ovation from the audience. Without Capron, however, the play soon closed and Peter was out of work again.

Back in Sydney again, Peter made an assessment of himself. Bobby Capron had opened a door for him that he had only begun to peer through. Without technique, dedication and experience, talent was useless. Peter's whole approach to acting underwent a change: he became analytical, critical and theoretical. He went to the Mitchell Library and read all the books that he could find on acting. A year later when Stanislavski's *An Actor Prepares* was published in Australia, he started to carry around a dog-eared copy, much the way his grandmother had carried around Krishnamurti's *At the Feet of the Master*.

Since the few theatres open in Sydney in 1936 only housed operettas and musicals and Peter could not sing (the gods had to stop somewhere), he was forced to return to radio. He was less than happy because he did not like radio nor radio actors and they did not like him. The radio actors were the only actors who worked regularly in those days (they tended to rush importantly from radio station to radio station with minutes to spare). They were a cliquey, superior lot who looked down on scruffy Cross rats. But when Peter showed up at the ABC his welcome was quite different from what he expected. The Sydney newspapers had publicised their home town boy's act of bravery and now the radio actors found Peter a very decent, very talented bloke. He was admitted to the club.

As a result of his new analytic and technical approach to acting, Peter began to take his radio roles seriously; he researched them with diligence and common sense. If he was playing a sailor, he would go aboard a steamship liner in Sydney Harbour and talk to the sailors, watch them at work, look at their sleeping quarters. If he was playing a painter, he would go to the National Gallery and sketch pictures. Fellow boarders got used to hearing different voices coming through the thin walls of his room. Even encased in the hated dinner jacket, he always wore one article of clothing that made him feel right for the part.

In the thirties, Australian radio actors were thought to be among the finest in the world and their vocal technique was highly developed. But at that time it had to be so. The control room left voice-levels entirely up to them; they were also left to do their own sound-effects. Footsteps were crunched in a boxful of gravel, doors were opened and closed and even the brng, brng of the telephone was trilled by actors. Peter quickly mastered radio technique and in a very short time he was gripping the arm of another newcomer, pushing and pulling him to and from the mike and saying at the end of the show, "I've got to teach you some technique, boy."

Like all the best clubs, the radio actors had their traditions and rituals. One strict tradition was their stance at the microphone. They stood, leaning back slightly, one shoulder higher than the other, one foot advanced; the script was held waist-high in the left hand (or the right in Peter's case as he was left-handed) while the other hand skilfully flipped the pages in order to avoid crackle. Many years later Peter was still unconsciously slipping into this posture.

One of the club's rituals was the midday swill. The members descended in a group upon the Hotel Australia, Sydney's biggest hotel, where they ravaged the free counter for bread, butter, cheese and celery; they then sat over their pints, airing their views until it was time to go back to work. It was a safe, pleasant, not unrewarding life.

Despite the wildness of Peter's life at the Cross, he never allowed it to impinge upon the discipline of his work — and the work came because of his voice. When transmitted over the air waves, it was pure gold. Then, just when directors were beginning to say "We've got to have Finch for this part", he disappeared.

Peter had got another chance to tour and he grabbed it. This time he was offered a part in a travelling tent show, an altogether different sort of touring date from *So This is Hollywood*. The entrepreneur was George Sorlie, a half-Jamaican, half-English actor, called "King of the Road"; Sorlie's tent shows were known all over inland Australia. On tour, the company would present six different plays a week. The schedule was rugged and the conditions were rough. Not only were the actors expected to help raise the huge tents each week in different towns, they were obliged to rehearse the repertoire for seven weeks without pay; Peter did not mind. At last he was a *real* strolling player.

Of the six plays in the repertoire with names such as *Ten Minute Alibi, Laughter of Fools* and *Married by Proxy*, the only one that stayed in his mind was *While Parents Sleep*, which in fact he only watched from the sidelines. It is a depressing little upper middle-class English comedy by Anthony Kimmins about absolutely nothing. A dull army colonel and his wife have two very dull sons — a guardsman and a naval officer. Into their midst comes the flirtatious Lady Cattering; in an attempt to seduce the duller of the two sons, she ends up in her underslip. No doubt Sorlie had counted on this spicy spectacle to drive the local cane-cutters wild. It did — but not exactly in the way planned. One night, when Lady Cattering's dress snaked to the floor, eleven hundred cane-cutters rose and whistled. She had forgotten her slip. The happy sound of this bawdy audience was to ring delightfully in Peter's ears for many months. However the natural elements were against them; the rains came in floods. Attendance stopped and the players, no longer able to stroll, slushed their muddy way back to Sydney.

Due to his recent defection Peter found the atmosphere strained at the ABC. He then turned to the five commercial stations. At one station he did a series of fifteen-minute serials with such titles as *The Purple Spider, Sulieman Strikes Again, Master of the Gobi Desert* and *Leaves from Another Woman's Diary*. The recordings were done in a day, often from one morning to the next. Peter found it a great lark.

Then he got a break. For another commercial station he played the brave, mutinous, gently-born Fletcher Christian, defying the lash-happy sadist Bligh in the serial *Mutiny on the Bounty*. Peter clicked with the public in that special way that announces the birth of a star.

In Peter's dreams, fame was always Elsewhere, mostly in Hollywood, occasionally in London. It never occurred to him that he would find fame in Australia and through the medium of radio.

All over the world in the thirties, radio was having the enormous impact on family life that television has today; it was perhaps even stronger as it was people's first experience of having the voices of complete strangers invading their homes, strangers who would become friends and favourites.

There are only a handful of truly great actors' voices from the past decade: Orson Welles, Walter Huston, Leslie Howard, James Mason, Sir John Gielgud and Robert Donat come to mind. And Peter Finch. Needless to say, there are many other distinctive actor voices like Cagney, Fonda and Bogart, but they are not voices to whom Shakespeare can be trusted.

One can describe these great voices technically; clear surfaces, inaudible breathing, sibilants that never hiss, fricatives that never explode. And one can note the glories of their phrasing, emphases, colours and diction. But the true excitement of the voices lies in their immediacy and intimacy — and these are mystery factors buried deep in the roots of an actor's personality.

In Peter's case these qualities were often remarked in his everyday life. He had a way of talking to *you* and to you *only*; he was entirely concentrated and undistracted, no matter what else was going on. It was as if he had no peripheral vision. This was a gift that remained with him throughout his kaleidoscopic life: the intense focusing on what was directly in front of him, knowing that it might have the power to change his life. He never talked *at* a person, he talked *to* him — *into* him, in fact. His voice seemed to snuggle confidingly in one's ear.

The Finch voice was now heard regularly in every home across the nation; Peter quickly became a favourite. Eventually the ABC found him desirable again and he was signed up for an exclusive radio contract at è16 a week, an excellent salary for those days. Only one other performer was paid as much, Neva Carr-Glynn. It was not only Peter's voice that the public became familiar with, it was Peter Finch as well. The radio weeklies and the entertainment magazines seized on him as a personality and ran his photograph along with interviews. From time to time he would say, "I have one big ambition, to play in a French film", or "My ultimate aim is to go to London." And in several versions, rewriting history, he reminisced about his happy childhood. The newspapers began to review his performances. Early on, they said that he had "actor-star quality". They raved about "the smooth treatment of his vowels and consonants'', they said that ''the Finch voice drips from beginning to end with sex-appeal''. One critic took the plunge: ''Peter Finch is a great actor. I realize that this is a foolish thing to say and the fact that I have said it increases my admiration for Peter Finch.'' Newspapers headlined: ''Peter Finch stole the play.''

The Radio Times published photographs each week of its up-and-coming stars. Peter's photograph as *Mr Deeds* going to town, blowing a tuba with hat on the back of his head, made him a pin-up.

During the years on radio, Peter had his pick of leading roles. He played Dickens, Shakespeare, Chekhov, Dostoevsky, Tolstoy. He played in Noel Coward, Galsworthy, Sidney Kingsley, Maxwell Anderson, John Van Druten, Emlyn Williams, Norman Corwin, Archibald Macleish, Arch Oboler and Euripides. He was Hans Christian Andersen and Richard of Bordeaux. He was The Informer and Rembrandt. When his Private Eye serial *Paul Temple* went off the air, there was a national outcry. When Peter played Raskolnikov in *Crime and Punishment* in front of a studio audience, the actors as well as the spectators wept. ''Get on to Dostoevsky's agent,'' said the head of the network the next day to his secretary. ''See if he's free to write a thirteen-part serial.''

Peter had Australia literally by the ear. At twenty-four he was labelled ''Radio's Great Lover''. Because of the many different parts he played, he was known as the ''Paul Muni of Australia''.

And that is what is going to become of the little bootblack in *Counsellor-at-Law*. He is not going to become a capitalist or a Communist. He is going to become a film star like Paul Muni and win an Oscar.

CHAPTER 6

The Older Woman

In Peter's twentieth year, he became the lover of an older woman. This affair was to last, on and off, for the next six years.

There is a whole range of French literature devoted to the dissection of the passions of a young man trapped in the snares of a *femme fatale d'un certain âge*. The summit of this genre is Colette's masterpiece *Chéri*: since Colette, the phrase "older woman" has conjured up a picture of a wealthy demi-mondaine; a temptress; a fascinator. But that was Chéri's mistress Léa, not Peter's. True, Peter's Léa was older — she was thirty-five or forty — but she was short and plump and a little desperate. She was fair-skinned and her dark brown hair was worn in a short straight bob. Only her smouldering black eyes were remarkable. There was nothing notable about her conversation. She had a young son and a husband — a rather indistinct figure who had the good sense always to be off somewhere, doing something. She lived at the Cross in a large, spacious apartment with her mother as well as her son. She was a "fringe" sort of person — not of, but interested in the theatre. Peter's mates wondered what it was all about.

She loved him. She adored him. She fed him, clothed him; she could not let him out of her sight. She wanted to possess him, to keep him forever. And Peter found he needed to be possessed by women; he needed to be kept. But although he needed to be kept, he wanted to be free. For the rest of his life these conflicting desires were to bewilder every woman to whom he was seriously attached. Peter would give himself up to them utterly as a child might and then, when their backs were turned, he would disappear. Something or someone else had captured his attention.

Because of the existence of the off-somewhere husband, Peter and his mistress kept their affair secret. So of course it was the talk of Sydney. The talk apparently did not prevent Peter from having relations with girls closer to his own age. When they asked him about Léa, "How *can* you, she's so *old*!" he would reply, "You don't understand. You're just a child."

The truth was that though he might hint obliquely at voluptuous afternoons passed in Léa's bedroom, the liaison was first and foremost a domestic one. In the evening they would sit quietly together in the living-room and Peter would read his current script to her — and to her mother and son. He would discuss new movie stars that had captured his imagination. John Garfield was the kind of actor that Peter was determined to be: street-real.

They talked about books. They made dinner together. And at Christmas time, he dressed up as Santa Claus for her child. Yet if they ever appeared together at a party and she saw that Peter was getting too interested in a pretty girl, she would go up to him and say, firmly, "Come along Peter, it's time to leave." And though Peter might whisper frantically into the girl's ear, "Don't let her take me away. Do something," he always left.

CHAPTER 7

The Making of a Legend

28 September 1937 was Peter's twenty-first birthday. That day, the staff and actors of the radio play he was rehearsing presented him with a birthday cake. "This is the first birthday cake I've ever had in my life," said Peter and burst into tears.

That night he held a huge birthday party for all his friends at Elizabeth Bay House, an old Regency mansion that has now been reconstructed and refurbished, and is stiff with Victoriana — simpering statuary, ugly furniture, soupy brown paintings, artificial flowers under glass and even a rubber plant. But when Peter turned twenty-one, it was abandoned and derelict, standing only in its beautiful bare bones in the moonlight.

Seated on the floor, by candlelight, Peter's friends assembled to honour him: society girls and script girls, prostitutes, madams and spivs, painters and poets, directors, actors and writers, and others who wore no labels. Wine flowed and toasts were given.

Helen McPherson stood up. She was a brisk no-nonsense Scottish girl in her late twenties. She had looked upon Peter for a long time with a kind of exasperated indulgence. She had lent him the suitcase for his trip to Melbourne, she had found him a dinner jacket for his first radio show, and many times she had taken him into the cafeteria in her office building and given him breakfast. But though she was fond of him, she was outspoken about what she considered to be his faults — his instability, his hand-to-mouth existence, and his peculiar friends. And she was never taken in by him.

"Stop lying," she would say in the middle of one of his stories.

"I don't lie."

"Oh Peter, you lie like nothing in the world! Where do you think I'd be if I lied like you?"

"But you have family," he would answer.

Now she proposed a toast. "To a boy that I've known for some considerable time. To a person who at twenty-one has been through more than a man of sixty."

She sat down. The guests shouted for Peter to perform. He borrowed a lipstick from one of the girls, blacked out his teeth, and performed the death of Lenin. Helen watched. She had never seen Peter act. My God! she thought, the boy was good. The boy was really *talented*! It caused her to shift her opinion for a moment. If he was so talented, perhaps he had a right to his peculiarities.

That night Peter ran around hugging and kissing everyone as he always did when he was happy. He embraced Helen, saying earnestly, "I want to introduce you to my best friend. Everyone else turns their back on him but you won't because you understand."

She shook the man's hand and then, involuntarily, shook her own head. The man was Charlie, a wino. He was well known at the Cross. He slept on the pavement under newspapers.

A day later, in the afternoon, Helen came upon Peter on the street; he was staggering along under the load of some wine bottles. "You're drunk," she said crisply.

"I want you to come to my flat now," he said. "I want you to meet my — " he laughed, "my fan club."

Helen passed a half hour at the flat. As Peter saw her to the door, she turned to him and said, "Peter, those are the worst kind of hangers-on!"

"They *like* me," said Peter.

Nine-tenths of charm is availability. Peter's charm was as indiscriminately available to the worst kind of hanger-on as it was to people of real merit. Thus, along with being a success, he became a legend.

Success did not change Peter, it only made him more so. It only gave him more opportunities to work, to drink, to have women and to get further into debt. As was right and proper for a legend of his time, he was charming, sexy, gifted and broke. "He lived the way true artists are supposed to live," said one of his admirers.

As a legend he was idolised and emulated. Though Peter might seem on the face of it to be a most unlikely leader, nevertheless a leader he was and had been since childhood. It may have looked as though he was just going along with things in his passive easy-going way, but mostly it was Peter who was bending people to his will rather than the reverse. Using the lightest touch he had been able to manoeuvre even Paul Brickhill and Donald Friend into being consenting, albeit amused, foils for him. There was no calculation about it; he had a genuine affection for his troops. But at the same time he didn't have any qualms about exploiting this gift when necessary. There are a few teachers in Peter's life (and he sang their praises loudly) but there are no Svengalis.

One of Peter's most ardent legend-makers was Alexander Macdonald. Mac was a short, tough young Scot, full of snappy come-backs and bile, whose school days had been spent in a real Benedictine monastery in Scotland as opposed to Peter's imaginary one in India.

Mac first met Peter at the ABC where Mac was frustratedly employed as a continuity writer. From his office, where he sat fuming daily as he churned out sentences like, "We are now going to hear the Columbia recording of — ", Mac had occasionally noticed Peter striding down the corridor, flinging open the door of the office across the way, shouting into the room "Donnelly, you're a bad-tempered bastard!" and then slamming the door shut and departing.

"What's up?" Mac finally asked him. "Donnelly's not in his office."

"I know. He's hardly ever in. It's my game of Russian roulette," Peter explained. "I'm trying to see if my luck holds." His luck held. Peter never once found his victim sitting at his desk.

Peter and Mac became drinking mates and late in 1937 they became flatmates. After the obligatory number of moonlight flits from various boarding-houses, they settled into a comfortable flat in a solid three-storey brick apartment called The Blackstone on Onslow Avenue at the Cross.

It was by now clear to everyone in Sydney that Peter's relationship with money was not normal. Neither, at that time, was Mac's. By then Peter was earning good money on radio and Mac was earning six pounds a week. They would put their money in a communal kitchen drawer only to find four days later that the drawer was empty. And it was not only their money that was communal. Separate photographs of them taken during this period reveals each of them to be wearing the communal pin-striped suit. First up, first dressed, was their simple rule of thumb.

Mac had chosen to be a friend to Peter rather than a mate. Mates do not censure. Friends can and do; they censure with sharp criticism and follow up with good sound advice. Thus Mac had elected himself Peter's artistic conscience and his social arbiter.

The familiar and serious debate on art versus commerce, integrity versus selling-out was being held in artistic circles all over the world in the thirties. In America, the noisiest accusations of selling-out were hurled around among the New York actors just before they raced each other to Hollywood. In Australia, Mac presented to Peter the case for maintaining one's artistic integrity and making no concession whatsoever to commercialism more forcefully and frequently than anyone ever had done before. At the time, of course, Peter's one hope of selling-out was to the radio soaps and serials he was doing for the commercial stations. Before Mac started in on him, he thought they were rather fun but now he was ashamed and did them only when he had to. Eventually however, even this temptation was removed. Besides dramatic shows his contract with the ABC required him to do nothing but educational broadcasts and poetry readings.

Nevertheless Mac talked on about integrity and Peter listened. Just as Peter had responded to Bobby Capron when he pointed out the necessity of technique in acting he now responded to Mac when he pointed out the necessity of integrity. In the forty-eight films Peter subsequently made, which varied from sensationally good to sensationally awful, he never made one "just for the money" and he never made one whose intention was to degrade the human condition. Nor, unlike other distinguished contemporary actors such as Laurence Olivier, Robert Morley and Orson Welles, did he ever do a cigarette ad or a television commercial. "I've been lucky," said Peter looking back. "I like what I do and I choose what I do." "He was in that very select circle of great actors," said Paddy Chayefsky, "he dignified his parts."

Peter listened to Mac but he listened selectively, so Mac got nowhere as his social arbiter. This was possibly because he was suffering from a bad case of secret Peter-worship. It is very hard to growl in disapproval at the same time as wagging one's tail in delight.

Mac hated Léa, whom he called a cradle snatcher, and he excoriated Peter for being a spineless, gutless milksop and not breaking off with her and finding a suitable girl of his own age like Nona, Mac's girlfriend. "Yes, yes," Peter would say. "True, true." And went on seeing Léa.

And he hated Peter's hangers-on — those truckling, fawning, sponging sycophants, and advised him to give them the boot. "They're my friends," Peter would say. And went on seeing them. Peter's weakness was that he liked people who liked him, and if they worshipped him it did not really matter that he did not like them all that much. Mac's rage was at its most convulsive when directed against the socialites who had taken up with Peter. Mac referred to them scathingly in Australianese as "silvertails" (as opposed to the democratic "coppertails"). He jeered at Peter for allowing them to have him on their terms, for performing his best comic routines in return for a little food and drink. He was a performing seal, said Mac, a scullion in their Hell's kitchen.

Mac's attitudes towards the silvertails was not, in the thirties, an unusual one to have at the Cross or, for that matter, throughout Australia. Moneyed people held little place in Australian mythology. As they could not promise the rewards of privilege like the English aristocracy or the rewards of publicity like American café society, there was no point in knocking oneself out trying to get into their houses at Point Piper and Vaucluse. If the Australian rich felt they were different from everybody else, the message had not filtered down.

Peter's attitude towards the silvertails was uniquely Peter's. He did not really hate them. He merely despised them in the way that a professional despises patrons of the arts who do not know anything, cannot do anything and do not applaud until after they have been assured that it's good. But being Peter, he saw no reason to let them know how he felt. After all, they liked him.

One month, when Peter and Mac were more than usually broke, Peter would return to the flat night after night from the posh parties with his pockets stuffed with chicken legs and asparagus sandwiches. But the starving Mac was not pleased. His mouth full of asparagus he would work himself into a fury. "They only have to stuff a sandwich in you and out comes a funny story," he would splutter. "Are you an actor or a slot machine? And what do you get out of this? Not a sou — not a brass razoo!"

"Then how can I be selling out?" asked Peter a little wearily.

"You're not selling out," Mac howled. "It's worse. You're *under-selling* yourself!" And he put forward what he considered a brilliant scheme which was, very simply, that henceforth, after each of Peter's performances at a society party, Mac should tag along as his manager and pass around a hat.

"It won't work," said Peter immediately. Like every professional entertainer he knew his audience: either they pay at the door or not at all.

But Mac persisted and Peter gave in. The results were not

successful. It became painfully clear to Mac from the outset that although Peter was more than welcome in these houses of the rich, he was not. He was not acceptable, and even something of an embarrassment. Not bothering to control his sneers, Mac passed the hat around at the end of each performance, but the takings were slim. He decided the trouble was Peter's material. His jokes were too blue, and the silvertails did not go for gags about royalty. He urged Peter to clean up his act. Stubbornly Peter refused, just as many years before he had stubbornly insisted on keeping Shakespearean monologues in his repertoire for the gangland patrons at the Maccabean Hall. One host gave them a cheque instead of cash. In order to cash it they had to open a bank account, but it bounced. Seething, Mac broke the news to Peter in his office. Peter shrugged, walked over to the office across the way, flung open the door and shouted "Donnelly, you're a bad-tempered bastard!" The room was empty. His feelings relieved, he departed to continue entertaining the silvertails for free.

The failure of the scheme had one good result: it seems to have stirred in Mac the memory of some kindly old Benedictine monk of his schooldays suggesting that he stop trying to correct other people's sins before he had made a certain amount of progress with his own, for from then on, he began concentrating on his own career. He became a truculent gag writer, a savage critic and eventually a columnist for the Sydney *Daily Telegraph* where his anger mixed strangely with his sentimental, nostalgic references to the old Finch, Finchie, Fincho days with which he continually sprinkled his columns.

In 1941 when Mac married Nona, Peter was best man at the wedding. When Peter left Australia for England in 1948 he gave Mac his photograph with the inscription "To my best friend and cinserest (*sic*) critic." Whenever Mac travelled he took it with him. In his last years, as in his youth, he drank excessively. When he died in 1974 Peter wired the Journalists Club in Sydney to the effect that he and Mac had a pact that the one who survived longest should pay for a round of drinks in memoriam of the other. Peter enclosed the wherewithal.

"Australia", Peter always said, "was a period of friendships."

CHAPTER 8

The Camera Loved Him

In 1938, still twenty-one, Peter made his film début at Sydney's Cinesound (a converted skating rink) in *Dad and Dave Come to Town*, directed and produced by Ken G. Hall, an ex-public relations man turned film-maker who prided himself on catering to the public taste. Peter's operational plan, of course, had been to make his début in Hollywood, but wherever he made it the verdict would have been the same: the camera loved him.

Dad and Dave Come to Town, starring the popular comedian Bert Bailey, was part of a series. In this one, the innocent country bumpkins come to town and eventually outwit the city slickers. But these country bumpkins seem exceptionally thick: they cannot cross a street, they cannot turn on taps in the bathtub, they cannot work a drinking fountain, they think a microphone is a telephone and they cannot tell the difference between a mannequin and a live woman. In the country they are equally dense. Peter, as the boy from the neighbouring farm, comes to Dad to ask him for his daughter's hand. But as her name is Sally, the same as that of the sheepdog, Dad thinks Peter wants the dog. The cross-purpose conversation goes on in a dreamy, unhurried sort of way until it is straightened out by Dad's son, Dave, who is not much brighter. What the movie camera caught in its first glimpse of Peter was a young boy, lolly-pop-stick thin with marble-smooth skin drawn taut and shiny across the fineness of his bones. It caught the sensuality of his full chiselled lips, the hurt of his fawn-like eyes, his coltish grace. It also caught the young actor giving a very confident non-performance.

Also in 1938, Peter acted in two excellent plays on the stage of the Theatre Royal in Sydney: one a drama and the other a comedy. The first one which opened on 10 April was *White Cargo* written by Leon Gordon in 1923 and set in West Africa. This play is as tightly constructed as Sartre's *No Exit* and the message is the same: Hell is other people. It is perhaps more impressive than the Sartre play in that Gordon did not put his characters in an imaginary hell but a real one of tropical swamp and malaria and flies in which no white man can survive intact. After the cargo ship departs, leaving as its latest cargo Longford, a young ineffectual Englishman, the four white men still stationed there — the doctor, the missionary, the company man and the new boy — proceed to goad each other to the edge of madness. The doctor, never drunk, never sober, keeps himself going by boring the others to death with rambling memories of England; the missionary by his smarmy piety; the company man by his malice which is now directed full force at the new boy who quickly goes to pieces but attempts to rally by the only act of defiance against his persecutor of which he is capable. He marries a vicious twenty-year-old half-breed — the infamous Tondelayo, thereby plunging into further disintegration and death. Though Peter had only a small role in *White Cargo* he found himself identifying with the weak, stubborn, doomed Longford at an early stage in rehearsals, and intimations of his own weaknesses and instability began to haunt him. Hitherto he had always been glad of his intense involvement with his work but now he saw how dangerous it could be and how unable he was to do anything about it.

It was with relief that he went into the next play, a comedy, that opened at the Theatre Royal on 26 July 1938.

Personal Appearance by Lawrence Riley was first produced in 1934 on Broadway where it successfully starred Gladys George as the gorgeous, outrageous, real but much-larger-than-life movie star Carole Arden on a personal appearance tour (billed as "The deadliest of high-powered vamps. She always gets her man."), who finds herself and her entourage thrust unwillingly into a home full of ordinary folk in the hills of Scranton, Pennsylvania, while her fancy foreign car is being fixed. Carole, casting about for some mischief to occupy her while she waits, focuses upon a likely young man, ignoring the fact that he is already spoken for. It is then up to his fiancée and Carole's press agent/warder to save the young man from a fate worse than death.

Like all good American comedies of that time, its humour derives from the pitting of the dummies against the smarties.

Peter happily played one of the dummies, a yokel called Clyde Pelton, and gave an excellent bobbing Adam's apple performance, his own being very prominent at the time.

On closing night, Peter had some special visitors. Into his

dressing-room came his cousin Cynthia, now an air hostess, his cousin Florrie up from her property in Queanbeyan and his former jailor, his aunt from Greenwich Point. They went out for coffee and talked about the play and the noisy people sitting in a box who had distracted everyone. Cynthia raved about Peter's performance; Florrie thought the play was stupid and why would anyone want to go to Hollywood; his aunt complained about the clothes Peter was wearing. Peter and Cynthia had always had an affinity and he loved visiting Florrie at her property, but as he glanced at his aunt at the end of the evening he thought, she's aged. She's old. She can't get at me any more.

About a week later Mrs Ringland, a neighbour from the Greenwich Point days, phoned him to say how pleased she was with his success. She was teaching a class of blind children and would Peter come out one day and entertain them? It would be like old times. She'd never forgotten those times in her kitchen when he used to recite all those poems.

In a panic, Peter hung up. Mrs Ringland's voice had opened up a window and the Zombs had suddenly come flying in. The Zombs. He thought they were behind him but they were in front of him, they were all around him, filling the room. His mind went back to his aunt's parlour back in Greenwich Point. He remembered her advancing towards him with the riding crop. He remembered how often he had run out of the house down the street into the safety of Mrs Ringland's kitchen. She was the mother of his schoolmate Jeff and she had treated him like one of her sons. She was kind and she loved him. When his aunt permitted, she had taken him along with the rest of her children on treats like movies and concerts. And he had hung up on her.

Peter sat without moving in his chair for the rest of the day. One dreadful scene after another came back to him. Incidents he had never thought about came back to him in vivid and frightening detail. Only now they seemed even more vivid and more frightening. The re-experiencing of those six years seemed worse than the actual events. He wondered how he had got through it. And had he got through it? And if he had, why could he not move out of his chair?

At six o'clock Nona, Mac's girlfriend, came in bringing with her a boarding-school chum, Marie Amos. Peter looked at Marie and, apologising for still being in his dressing-gown, went quickly into the bathroom to shave. As Peter studied his face in the mirror he wondered for the thousandth time who he was. It was not a philosophical question, it was a precise one. Peter George Frederick Ingle Finch. Pidgifif. But who was he really? He was illegitimate, of that he was sure, or why would his parents have got rid of him? He speculated upon who his mother was. She must be Jewish, he thought. He looked Jewish and he had a great affinity with Jews. Or was he Russian? He felt that way about Russians too. But perhaps he was Indian — he had been in India in that Buddhist school or whatever it was. Certainly he was part Celt. His grandmother had been proud of her Scottish ancestry. "I can become anything," he had said to Rukmini. Peter finished shaving and went out to join Nona and Marie.

Mac had come home from work and the four of them went out to dine at the Cross. Marie sat next to Peter in the restaurant. She was an attractive fresh-faced nineteen-year-old who had just got her first job at the ABC in the Music Department and was finding every minute of it exciting. She chattered away revealing a trigger-quick intelligence. Finally she paused and remarked to Peter that he was very quiet and asked him what he was thinking about.

Peter had been thinking how his strongest emotional ties were with the irascible Mac, the possessive Léa and Charlie the wino and that he was fed up with them all. He was thinking about Mrs Ringland that morning and how he had hung up on her. Now he looked at Marie smiling at him and thought she could fit right into the happy Ringland family.

"I was thinking … you're respectable, aren't you?"

"I guess I am," she replied, adding, "I've heard that's not a very popular thing to be in your books."

"Oh I have a great longing for respectability," he said. "I'm thinking of retiring to the suburbs and breeding dogs."

Friends came in and joined them at the table. The place grew crowded and noisy. Abruptly Peter stood up. "I can't stand them tonight," he said to Marie, but as he left he called back to her, "I want to see you again."

"But you don't know where I live."

"I'll *find* you," he said.

But when he found her she would not let him see her. She had been in a motor accident, gone through the windscreen and her face was all bruised and swollen. He wanted to visit her but she was adamant. The first thing she had thought when she had recovered consciousness was — my face! Now I can never see him again. However, when her face healed he came round to her house, very properly dressed in the communal pin-striped suit and took her to dinner at Romano's, the swankiest restaurant in town. He told her he had taken another step towards respectability. For the first time he was having Christmas cards printed with his full name, Peter Ingle Finch. Twice they went to Romano's and twice to Prince's, the rival restaurant. "Now I'm broke again," he said cheerfully on their fifth date. "So it's back to the old Café de Wheels." Their romance began.

Almost everything in Sydney has changed from what it was once like in the late thirties — except the Café de Wheels which still stands, exactly as it was then, the world's tiniest diner, down by the docks. It sells the best hot meat pies in town. Peas-Pies-and-Pud, specifically: mashed peas on top of the pies with potatoes on the side. All night long (then and now) it conducted a thriving business with a vastly varied clientele, ranging from silvertails, to Crossites, to dockers.

Peter took Marie to the recording studio to listen to him playing *Romeo and Juliet*. She sat in the control booth amidst half-eaten sandwiches and cold cups of tea with the technicians who had seen it and heard it all many times before and were scanning the racing forms. Then Peter began the balcony scene. Slowly the men stopped reading and sat still, their eyes riveted on Peter. "That's *acting*," said one of them quietly.

At first Marie did not find Peter wild; on the contrary, she found him kind and sensitive. For a long while after her accident she was terrified of cars and he would instinctively shield her face with his coat and tuck her head into his shoulder whenever they were in a car driving too fast. For her part she would sit with him for long silent spaces until he got over his attacks of the Zombs. She was with him one day when he picked up his salary at the radio station and left prepared to pay back some money he owed. They ran into a broken-down old actor who asked Peter for a loan. Peter gave him his entire salary. "You're very kind," Marie said. "No," he corrected her. "I'm not kind. I'm only kind provided it doesn't inconvenience me. I don't put myself out for people and I hurt them."

At the beginning of 1939 he was starting to behave erratically again. One afternoon he rang Marie at her office every hour on the hour to fix the time of their meeting for that evening. "I can't wait to see you," he kept repeating, but when she went to meet him he was not there. He turned up a week later. When she asked him where he had been, he told her that while he had been waiting for her a bloke he knew had come by in a truck on his way to Broken Hill (a famous mining town 735 miles away). And as he had never seen Broken Hill, Peter explained, he had just had to go along.

Upon awakening one morning at eight o'clock, Peter realized that he had a nine o'clock broadcast and that he was still drunk from the night before. In order to sober up as well as arrive on time he jumped into the bay, swam a mile across Sydney harbour, surfaced at the Botanic Gardens and arrived barefoot and dripping at the studio ready to work at nine.

This incident triggered off another what-are-we-going-to-do-with-that-man-Finch? meeting among the ABC staff; these were becoming increasingly frequent and invariably ended the same way. It was agreed that yes, Finch was wild, scruffy, hard to get a hold of and did very peculiar things — but, from the first rehearsal on he was always on time, thoroughly prepared, thoroughly concentrated and the only actor who always presented the director with three different interpretations of the role. Case dismissed.

Marie was becoming more and more confused by Peter's behaviour. She sensed that when he left her each night on her door-step he was not going straight home. One evening at a party, Léa (of whose existence Marie had not been aware) suddenly appeared, uninvited and distraught. She began to make a scene. "Save me! *Do* something," Peter pleaded to Marie. Marie stood immobilised and Peter left with Léa. He and Marie quarrelled the next day, she walked out of his flat, and the following Monday she picked up the Sydney *Herald* to find on the front page the announcement of Peter's engagement to a society girl. That lasted a week and left behind a wake of shattered hearts and Peter reeling under the blow of a three-day hangover.

In 1939 Peter made another film at Cinesound, again directed and produced by Ken G. Hall, *Mr Chedworth Steps Out*, with the great character actor Cecil Kellaway in the title role. Chedworth is everybody's victim. He is underpaid, in debt and exploited by his children and his social climbing wife. He finds a satchel full of money in the basement of a building where he has been reduced to being janitor. He steals it and puts it in his tool shed. He then starts dipping into it thereby setting off a complicated plot full of gangsters and counterfeiters. Cecil Kellaway, as always, gives a faultless performance as bouncy and endearing as any well-beloved cartoon animal of that era. Peter as his delinquent son has still not quite got the hang of giving a consistent film characterization. He is at once aloof and engaged. That is, he manifests his delinquency by holding himself aloof from the family squabbles at meals while at the same time he reveals himself touchingly eager to act with anyone the script allows him to. His most outstanding characteristic is his air of extreme youth. This is not surprising for an ordinary twenty-two-year-old, but this quality of youth was one that Peter was to project powerfully until well into his thirties.

On 3 September 1939, twenty-five days before Peter's twenty-third birthday, England declared war on Germany. Immediately thereafter, Prime Minister Menzies announced to Australia that they too had joined the fight. And so again, as in 1914, the Australian people — uninvolved, unimplicated and living on the other side of the world from the Allies — were rushing to the aid of the mother country.

Now that war was a fact rather than a possibility, the various attitudes held by young Australians as they had watched its approach hardened into convictions. There was a feeling of antipodean rage at being dragged once more into some far-away dispute only to be decimated as they had been at Gallipoli in 1915. But there was the opposite feeling as well — a patriotic one, the "have-a-go" boys, for country, glory and adventure. And there were those who saw the army as a chance to advance their careers in some administrative desk job capacity and joined up eagerly. The artists — actors, musicians and writers — felt on the whole that their best plan was to sit tight until the entertainment units were organised: that was where they belonged and that was where they could make their best contribution. Peter as usual had his own feelings. Emotionally he was a pacifist. Philosophically a Buddhist, he was against violence and killing. Politically he was of the Left, and pro-Russia, which at the time had signed a treaty with Germany.

The ABC claimed top priority for Peter's exemption from the Armed Services. There were war documentaries to be made, war bonds to be sold and propaganda talks to be given. As an actor his value to the Australian people had been sealed by his unique contract with the ABC.

At the end of 1940, the ABC released Peter to make a war film again for Cinesound, *The Power and the Glory*, directed by Noel Monkman and scripted by Monkman and Harry Lauder Jr. It is a story about German spies penetrating Australia. Seen today, the opening sequence, which shows how a bunch of Australian actors who had never seen a German in their lives reacted to Nazi staff officers at headquarters, is as unintentionally funny as anything ever shown on film. They wear monocles and shout bits of reinforcing ideology at each other while they stab at wall maps with sharp letter openers and pound on desks cluttered with basic Nazi paraphernalia and bordered with bands of swastikas. It is not meant to be but is a brilliant satire on the Hollywood Nazi movies of the period, though even Mel Brooks would not have had the inspired bad taste to cast as head Nazi an actor who is so obviously Jewish. The scenario of *The Power and the Glory* is funny enough to merit a few words of description.

Between grindings of teeth and clickings of heels we learn that a kindly scientist and his bemused daughter have invented a special gas which is not only able to heat up the house in winter as hoped but is, dismayingly, able to destroy the world as well. Moreover, as the camera takes us into the scientist's laboratory, we learn also that his creepy-crawly female assistant (a superbly overacted performance) has tipped the Nazis to the good news thus precipitating our hero and heroine into Australia.

In the land of the kangaroos, they settle down deep in the bush to rebuild the laboratory and re-invent the gas for humanitarian purposes. The daughter admires the scenery, goes swimming, falls in love, sings, dances and so forth. But there is a spy in their midst — skinny, coltish Australian pilot called Frank Miller, alias Frederick Muller ... alias Peter Finch! In the end it all turns out as it should. After a spectacular aerial dogfight, staged by the Royal Australian Air Force, the bad guys are dead and the good guys are swathed in bandages.

Peter, as the arch villain, gives a surprisingly chilling performance. Again there is that impression of extreme youth. The face he presents is not the smooth mask behind which lurks unspeakable evil, but the smooth mask of an innocent child behind which lurks nothing but impulses. It is, one might say, a quick sketch for Iago — or Dorian Grey. His deceptions seem antic, his intentions without motive and therefore doubly dangerous. Only his smile is not innocent. And it is not young. It is the beginning of Peter's particular smile which one notices again in his subsequent work: a spontaneous click that registers his instant recognition of what he was later to call "human frailty", glimpsed either in himself or others.

Peter at twenty-three was wise to the ways and waywardness of himself and others in the world. He not only accepted the fact of waywardness, he was attracted to it. As he would say all his life, "I am fascinated by human frailty". And "Is this true to human frailty?" was the first question he asked himself upon reading a script.

Now, with the progression of the war, he was having increasing difficulties coping with his own frailties: drink, women and debt, against the increasing burden of his work at the ABC. His wildness was beginning to spill over into his work. He was not always sober during his performances and when he was they were slick and facile.

Peter watched the ABC staff thin out as the men enlisted, and he watched the streets of Sydney fill up with soldiers on leave. One day he showed up for rehearsal; the next day he did not. Peter had disappeared again. On 2 June 1941, aged twenty-four, Peter had enlisted in the army. He had become Gunner Finch, NX26035 in the Light Australian Artillery Anti-Aircraft.

When he turned up at the Cross on leave, his skinny legs showing under his khaki shorts and swimming in his army boots, to the queries of why he had joined he would reply, off-hand, "Old Cece Perry (another actor) and I got drunk one night and just decided to", or "It was the only way I could get out of paying my debts." But he had been drunk before and he had been in debt before. He probably came closer to the truth when he told Marie whom he met again at Mac's wedding, "I didn't see why I should stay out when everyone else had to go."

1 Peter's famous grandmother, Laura Ingle Finch, c. 1905

2 Peter's grandfather, Charles Finch, c. 1900

3 Peter's mother, Betty
Staveley-Hill

4 Captain George Ingle Finch at
the base of Mount Everest before
his ascent, 1922

5 An early photo of Peter

6 *Left:* Peter (*l*) and his grandmother (*far l*) at a wedding in Vaucresson, early 1920s
7 *Right:* Peter and Friend in Vaucresson, 1924

13 Sergeant Finch of Finch's Follies:
the medals were Coca Cola bottle
tops Darwin, 1941-2
14 Peter on radio—he received the
Macquarie award for the Best Radio
Actor in 1946 and 1947
15 Tamara in Balanchine's ballet
Cotrillion, 1940s
16 Peter with Tamara, 1943
17 Tamara in *Scheherazade*, 1944

18 *Above:* On tour with the army players in *French Without Tears*, 1944-5—Peter, as always, the centre of attention
19 and 20 Peter and George Heath among the Aborigines. "They touched the primitive chord in me that had always been there."

CHAPTER 9

War and Tamara

Peter did not have a "good" war or a "bad" war. He had very much his own war. Gunner Finch stepped on to the *Queen Mary*, now a troop ship, to go to the Middle East, but Entertainer Finch landed in the grand ballroom to convulse the troops.

They arrived in Palestine and were then sent to the Gaza Strip to await further instructions. As a soldier, Peter was cheerful, carefree and fearless in disobeying orders. The troops had been ordered not to fraternize with the Arabs, who might be hostile, as the army wanted no unprovoked incidents, yet Peter disappeared for three days and came back with five close Arab friends. The officers were not amused by this incident, nor were the enlisted men. There was a feeling of natural resentment among his fellow soldiers towards one who made up his own special rules. Besides, at close quarters, Peter had become decidedly whiffy because he never bathed. A conference was held at the end of which they dragged him under the showers.

After a while the unit sailed to Ceylon to fight the Japs. When they got there the Japs had not arrived and neither had their gear which was following in another ship. They sailed for Singapore via Sumatra, but before they arrived, Singapore fell and they were ordered back to defend Australia. They landed in Adelaide, proceeded to Darwin and there they saw action. The Japs attacked: their bombs rained on Darwin. Australia had no effective fighters yet and the Jap bombers flew too high for the light ack-ack guns. Again and again the Japs attacked. The nation was shocked. For the first time in history an enemy had attacked Australian soil, bombed a city — killed and killed.

As one soldier in Peter's unit put it, "When that first bomb landed in Darwin I was in Alice Springs, nine hundred and fifty miles away, in five minutes." And this feeling, if not this activity, was shared by most of the men. Peter proved his mettle and organised an entertainment unit. The subsequent show with its sketches, songs, dances and high quota of bawdiness quickly gained popularity and ended by playing to audiences of four thousand troops. Peter liked to include in each show his own lament to victims of the clap which began:

> So full of innocence and pure was I
> So strong and young and keen of eye
> That in this blissful state I thought
> The testes were but made for sport
> And initiations of the penis
> Invocations to the shrine of Venus.

The show became famous with both Australian and Allied servicemen in the Northern Territory and was known as Finch's Follies (or by some, Finch's Folly). During air-raids soldiers who were not assigned active posts sat through the show rather than dispersing for shelter.

Peter's work as a morale builder had won him the affection of the servicemen as well as the gratitude of the officers. If his rifle had not always been rusty, he would possibly have been decorated.

At the end of December 1942, after serving eighteen months on active duty, Sergeant Finch was granted leave and at the same time seconded to Sydney to make war bond appeals at cinemas and propaganda films for the Department of Information. Before he left he went up to one of his mates in the show and said, "When you meet me in Sydney don't say anything about this, will you? Because down there I'm not a comic, see, I'm Shakespearean."

It was summer time in Australia and upon arriving in Sydney Sergeant Finch went straight to his favourite beach at Redleaf, spread out his very dirty towel and jumped into the water for a refreshing swim. When he came out he was delighted to see his old mate Hal Lashwood seated on the towel next to his. It was a happy reunion. They were both good actors, both good-looking, both successful with women, and they both held the same left-wing political beliefs which had become increasingly important to Peter. But all this counted for nothing when Hal introduced Peter to the dark-haired young girl he was with, a ballerina named Tamara Tchinarova.

She was wearing a white bathing suit with a blue Tahitian print and Peter fell for her from a great height. In his own words: "I was enraptured by her Georgian face of high cheekbones and narrow forehead, her dark long hair and her extremely good figure with long perfectly shaped legs. Her Russian accent was delightful.''

As he and Tamara talked to each other, or rather as he talked to her for she was mostly silent, only glancing sideways at him from time to time and answering him monosyllabically, the word had spread up and down the beach that Peter was back and all his mates gathered round to welcome him. They might have saved themselves the trouble. Peter's vision was focused on Tamara, and he was virtually unaware of everyone else; Hal Lashwood eventually left for a rehearsal but it is doubtful whether Peter noticed.

Tamara, glancing at Peter, was puzzled. This very thin young man in an old pair of bathing trunks with moth holes, held up by an old necktie around the waist, this young man who was so skilfully deflecting his friends' attention away from the two of them was charming, interesting, full of jokes and obviously very popular — she had vaguely recognized his name — but he was also a wreck. He was shattered and frightened; his expressive eyes were sunk in hollows.

When they began walking back to her flat, Tamara found out why. An air-raid alert went off, a testing siren in case the Japs should begin bombing Sydney. The city folk paid no attention but Peter grabbed Tamara and started running until he found a shelter where he collapsed, shaking violently. He was having a delayed reaction to the months of steady bombings in Darwin. If Tamara had been drawn to him earlier by his charm and personality, she was even more drawn to him by his helplessness as he sat trying to control his nerves.

Afterwards, as they continued along to her flat, Peter thought he had never in his life met a girl so young in years with the maturity of this graceful silent creature. Even with the little she said, even without knowing much of her history, he knew instinctively that they were equals in their struggle for survival.

This feeling was reinforced when he walked into her home and was introduced to her very Russian ''Mumma'' or ''Mummushka'', who with overflowing Russian hospitality offered him tea and cakes over the samovar. The sitting-room was tiny and cramped; there were costumes hanging on the walls. Mother and daughter had come to Australia with the famous Colonel de Basil Monte Carlo Ballet in 1938 and had been stranded because they carried ''enemy alien'' Romanian passports. Mumma, formerly the company's wardrobe mistress, now sewed costumes for the J.C. Williamson touring company when she could, while her daughter Tamara, a prima ballerina with the company, was working as a photo colourist. Peter approved. He had always known it would happen this way, that he would find his princess not in a palace but in humble circumstances where he himself felt most happy and free. The Tchinarovas were very poor but he saw they were not stricken with poverty, they were resourcefully, industriously struggling against it. Added to that, the family constellation of mother and daughter had always been an irresistible one for Peter.

By the time he finally left them that evening both Tamara and Peter, mutually bewitched, felt they had known each other all their lives.

Peter slept very little that night and the next day, as early as he dared, he turned up on the Tchinarova doorstep. A week later he moved into the bedroom that the Tchinarovas had previously rented to lodgers.

It is doubtful if Peter was ever aware of how far back his obsession with Russia began or in what curious ways it kept surfacing. Yet it had always been there from his earliest days in Vaucresson when Russian emigrés flooded into Paris and Peter listened to their thrilling tales of narrow escapes from the Bolsheviks. It surfaced when he told Rukmini that he had Russian relatives, and when he did that odd production of *The Tragedy of the Romanoffs* for the Boy Scouts, and on the road when he became a Russian polo player, and in his choice of Lenin for his twenty-first birthday party performance. It caused him to embrace Soviet politics and the most important Russian literature: Chekhov, Dostoevsky, Tolstoy, and Gogol. It would continue for the rest of his life.

Now he was in a Russian home, in love with a beautiful Russian girl who, except when she talked Russian to Mumma, was mostly silent.

One day he discovered what was behind her silence: Tamara could not speak English. She was in the sitting-room holding an enormous book in her hands and she was in a paroxysm of frustration. Peter asked her what was the matter. She explained that although she was fluent in French and Russian, her English was non-existent. "I am trying to read this book," she said in exasperation. "It is called *Gone With the Wind*. It is over a thousand pages long and by the time I am finished I am sure I will be able to speak English. But it is so difficult, so full of apostrophes and American expressions of the South!'' She threw down the book. Peter laughed, more delighted with her than ever, and told her she was going about it in entirely the wrong way. He went out and came back with a copy of *Winnie the Pooh*. ''And,'' says Tamara, ''he opened for me a whole wonderful world of English children's literature.''

Everything they did seemed to be of mutual benefit, every interest they had seemed to dovetail. They had both had an uprooted childhood. Like Peter, Tamara was self-educated, enthusiastically so. Born in the tiny country of Bessarabia in 1919 when it was still part of Russia, her father had been an officer in the Tsar's Black Guards (''the Regiment of Death'') who disappeared during the Revolution. Her mother, with Tamara aged five, had fled to Paris. There Madame Tchinarova had become wardrobe mistress to the Diaghilev Company and Tamara had left school at twelve to become a ballerina. Travelling all over the world with the de Basil Company, working her way up from the corps de ballet to principal dancer, Tamara found that her greatest recreation and enjoyment was reading. Her zest matched Peter's. In exchange for A.A. Milne and Lewis Carroll, she introduced him to Balzac and Molière.

Peter was only on temporary leave, but when it was discovered that he was in Sydney, radio scripts came pouring in. Though unable to accept them he enjoyed reading them to Tamara. One day, as he was reading a particularly romantic one he stopped suddenly and said to her, ''By the way — let's get married. No, it's not a line in the script. Let's get *married*!'' Tamara was taken by surprise. She had not thought of marriage. She had been content, in her Russian way, to go from one day to another and asked for time to think it over. How long, Peter wanted to know. A couple of days, said Tamara. Then, deciding to accept, Tamara sat down and carefully composed a little speech for this special occasion. She never got to say it. Peter was looking over a script. Tamara began ''Well, I have decided — .''

''Good,'' said Peter. ''I thought you would.''

That settled, their fortunes immediately began changing. The army prolonged Peter's leave and continued to use him in short Department of Information films and in selling war bonds. For Tamara, the ballet was starting up again and discussions were in their initial stages. Under the directorship of Borovansky, the former leading character dancer of the de Basil Company, she and eleven others of its members who had stayed on in Australia were forming a new company that was to become the nucleus of what is today's Australian Ballet. Tamara would be doubly valuable to the company, serving as both a prima ballerina and, thanks to her excellent memory, as a choreographer who could revive the great ballets of the de Basil repertoire as danced in former years.

In February 1943, Peter was given further leave to do a film called *Red Sky at Morning* adapted from a prize-winning Australian play by Dympha Cusack set in New South Wales in 1812. It was written and directed by Hartley Arthur for Austral-American Productions. Among the different characters collected at an inn one stormy night are an escaped convict, who is an Irish political rebel (played by Peter), and a beautiful, tempestuous run-away wife. Overnight they fall in love and flee together from their pursuers in the morning. The film was not successful and it is doubtful if it even had a release but Tamara went with Peter to see a rough-cut. For the first time she saw Peter on the screen. She was, in her own words, "besotted by his work". But by the same token she was upset watching what she described as a "tremendously talented man just running wild". By then she had had glimpses of the way he drank with his mates at the Journalists Club which was close to where she and Peter lived with Mumma on Phillips Street. Trained since childhood in the highly disciplined world of the Russian ballet (than which there is no stricter discipline, no stricter time-keeping in the world), she could not understand how Peter could keep "wasting his health and wasting his time drinking".

"That's what Australian men do," explained Peter. It was the custom of the country. Tamara held fire. Perhaps, she thought, she could influence him by example.

CHAPTER 10

Love and Peace

On 21 April 1943 Peter Finch, aged twenty-six, married Tamara Tchinarova, three years younger, in a Church of England service at St Stephens in Bellevue Hill, Sydney. At Peter's insistence it was a double ring ceremony, though this was a very un-Australian, and, one would have thought, a very un-Peter-like thing to do. For her bridal dress Tamara wore a pale blue crêpe gown cut on the bias and falling into a cloche effect which had been lovingly (and cheaply) made by Mumma. Peter shook like a leaf throughout the service and forgot his lines. They saved a pound by dispensing with the "Here Comes the Bride" organ music.

Peter's worldly goods at the time consisted of an army kit-bag containing one enamel mug, one aluminium spoon, one packet of emergency dressings, a bar of chocolate, one pullover and a pair of bathing trunks. He also had the traditional shirt on his back. "Peter had this ability to leave things everywhere," says Tamara. "If he had three shirts he would lose one, give one away and the other would be the one he was wearing." So every night Tamara washed and ironed the nuptial shirt for his use the next day. His army leave pay was six shillings a day and Mumma, who had saved up fifty pounds, gave Tamara thirty of it for a wedding present; twenty for a wedding outfit and ten for a month's rent in a "honeymoon" flat.

For a while they lived in blissful poverty. Peter was happier than he could remember — as far as he was concerned, every possible condition of true happiness had been fulfilled. He was young, he was in love, he was being looked after, and he was poor. For Tamara, it was Paradise.

When Peter's leave was up he was offered the choice of going back to his old ack-ack unit in the Northern Territory or being transferred to the entertainment unit whose main headquarters were an immense broadcasting studio in Pagewood just outside Sydney. Peter hardly gave it a thought. Of course he would go back to Darwin and his old mates.

But when he got to Darwin he found that the bombings had stopped and the Jap planes had vanished. Were they going to sit out the rest of the war in the gun pits, he wondered. He was also wondering about something else, something that surprised and disturbed him. All his life Peter had been able to slip out of one set of circumstances and into the next with the greatest of ease. But now suddenly, for the first time, what mattered to him most was not what was here in front of him but what he had left behind. He had known, of course, that he would miss Tamara, but he did not know that he would miss her *that much*.

Peter put in a request for a transfer to the entertainment unit back in Sydney. When it was granted, his Battery Major delivered the valediction: "I'm deeply sorry you're going, Gunner Finch," he said. "You were a bloody awful soldier but you did make me laugh." A neat summing up of the army's reaction to twenty months of The Good Soldier Finch.

Returning to Sydney, Peter went immediately to Mumma's flat where Tamara was staying. It was a heart-warming reunion: Mumma bustling over the evening meal and Tamara so transparently overjoyed at seeing him. They sat down to a feast of fried pepper steak, zuop and peasants' caviar. Afterwards Peter sat back in his chair, beaming. At last he was in the bosom of his *own* family.

The next day he and Tamara went flat-hunting. They made an unfortunate choice: a flat above a Chinese restaurant. When they discovered that it had rats, they removed themselves to Mumma's. Poverty was one thing; rats were something else. Eventually they found a place at the Cross, a third floor walk-up in William Street. In a fit of domestic inspiration, Peter painted the bathroom walls silver and the bathtub green.

The Borovansky Ballet was meanwhile going ahead full-steam and Peter watched with awe the care and attention given to every aspect of it: the production side, the décor, costumes, lighting plots and orchestral arrangements as well as the energetic rehearsals and strenuous exercises at the barre.

Peter loved watching Tamara working out at the barre. He always admired physical activity of any kind but, more important, he was now dumbfounded at seeing what *real* discipline involved.

Since Peter knew nothing about the ballet, he was also astonished at how they were able to raise money to supply the best of everything. The truth was that of all the performing arts in Australia the ballet was (and is) the most popular as well as the most respected and revered. Also, young Australians, with their early athletic training, are exceptionally well-suited to ballet dancing. With the combination of the expert dancers like Tamara, a well-trained corps de ballet of Australians and the driving genius of Borovansky, the company's success seemed a foregone conclusion.

By contrast, Peter would drag himself out of bed every morning at 5.30 a.m., arrive at the entertainment unit at Pagewood, line up for parade or drill and then ... just *sit* for the rest of the day with his old friend and fellow actor Redmond Phillips, the two of them alternately hysterical or bored witless as they pretended to be thinking up skits to perform for returned soldiers and officers in mess-halls around the countryside. They usually settled for going around the camps doing expanded versions of Peter's old party pieces. Redmond, naturally, played the stooge.

What energy Peter had left was consumed by his hatred of a commanding officer, a petty tyrant whom the men had dubbed, with heavy sarcasm, "Our Leader". Peter christened him *Tyrannosaurus Resi*. This, he assured his mates, was a particularly fearsome beast that lived in palaeolithic slime. Of terrifying shape, possessed of cunning and sadistic tendencies, it struck fear into the hearts of all its prehistoric contemporaries; nevertheless, despite so many unpleasant attributes, the creature's brains could not have filled to the brim a modern egg-cup.

Peter and Our Leader clashed on sight. Our Leader enjoyed barking out at parade "All Buddhists, one step forward!" Pointing at Peter's skinny legs poking out beneath his khaki shorts he would sneer "Upon these slender stalks rests the flower of Australia." Peter revenged himself by "soldiering on", an army term which means being as troublesome as possible without actually breaking the rules. He also deployed a childhood weapon that he was never to let go: he would make hideous faces behind Our Leader's back. It seems obvious that in Peter's mind the new tyrant closely resembled the earlier one in Greenwich Point.

If it was impossible for the army to make Peter toe the line in situations of potential danger, it could hardly have had much luck in situations of safety such as his present one sitting around an old broadcasting station in Pagewood with a lot of equally disgruntled mates. Our Leader did not understand this. He tried to render Peter's situation unsafe and thereby bring him to heel by threatening to send him with entertainment units to New Guinea or the Solomon Islands. Peter countered by threatening to get himself reassigned to the ack-ack. It was stalemate. Our Leader knew that sometime in the near future he was going to have to send full-scale entertainments to hospitals and camps and that when he did he would need Peter. Finch's Follies had proved that Peter had that special ability to make men want to work with him.

When the Borovansky Ballet opened in Sydney and triumphed, Peter and Redmond Phillips were still touring army camps with their comic routines. For Peter, the experience was becoming an increasingly unhappy one. He was much in demand but he was disgusted. He was merely doing what he had always done, what it looked to him as though he was going to have to do *ad infinitum*: sing for his supper. Every success was a failure that added to his prison sentence. And on top of this was the galling fact that by now most of his mates from the ack-ack unit had been demobbed.

Peter began drinking heavily. He drank at officers' messes where the hospitality was lavish; he also drank at the Journalists Club which had become his favourite haunt. Tamara had known Peter only five months before they married but it was more than enough time for well-meaning friends to alarm her with details of the notorious Finch legend. Proceed at your own risk, they warned her — he's slept with every woman in Sydney, you know. She prepared herself for trouble with women, but when trouble came it was with men, not women.

In those days, the Journalists Club was the all-male stronghold of Sydney's intellectual life. For its members — journalists, political cartoonists, writers, poets, musicians and visiting celebrities, it was a home away from home. For some of its members it was simply home. Because of the different newspaper deadlines, the club was open round-the-clock. It had a refrigerator and a gas-ring where you could cook yourself a steak and French fries, thus fortifying the liver between the rounds of drink. It was also possible to sleep there, if you were not too fussy. In fact, days could be passed without leaving it. This club finally received the unique accolade of being successfully named in a famous divorce case as co-respondent.

For the inhabitants, the club was fun and lively and there was always something going on. Depending on the time of day, the membership might seem to be composed either of a refined group of cranky professors arguing over word derivations or of a bunch of aggressive drunks telling each other to step outside and say that again. There was, of course, a certain overlapping of groups.

There was a nearby tram that left for the Cross at two a.m. Wives in their beds listened anxiously as it rattled by; if the husband did not show up then, the wife knew (or hoped) that he would be on the four a.m. tram, the last. If the Great Australian Male did not turn up for four or five days, his wife never dreamt of inquiring where he had been. She knew that a woman's place was always five paces behind the man, carrying the bundles. Australian society was what might be called a *mate*-riarchy: if the Australian male did not drink with his mates every night he was "a social outcast". It was an article of faith that a man who spent a lot of time with his wife or girlfriend was a "sissy" or a "bloody poofter" while a man who got drunk every night with other men was all man. A curious footnote to this aspect of mateship comes from the Australian pundit Max Harris in his book *The Angry Eye*: "Historians", he writes, "have come to accept fairly calmly the notion that the Australian philosophy of "mateship" emerged from what was perhaps the world's only homosexual ordering of Things."

Peter was an Australian by conditioning if not by birth. Wholeheartedly he accepted this part of the Australian philosophy. It suited him. He very much wanted to be one of the boys.

Tamara was distressed, horrified and extremely worried. Her European background combined with the male-female equality that had always existed in the world of ballet meant that she was ill-suited for playing at docility in the Australian manner. When Peter was virtually carried home by his laughing mates she lashed out at them. She seemed not to admire them. This was a brave but hardly popular attitude. It also raised the tricky question of just how much collusion was going on at the Journalists Club. A former *habitué* remembers seeing Mac, yellow with hepatitis, having his glass of plain soda water firmly swept away while a medical doctor member refilled it with "healing" whisky. In just such a spirit would Peter, protesting that he was sticking to beer for the evening, have his drink spiked without his knowledge because he was "so much more amusing when he was a little boozed up".

Tamara was worried about Peter, but she also had other things on her mind. The successfully established Borovansky Ballet was now being offered choice dates in the main cities of Australia and she herself was also having a great personal success. She was dancing leading roles in *Les Presages*, *Giselle*, *Scheherazade*, *Les Sylphides*, *Swan Lake* and *Blue Danube*. Reviews spoke of her as "dark, handsome and exciting", as "delicious", as "cold, glittering and elegant". Over and over again, the critics referred to the "tall, dark beauty of Tchinarova".

So Tamara danced in Adelaide, Canberra, Plymouth, Newcastle and Melbourne. And Peter drank at the Journalists Club, each night further putting off the evil hour when he would have to return to his empty flat and empty bed.

Fortunately, two outside events conspired to steer Peter back on to his appointed course: it was at that point in the war when American troops landed in Australia by the thousands taking over Sydney and, more particularly, the Cross. In the resulting holiday atmosphere, Kathleen Robinson, a wealthy, influential patron of the theatre, decided that the time was ripe to re-open the Minerva, a theatre well-situated at the Cross, and to present a season of English and American plays for this new audience. Since there was nothing going on at Pagewood at the time which could involve Peter, he was able to secure a temporary release and join the Minerva Company.

It was a welcome liberation. All of Peter's energy that had been frustrated at Pagewood and dissipated at the Journalists Club could again be channelled into what he did best: acting.

For the whole of Peter's life, his recuperative powers were nothing short of magical. He might be idling passively down some matey, alcoholic Lethe, when suddenly Peter Finch, the actor, would sight Opportunity, grab it, and be instantly, buoyantly transformed.

Peter's first part at the Minerva was that of District Attorney in a courtroom melodrama, *The Night of January 16th*, by Ayn Rand at her battiest. It contains perhaps one of the great gimmicks of all time: the jury is chosen *from the audience* and the actors play out the alternative endings to the verdicts "guilty" and "not guilty".

Did Karen Andre, "efficient secretary and notorious mistress" of tycoon Bjorn Faulkner, push her lover out of a fifty-storey penthouse apartment — or did he just jump? The audience is asked to decide. But the entire play is permeated with the significance of Ms Rand's real question: if Karen Andre *did* push Faulkner, well, why the hell *shouldn't* she? After all, she was only doing what all proud, passionate, red-blooded women-in-love would do if they weren't such a bunch of namby-pamby sheep.

Peter, as District Attorney, a part rich with high-flown denunciatory speeches of deepest purple, attacked his role with gusto. In theatrical parlance he "made a meal of it". Calling on memories from his copy-boy days at the Supreme Court when he watched those forensic artists, Dovey, Boyce and Windeyer, he drew from them his tone, his flamboyant gestures and his timing. Then, with these staples as a base, he invented a moment of his own. And what a moment it was! It was so electric it brought many happy customers back to the theatre to enjoy it again.

The District Attorney is cross-examining the witness. He is making points but he is not getting what he wants. Discouraged, he turns from the witness box and slowly walks the long way across the stage. He is just about to resume his seat. But ... suddenly, he turns full front, facing the audience, allowing them to see *very gradually* a devastating new thought dawn in his mind! He swings around to the witness. He barks a telling question at her. It hits home. The witness collapses and the audience applauds. Brilliant Peter Finch!

Peter opened in *The Night of January 16th* on 19 June 1944. Reviews unanimously agreed that Peter was "brilliant". The unanimity was such that from then on in Australia the word "brilliant" was permanently affixed to Peter's name whenever it appeared in print. "Brilliant Peter Finch" was varied sometimes with "Peter Finch, Australia's most brilliant actor". It even turns up in a novel of the time. One character says to another, "That's Peter Finch," adding (compulsively it would seem), "He's *brilliant*."

After *The Night of January 16th*, Peter got a break that afforded him not only the chance to play a good part in a film, but enormous personal satisfaction. The director-producer-writer, Charles Chauvel, the discoverer of another Australian, Errol Flynn, in 1933, in his film *In the Wake of the Bounty*, cast Peter in his big morale-boosting war film, *The Rats of Tobruk*. Chauvel had previously dismissed Peter for work in his films as "not being an Australian", or even "an Anglo-Saxon type". Now Peter was cast as one of the leads — and an Englishman.

The film's grim, if honest message seems to be that if one managed to live through the siege of Tobruk one would probably be killed in New Guinea. Peter as the English soldier does not live through it but before he dies he manages effectively to quote both the stirring "We happy few" speech from *Henry V* to the trapped Australian soldiers, and several lines from *Romeo and Juliet* to a hospital nurse, making them both sound like natural and inevitable pronouncements from his character.

"I am not a comic, I'm Shakespearean," Peter had told his ack-ack mate. Yet there was Peter in his next play at the Minerva, Terence Rattigan's wartime comedy, *While the Sun Shines*, as the silly-ass Earl of Harpenden (now a sailor in His Majesty's Service). It was a role that required nothing but a display of aristocratic frenzy in order to succeed.

If *The Night of January 16th* was crypto-Fascist, *While the Sun Shines* was overtly homosexual. The men only get into bed with the men — never with the women. In the opening scene we discover through the butler that the Earl has picked up a drunken American Commando and looked after him by taking the Commando home to bed with him in his bedroom off-stage. Why, one wonders, when there is a perfectly good sofa on the set?

Later, in Act III, things are manoeuvred so that not only the Earl
and the Commando, but a newly arrived French Lieutenant all
march off to the bedroom to spend the rest of the night together.
However if Terence Rattigan thought he was pulling a fast one on
his Aunt Edna, he should have known better. Aunt Edna had plenty
of nephews at Harrow and Eton. She knew boys will be boys.

It must be said that empty as it was, *While the Sun Shines* proved
a very popular success and the audience much enjoyed the sight of
Peter as the Earl falling in and out of love with the two girls (one
wide-eyed, prissy and high-born; the other, good-natured, sluttish
and low-born) in alternate speeches to them.

Peter, himself, found the play both exhausting and unrewarding.
But it was not only the play that was upsetting him; while this piece
of artifice was taking place on stage, events in his real-life drama
were driving him towards crisis.

Superficially, the same things were happening as before. Whenever Tamara went on tour Peter went on drink. Eventually, the
drinking began to overlap Tamara's homecomings. On the sidelines, friends watched the couple with interest, either with glee or
with sorrow, depending on their natures. But all predicted disaster
for by now they knew Peter inside out, were well acquainted with his
ways and waywardness.

What they didn't know was that Peter had a secret weapon,
known only to Tamara. It was his deep, powerful, and, as he felt,
once-in-a-lifetime love for his wife.

When Tamara was on tour, Peter poured out his secret feelings in
his love letters to her. Love letters are traditionally short on hard
news and Peter's are no exception. Outside events rarely obtrude.
VE day and VJ day are not mentioned. Peter's letters describe
intimately what he feels about Tamara, and what he hopes she feels
about him, and what they should feel about each other. There are of
course, from time to time, passing references to a film he is making,
a play he is in, a ballet she is dancing, an evening spent with
Mumma, a complaint about a friend he suspects of spreading false
rumours that may get back to Tamara. ("They'll go to any lengths
to keep the 'wild young Finch' tradition going on"); and there are
increasingly bitter references to Our Leader. But the overwhelming
impression one receives is of the wrenching pain of a man separated
from his wife. For Peter had no family. All his love was focused on
Tamara. "Don't forget, my darling, you are my everything — my
mother, my sister, my lover, my companion," is the orphaned cry
that is sounded from Peter's earliest letters to Tamara and haunts

the entire correspondence.

The particular love poem he chooses to copy out and send to her is the mighty *Song of Songs* which begins significantly, "Thou hast ravished my heart, my sister, my bride".

After *While the Sun Shines* closed, Peter reported back to Pagewood and to what he called "the petty war of nerves that flourishes there". Our Leader had him working on a series of skits for army camp entertainments. Besides prodding and goading, Our Leader had apparently embarked on a course of self-improvement and was nightly skimming the dictionary. When Peter submitted one skit for his approval Our Leader, suspicious that he had detected a *risqué* double entendre therein, stopped the show and thundered, "I will not tolerate any contentious invidiousness!" Peter didn't know whether to laugh or cry.

Peter was again released for a few brief weeks to make a film called *A Son is Born*. He was, if it is possible, even unhappier during this time. He played a shiftless, useless travelling salesman with nothing on his mind but booze and pinball machines. Completely indifferent to his wife, it amuses him to steal away from her their son's affections. They jog along in misery for a while until she throws him out whereupon the son insists on going with Daddy. With a smart new job and smart new clothes, the wife gets herself a smart new boyfriend and the next thing we know, Peter is dying in hospital, having crashed his car while drunk. Peter sends for his wife and then follows a refreshingly unheroic death-bed scene with no last minute apologies, conversions or transformations. When Peter tells his wife to look after the boy he does so with the urgency of a man who has little breath and less interest. Immediately afterwards, he turns away from her to get on with the serious business of dying. The film then continues on its soap-sudsy way. It was a bad film which did no one any good and depressed Peter unutterably. Peter always lived his parts and this was a part *no one* would want to live.

"Will the *real* Peter Finch please stand up?" People were to demand later in Peter's life, impatient at his chameleon-like changes. And, "Who was the *real* Peter Finch?"

As the real Peter Finch was a little boy so frightened in his own skin that he jumped out of it and into that of others, one must always take into account the role Peter was playing to match it up with his feelings and behaviour at the time. It is perhaps a cliché to say that this role in *A Son is Born* exacerbated his already discouraged state of mind but the facts show that it did.

He wrote to Tamara: "I feel I am no good and fast losing my

talent if I ever had any. I'm getting worried, I'm nearly thirty and I don't seem to have achieved much. I must do something solid soon, a book or a play or a good production. I don't want to float around as a fairly good actor all my life. Please God, before I get too old I will find somewhere to really learn about the theatre. I don't want to be a failure for your sake. You know I am an artist somewhere underneath, don't you?''

But along with his despondency, one also sees in his letters to Tamara of this period something that he cannot face but which is nevertheless lurking: it is a growing resentment that her star is rising. He jokes about it but there is always an edge to the joking. He asks her not to forget in spite of all the flowers she receives and the shouting and the painters painting her that in the background Peter stands, her lover and her husband. He jokes that he will be turned away from her stage door, and that people passing will say pityingly ''That's him, the ballerina's husband, Mr Tchinarova.'' And he signs himself ''Fincharova''.

In the middle of April, Tamara returned from an engagement but only just to catch her breath. The Borovansky Ballet's next touring date was New Zealand. It would be the company's first time out of Australia. Since Tamara's passport (she travelled with the ballet under a Romanian one) classed her as an ''enemy alien'', she needed Peter's signature on her travelling documents. They had had a series of rows and the night before her departure he stamped out of the flat without signing the papers.

Tamara was frantic. She telephoned all Peter's friends and all his haunts. When she found him, he was drinking in the mess at Pagewood with Redmond Phillips and Ralph Patterson. Peter refused to come to the phone. Patterson talked to Tamara and promised to see what he could do.

''I don't care whether she goes to New Zealand or not,'' Peter mumbled drunkenly. ''It's nothing to me. I don't give a damn.''

Phillips and Patterson wondered what was going on. If Peter didn't give a damn whether Tamara went to New Zealand, why didn't he just go home and sign the papers? What was going on was that for the first time in his life, Peter was feeling the sharp pangs of jealousy, envy and — it must be added — a certain amount of spite. Phillips and Patterson concocted a scheme whereby they would pretend to be so drunk they needed Peter to guide them home. Once at the Cross, they re-routed themselves to Peter's flat. In front of his house, Peter miraculously seemed to sober up and resolutely went upstairs where Tamara was waiting in agitation.

Peter signed the papers. He then announced to Tamara that he felt they were no longer temperamentally suited and he wanted his freedom. Then he passed out.

Not many hours after Tamara's departure, Peter started to feel the stirrings of remorse. One of his favourite assignments at the BBC had been running the children's programme. Dipping into his early childhood, he had composed a series of delightful poems for broadcast about the adventures of a little boy called "Peterkin" which was, of course, Peter's grandmother's pet name for him. Now a fragment of verse kept spinning painfully around in his mind:

Up to dream climbed Peterkin
Up for the Princess' hand to win
And fly to far Cathay..........

He remembered writing it and sighing at the hopeless dream of ever meeting his Princess, of ever winning her hand. Well, he had met his Princess. He had reached up and grasped for her hand. And then, drunkenly, he had lost his footing and tumbled down the mountain.

Peter wrote to Tamara in New Zealand. He attempted a light, rueful tone. He'd behaved like a bastard, he knew, but whatever he'd said he didn't mean — he'd been silly with drink. She would forgive him, wouldn't she?

Tamara didn't answer.

Anxiously, Peter wrote again. This apology was more strongly worded. He had gone to Mumma's but it tortured him because there were so many photographs of Tamara there. But then, every corner and street and person in Sydney reminded him of Tamara. And he'd rushed home from camp this evening and the damn letterbox had been empty again. He reminded her of their early days of courtship and the "thousand happy moments" they had had. Most importantly, he had given up drink, he was seriously going into battle against a "fourteen-year-old habit". "I must love you a lot because I have never even tried before." And he ended the letter. "For she has fled away again and left for my safe keeping exquisite pain."

Tamara did not answer.

Peter wrote to her again. "Funny to think of you an ocean away ... " he started. And suddenly one can almost *feel* him seize with terror. It is as if every abandonment he had ever known: mother, father, grandmother, parted from him forever by the ocean, had rolled into one — to become Tamara's desertion.

Though she was only in New Zealand, she had crossed an ocean and she might as well be on the other side of the world, leaving the orphan wailing impotently across the seas.

"The only thing to do is think across the ocean," Peter continued. "Think so hard you can feel me wanting and longing for you. I can't fight an ocean. I can't call out and run across and hold you. It's like pouring immotion (*sic*) into a turbulent sea that engulfs it and tosses it away leaving you an empty shell. I have awakened in the last three nights in a terror that I might die — that everything might go black before you were with me helping me to face it."

Now Tamara answered. He had been playing Russian Roulette with her for too long and she gave it to him with both barrels. She described how much she once loved him; how terribly she missed him during her long, lonely tours, crying every night into her pillow. She described how insignificant and unwanted he made her feel in comparison with his drinking friends. She told him how selfish he was, never considering that ballet had always been her life and that he made it impossible for her to perform well with his behaviour and all the rows he caused. Furthermore, he had said that they were temperamentally unsuited and that he wanted his freedom. Very well, he should have his freedom. She was glad to be rid of him.

Peter then poured over Tamara a torrent of letters pleading his case with all the considerable eloquence at his command. He told her he knew now how much he had hurt her, he knew now so well because he felt the pangs himself! And how could she be expected to know he loved her so much when he had always expressed just the opposite? He only knew now that there was an ache in him stronger and clearer than he had ever felt before. And for the first time, he openly admitted he was jealous of the ballet and the people she might meet when on tour. If only she would come back to him he promised to make her feel needed and wanted. He emphasized he was not drinking. He realised now that he and Tamara could have been the happiest couple in the world if only drink had not interfered. And finally he threw himself at her feet, "Darling I'm pleading, all I know is that I am your man. All yours for all time. If you leave that is the end of life and me. And my heart will shrivel up. Try to accept my humility as a gift. A thousand words will not express or convince. There are only three: I love you."

Tamara relented.

And Peter answered joyfully, "When we come together again I am going to chain you to me with leg shackles and never let you out of my sight again."

CHAPTER 11

Peter Determines

Peter went on the wagon and made some interesting discoveries.

"Change," said the Buddha, "all is change." For Tamara, Peter was determined to change, to reform in the basic sense of the word: to *re*-form. But the habit of chaos was strong in Peter and what he had thought of in the past as "freedom"— his random, please-yourself-behaviour — was actually a firmly entrenched routine.

An added difficulty was his "legendary" status. Like all legends, Peter had been something of a crowd pleaser, a hanger-on pleaser, and these people deeply resented their legend being taken away from them. As Peter wrote to Tamara, "The drunks have stopped inquiring if I'm coming on a party. One loses a few doubtful friends when not drinking. They laugh and whisper that this wife of his has made a cissy (*sic*) out of him. If they only knew, his wife is making a reasonable human being out of him."

Peter was discovering that an artist must not only be able to understand — he must be able to withstand. Peter withstood and stayed on the wagon. He was too scared of losing Tamara to fall off.

At the end of April 1945, Peter was directing members of the entertainment unit in plays to tour hospitals and army camps. He suggested they do Shakespeare. It was vetoed. He suggested Odets' *Golden Boy*. It was vetoed. Instead, two popular plays of Rattigan's were chosen: *French Without Tears* and (for Peter, his second time around) *While the Sun Shines*. Peter was less than happy with the choice but he went at his directorial chores with characteristic zeal, even going so far as to harbour expectations of perfection. He overworked his cast and worried himself sleepless when the "actors" (most of whom were non-actor enlisted men) fell short of his standards. In fact, two enlisted men fell so far short they had to be replaced at the last moment by Peter himself in each play. Valiantly he tried to impose discipline. He inflicted a fine of ten shillings for each missed entrance. In doing this he was perhaps on the wrong track altogether, for the troops, Peter discovered, mainly attended plays in the hopes that something would go horribly wrong on stage.

They were seldom disappointed. Rattigan in his two plays had provided his actors with enough fast entrances for them to be easily missed by anyone stealing a quick drag off a cigarette in the wings.

As they travelled over Australia Peter had one thought uppermost in his mind: he wanted to get out of the army and be with Tamara. Peter had been in the army for four years. All his ack-ack mates had been discharged and he felt like the oldest living soldier in the world. "I shall go straight out of the army into the old men's home," he wrote to Tamara.

On 6 August the atom bomb was dropped and the war was virtually over. Discharge from the army worked on a point system and Peter, counting his enlistment, his overseas service, his years in the army and his marriage, had all possible points. But since he was classified as "key personnel" those points could go for nothing when the tour of Australia was over. The show's next stop, he knew, was to be New Guinea.

At the end of August, Peter abruptly landed in hospital. His mates wondered if he was faking. Judging from Peter's past life, he was perfectly capable of it, but medical tests showed him to be genuinely ill with urethritis. In the hospital where he saw the medical specialists he also saw a psychiatrist or, as he would write to Tamara "a siciatrist" who pronounced him severely run-down due to emotional strain. In any case the infection coupled with his mental condition seemed real enough to the army to keep him in hospital for two months.

Occasionally he was let out for an evening. These he spent with Mumma. After one such evening, he wrote to Tamara:

My own Darling!
I have no news so this is a love letter to the one and only woman I have or ever will love. Mumma and I saw *Romeo and Juliet* (the film) last night and I grew angry that my love for you could not bring forth those tender epithets. I must do it haltingly. Darling all I know is that my blood knows of you and runs through its course till I can feel it loving you as my mind does.

Do you know that feeling? That feeling that your body belongs to your beloved and when she's away it waits like a hand to be gloved again. Sometime at night just before sleep I feel a great wave of loneliness and love and I try to see you in the room — your back through the door at work in the kitchen or when you stand at the dressing table and push back your hair — your legs when you put on your shoes. The way you eat, put on a necklace — all these are as vivid to me as if you were here because my love has made me love all those simple actions. I can feel your body beneath my hands and know every inch so well, your breasts and thighs and buttocks and legs — and I can feel you touch me. But alas all this is in memory and I long for you —

I want to give you so much in life and feel so inadequate. I want to surround you with beautiful clothes and pleasant surroundings but I'm afraid I'm not the man who will succeed the easy way and so must only offer you at the moment my love and my brain. Darling my whole mind is yours as well as my body. I have not shut off part and can share all my feelings and mental progress with you and all my fears, doubts and misgivings and joys.

What a rare love that is that belongs to both of us. It means we have not only arms and breaths and lips but Chopan (*sic*) waltzes, old books, rare foods, a spring morning, looking on trees and still water, the surge of feeling at an encounter with some historic spot, the feel of sun and surf, the vital words of a poet, the wisdom of philosophies — all these!!!!!! to bind us and entwine us till time will wither us as gently as old autumn leaves and blow us gaily into the dark pathways of after life.

While life lasts let us make it *we* not you or I but as one person, as rich and as full and as *honest* as it should be. To hell with fame and chatter and scandal and striving after ambitious goals. Let us be always true to life and as long as we have each other what can be more of existence but existing harmoniously?

I love you and want you terribly,
Peter

This letter is remarkable not only for revealing what tender poetic heights Peter could reach under Shakespeare's inspiration but that, in this mood of harmony and peace with himself and Tamara and the world, he is able to do so with only one word misspelled.

CHAPTER 12

The Mercury: Actor as Teacher

On 31 October 1945, Peter was discharged from both the hospital and the army.

In post-war Sydney, there was a bright optimistic feeling among the actors — they were civilians again. They had come through the war alive and the world seemed to them to be at peace and at plenty. And now, at last, *life*. They couldn't wait to get on with it. They couldn't wait to begin acting seriously. But there was still the old problem: where were they going to act?

The Sydney theatre scene was discouraging as before: Romberg-type operettas were firmly entrenched in the J.C. Williamson playhouses. How then could they prevent themselves sinking back into the quagmire of radio?

A chance meeting in a coffee bar at the Cross between Peter and Sydney John Kay, a German refugee composer-musician and theatre zealot, sparked off an idea that eventually grew into what they would call the Mercury Theatre, after Orson Welles' famous Mercury Theatre in America.

If, when Greek meets Greek they open a restaurant, why, when ex-serviceman-actor meets ex-serviceman-actor, shouldn't they raise their sights and open a classical repertory theatre? Such was the proposition that Peter and John Kay laid in front of the best and most experienced ex-servicemen-actors in Sydney.

Peter gave John Kay most of the credit for the idea. "All the publicity I got was out of balance," he said. "The real soul and force behind the Mercury Theatre was John Kay. He infected me with his burning passion for drama; his titanic energy was a contagion. We were wild-eyed with fanaticism, desperate that something be done to drag the Australian theatre from the doldrums it had been wallowing in."

Along with Alan Asbolt and John Wiltshire, Peter and John Kay carefully chose their company. Everyone put money into it: their savings, their army mustering-out pay and their radio earnings. Then they looked around for every penny they could beg, borrow or steal.

They saw themselves as idealists who were prepared to go all out for their ideal: to go from the ridiculousness of Sydney theatre as it stood to the sublimity of unknown European classics. Peter was in highest spirits; he was not only involved in an idea, he was at the helm of it. He had found a cause he believed in.

On 19 July 1946, at the Conservatorium, a large auditorium that was part of the Sydney School of Music, the Mercury Theatre made its début in three one-act plays: *Diamond Cuts Diamond*, by Gogol (in which Peter acted), *The Pastry Baker*, by Lope de Vega (which Peter directed) and *The Broken Pitcher*, by Heinrich von Kleist (in which Peter also acted). It was a *succès d'estime* but a commercial flop, and a limited engagement of three nights after which they were refused bookings in every other theatre. "The dead hand of commercialism was too heavy for us," said Peter.

It was John Kay to the rescue. "We will open up a school," he announced. He knew of a deserted house on the quay where students could build a theatre while being charged for lessons given by Peter. Peter was in eager accord. The wild quixotism of the scheme appealed to him. He had written to Tamara during rehearsals of the Conservatorium programme: "For the first time in my life I am doing what fate meant me to do — I am a classasist (*sic*) at heart."

Peter's sense of well-being was not only caused by his Mercury activities but by Tamara as well. Immediately after his release from the army he had travelled with Tamara and the Borovansky company to Tasmania. There, on a picnic by a gorge, as Peter and Tamara lay on rocks gazing at a mother eel desperately trying to save her babies from drowning in the waterfall, Tamara announced that she had made a decision. When her year's contract with Borovansky finished she was giving up the ballet. Since the age of twelve ballet had been her life, but now she thought differently. Peter was her life. All her ambition would be transferred from her career to his. She would furnish him with drive and stability. But: he must stick to acting; that was his true *métier*.

Peter, at this point, had been experiencing the malaise that overtakes practically all natural and instinctive actors who have started very young. Arriving at a certain stage of recognition they ask themselves "Is this really what I *want* to do — or did I just take the easy way out?" Peter had begun to dismiss his acting talent as mere facility and to despise it as such. He knew he had a gift for writing and poetry. He yearned to be a writer or a poet — not *just* an actor.

Tamara insisted that he could write or paint or anything else he wanted to do but that it must be done on the side. Acting should come first. Peter, mindful of her sacrifice, agreed. They were both content. For Tamara, that day in Tasmania with its decisions was "the happiest day of my life".

In September 1946 the Mercury School opened, and the teaching of its students proved to be a vital step in the development of Peter's own craft. The ease with which he became an instructor gave him confidence, though teaching others how to act was, after all, something he had done all his life from primary school to the Boy Scouts to the Army. But the really exciting aspect of this project for him was that it enabled him to clarify and reinforce many theories about acting which he had formulated over the years by testing their validity on the students.

Former students give Peter highest marks; he was both authoritative and inspirational. He was strict about their voice lessons and breathing exercises. No matter how thin Peter became, his expanded diaphragm was always visible. "Feel that," he would say, proudly patting it, to the students. "That's good breathing!"

Actress Shirley Cameron, a former Mercury student, remembers Peter lecturing his pupils: the boys listening spellbound and the girls crying as Peter talked, "because it was all so true and beautiful ... And it *was*."

There was a theatre rat that only materialized when Peter was on stage. It would sit up in a corner on its hind legs in frozen attention while Peter spoke. The students named it Peter Rat.

The students performed set speeches from the classics and from the moderns as well — particularly Peter's favourite, Odets. Peter stressed the necessity of establishing that magical connection between the actor and the audience: "The audience must know at every moment what you are thinking or what you are hiding." Long before the word "sub-text" had become theatrical jargon, Peter had his students doing scenes in which they spoke not the written dialogue but the inner dialogue — what was actually going on in the character's mind.

The exercise that revealed most easily the sort of actor Peter was seeking to become, was the one in which he made each student pretend he was in an art gallery. As the student looked at each painting, the others were to guess what sort of a painting was being looked at. This exercise struck at the very heart of Peter's art. It could only be performed successfully by employing the most intense sensitivity in an imaginary environment. This was what Peter was always striving for and this was what he was to achieve so peerlessly in later life as in — for a specific example — the film *Make Me an Offer* when, as an antique dealer, in a long silent scene in an attic, Peter Finch's gaze reflects back the beauty of a black Wedgwood vase.

During this time, adding fuel to the fire, Peter was discovering the French cinema in its golden age. The Savoy Theatre — where long ago Peter had played the bootblack in *Counsellor-at-Law* — was now a foreign language cinema and here Peter sat enthralled through such masterpieces as *La Grande Illusion, Un Carnet de Bal, Kermesse Héroïque, The Baker's Wife* and *Les Enfants du Paradis* — and sat enthralled through them not less than fourteen times each.

The great French actor, Louis Jouvet, replaced John Garfield as Peter's idol. And not far below on his list of deities were Jean Gabin, Jean-Louis Barrault, Harry Bauer, Jules Muraire, Raimu, Pierre Brasseur and Gérard Philipe.

As Peter studied these actors closely, trying to analyze why their performances had such a powerful effect on him, he was struck first by the importance these actors placed on their eyes. "In a film the audience can see the actor's thoughts in his *eyes*," Peter said in an interview in *Films and Filming* in the '70s. "You can flit several thoughts through your mind and if you're *really thinking* them, it happens in the eye."

Peter was also struck by the French actors' total familiarity with the environment in which their characters were placed, no matter how out-of-the-way the environment. And he was struck by the way these performers established a thorough knowledge of the jobs or professions they were portraying. What French actors were able to convey so superbly and uniquely, Peter saw, was the weight of imagined experience. It was something they'd worked at; that was important to them. You did not wonder, watching them, as in so many American films, whether a character had won his job in a card game the night before.

Sitting in the Savoy Theatre and watching the French cinema through 1946 Peter learned his French lessons well. He never forgot them. All his life he would owe more to the French style of acting than to the English or American style.

CHAPTER 13

Eureka and the Aborigines

For most of 1947, the Mercury Theatre suspended its plans and operations. The alluring reason for this was that *Eureka Stockade*, an historical epic film about a miners' uprising during the Australian gold strike in 1870 was being shot on location in Singleton, New South Wales. For ten months, work on this film virtually emptied the Sydney bars and cafés of actors and their girl-friends. Like lemmings to the sea, they beat a path to Singleton for this Roman holiday.

Englishman Harry Watt was the film's director, and the film's producer was England's Ealing Studios. Two years before in Australia, also with Ealing Studios, Watt had directed a highly successful film *The Overlanders* which made a star of bit player Chips Rafferty overnight. Watt was a blunt, no-nonsense documentary man. Of his initial arrival in Sydney in 1945, when he was looking around for actors, he says, "The first one everyone mentioned was Peter Finch. There was no doubt about it, he was their leading actor. But I also heard that he was a drunk and I wasn't interested in putting up with that sort of thing. So I used Chips Rafferty in *The Overlanders* instead. Maybe Finch would have been better, I don't know. But I do know that a big change came over Finch in the next two years and I think Tamara was responsible for it. So when I did *Eureka Stockade*, since Finch was interested in every aspect of film-making, I gave him a job as one of my assistants plus a small part as a government official. He was eager to try anything. I cast Chips in the lead again. We began shooting. About four days out, Les Norman, the associate producer, came to me and said, 'I don't think Chips is going to make it. You ought to use Finch instead.' We argued. I think now he was right but I was stubborn. And Les finally got his chance to use Finch years later when he directed him in *The Shiralee*."

The filming of *Eureka Stockade* was held up by rain. During the months they waited for the weather George Heath, the cinematographer, contracted to make a documentary on the Wangarri tribe of Aborigines in Arnhem Land. When Peter heard of this project he was wild to go along: the Aborigines, their lore and their mystery began to occupy a great deal of his thinking and reading.

Peter proposed himself to Heath as his assistant. Heath was undecided. Peter re-proposed himself to Heath wherever he could find him and then nightly on the phone for several weeks. "That's Peter," Heath's wife would say every evening at 6.00 p.m. when the phone started ringing. After a great deal of this, Heath accepted Peter's proposal.

Peter did an odd thing when signing the contract to be Heath's assistant at twelve pounds a week. He signed it Peter *George Ingle* Finch, using two names that had not appeared in his signature for many, many years. It seems clear that his coming adventure in the land of the Aborigines reminded him — was perhaps even inspired by — of the shadowy image of his father George Ingle Finch and the latter's adventures climbing Everest. In the twenties, George had written what was to become a standard textbook on climbing: *The Making of a Mountaineer*. He had also contributed his thrilling account of his party's ascent in 1922 in the book, *The Assault of Everest*. These two books with their photographs were Peter's only tangible contact with his father and he had devoured them.

In the light of this, it is interesting to contrast the different attitudes held by George Ingle Finch and Peter George Ingle Finch towards the "natives" of the Himalayas and the natives of Arnhem Land — always keeping in mind that George Ingle Finch's expedition was undertaken in 1922 and Peter's in 1947. The two men differed of course in generation and upbringing. They also differed in objectives. George's objective was to climb a mountain; Peter's seems to have been to make friends. But the difference goes far deeper than that.

George always kept his distance. In *The Assault of Everest*, he had this to say about confronting the Tibetans: "If one wishes to converse with a Tibetan it is always advisable to stand on his windward side. A noble Tibetan once boasted that during his entire lifetime he had two baths — one on the occasion of his birth, the other on the day of his marriage. If you wish to hold converse with a Lama, it is advisable not only to stand on his windward side but take care that the wind is exceptionally strong. Lamas do not marry. The odour of sanctity is pervading."

Peter, on the other hand, took three giant steps and landed in the middle. "I'll never forget those months with the Wangarri Tribe," said Peter in an interview in 1956. "Those wonderful, humane people. Primitive, yes, but with a code of behaviour that puts to shame this thing we call civilization. They taught me more about human beings than I'd picked up in the years before."

And in further contrast:

George Ingle Finch (*Assault of Everest*): "I watched the porters scurrying back down the rocky ledge singing as they went snatches of their hillside ditties. Splendid men!"

And Peter Finch (interview, 1956): "Going with the clan on a two-hundred mile walkabout, I made myself useful mainly as a pack horse."

Peter never rationed his enthusiasm. With him there was never any danger of it being in short supply, though there was always a very great danger of it being short-lasting. His enthusiasm for the Aborigines and his stay with them, however, burned deep in him. It was an enriching experience which he talked of all his life.

Something wild and untamed in Peter responded to primitive people. "I'm a bit of a primitive myself," he said. "I don't know whether it was my amazing experience with the Aborigines that turned me that way or whether it just happened to touch a primitive chord in me that had always been there."

After Peter returned from his two and a half months in Arnhem Land with the Wangarris, he began regaling — or to use his own Australian word — "ear-bashing" his friends with stories of his adventures with these fascinating Stone Age people. He told of wading waist-high in crocodile-infested waters singing at the top of his lungs to show he wasn't scared. He told of waiting in suspense with the two other white men, Heath and Evans (a Native Affairs Patrol Officer), while the Wangarri chiefs kept a forty-eight hour surveillance on them to decide if they were acceptable. Peter and his friends passed the test and were invited to accompany the Wangarris over the land, and they were given permission to use the camera. Peter and the Wangarris went on a walkabout covering over two hundred miles, never spending more than one night in the same place.

Some fifteen years beforehand, during the Great Depression, Peter, still only a boy, had gone on his own version of the Aborigine walkabout. Like them he had learned to "live with the land and from the land". And it was during this walkabout — that had brought about in him a spiritual awakening — that Peter had also grown up.

Now Peter had gone on a *real* walkabout and with the very people who were the source, so to speak, of the inspiration. No wonder this tribe and their wandering way of life always remained for Peter a "Paradise Lost".

Peter also ear-bashed his friends about the feasts he shared with the tribe consisting of snake, mud oysters, lily roots and wild honey. He acted out a kangaroo hunt for which the Wangarri hunter wears a kangaroo mask and expertly mimes the movements of the kangaroo in order to get within spearing distance of the animal.

Out of friendship, the Wangarris made Peter and Heath "honorary members" of their tribe. This friendly act was alchemized by Peter's tongue into being made "blood brothers" of the tribe, an entirely different procedure from the former involving a ceremony both painful and bloody and one which leaves large, noticeable scars on the chest. Aborigines today agree the Wangarris would have been too polite and too diplomatic to have inflicted this ritual on strangers. Yet many years later, Peter writing to Heath, always signed himself "Your blood brother".

Peter, back from the Aborigines, now felt himself as much drawn to the simplifying influence of the primitives as he was to the civilizing influences of the classics. And these opposing forces added further complexity to this already complex man.

For the time being, however, the classics appeared to have won.

CHAPTER 14

"And if you ever come to London, look me up."

When at the end of 1947, *Eureka Stockade* had folded its tents on location and stolen away, everyone returned to Sydney.

John Kay and Peter came together again to decide on the Mercury Theatre's future plans. Again there remained the giant stumbling block of not being able to secure a theatre, but both men had too much ambition to abandon their dream. They finally decided that if they could not get a theatre to which to bring people, they would bring a theatre to the people. Peter had done it with tent shows and army tours with contemporary commercial imports. Now he was determined to do it with classics.

They would tour all over Australia. They would play in schools, in factories at lunchtime and at surf clubs. They would play anywhere that would have them. John Kay designed an ingenious folding stage and proscenium which could be packed with all the props and scenery in a single truck and, with the actors going on ahead, could be set up anywhere in fifteen minutes.

The play they chose to dazzle the masses with was Molière's *Imaginary Invalid*. This was aspiration indeed! Everywhere in the world, except at the Comédie Française, Molière is known as instant failure; uncommercial and unpopular. Peter and his company were blissfully ignorant of this, and their enthusiasm and their high standard of acting blinded both actors and audience alike to the bald fact that the irascible eighteenth-century French playright was box-office poison.

Peter's performance in the leading role of Argan, the imaginary invalid, had a great deal to do with the play's success. His Argan was exuberantly cunning and foxily sly in his hypochondria. He was bursting with rude health and in the prime of his life. Peter also brought a charm to the role that Molière's invalid severely lacks. As always, the Peter Finch name got star billing on the programmes and on the billboards.

On 19 August 1948, Al Thomas, an actor with the Mercury Theatre, stood, stripped to his jockey shorts, helping put up the scenery for the lunchtime performance at the O'Brien glass factory outside Sydney. He tripped over a flat, fell and found himself looking up into a pair of the greenest eyes he had ever seen.

"Oh! It's you," he gasped.

"Yes," said Vivien Leigh, smiling down at him. "It's me. We've come to see your Peter Finch."

The newly knighted Sir Laurence and his wife Lady Olivier were at this time on the last lap of their famous 1948 Australian tour with the Old Vic. It was a brilliant idea to send this glamorous young couple to post-war Australia to hold the Empire together and keep the flag flying, and once it was presented to the Oliviers they put it in motion enthusiastically. No two people of that era could have pleased Australia more. Wherever they went, their reception was overwhelming. They were adored and revered as royalty. In fact royalty is exactly what they were: the king and queen of the English theatre, to say nothing of the king and queen of films where they were worshipped to the extent of idolatry as Heathcliffe, Henry V, and Scarlett O'Hara.

The other Old Vic players had been as carefully chosen for the tour as had been the plays presented: *Richard III*, *The Skin of Our Teeth* and *School for Scandal*. Each play showed the actors to advantage and the stars to perfection. It was the best theatrical company Australia had ever seen.

The tour was gruelling for the Oliviers. It not only included playing all the main cities of that vast continent but involved being sparkling and gracious at huge press conferences and private interviews, and each opening night was followed by many weeks of receptions.

Before they sailed for Australia, Olivier, the youngest actor ever to be knighted, was told by the British Government that they were being sent as goodwill ambassadors. Larry and Vivien played their parts to the hilt. Inevitably, the going got tough. The endless rounds of Government House festivities, exclusively peopled by the "blue-rinse-brandy-crusters set" — brandy with frozen sugar — began to pall on the Oliviers. In spite of their goodwill, in spite of the very best will in the world, they deeply felt the need for spiritual nourishment. And for theatre people the world over, spiritual nourishment means theatre. In every city the Oliviers asked the same question: "Where is your theatre?" — and always they received the same embarrassed answer. Except for tours of commercial English or

American imports, there wasn't one. "Who are your best actors?" they asked. And then the name Peter Finch began cropping up.

Not that any city but Sydney, and once briefly Melbourne, had ever seen him on stage, but all Australia knew and loved and listened to his golden voice and marvelled at the incredible versatility of his radio performances. Finch, the Australians told the Oliviers enthusiastically, had won the Macquarie Award (Australian radio's Oscar) twice running in 1946 and 1947, once as a Frenchman and once as a Russian! Peter Finch was their best actor. He was brilliant.

The Oliviers tucked away the name in the backs of their minds and when they arrived in Sydney and heard that Finch was touring in a company which performed lunchtime classics in factories, they were intrigued.

One day John Kay said to Peter, "I'm going to try and get Olivier to come and see one of our factory shows."

"No, you're not!" said Peter quickly. "He doesn't want to see a tatty show like — no, sorry, I don't mean it's tatty, I mean — for God's sake don't ask him!"

But Kay did. And the Oliviers came.

"We've come to see your Peter Finch," Vivien Leigh had said as she left Al Thomas and walked into the audience where she and Olivier sat amongst the sandwich-munching typists and workers.

Peter peered through the audience and saw the Oliviers. He felt paralyzed. "I never thought they'd come," he murmured to himself. He felt sick and he began shaking. Then he steadied himself and added up the pluses on his side. He felt good and he felt right in the part of Argan. He had played the role successfully many times. He had even played it at that particular glass factory before. The Mercury had actually been invited back. And, in any case, he reassured himself, he had nothing to lose. He knew that he would manage something and he prayed that it would be good.

Olivier, watching Peter from the audience, leaned forward in his seat. He felt the prickle in his spine that he always felt when in the presence of exceptional talent. Under Peter's make-up, Olivier saw an extraordinary thirty-two-year-old actor shining through; he heard an extraordinary voice, controlled, supple, fluid. Under the charm of Peter's performance, Olivier saw an authority that said: I *belong* on this stage. This stage is *mine*.

No one in the company was prepared for Sir Laurence's enthusiasm afterwards. He bounded up on stage calling the Mercury Theatre the most exciting thing he had seen in the theatre for years;

he said it reminded him of the lost days of the medieval strolling players. Then he singled out Peter. "And you", he said, "are a damned good actor."

Peter, rooted to the spot, could only giggle with nerves.

"Don't giggle," said Olivier. "You're damned good." Then came Olivier's famous words, "And if you ever come to London, look me up."

Peter was so dazed by the encounter, it is doubtful if he even heard the words. But others did and, of course, they repeated them. And with each repetition the words got a little more distorted so that by the time the press got hold of Olivier's casual remark, Peter was reported to be under contract to Sir Laurence and sailing back with him to England immediately.

It did not happen in quite that way — although, in view of subsequent events, it could be argued that the press was clairvoyant. For, after meeting again at an Actors Equity reception, a friendship sprang up between Sir Laurence and Peter based on admiration on Peter's part and fascination on Sir Laurence's. In fact, Olivier was so fascinated by every aspect of Peter's colourful past as well as his talent that it seemed to many people that he regarded Peter somewhat as his *alter ego*; they were totally different yet somehow alike — the two sides of the same coin one might say. Olivier was serious, earnest, ambitious; Peter, relaxed, funny, happy-go-lucky. But both were basically shy men and both were supremely sensitive artists.

Moreover with Peter, the Oliviers could have fun. During their brief stay in Sydney, they managed to an increasing extent to slip away from the blue-rinse-brandy-cruster functions and meet up with Peter in some low dive of his choosing where, with Finch and his mates, the Oliviers could happily let down their hair.

By the time the Oliviers left Sydney for the next leg of their tour, Olivier's "If you ever come to London, look me up" had become "Now don't forget, Peter, when you come to London you must promise to get in touch with me."

In the '40s, if you were a success as an actor in America, you bought a house in Connecticut. If you were a success as an actor in England, you became a member of the Garrick. And if you were a success as an actor in Australia — you left!

Two and a half months after meeting Olivier in Australia, Peter Finch left. If one listened to what he said at this time, one would have concluded that he was very reluctant to leave Australia and his mates, and reluctant to exchange Australia's classless society for

England's class-ridden one. And, although Peter had been given a grim lesson in reality when certain Sydney businessmen who had promised Olivier backing for the Mercury Theatre disappeared the moment Sir Laurence left, one would also have concluded that Peter was very reluctant to leave his "strolling players" troupe.

What he did was to accept a role in a radio soap opera that he had scornfully turned down many times before but which offered him the highest sum ever paid to an actor on radio. And this sum, along with £1000 that Tamara had secretly saved up for just such an opportunity, made the trip to England possible.

At the end of October 1948, Peter and Tamara embarked for England on a P & O line ship, the *Esperance Bay*. They were given not one but three farewell parties. At the last of these, Peter climbed on top of a ladder and delivered his farewell address.

"It is a far, far better thing I do than I have ever done..." he declared amidst cheers from the guests.

Just before they left, there came a voice from the past on the telephone. It was Peter's aunt who had looked after him as a boy in Greenwich Point. She wished to see him. When he arrived she thrust a packet of letters in his hands. "These letters have to do with your mother and father and you," she said to Peter, and told him that his father was a Professor at the Imperial College in London.

On the *Esperance Bay*, after the well-wishers had stumbled out of their tiny cabin and the Finches had set sail for England, Peter took the packet of letters out of his suitcase and chose one at random. It was from his father to his grandfather.

20th June, 1915

My dear father,
I have some quite startling news for you—I was married last week quietly by special licence to Miss Fisher to whom I have been engaged but a comparatively short time...

He read another and another. Then he read the letter from George to his father:

Betty and my son was born on the 28th of September last. His name is Peter. He is a splendid boy and you will be awfully proud of him.

Peter read all the letters, and the more he read the more confused he became and the more he determined to find his mother and father in England.

Part Two

CHAPTER 1

The Stranger Returns

The two strangers, the Australian actor and his Russian ballerina wife got off the *Esperance Bay* at Southampton on the 17 November 1948. After a skirmish at the docks — the customs officials very nearly confiscated Peter's cherished record album of Gandhi's anti-British speeches — they caught the boat train to London where they took a taxi to their hotel.

That winter the weather was exceptionally cold. England was still suffering its period of austerity. Clothes, food and heating were severely rationed. Bomb sites presented yawning gaps of rubble.

It was thirty-three years since Peter had been born in London in a nursing home on Cromwell Road. He had returned — but as an utter stranger.

The taxi drove them down Shaftesbury Avenue through the theatre district and Peter studied the passing hoardings: John Gielgud in Christopher Fry's *The Lady's Not For Burning*, Gertrude Lawrence in *Septembertide*, Paul Scofield in *Adventure Story*. Would his own name ever be up there with theirs? Peter shivered in the unheated taxi. In Sydney he might be a legend but in London he was a blank page.

Nevertheless, by the time the two strangers had alighted from the taxi at their hotel, the bustling Regent Palace overlooking Piccadilly Circus, walked through the lobby crowded with other strangers and taken the lift up to their room, their spirits had risen. They had made it! They had made it to London, the Mecca of Theatre! In their tiny room they bounced on the bed with glee and excitedly began ringing the few other Australians they knew in London who welcomed them with delight.

Then Peter rang the film director, Harry Watt. They had by now become good friends and Peter loved recounting the story of his close-up in *Eureka Stockade* when his "thinking" technique had not worked: he was thinking beautiful thoughts; marvellous things were going on inside him — and absolutely nothing was showing on the outside. Watt came up to him and said, "Would you mind breathing from time to time so we can tell that you're alive?"

Watt, however, watching Peter's work in *Stockade* and especially *The Imaginary Invalid*, had become a staunch admirer of the Australian actor and had urged him to try his luck in England where, the director pledged, he would do what he could to help Peter. He proved to be as good as his word. Upon receiving Peter's phone call he immediately said he would undertake not only to introduce him to such eminent Ealing directors as Basil Dearden, Alexander MacKendrick and Robert Hamer but to convince the head of the studio, Sir Michael Balcon, that Peter must be given a screen test.

Still on the wave of Watt-induced euphoria, Peter impulsively put in a call to the Imperial College. In much too short a time for him to realize fully the immense significance of his act, he was talking to Professor George Ingle Finch. The stunned professor made an appointment to meet Peter at the Regent Palace for tea in three days' time.

Tamara and Peter spent the intervening days on a pilgrimage to the family seat of the Finches in Little Shelford, Cambridgeshire, wandering round the house and the village Peter had so often heard about in his youth. In spite of the cold weather he sat silently on the ground in the family graveyard for an hour. Here are my roots; here I will be buried, Peter thought with a kind of pleasurable melancholy. He could see the tombstone: Peter George Frederick Ingle Finch. Pidgifif.

Peter had brought with him from Australia his copy of George Ingle Finch's *The Making of a Mountaineer* which he read again and again in those two days, wondering if he was too old to start climbing mountains or if his father would suggest they go off together to some practice mountain where he would teach Peter the art and science of climbing.

On the day of their meeting the receptionist rang Peter to say there was a Professor Ingle Finch coming up to the room. The professor had arrived a half an hour early. The Finches had expected to meet him downstairs. Tamara had been lying on her bed exhausted from a day of flat-hunting. Quickly she put on her shoes, arranged herself, and tidied up the room. She describes the events that followed:

"The Professor came into our tiny hotel room and immediately it was awkward as there weren't enough chairs. So one of us sat on a bed. He was tall, straight, handsome, grey-haired and very thin. He wore a monocle. He was very dry and abrupt in his speech. It was a very inarticulate meeting. I cannot say it was a cold meeting but it was full of 'undercurrents' and without any real communication. Peter became very emotional, he was very moved at meeting his father. He was full of questions which the Professor evaded answering. If one asked the Professor a direct question he would answer very straight to the point without emphasizing anything; without elaborating anything. Just the correct answer. To 'Where is my mother?', the Professor said, 'I have had no communication at all with her. You understand that when contracts are broken' — that's what he said, 'contracts' — we couldn't understand what that meant — 'you cannot continue to have communication. You'll have to find out yourself where your mother is.' So Peter said 'How can I find out?' and the Professor said, 'I believe there was a trust fund set up for you by your maternal grandfather, Frederick Fisher. You would have to look it up in his name.'

"And then we went down in the lift, prepared to have tea with him. He stopped at one of those glass cases in the lobby that have displays of cheap jewelry and looked at it for a moment and then said, 'Trash!' so violently his monocle dropped from his eye. We were taken aback.

"We had tea and the conversation went 'Where do you live now?' and 'How long will you be here?' — that sort of conversation which did not go into depth at all. The tea lasted not more than half or three-quarters of an hour. We just had self-conscious conversation about everything and saying nothing. He told us that he was married again and had three daughters. And he complimented Peter on the beauty of his wife, I think. And he wished Peter good luck. And then ... he left."

Peter and Tamara sat silent among the tea things in the busy lounge of the Regent Palace for a very long time staring at the glaring geometric patterns on the hotel carpet. When Peter finally spoke, Tamara could barely hear him. "I don't think I'll bother to look up my mother," he said quietly.

The English are very strange, thought Tamara.

On the ship coming over to England, Tamara and Peter had read and re-read and puzzled over the packet of letters Peter's aunt had given them. They had hoped to find therein some explanation of the peculiar circumstances that had resulted in a young boy being left to grow up in Australia when both his parents lived in England. There were letters from George to his parents, copies of their letters to him, and one single letter from Peter's mother Betty to her then mother-in-law. But though Peter and Tamara thought they now understood how unhappy the marriage had been and how bitter the divorce, Peter himself felt there was still some mystery, some never-to-be-mentioned Finch secret he had not penetrated. Because really, was it possible for a father to behave as his father had just done to his long-lost son?

Later on, Peter would put a good face to it. "The feeling of wanting to see my father was born more out of curiosity than yearning," he told Douglas Keay in an interview thirteen years later, "and the meeting with him turned out to be no more than I expected. We faced each other like complete strangers. We did not talk long."

But that afternoon in 1948, sitting in the lounge of the Regent Palace after his father left, Peter was paralyzed by the blow. The human comedy? The human tragedy? It was all the same, he thought. It was all human frailty. And he smiled his particular smile as he wondered how his father would have reacted if he had tried to touch him for a fiver.

CHAPTER 2

The Train of Events Begins

Early the next morning, Peter went walking alone through the cold, damp, grey streets of London crowded with unfamiliar faces. What he saw did not reassure him. Was it because of his father's rebuff, he wondered, that the people looked so unfriendly, that he suddenly saw so clearly the extent of his folly dashing 12,000 miles across the sea on what was very probably a wild goose chase?

Olivier was now constantly on his mind. He tried to remember Sir Laurence's exact words to him. Had he said "Be *sure* to look me up" or just "Look me up"? And what did it matter anyway? Olivier's words, whatever they were, now seemed to be no more than the vague, kindly utterances of a famous theatrical visitor grateful for a spot of theatre talk in a strange country.

Peter had written to Olivier from Australia giving the date of their arrival in London and the name of the place they would be staying. The Finches had been in London for five whole days! Surely Sir Laurence would have rung by now — that is, if he hadn't already forgotten or regretted his hasty words. For why should Peter expect England's greatest actor to concern himself with an Australian newcomer when his own father had not?

The thought of Olivier made Peter dash back to the hotel. He asked hopefully at the desk for his. messages. There were none. Upstairs in his room, he sat huddled by the phone for the rest of the day *willing* it to ring. Later he said, "All that freezing December and half of January I sat staring at the phone. It crouched there silently like an ugly black frog that refused to croak. I practically went down on my hands and knees praying for it to ring." But as for contacting Olivier himself as Tamara urged him to do over and over again — Peter simply did not dare. The Finches spent a cold anxious Christmas.

During those freezing first months the telephone did, of course, ring occasionally — though it was never the shining knight. And Peter himself made a great many calls. As a result of one to the ABC's office in London, he was introduced to the key man at the BBC — another Laurence, not Laurence Olivier but Laurence Gilliam, Head of the Features Department of the BBC, who claimed the distinction of giving Peter Finch his first chance in his native land.

Anyone wide awake enough to switch on the BBC very early one morning in December 1948 would have heard the golden Finch voice making its début in England: Peter was reading the meat marketing report. An even more ignominious incident followed. In the beginning of dark January, he was employed by an Australian commercial radio company to record the quaint and colourful cockney sounds of barrow boys calling out their wares.

Peter arrived in Berwick Street, a well-known market centre, at six o'clock one evening carrying heavy recording equipment. He went to a pub and politely asked permission to use one of their outlets. When it was granted he plugged in his cable, but it was the wrong voltage, and he fused every single light on Berwick Street. In the blackout, the air was heavy with abuse. If only he had been able to record *those* quaint and colourful cockney sounds, thought Peter as he dragged himself and the miserable recording equipment back to the hotel.

He was very close to giving up. That week he stopped asking for messages whenever he came back to the hotel. One day he didn't go out at all. Tamara was still out looking for a flat they could afford, though at times they each silently wondered why. In the afternoon there was a knock on the door. It was a bell boy with a huge floral arrangement for the Finches. Where's the funeral? Peter wondered gloomily as he reached for the card. The flowers were from the Oliviers! The card contained a "belated welcome" and an invitation to drinks at their home, Durham Cottage in Chelsea. Joyfully, elatedly Peter raced through the invitation, but when he came to the date, he sank dejectedly on the bed. It was a fortnight away. A fortnight! How was he going to live that long?

He lived. But it was for a further disappointment. When the Finches, looking their most festive, arrived at the Oliviers for drinks they discovered about a dozen other people there as well. Drinks were sherry and biscuits, and half an hour later the party was over as the Oliviers had to dash off for a dinner engagement. Before leaving, Olivier sought out Peter and told him he had recommended him to his own agent Cecil Tennant, head of the powerful Myron Selznick agency. Then, as a parting shot he added, "You're all right, Peter, aren't you? Give us a ring sometime."

So disheartened that they were unable to speak to each other, the Finches taxied silently back to the new flat Tamara had found in Powis Terrace out in what was then considered the unfashionable wilds of the Bayswater district of London. But one day not long after the Olivier party, when the phone rang in the Finches unfashionable flat, it tolled, at last, with the unmistakable cadences of destiny. Stalwart Harry Watt was on the phone. He had been unceasingly busy on Peter's behalf. He had already taken him out to the Red Lion, the pub favoured by Ealing directors, where he had introduced the Australian as his protégé. Now Watt had arranged the promised film test. "It's not for any specific part," he warned Peter. "It's just to give Michael Balcon an idea of what you can do."

Shortly thereafter Peter showed up at Ealing for his film test. The director Basil Dearden, who was supervising it, suggested that Finch do his test with a scene from *Train of Events*, a film Dearden was preparing to shoot. The role was that of a young Shakespearean actor who has decided to murder his wife. Playing opposite Peter in the test as his wife was Diana Graves.

Peter was terrified at the beginning of the test but said later, "Diana soothed much of my terror away by her friendliness and humour." Besides Diana Graves and his talent Peter had something else working in his favour: he had ten years of radio experience behind him. Radio actors, most of whom have perfected their instant sightreading-acting technique, are notorious for giving brilliant first readings.

When Sir Michael Balcon saw Peter Finch on film as the murderer he was so impressed that he cast him in the same part in *Train of Events*.

As always, Peter researched his new role diligently. The aspiring Shakespearean actor aspect of the character he felt to be well within the limits of his knowledge, but the man's murderous side that leads him to dismember his wife and stick the pieces in a travelling basket that he has to keep close by him on a train to Liverpool was a bit beyond Peter's ken. Therefore he spent a day at Scotland Yard's Black Museum immersing himself in the ghoulish exhibits of severed heads, cleft tongues and reft thumbs. His thoughts sufficiently bloody, Peter was now ready to embark on his new role.

On the *Train of Events* set on the last day of shooting, destiny was on the phone for him again, this time foretelling an even more glorious future. It was Sir Laurence Olivier at the other end. Olivier, far from forgetting Peter, had been keeping track of his progress and had heard excellent reports of the Australian's performance in *Train of Events*. He told Peter he would be sending round a script to him that evening, a new James Bridie play *Daphne Laureola*, which he would very much like him to read.

Olivier's first attempt as a producer had been in 1947 when he presented the American hit comedy *Born Yesterday* in London. It had whetted his appetite for becoming a fully-fledged actor-manager. Now he was fulfilling this ambition by forming his own permanent company known as L.O.P. (Laurence Olivier Productions) with Vivien Leigh, Sir Alexander Korda, Roger Furse, Anthony Bushell and Cecil Tennant (as managing director). L.O.P. was to make its début presenting Dame Edith Evans in *Daphne Laureola*.

At midnight on the day Olivier had talked to Peter, the Finches' doorbell rang. It was the fastidious Cecil Tennant in dinner jacket who had made the trek from the civilized West End out to the wilds of Bayswater to deliver the *Daphne Laureola* script to Peter. He told him to look over the role of Ernest Piaste and asked him to be at Wyndham's Theatre the following Tuesday morning at 10.30 to be ready to read with the understudy to Dame Edith. That would give Peter two whole days to study the part, Tennant said. And two whole nights, thought Peter wildly.

Before departing, Tennant looked round the Finches' large bedsitter rather as if he were trapped in an opium den and finally, unable to contain himself, he exclaimed: "Dear boy! You *can't* live here!"

"Why not?" asked Peter.

Tennant looked at him. "*It's the wrong side of the park*," he explained gently.

CHAPTER 3

"You don't know me. My name is Edith Evans."

The instant the door closed on Cecil Tennant, Peter grabbed the script and leafed through to Bridie's description of Ernest Piaste: "He is a shy, young man of about twenty" Peter read, "with a sort of middle European look about him. He is, in fact, a Pole." The thirty-three-year-old Australian actor had been asked to read for the part of a twenty-year-old Pole. It was a prospect that would have dismayed many a thirty-three-year-old actor but Peter Finch knew his thin body and his smoothly neutral face still bore the stamp of extreme youth. As for the accent, there was Tamara's rich Russian accent which after all, Peter reasoned, was Slavic — ergo, Polish. Wasting no time in doubts he went straight to work on the script.

Tuesday morning finally came and Peter presented himself at Wyndham's at ten-thirty. Inside the theatre it was dark and chill, lit only with one work-light on the stage. Peter stood in the centre of the stage rigid with fear as he looked out into the black abyss across the front lights hearing but not seeing people mumbling in the auditorium. He heard the creaking of the seats as they were tipped down — and occupied by (unknown to him) — Laurence Olivier, Vivien Leigh, Dame Edith Evans, James Bridie and the director Murray Macdonald.

Soon Peter was joined on stage by the understudy to Dame Edith Evans. Peter thought his eyes must be playing tricks — the understudy was none other than Diana Graves, the actress who had so successfully helped him through his screen test at Ealing! Whether or not Peter was able to persuade himself that the presence of Diana was a sign from above is unimportant. What mattered was that he was able to catch fire from her and that this stroke of good fortune enabled him to rise to the occasion. That — and his radio training.

Peter heard the words, "We're ready when you are, Mr Finch."

"Then there was that awful moment," said Peter later, "when you hear your own voice making, it seems, the impact of a mouse's squeak in the silence."

And then the actor took over ...

After a time Peter heard another voice, Olivier's, echoing from the darkness, "Thank you, Peter. Just a minute."

It was the longest "minute " Peter had ever endured. Carefully he examined his shoes and wondered whether he should stand or sit or stay or go. And through it all he felt Diana's good wishes flowing out to him, almost tangible in their intensity.

Finally a rich, lyrical, startlingly beautiful voice called from the dark, "You don't know me," the voice said. "My name is Edith Evans." Peter heard steps getting nearer until he was conscious of a face looking up at him from the orchestra pit. "I'll see you at rehearsal next Tuesday," Dame Edith said to Peter, "and I'm delighted."

Diana squeezed Peter's hand hard. The role was his. But it was the unexpected, overwhelmingly kind gesture that England's greatest actress had made towards him that caused the tears to start in his eyes. And he found himself crying just as long ago he had cried at the unexpected present of his first birthday cake on his twenty-first birthday.

A lot had gone on behind the scenes before Peter was given the role of Ernest Piaste in *Daphne Laureola*. Bridie and Dame Edith had submitted the play without success to several managements before L.O.P. and it seems fairly clear from subsequent events that Olivier's gamble was based on other considerations than the script alone: foremost on Dame Edith's magic, but also on Olivier's extra-ordinary intuition that the unknown, untried Australian actor was going to pull off the difficult but vitally important role of the young Polish student who falls instantly and totally in love with the dipso-maniac Lady Pitts. To play Ernest Piaste successfully required both sensitivity and virility and Peter Finch filled both these requirements at a time in the West End when sensitive young actors were a dime a dozen but virile young actors were as scarce as hen's teeth.

To direct *Daphne Laureola*, Olivier chose someone who had already worked with Dame Edith — the experienced Murray Macdonald, known for his elegant, precise, well-paced style.

Of the behind-the-scene manoeuvres Macdonald says: "Larry presented me with Finch as a *fait accompli*. That was who he wanted for the part and that was it ... I was handed Finch and I was stuck with Finch and thank God he came through. He and Edith clicked instantly. I think it was because they were both intuitive actors. I know everybody thinks Edith was pure technique but that wasn't true. She was pure instinct. They both worked intuitively and they respected that in each other and they sparked off each other. Edith adored Finch. She was over the moon about him. To her he was 'my boy' and sometimes when she'd suspected he'd had a drink or two, 'my naughty boy'."

Charles Vance who was then stage manager for the company, remembers Dame Edith and Peter in rehearsal one day reading along a scene together when both, suddenly overcome with the realization of the wisdom and wonder of the words they were saying, simultaneously burst into tears. Murrary Macdonald watching from the stalls was very patient. "All right you two," he finally said. "Now that you've both had a good cry, do you think we might get on with the acting?"

The weeks of rehearsal went by smoothly and happily for the cast. Edith Evans always used the simile of a tennis game when discussing acting: an actor, like a tennis player, could only play his best game with players of his own class. With Felix Aylmer playing her husband, Sir Joseph Pitts, and Peter Finch as Ernest Piaste, Dame Edith was among players of her own class. "In the absence of friction," Jean Batters writes in her memoirs of the actress, "Edith learned her lines with unaccustomed ease."

Behind the scenes, however, a very different mood prevailed. From the start neither Olivier nor the others in L.O.P. had had any great faith in the play and they were not encouraged to change their minds by what they saw when they dropped into rehearsals from time to time. This view manifested itself in the building of the sets which were of a rather flimsy nature as L.O.P. were sure the play would not run long enough to warrant anything sturdier. It led also to the decision to "open cold" in the West End and not have the usual shakedown tour, the assumption being that the provinces wouldn't like it and that bad provincial notices could demoralize the cast — if they didn't kill the play before it had a chance to reach London.

Luckily the players knew nothing of this and Edith Evans' mood of optimism and affection was exactly reflected in the note she sent Peter three days before opening night:

I do hope Peter that you are not missing your Sydney Harbour too much and that your reception on Wednesday night will tell you the Bows and Bells tailcoats and striped trousers are warm hearts and most friendly souls. I am so happy to have you as a partner and a colleague. I hope that you are pleased too.

Love,
Edith

The night of the dress parade, when the actors lined up on stage to have their various costumes approved by Macdonald (fortunately L.O.P. had not stinted on Edith Evans' clothes, she was dressed gloriously throughout by Molyneux), someone pointed out that Peter still had on his wedding ring.

"I know," said Peter, "it won't come off. I've never had it off. I prefer not to have it cut or sawn off if you don't mind," he added firmly. So they fitted him with a signet to wear on it: just the thing for a young Pole in a vaguely aristocratic ambience, it was argued. That was easy. That presented no problem.

The problems came at the final dress rehearsal the night before the opening. The last dress rehearsal is traditionally a disaster and *Daphne Laureola*'s was well within the tradition. Not only was the whole cast terrible but the technical problems seemed insurmountable.

Peter remembered that night vividly: "Laurence Olivier watched the performance from the stalls and said afterwards that dress rehearsals always went badly and a bad dress rehearsal generally indicated a successful first night. But while his words were meant to be encouraging his ashen tortured expression betrayed his true feelings.

"Later he came to my dressing-room. 'I hope I haven't made a mistake by giving you this part,' he said. 'Whatever happens, take it in your stride, dear boy.' "

All day long on 23 March Tamara watched her suffering husband helplessly. Peter would eat nothing. He shook. He was sick and weak. He kept running to the bathroom. Finally, late in the afternoon, he went over to the theatre for a line rehearsal. By now Tamara was beginning to suffer as well. With relief she greeted the arrival of her friend Lynn Foster, the Australian script-writer, who was to accompany her to the theatre. Tamara put on her turquoise satin gown, specially bought for the occasion, but when she regarded herself in the mirror she was dismayed. Though little more than a month pregnant, in her clinging satin dress she was "showing". Searching frantically through her bureau drawers she found an old black lace mantilla from her dancing days and draped it concealingly around her dress. They were almost late for the opening.

The *Daphne Laureola* opening at Wyndham's was the most glittering first night since before the war. The presentation by Sir Laurence and Lady Olivier of a new play by the distinguished playwright James Bridie with the great star Dame Edith Evans was a welcome excuse for all first-nighters to discard the nonsense of their utility clothes and get down to the serious business of outdazzling each other in dresses, furs and jewels.

At length everyone was seated. The lights dimmed and the curtain went up revealing a small Soho restaurant peopled by various diners and a writer. Edith Evans, dressed in a gorgeous Molyneux, was seated alone conspicuously drinking double brandies at a rate sufficient to alarm the waiter. Tamara watched tensely. The dialogue began. The audience laughed where they were supposed to. Slowly Tamara relaxed, thinking to herself with surprise, "It's playing so much better than it reads."

Then Peter Finch came on stage. To Tamara he looked very young and very good looking — and very frightened. "Then he spoke," says Tamara, "and there was the magic of his voice and the way he looked at Edith ... it *lifted* the play ... "

Edith Evans lifted it even further and in their scenes together they reached the heights. They were playing, as Dame Edith might have said, centre court at Wimbledon. Ernest Piaste looking at Lady Pitts made everyone in the audience see what he saw: that she was the most fascinating woman in the world.

It was of course Edith Evans' play from start to finish: acknowledged as one of the finest performances of her career. In Lady Pitts, Bridie had presented a recognizable type (recognizable on stage anyway): the elegant, magnetic, superior, resourceful woman, and then he had added to her character an extraordinary "but" which sets the play in motion and carries it to its conclusion: *but she drinks!* Why? The explanation and the consequences of her drinking — in other words, the plot, is fairly muddled but the presentation of this character is always riveting. Olivier was right in his misgivings about the play and Dame Edith was right in her optimism. *Daphne Laureola* was that intensely thrilling but rarely-to-be-seen-today kind of play: a "vehicle" for a star which works only if the star is of such magnitude that she blinds as she dazzles. Dame

Edith that night blinded and dazzled, causing Harold Hobson to write of her in *The Sunday Times*: "I believe the very constellations will look down with jealousy. Every smile is like the rising of the sun and every syllable she speaks is like a song."

The first-act curtain fell to thunderous applause. The audience left their seats and began milling about the lobbies and bars.

What happened then was so exactly like what used to go on in those star-struck, stage-struck movies of the 30s and 40s, right down to the last cliché, that it was hard to believe it was not all happening for the benefit of the camera.

"What a pleasure and a delight are the intervals of a play that is a crackling success from the start," wrote T. C. Worsley in the *New Statesman*. "And how this reflects itself at once in the high edge of chatter, the confident nods between acquaintances at the bar, the exciting re-telling of this or that memorable stroke!"

Theatre World bubbled: "The excited audience welcomed a new young actor to London in the person of Peter Finch. 'Who *is* Peter Finch?' was the question on the lips of the play-goers at the *Daphne Laureola* opening as they jostled each other during the interval. None of them had seen the young man before and they admired the assurance with which he carried off this intricate new Bridie characterization."

In using such heady language, these reporters were not taking poetic licence. As *aficionados* of first nights know, this could happen, this does happen, and this *did* happen on the opening night of *Daphne Laureola*.

At the end of the play the audience went predictably wild. When Edith Evans came out to take her bow they rose in her honour with deafening cheers and applause. Dame Edith slowly made a deep curtsey to the audience. Up went another roar and another. And another. That night she took sixteen curtain calls.

When Peter came out to take his bow and turned to leave, the audience shouted "More! More!" Hearing this unfamiliar sound, Tamara turned to Lynn Foster and asked anxiously, "Are they booing?"

Olivier, still slightly streaked with make-up from his performance in *Antigone* at the New Theatre dashed across the street to Wyndham's in time for the curtain calls and enthusiastically, if astonishedly, joined in the cheering.

At the opening-night party given at set-designer Roger Furse's house, Peter was delirious and behaved in an appropriately delirious manner. Among the guests were Sir Alexander Korda, Tyrone Power, John Mills, Emlyn Williams and Joseph Cotten. Peter asked Cotten politely if he hadn't see his face somewhere. Then he introduced Eric Linklater to everyone as A.A. Milne (the well-known preceptor of Tamara's English lessons) and after that he fixed Sir Laurence's tie to his own particular liking and spent the rest of the night ear-bashing the patient James Bridie with long selections of Banjo Paterson's Australian poetry.

At four o'clock in the morning Peter, in bed but still awake, was phoned by the company's press officer David Fairweather. He was calling from a booth outside Kensington tube station in his pyjamas. He had bought the morning papers at the news-stand and he was "weeping with joy". Peter leapt into a cab similarly attired and joined Fairweather at Kensington tube station.

Fairweather shoved *The Daily Telegraph* at him first. W.A. Darlington had written: "I haven't much idea what Bridie is saying but I agree with every word of it. The events of the play are crazy and the symbolism obscure but I have not enjoyed a play more in a very long time." After a tribute to Dame Edith Evans, Darlington adds only eleven words about Peter Finch, but for a young actor making his London début they could not have been better chosen. "Peter Finch as the Pole makes a name in a night."

Other newspapers were more specific, calling Peter's performance "the most tender acting on the stage in years". He was "quicksilver". He was "fire and romanticism". His performance was "sensitivity at its greatest".

Beverly Baxter remarked shrewdly: "I think this is the best acting Edith Evans has ever done but her triumph is aided in many delicate ways by a young Australian actor Peter Finch."

None knew this better than Edith Evans herself. She was a formidable woman, often cold and aloof, and she did not bestow her friendship easily. But five years after *Daphne Laureola*, when she wrote to Peter to thank him for his opening-night good wishes in Christopher Fry's *The Dark is Light Enough*, she added "I wish we could be in a play together soon." And it is that word "soon" that lifts her note from the general to the specific. In 1956, at the age of sixty-eight, after her triumph in *The Chalk Garden* she wrote to Peter, "It was nice to see you again. I wish we could be in a play together. I shall always remember one scene we played together in

Daphne in the last act. You were so fine.''

Australia, as might be expected, took Peter's success in a bigger way than everyone else. On 24 March 1949 every news hoarding in Sydney's streets bore in thick black letters the *Sun's* legend. SYDNEY ACTOR HAILED IN LONDON. (The *Sun*, of course, was the newspaper from which sixteen years earlier its inept young copy boy had been fired.)

CHAPTER 4

"Call me Betty"

Back in his flat in Bayswater, Peter slept till noon. Did he awaken to stardom? It is at this point that the film fades out, The End appears on the screen, the credits roll up, the lights come on and the audience leaves. Reality takes over.

Therefore Peter did not awaken to stardom the next day. He awakened to the second night performance of *Daphne Laureola* and to Dame Edith's warning to the cast that this performance must be as fresh as on the first night. For Edith Evans every night was a first night and she made sure that everyone's tennis game was up to hers for the three hundred and sixty-seven performances during the eleven months that *Daphne Laureola* was to run.

In 1945, still frustrated in the army, Peter had written to Tamara in words like a prayer: "Please God before I am too old I will find somewhere to really learn about the theatre."

Now Peter's prayer was being answered. It was of course impossible to act with Edith Evans every night and not become aware of what one did not know. For her part, Dame Edith was tremendously keen that Peter should learn from her. Sometimes she helped him by stating theatrical truths in a vividly metaphorical way. After several performances during which they were losing laughs she told him "You're pressing too hard. The art of comedy is to fire powder puffs out of a cannon. You were firing cannonballs." More often her advice was practical. During the long run of the play, she willingly gave up her mornings to go down to the theatre to coach Peter through Shakespeare and the classics. And Olivier contributed his part towards the theatrical education of Peter Finch by sending him to his own voice coach, the great Elsie Fogarty.

Peter was now under a five-year contract to Sir Laurence Olivier beginning at £30 a week (about £50 in present-day terms) and rising finally to £90 a week. To be near the theatre — and, no doubt to the relief of Cecil Tennant — the Finches moved from the "wrong side of the park" right into the dead centre of the theatre district. Their new address was Burleigh Mansions, St Martin's Lane.

Though Peter was by no means a star, he was something perhaps equally exciting: a "discovery". As such, illustrated articles about him appeared in many magazines. Peter studied these articles intently but not for self-glory; his thoughts were on that woman who was his mother, wherever and whoever she might be. Might she have chanced to see this article or that one? Might she have recognized his name, his story, his photograph? Often in his dressing-room after the show he found himself tensely waiting for someone to be announced who would reveal herself to be his mother. After *Daphne Laureola* had been running for six months he came to the decision that he could no longer put off finding out what had happened to her.

It was in August, Tamara remembers, when she was six months pregnant, that Peter turned to her one day and said, "Let's do something about finding my mother." They went to a Trusts Office in the city and found that there was a trust made by Frederick Fisher for the descendants of Alicia Gladys "Betty" Ingle Finch, Peter's mother. The Finches asked the man in charge for her present surname. Officially he was not allowed to disclose the details of her circumstances but the Finches persevered. Peter showed his birth certificate: Peter George Frederick Ingle Finch. "Just a minute," said the man. He went away and came back with a folded scrap of paper which he pushed into Peter's hand and then said, raising his voice a little, "I'm afraid there's nothing I can do for you."

Outside the office Peter quickly unfolded the piece of paper. It said: Mrs Betty Staveley-Hill, Carbis Bay, St Ives, Cornwall. Back at their flat, he put a call through to Mrs Betty Staveley-Hill in great excitement. "There was a short conversation," says Tamara "and a very stunned reaction on the other end of the line. Mrs Staveley-Hill said 'Come and visit me. I live in a cottage in Cornwall. I'll be waiting for you at the St Ives station. Find out the train times.' "

As Peter had only Sunday night off from the theatre, the Finches caught the one train they could: the 11.30 Saturday night train which left after the show. There were no sleeping cars and the exhausted actor who had done two performances that day and his pregnant wife had to sit up all through the night. Early in the morning they were told to change trains for St Ives. Dead tired they dragged themselves on to what turned out to be an excruciatingly slow train and arrived at the small station of St Ives at eleven o'clock in the morning. They had been travelling for twelve hours.

The station platform was empty. There was no one waiting for them. Dazed they wondered if they had got it wrong. They confirmed with the station master that Mrs Staveley-Hill did live there. There were no benches and no taxis or any other kinds of transportation in sight. They waited.

Half an hour later a car finally drove up with two passengers in it. Peter stepped forward, prepared to meet some grey-haired plump cosy soul. Instead the woman who got out of the car and came towards him was petite and slim with shoulder-length ash blond hair and sunglasses hiding her eyes. She wore smart country clothes. With her was a big hefty blond girl of about thirteen. The woman went up to Peter and held out her hand.

"Call me Betty," said his mother casually, and introduced her daughter Flavia, Peter's half-sister. Flavia was at an age where she was totally infatuated with animals. Her only remark on being told a half-brother from far off Australia was about to visit them was, "Will he have a parrot on his shoulder?" Surreptitiously now she stole a look at his shoulder.

They all got into the car and drove until they arrived at Betty's cottage which was perched on a rock overlooking the bay. Tamara remembers the conversation during the drive. "As with Peter's father, it was completely about nothing — the air, the sea, the seagulls ... Really it was as if we had seen each other just last weekend. There was no mention of the past and since that was the tone established, Peter responded with social conversation of his own. The seagulls were calling to be fed — so we fed them."

Peter recalled to Douglas Keay in an interview in 1961 what followed: "Then we went indoors and had tea. The kind where cups are balanced on knees and conversation seems just as precarious. Talking was like trying not to go on the same circular road twice. I kept sneaking looks at my mother. I decided she reminded me of pictures I had seen as a boy of Gladys Cooper. I could imagine her having been among the bright young things of the twenties. At heart she still is."

"Then", says Tamara, "a young man on a bicycle came by. He

had lost his way. Betty or Flavia, I forget which, pointed out where he had taken the wrong turning but suddenly everyone was urging the cyclist to stay a little longer, to have some tea or a drink as if it were a Chekhov play. We were all so wrapped up in our own thoughts, in our own emotions, we couldn't connect with anyone else. But on the surface absolutely no feelings were shown.

"We found out that Betty had separated from her third husband, Alexander Staveley-Hill, and was now living alone with Flavia but that was all. We were given a room upstairs and I lay down to rest and after a while Betty came into my room and said she was very happy to see us. And I said — I just had to — I was exploding inside — I said *'But what was your first impression of your son? What do you think of him?'*

" 'Oh,' said Betty, 'one thing that I noticed immediately — I noticed that he was wearing a signet ring on the wrong finger.'

"I thought, she hasn't seen her son in thirty years and this, *this* is her first impression?"

The English are very strange, thought Tamara.

Downstairs in the sitting-room Peter was due for another shock. Betty told him that he not only had a sister Flavia but a brother, Michael, who was three years younger than he. Michael had a pig farm not far away and was coming to join them later. When he arrived, as Peter described it, "I took one look at Michael looming large in the cottage door and thought: Him I'm going to like." After he'd been in the cottage ten minutes, Michael said quickly, "Peter, you and I are going to leave. Come on let's have a drink!" And they drove off to the local pub.

In the pub Peter and Michael wondered at their lives, each so different from the other's. Educated at Harrow, Michael had become one of the youngest Wing Commanders in World War II and had been awarded the D.F.C. and bar. He had been a test pilot. Now he was a farmer. In spite of their different careers, they took to each other at once and with Michael, Peter gained a much loved younger brother and friend for life. By the time the two of them were ready to return to their mother's cottage, Peter was feeling considerably more informal.

At the age of fifty-six, Betty Staveley-Hill beheld her eldest son almost, one might say, for the first time in her life. Looking back at that reunion in the small cottage in Carbis Bay, Mrs Staveley-Hill, now eighty-seven years old, says: "Wasn't it lucky that Peter and I liked each other from the start? Suppose I'd hated actors? Suppose we'd hated each other? Peter said to me that first evening in Cornwall, 'I don't want to come back into your life if it's going to embarrass you.' I said, 'Embarrass me all you bloody well like.' He was like that — always considering me first."

One may think that no stranger relationship could come to pass than the subsequent friendship and even love of a son for a mother who had not ever inquired after him in all those years; who knew nothing of his existence in Australia other than that he had arrived there as a child; who had pretended to herself and to her friends that this child was dead so that, in her words — "I could forget him and go on living."

To understand this relationship one must understand that if Peter's whole life had taught him nothing else, it had taught him to accept things as they are and make the best of them, and that this quality of acceptance was something he very much shared with his mother. They also had humour, eccentricity and charm in common. Like Peter, his mother was an original. As a young woman no one had ever known what she might say next — it was always the first thing that popped into her head. And now in middle age, this had not changed. She was audacious, spontaneous and popular. If she liked you (and that was a big "if") she could be an extraordinarily sympathetic listener. She could also be, some said, extraordinarily extravagant and selfish. She had never in her life lacked for a beau. She had a natural talent for getting along with men and getting around them. Olive Harding, Peter's agent, dubbed her "a man's woman".

Wisely she chose not to "mother" Peter as they grew closer together over the years. "They were close but they were like sister and brother rather than mother and son," says a friend.

Once, however, Peter did confront his mother with the past. They were sitting in the Finches' flat: Peter, his mother and an intimate friend of his, the actor Alan White, newly arrived from Australia. Peter was drinking. Suddenly tears began pouring down his face.

He turned on his mother and burst out, "How *could* you have done it? How *could* you have done it to me?"

Mrs Staveley-Hill looked steadily back at him. "When you are as old as I am and have made as many mistakes as I have," she said evenly, "you can ask me that question."

This statement, which contained both an acknowledgement of guilt and a challenge (if not an answer), caused Peter, as he later put it, "to consider that my parents were not just my parents — they were people as well''. At the time he must have felt that his mother, in answering him thus, was being truthful — and perhaps rather brave. Or, on a much deeper level, some profound primal fear may have begun stirring in him that warned him if he pursued this course with his mother he might lose her again, this time for good.

In any case, throughout his life, Peter was to remain amused, interested and impressed by his mother. He was also to contribute substantially to her upkeep. When one says he was attracted to her as a *person*, one has, perhaps, got to the bottom of it.

As for Mrs Staveley-Hill, it is interesting to note that she always preserved a certain ironic, comic style in her semi-public remarks about her relationship with Peter, perhaps to deflect the tragic ambiguity of emotions that must always have existed between mother and son.

When Yolande Finch, Peter's second wife, in pursuit of back alimony, had a friend telephone Peter's mother to ask for his address in Jamaica, Mrs Staveley-Hill said that she did not know it. Pressed, she told the caller firmly, ''I am responsible for my son's birth — and nothing else.''

At Peter Finch's memorial service at St Paul's in London, Charles Vance spotted Mrs Staveley-Hill in the crowd outside the church. Giving her his arm, they walked up the steps. Reporters converging stopped them.

''Either of you connected in any way with the deceased?'' one of them asked.

Mrs Staveley-Hill drew herself up. ''They tell me I'm his mother,'' she said. And swept in.

CHAPTER 5

The Australian Bum

The film *Train of Events* which Peter had completed before rehearsals of *Daphne Laureola* was released in August of that year. Although the critics' reaction to it in general was mild, it was another personal triumph for Peter. The *Evening Standard* critic said: "Peter Finch is new to the screen but brings to it all his talents from *Daphne Laureola* without mislaying one of them. He proves once again his capacity for odd character and his beautiful control of voice and expression. He is worth all the rest."

And Alan Dent in *Illustrated London News* wrote: "The one thing I am likely to remember for any length of time is Mr Finch's bitter brooding study."

C.A. Lejeune, at that time England's most influential film critic, predicted accurately that: "Peter Finch is likely to become a cult." And in fact a cult he became.

In October Peter also became a father. On the 27th of that month Tamara gave birth to a baby girl whom the Finches christened Anita after her maternal grandmother, Mumma, who was still in Australia. At the christening, which she felt strongly should star the baby Anita, Tamara noticed, half irritated, half amused, that Sir Laurence could barely get through the performance of his duties as the baby's godfather in his impatience to take Peter aside and pull out from his bulging pocket the script of a new play he wanted him to look over.

Shortly afterwards, the Finches moved house again, this time to Dolphin Square, a huge block of flats overlooking the Thames. During the war the flats had been taken over by army and navy officials. Now, in peace time, they were inhabited by artists, writers and actors. The Finches were amused to discover they were living in the flat once occupied by General de Gaulle. Comfortably housing their family of three, the flat was let for £8 a week.

During the long run of *Daphne Laureola* Peter accepted only two parts in films — both very small. He played an RAAF officer in the prisoner-of-war escape film *The Wooden Horse* and a young Pole in *The Miniver Story*.

Even by the high standards of his past life, Peter's first twelve months in England might be considered something of a peak. The Australian orphan now had four blood relatives close to him: his mother, his sister, his brother and his child. He had made two successful débuts — one on the English stage and one in the English cinema. He was the protégé of the greatest English actor and he was playing opposite the greatest English actress. He had a wife who loved and understood him, and a baby girl he doted on.

But one night when a young fan burst into his dressing-room and began rhapsodizing over his performance, insisting it was "the most moving, the most marvellous, the most glorious — " Peter cut her off in midstream by saying with absolute sincerity: "I'm not an actor. I'm an Australian bum. And a poet." In that statement, Peter revealed again the permanent conflict in his life: those two opposing forces that would always be at war within him. There was his craving to be a bum, as he said, a vagabond; to live simply from the land and with the land, and sleep under the stars in a different place every night. But pulling him in the opposite direction was his craving to be a poet. Yet even though he might have become a good poet — indeed it was the distinguished Australian poet Kenneth Slessor's published opinion that Peter Finch had the makings of a "first-rate" poet — deep inside him he always knew that his poetry could best, in fact could only, be expressed in his acting.

CHAPTER 6

Running in Place

Daphne Laureola closed in February 1950. The very next month Peter was rehearsing in the play Olivier had been so eager for him to read at Anita's christening. It was called *Damascus Blade* and it starred John Mills.

"It was a terrible play — really frightful," says Bridget Boland. "I know because I wrote it. We kept touring up and down the country — Bristol, Newcastle, Glasgow, Edinburgh, Brighton — with me out front every night watching and rewriting, trying to get it right. We never did. As it got worse and worse, John Mills and most of the others adopted that rather tense, aggressive attitude I've seen actors in bad plays assume towards the audience. A sort of I'm-going-to-ram-this-down-your-throat-whether-you-like-it-or-not attitude. But Peter never did. Of course he had only one big scene but the audience loved him. In Glasgow we thought, well it's because of his rough down-to-earth exterior, Glaswegians like that. But in patrician Edinburgh they liked him too. I asked him once, 'How can you go on stage every night and do what you do, knowing the audience hates this play so much?' 'Oh well,' he said, 'they've paid. I've got to give them their money's worth.' As the play dragged on all the actors began feeling sorry for themselves but Peter felt sorry for *me*. We became good friends and when later I moved to Rome he came often to visit me."

In June the *Damascus Blade* finally stabbed itself to death in Brighton and all concerned called it a long hard day and fled with relief back to London. The next play Olivier chose to cast Peter in was *Captain Carvello*, by Dennis Cannan. He did not, however, cast Peter in the title role as might be expected but put him in a supporting part as the bearded, garrulous middle-aged Professor Winke. Again, as in the casting of Peter in the small role of a revolutionary hidden behind large spectacles in *Damascus Blade*, this seemed a curious misuse of the special brand of Finch charisma which had proven both in *Daphne Laureola* and *Train of Events* to be, in the words of the long-ago Australian critic, "dripping with sex". *Captain Carvello*, an uneasy blend of high comedy, low farce and verbosity opened at the St James Theatre on 9 August 1950. It scraped by with polite notices and, "under the magisterial wing of Sir Laurence Olivier" as *The Sunday Times* put it, managed to stretch out a run of seven months. But *Carvello* was a severe disappointment to playgoers who had come to the theatre with the sole expectation of falling under the Finch spell again. Of Peter's performance the *Daily Telegraph* critic wrote, "Peter Finch made quite a nice piece of work as Professor Winke." And that just about summed it up.

Immediately after *Captain Carvello* closed, Peter worked forty-eight hours round the clock, learning a huge role in order to take over the lead from Dirk Bogarde in a mediocre Anouilh play, *Point of Departure*, in the middle of its run. Next he found himself bewigged and bearded as the Sheriff of Nottingham in Walt Disney's film *Robin Hood*. For research, he went to Nottingham, studied ninth-century records and roamed around its Sherwood Forest for days. Peter made such an impact on the early rushes that he ended up with a part three times its original size.

The filming of *Robin Hood* was noteworthy for Peter mainly because during this time he suffered a major artistic disappointment. "Most actors want to play parts they are not suited for," says Peter's friend Alan White, "but the parts that Peter burned to play — Till Eulenspiegel, Peer Gynt, Robert Louis Stevenson and Don Quixote — were all parts he would have been magnificent in. They were all, like him, seekers after the romantic quest." To play Don Quixote had always been Peter's most cherished artistic dream. He had often talked about it to John Kay during the Mercury days in Australia and to Olivier in England. Now he talked to the producers of *Robin Hood*. They listened to Peter with interest and, watching Peter's work, they daily became more enthusiastic about the project. Beautiful colour stills were taken of Peter as Don Quixote in full costume and make-up with James Hayter as Sancho Panza. If it is possible for one to judge how good an actor is going to be merely by stills (and it is surprising how often it is), Peter would have been "brilliant" as Don Quixote.

When the producers saw the stills they became even more enthusiastic. Peter himself was by now in a state of high excitement as his dream seemed to be taking the shape of reality. All the project needed to get underway was the O.K. of the great Walt Disney who was shortly arriving in England to view *Robin Hood*

At last the all-powerful Disney arrived in London. He was given a special private showing of the rough-cut *Robin Hood*. And ... and ... he was observed to be *drumming his fingers throughout*! It was the Emperor's thumbs down.

Don Quixote was abruptly cancelled. Its death, still-born, marked Peter's first realization that Australia did not have a monopoly on artistic frustration.

After chasing Robin Hood around Sherwood Forest for four months Peter, suffering from exhaustion and disillusionment, was fervidly planning on a long rest to catch his breath. Sir Laurence, however, had different plans for him which were equally fervid. He had managed to capture that elusive magic balloon Orson Welles and tether him down to appearing as Othello at the St James Theatre for a limited engagement of nine weeks. Peter Finch, Olivier had impressed upon Welles, would be his perfect Iago.

When Olivier disclosed this plan to Peter, the latter, instead of reacting euphorically to the news, plunged into dismay and confusion. In his fatigued state it seemed to him that since his triumphs in *Daphne Laureola* and *Train of Events* he had been running and running but in some curious way he was still in exactly the same place. He was still a "discovery"; he was still "promising".

When tempting offers of films and plays had come pouring in after his initial success, Olivier had advised him to turn them down. "You're not ready," he had said. Peter, always the first to admit that he had much to learn, had taken Olivier's advice, had turned down these offers and had accepted instead the roles assigned to him by Sir Laurence "for his own good" — including the Sheriff of Nottingham. These unrewarding roles that he had been playing were, as Peter saw it, part of his training period. But was it possible, he wondered, that all this training was in fact weakening him?

Now with the offer of Iago it could be presumed that at last Olivier felt Peter to be "ready". To make his début in Shakespeare on the London stage in one of Shakespeare's longest and most fascinating roles opposite Orson Welles, was, Peter knew, a very big chance and a very big challenge.

But suppose he turned it down as he'd decided to? Then he would be free to take his wife and child, whom he rarely had a chance to see for any length of time, and go off somewhere with them on a long sea voyage. Or to go to the Continent — see places he had only read about. And paint. And write poetry. He had not had a week off from work in two years.

Yes; suppose he turned down this big chance? Then what? The answer was simple: he would never have it again. "Under the magisterial wing of Sir Laurence Olivier" ... Orson Welles ... Shakespeare ... Iago.

"I'm exhausted," he told an interviewer after he had decided. "But Larry thinks it would be a good thing if I went straight into rehearsals of *Othello*. Since my boss works harder than any man I know, who am I to argue?"

Peter had decided that his new assignment — and his first with Shakespeare on stage — was a train of events he *must* be on.

THE  SUN

"FOR AUSTRALIA"

THURSDAY

(Printed and published by Associated Newspapers Limited, at the registered office of the company, 60-70 Elizabeth Street, Sydney)
THURSDAY, MARCH 24, 1949

SYDNEY ACTOR HAILED IN LONDON

21

22 Peter as Ernest Piaste in *Daphne Laureola*, 1949 "Peter Finch as the Pole makes a name in a night."

23 Peter drinking at the *Salisbury* pub during a break from rehearsals of *Daphne Laureola*

24 Peter and Sir Laurence Olivier celebrating the success of *Daphne Laureola* at the opening-night party
25 And then Olivier inexplicably cast Peter to look like this in *Damascus Blade*, 1951

26 *Train of Events*, 1949: "Peter Finch is likely to become a cult."

27 Don Quixote—the part Peter hoped to play but never did

28 and 29 Peter Finch, 1950

30 Peter and Tamara fencing on the roof of their flat in Dolphin Square, 1950

31 Peter and Vivien Leigh in Ceylon working on *Elephant Walk*, 1952—the beginning of a Romance

32 Peter with Elizabeth Taylor who took over Vivien Leigh's part in *Elephant Walk* when Vivien became ill

33 Peter as Flambeau in *Father Brown*, 1954—a ravishment to the eye and mind

34 *Robbery Under Arms*, 1957—Peter's only relationship was with his horse Velox

35 and 36 *The Shiralee*, 1957:
Peter as an Australian Bum
saddled with his "shiralee", his
young child

CHAPTER 7

Success! Success!

In the '50s a small basement club called the Buckstone, located on Suffolk Street opposite the stage door of the Haymarket Theatre, had neither signposts nor a sign to indicate where it was. It needed none. Everyone in the know already knew not only where it was but what it was, namely the most popular eating and drinking theatrical club in London. Run by a cheerful plump actor named Gerry Campion (who played Billy Bunter in the popular TV series), its customers ate cheaply and well and drank, equally cheaply, a lethal cider of high alcoholic content which tasted like steel shavings and exploded into the nervous system like dynamite. The Buckstone also functioned as a pipeline through which flowed the freshest, straightest and latest theatrical news.

The pipeline almost blew up when the *Othello* casting news rushed through. Orson Welles, it seemed, was definitely *not* interested in auditioning any actors who had *already* played in Shakespeare! He emphatically did not want anyone who had been tainted with what he called "Old Vic elocution-type renditions of Shakespeare's 'purr-trih' forced through strangled, tremulous, pear-shaped tones".

In America, there would have been a line a mile long of first-rate actors who had never played in Shakespeare for Welles to choose from. But in England, where Shakespearean productions yield one third of its theatres' annual harvest, to find an actor of quality whose tongue had never tasted of the Bard was well-nigh impossible.

Therefore actors auditioning for Welles found themselves in the curious position of fibbing *downwards*, so to speak, instead of *upwards*, as is more usual. They actually had to deny themselves certain achievements.

Othello's obstacle course had begun. When Welles, mid-way through auditions, realised that this no-Shakespeare hurdle was too high for certain actors that he wanted, he lowered it for them by making them give their solemn promise that they had never in their lives ever played in — or indeed had ever given a thought to playing in — *Othello*. Good-naturedly, the actors complied.

In the case of Peter Finch, Welles was safe. The only Shakespeare Peter had ever done professionally was in radio in Australia. And that, of course, did not count.

Maxine Audley wisely said nothing to Welles about the fact that she had already played Emilia, Iago's wife, in Nottingham Repertory, when she got the part. How many other actors adopted similar tactics is not known.

In due course the casting of *Othello* was completed and the rehearsals were scheduled at the St James Theatre.

In agreeing with Sir Laurence Olivier to act in and direct *Othello* as his first stage production in England, Orson Welles, boy genius, now aged thirty-six, must have felt he would be putting his genius on the line or his head on a block. Welles had not seriously performed on stage for twelve years, not since his Mercury salad days on Broadway, before *Citizen Kane* and Hollywood. In taking on *Othello*, he was taking on a part that no white man in living memory had triumphed in unless he sang it. Furthermore, Welles would be working with actors who were strangers to him, not his familiar and expert Mercury Players who knew him and his idiosyncratic ways and had worked with him for years on Broadway and Hollywood.

One of Welles' sayings was: "Nothing is so secure as no-talent." In other words, talent by its very existence generates insecurity. And if insecurity can be generated by talent — what can be generated by genius? Panic? Was there some fear on Welles' part that he might fail? Or that, if he *did* fail, might it not be better for him to have some good reasons for the failure? Perhaps he could not forget John Gielgud saying to him incredulously, "You're going to do *Othello*? (pause) On the *stage*? (pause) In *London*??" All this speculation is by way of trying to understand Welles' extraordinary behaviour during his production of *Othello*.

On the morning of the first rehearsal, the cast assembled: outwardly all warmth and grace towards each other while inwardly scrutinizing and measuring each other's potential for friendship or enmity. Maxine Audley, sultry and handsome in the grand manner, and Peter sized each other up at once as potential friends and allies.

At lunchtime the two went off to the Buckstone together where, over the potent cider, they discussed the morning's events. They both expressed their admiration for The Great Man, spoke glowingly of his magnetic personality, his voice, his presence, his knowledge, his humour. Then Maxine leaned back in her chair, lit a cigarette and said, "Well, what do you think of the cast?"

Peter thought for a moment. Then he said, "How tall are you?"

"Five foot four," said Maxine puzzled. "Why?"

"You're five foot four," said Peter. "And Welles got a Desdemona who's under five feet. I'm five ten — and no one else in the cast is taller than I am. Except, of course *him*. He must be about six foot two tall and six foot two wide."

"So?" asked Maxine.

"So?" repeated Peter. "So we're going to look like a bunch of midgets next to him on stage!" They both laughed at the low cunning of it.

In the early days of rehearsals, the cast adored Welles. They found him magical. They found themselves learning a great deal from him about making sense of Shakespeare as he determinedly steered them away from the orthodox readings and forced them to sound like human beings. He talked of the importance of this a great deal.

Welles, they were beginning to discover, loved talking about anything a great deal. Sometimes he would even stop a rehearsal because he had thought of a good story about John Barrymore and, if the mood was on him, he would be quite happy to abandon rehearsal for the rest of the day so that they could all sit around swapping yarns. Eventually the cast began to worry. Precious time was slipping away, though the actors would not have dreamt of pointing this out to Welles.

"At that time," says Maxine Audley, "we were all very disciplined actors. I mean we did what the director told us and shut up. It was not like it is now when English actors, from the first day of rehearsals, contribute their own ideas of their parts. In those days one was given a part and thanked God for it or Orson or whoever and just waited for the director to tell you what to do or where to move."

The sight of so much docility on the stage one day caused Welles to lose his head. He found a twenty-foot pole in the orchestra pit and with demonic glee wielded it across the stage from side to side. As the actors dodged and leaped into the air to escape being crippled, The Great Man roared, "To hell with the Method! This is the Welles way! Act, you sons-of-bitches!"

Next, the actors — by now thoroughly unnerved — were told of a new rehearsal schedule. They would be rehearsing from noon to six o'clock straight through without a lunch break. Six hours without a break was a long stretch, but at least it looked as though Welles meant to get down to work. So far he had done no rehearsing with himself on stage together with the cast. He had planted his understudy there in minute and exact positions and only once about every three days would he get up on the stage as Othello. This was usually in his scene with the Senate. He would begin his speech to them "Most potent, grave, and reverend signors ... " and then cut to the end of the speech, leave the stage and yell for his understudy to come back.

The day the noon-to-six o'clock rehearsals began the actors were in for another shock. Promptly at one o'clock, a picnic hamper arrived for Welles accompanied by a silver bucket of iced wine. Rehearsals then stopped while Welles opened the hamper to reveal a large plate of oysters and a plate heaped with thinly sliced buttered brown bread. Welles uncorked the wine and sat in the stalls partaking of his feast while the rest of the cast stood on stage watching him with watering mouths and gnashing teeth. For the remainder of the rehearsals, the actors may have missed *their* cues, but the picnic hampers, they swear, never missed *theirs*.

One day, to his astonishment, Peter actually discovered himself acting with Welles on stage. It was a disconcerting experience. He found himself being ruthlessly upstaged by Welles who was pulling out every old trick in the book to draw attention to himself and away from Peter. Peter, the Australian without the English tradition of stage docility, finally spoke up.

"Fuck *yew*!" he said, giving the phrase its full, rough Aussie ring.

The Great Man stopped in his tracks.

"This scene isn't going to make sense, Orson, if you play like that," Peter explained.

Welles' sunny smile was devoid of guilt. "Look kiddo," he said, "I know all about the part you're playing. Iago usually steals the show and I am going to make damn sure that you don't!"

By now, the Buckstone had taken on an almost carnival atmosphere as the acting profession crowded in there daily to get the latest bulletins from the *Othello* company. Happy hours were passed by resting actors during the afternoon and evening, spinning out fantasies of "What will Orson think up next?"

As always with Orson, no one could possibly have guessed. A week before they were scheduled to open on tour in Newcastle,

Maxine, Peter and some of the rest of the cast trailed into the Buckstone at lunchtime. A crowd quickly gathered around them wanting to know what they were doing there and why they were not working straight through till six.

"Orson's gone," said Peter.

"They don't know where," said Maxine.

"They can't find him," said one actor.

"Just disappeared," said another.

"But what about Newcastle? Don't you open there in a week?" someone managed to gasp.

"What about it?" said Peter in a hollow tone.

Orson the Magician had disappeared into thin air. He stayed missing for four days. On the fifth, the Maestro-Playboy reappeared just as magically at the St James and casually announced by way of explanation that he had attended a party in Venice. Then he called a rehearsal. At the end of it he said, "You're all terrible."

A common dream, or nightmare, that a great many people suffer from (not just actors) is the one in which they are on stage in front of an audience but the play they find themselves in is not the play they have been rehearsing; it is something dreadfully different. It is called an "anxiety dream" from which the dreamer thankfully awakens.

On opening night in Newcastle the *Othello* cast was having what might be called an "anxiety reality" for though they were awake and in front of an audience, the play they were in was not the play they had rehearsed.

First of all Welles did not know his lines. Second, he came on from totally different places than those which the cast had been led to expect from rehearsals. And third, he stood and moved around in totally unexpected places. If that was not enough to confound the cast, he had one more surprise in store for them. He was wearing *four*-inch lifts on his shoes raising his height — to say nothing of his bulk — and forcing the dwarfed actors to stretch their necks painfully whenever addressing him.

"What with one thing and another, we were all on our toes," said Maxine Audley recollecting from a tranquil distance of twenty-seven years that memorable first night in Newcastle. They got through it. Following the final curtain, however, the actors had not got the heart to turn and reassure each other with those immemorial words of the theatre: "I'm sure the audience didn't notice a thing."

Astonishingly, one critic in Newcastle "didn't notice a thing". The Newcastle *Evening Chronicle*, after expressing its appreciation that Welles had chosen to honour its town with his stage début in England, added that as Othello, Welles gave a "fine forthright presentation". As for Peter Finch, he "did well as Iago but at moments was too robust to convey the truly detestable snake".

After the first night, still huddled together like survivors of a shipwreck, the cast made their way back to their quarters at the Turk's Head Hotel opposite the theatre. There Welles surprised them by offering them a nightcap in his suite.

"Oh-oh," said one of the actors as they filed in after Welles. "It's anecdote time."

And sure enough, after the brandy had been passed around a couple of times and everyone was feeling nice and mellow and Orson had relaxed his bulk into an easy chair and was puffing away on his mammoth Romeo y Julietta cigar, he removed it from his mouth and began to tell a story.

The story he told was a pretty good one: the one about his 17,000-mile tour of America in 1933 in Kit Cornell's company when they were reviving the road which had been dead for a couple of decades. They were doing *The Barretts of Wimpole Street* in Sioux Falls, South Dakota, and someone had smuggled in Basil Rathbone's monster German shepherd Moritz to be substituted for the cocker spaniel Flush, in the second act. So when Kit sits up and calls "Flush", Moritz unwinds and steps out of his basket and ...

It was a good story, well told. Welles was a brilliant raconteur. At its conclusion, the cast laughed appreciatively as well as politely and the brandy went round again.

"Y'know Jack Barrymore — " Orson began and then paused to take a puff of his cigar. And into that pause, deftly slipped Peter.

"Did you say 1933, Orson?" Peter asked pleasantly, not seeming to realize that he had interrupted The Great Man in mid-sentence. "Let's see. That must have been around the time that I was a swagman. 'Swaggies' they called us in the Great Australian depression. I was just a kid but we had a ball keeping one jump ahead of the cops. One day when my mates and I were out on the track in the sweltering midday sun out in the God-forsaken mulga, we were tucking into our only meal for the day, mutton and johnny cake and drinking tea out of an old battered leaky billycan, when all of a sudden we saw getting closer and closer to us a sort of cloud of dust rising and heard the pounding of hooves like thunder. Well, we wasted no time, we ..."

Everyone was staring at Peter. He had always been so quiet when Welles was in a story-telling mood, never saying anything, simply listening. Now Peter was not only talking, he had actually interrupted Orson to do so.

Peter continued talking, leaning forward in enjoyment of things to come — easy, relaxed, confident. For Peter was a story-teller in the Australian tradition, accounted along with the Irish as the finest in the world. Swiftly and economically he established the basic facts of his tale and then fleshed them out with perfectly mimed characterizations of the people he was talking about bringing them all to vivid life. At times he plunged ahead with his narrative; at others he held it tantalizingly back. It was all at his fingertips: the timing, the emphasis, the throwaway line. Carefully, unhurriedly he built up each climax and then ... left it hanging in the air for a while. After this he rolled on a touch of humour expanding it into a wild hilarity and always ended on a haunting note of pathos.

Theatre people love stories about theatre people. Stories about rogues and vagabonds triumphantly living off their wits, putting it over on the audience, and never giving a sucker an even break, appeal strongly to people who deal in illusion. There *is* no business like show business and its jokes are first class, as for example the quintessential one about the veteran Thespian inquiring with dignity of his dresser just before going on, ''Where is the stage and who is playing Juliet?''

Orson's showbiz stories were funny and fascinating and they had a background that was familiar to the cast. Yet contrasted with Peter's tales (and Peter's delivery), they seemed mere tinsel. Peter was making reality even more seductive than illusion as he told them about life in the raw in a strange, rough, faraway land. He took them right out of themselves and he kept them there. They drove cattle in the outback. They lived among the Aborigines. Down-and-out at the Cross, they wandered through the brothels of the Dirty Half Mile. From the rich mosaic of his life he plucked out events seemingly at random and polished them so highly that they shone before his listeners' eyes.

When Peter finished talking there was silence. Not a word was said. Finally Orson shifted his bulk in his chair and chomping on his cigar wondered aloud if anyone wanted another drink. No one did. More silence. Everyone remained still, Peter noticed, except for one actor who had raised two discreet fingers to him in a V for Victory sign. Maxine was doubled over, her eyes shut and her mouth tightly compressed, and she seemed to be having some kind of fit.

Dreamily, the cast filed out of Orson's suite like satisfied, sleepy children who have just been told their favourite bedtime story. Halfway down the corridor, Maxine, unable to control herself any longer, began laughing hysterically. "You've done it!" she gasped at Peter. "You've done it! You've won by a knockout."

"Done what ... ?" began Peter innocently. But by now Peter and Maxine and three or four other actors were hysterical with laughter. They repaired to Peter's room where they settled down to some serious and rowdy carousing.

Every night until the end of their run in Newcastle, after each performance of *Othello* the cast would assemble in Welles' suite for what they privately called "The Turk's Head Tournament". The brandy was passed around and the two contenders, Orson and Peter would warm up with a few one-liners and then square off for the main event. Orson opened his bag of reminiscences of his Dublin Gate days, New York Mercury days and Hollywood days, and Peter talked about the life and death struggles he had witnessed during his days as a court reporter (sensibly he had elevated himself from copy-boy), going into the outback, and his two thrilling years in an Indian monastery as a boy Buddhist.

Each night the cast would silently but unanimously confer upon Peter the *Scheherazade Golden Tongue Award*. It was unbeatable, his "full Waltzing Matilda thing". After each story session a hard core, composed of Peter, Maxine, and several other more hardy types would retire to Peter's room and whoop it up somewhat boisterously for Newcastle in the early hours of morning. On one such morning the irate manager appeared and, notwithstanding Peter's golden pleading, threw Peter and his fellow-revellers out of the hotel. At three o'clock on that morning, a scraggly little band of merrymakers, clutching bottles of brandy and suitcases, could be seen tramping the wet streets of Newcastle seeking refuge. When at long last they found a hotel willing to receive them, they discovered to their astonishment that it was a *temperance* hotel. "I really learned something that morning," Maxine recalled. "Temperance hotels don't *serve* drinks but they don't mind if you bring your own!"

The whole escapade had a far-reaching effect, however. Shortly after the *Othello* company left, the patrician Gladys Cooper and her very respectable company came to Newcastle and were brusquely turned away by the Turk's Head Hotel with the explanation that they "didn't take any more theatricals".

Not surprisingly, Peter's opening night as Iago in Welles' *Othello*, on 18 October 1951 at the St James Theatre in London, was rather different from his opening night as Ernest Piaste in *Daphne Laureola*. It was hardly championship tennis that the audience was watching; it was more like watching a match of *sauve qui peut* between Welles and what by now could no longer be called the "supporting" cast.

The next day and on the following Sunday, the critics all agreed that the production of *Othello* was visually superb. Sets, costumes, lighting and the use of a travelling curtain to wipe away each setting in the manner of a cinematic dissolve all won critical applause. The first sight of Welles as the Moor, huge and towering in his splendid garments and close-cropped military head sent chills of anticipation up critical spines. Then, one by one, the critics stopped applauding and began to cavil. Harold Hobson in *The Sunday Times*, gave up at the halfway mark. Until then, he felt, "the game had been played with such mounting intensity, with such suggestions of splendours and thunders to come that I thought Mr Welles was going to win and for very high stakes. But thunder after rumbling for so long as to loosen one's hair never breaks. By the end of the evening the game had been lost."

Kenneth Tynan in the *Evening Standard* was more descriptive and also more severe about Welles' performance: "He gave a performance glorious to the eye; but it was a performance of a magnificent amateur. His voice, a musical instrument in one bass octave, lacked range; he toyed moodily with every inflection ... he positively waded through the great speeches ... his bodily relaxation verged on sloth. Welles' performance was one huge shrug." This, in varying degrees of leniency or harshness, was the overall opinion of Welles as Othello.

Of Peter Finch's Iago, opinions were of such diversity as to make one wonder if the critics had all seen the same play on the same night. On the one hand Hobson found "Finch's sinister and swift moving Iago excellent". On the other, Tynan found it "charmless" and "bantam weight". Peter's best review came from Stephen Williams in the *Evening News*: "This I take it is exactly the Iago Shakespeare (and Cintho before him) imagined: a dirty muddy-mettled rascal who revels in obscene images with the relish of a slum boy writing rude words on the wall."

One critic, a long-standing member of the Buckstone, who had been following the *Othello* saga from its inception with the same breathless excitement as the rest of the members, concluded his negative review of Peter as Iago with the words, "He will improve." This no doubt, was code for "I know what you've been through, old boy." A sort of consolation prize. And Peter did improve. Three nights later Cole Lesley saw him and pronounced him "magnificent". A week after the opening, literary critic Francis Wyndham said, "The production was a shambles but after I'd seen it I remember being glad I had. And the reason was Finch's Iago. He was *Iago*! That spark I'd seen in *Daphne Laureola* was there again."

But there are no consolation prizes in the theatre. The opening-night exam — and to a far lesser degree, the second night one — are the only exams that count. Peter had not been at his best on opening night, and he knew it.

Afterwards, Peter and Tamara gave a party in their flat at Dolphin Square which was in full swing by the time Peter arrived. As he came through the door someone handed him a drink and, looking around, he was suddenly startled to see at the other end of the room his earliest boyhood mate from Greenwich Point; his fellow copy boy on the *Sun* with whom he had shared so many youthful fantasies of achievement: Paul Brickhill. Peter caught Paul's eye and they looked at each other for a long time, their thoughts going back into the past and then returning to the present. Paul Brickhill was now a successful writer and Peter a successful West End actor.

Slowly Peter raised his glass to Paul in an ironic salute and over the noise he called out with infinite mockery, "Success! Success!" Paul raised his glass in the same spirit and returned the toast, "Success! Success!"

CHAPTER 8

The Happy Time

Just before Christmas *Othello* closed and Peter realized that now was the time for that long, extended restorative sea voyage. But Olivier, in America where he and Vivien Leigh were playing in a season of Shaw's *Caesar and Cleopatra* and Shakespeare's *Antony and Cleopatra*, had become enamoured of a successful comedy currently running on Broadway called *The Happy Time*. The comedy was about a French Canadian family and Olivier sent the script to Peter designating him for the part of the papa. The play would be opening in London on 30 January and it meant starting rehearsals almost immediately. Peter did not tear up the script; instead he sat down, read, took a deep breath and accepted it. Bruised though he was from the *Othello* experience, this was a different set of numbers. He liked the play. It was a comedy and he loved comedy. He was a stage actor. Stage actors should act on stage. His boss wanted him to play in it and after all, as he had remarked previously, his boss worked harder than any man he knew, so who was he to argue? Nevertheless, at the first rehearsal he looked around him with a new alertness for any potential troublemakers in the company.

The Happy Time rehearsals were mostly happy times for Peter. The seven other actors were highly experienced, civilized professionals. The gentle, sensitive director was George Devine, then of the Old Vic, who also took a role in the play.

Let us now praise superlative actors. At that particular time, London was bursting with a group of high comedians (mis-called "light" comedians) whose equals could not be found the world over. These men, whose names meant nothing to the general public, but whose appearances lit up the stage or screen whenever they appeared, could sketch to perfection a whole character with the tilt of a chin. By extracting the last nuance of feeling from a line they could show the audience not only who they were but what they were up to. They were the backbone of English comedy. One could say they were English comedy. They were "high" comedians in the sense that the laughs they got were never broad, cheap, low or easy ones. They worked constantly and they were never less than at their best. Among the names that come to mind are: Wilfred Hyde White, Robert Coote, Guy Middleton, Raymond Huntley, Ernest Clarke, Richard Wattis, Ronald Culver, Robin Bailey ... and Ronald Squire. Ronald Squire, a mild middle-aged pixie with a dauntlessly jaunty manner, whose features seemed to have bunched themselves obsessively into the centre of his face as if to synchronize his thinking, was also in *The Happy Time*, playing the amorous grandpapa. Of all the high comedians Squire was the acknowledged king.

Peter was happy working with the congenial cast and director of *The Happy Time* until it slowly began to dawn on him that he was not extracting enough comedy from his part. He had had trouble before with comedy in England. Now he remembered Peter Fleming's review of *Captain Carvello* in the *Spectator*: "Peter Finch does not give the impression of being a natural comedian." Could Fleming be talking about Pidgifif, the school clown? The life and soul of every party in Sydney? The best stand-up comedian at the Cross?

Off-stage Peter knew he was a very funny man. At the pub during the rehearsal breaks of *The Happy Time*, he had the cast on the floor with laughter. But then, back on stage — nothing.

"Dying is hard," said the great actor Edmund Gwenn on his deathbed, "but not as hard as playing comedy."

During rehearsals, and later standing in the wings during the performances, Peter studied Ronald Squire's art that concealed art at every possible chance, trying hard to learn this most exquisite brand of comedy, trying to absorb its lessons of timing, presence and style. Kenneth More, too, had stood in the wings watching Squire in his time, but More had been able to put into practice what he saw whereas Peter could not. Was it because More was English and Peter, as an Australian, missed the finer shadings? Peter wondered if by chance he had lost his comedic gift in crossing the ocean. "Peter could not get his feet off the ground," said Olive Harding, his agent. "He was wonderfully funny as a person but the minute he put his feet on stage or on a set they were solidly planted there."

Comedy necessitates the wearing of a mask. Perhaps since Peter had arrived in England and had every fantastic thing possible happen to him in the form of long-lost parents and success with Olivier and Orson Welles — things he could only cope with by wearing the mask — perhaps something in him needed the relief of leaving *that* mask in the wings and stepping on to a stage, vulnerable and earnest. For whatever reason, a burning sincerity was to mark his performances for the rest of his life.

Though Peter was now aware of his deficiency in comedy he still loved it more than any other genre in acting. This was to be revealed constantly in his future interviews:

What is your Christmas wish, Mr Finch?

"To create a really good comic character on the screen."

What are you going to do next?

"A comedy, I hope."

Why have you never played in a comedy?

"It must be my sad face. I'm never offered one."

What made you decide to do Network*?*

"It's a comedy."

During *The Happy Time* Peter finally put his case before Ronald Squire. "My part isn't working. I can't get the comedy. What shall I do?"

"Lighten it, dear boy," replied the Maestro instantly. *"Lighten* it."

"How?" asked Peter in despair.

Squire studied his face carefully. "Well," he said after a while, "whenever you feel you're getting too heavy, you might, you know, try raising your eyebrows."

Peter found a mirror backstage. He practised raising his eyebrows. Yes, that felt good. It really felt lighter! His eyebrows still raised, he smiled. Ah, that was even better! He used it.

He used it for the rest of his life. One can see how he incorporated this expression in film performances so that whenever he felt himself becoming too heavy, he raised his eyebrows. Sometimes it made him look endearingly like the young Bing Crosby.

The Happy Time was a warm, sentimental, ethnic comedy. Warm, sentimental, ethnic comedies do not, on the whole, succeed in England; and this one was no exception. It was slight and light with nothing much happening apart from papa explaining the facts of life to his eleven-year-old son. The family, all quaint and colourful, had not much connection with each other or with whatever plot there was. Produced by L.O.P. in England but by

Rodgers and Hammerstein in America, one critic suggested that the libretto had been performed before the score had arrived.

Peter got what's known as "mentioned" by the critics. *The Daily Telegraph* remarked that he showed himself "a very complete actor" and *The Observer* mentioned his "quick charm". To a man, both audience and critics left the theatre on the opening night enthusiastically whistling the glint in Ronald Squire's eye and the tilt of his straw hat.

In spite of Squire's glint and hat, *The Happy Time* closed on 6 March 1952, one month and six days after it opened. Sir Laurence Olivier sighed. "The life of a theatrical manager is one where hope is constantly at odds with better judgement," he said. By the end of the run Peter was exhausted, having managed to squeeze two brief film performances — in *The Story of Gilbert and Sullivan* and *The Heart of the Matter* — into the same period. He slept for twenty-four hours and did not leave his bed for a week.

It was around that period late one night at the Buckstone after the bar had closed that some actors sprawled around the back room were working themselves into a lively bull-session concerning the merits and demerits of other actors who were, needless to say, absent. In the smoke- beer- and cider-scented room, the name of Peter Finch was brought up.

"It makes me angry when people ask me what's happened to Finchie," said one actor. "Nothing's happened to him. He never stops working."

"That's not what they mean," said another. "I know what they mean. What's happened to him since *Daphne Laureola*? People are not keen on having their expectations raised only to be dashed. Look, here's the way I rate him: gallons of charm, yes. A beautiful supple voice, yes. Intelligence — I give him full marks — *but* — "

"But you're forgetting the most important thing," a young, recently out-of-work actor interrupted irritably. "*Luck!* Peter Finch has *Luck*. And that's all there is to be said."

The oldest actor there spoke in sonorous, measured tones. "I would define Finch as a *useful* actor. A fine actor. Predictable perhaps, but always sound. A good journeyman actor but not, I think, a star."

"What the hell's the difference?" said the club's most aggressive actor. "Finchie's the nicest chap I know. In fact, he's the nicest damn chappy in this whole bloody profession. Give you his last fiver."

At this point they were all so much in accord that they would have forthwith drunk a toast to Finchie ... if only they could have wheedled the stuff out of Gerry.

Sometime later that week a not so different conversation was taking place between Antony Bushell, one of the founding members of L.O.P., and Paul Brickhill over dinner after their golf game.

"You know, with Peter Finch, we thought we had another Olivier," said Bushell. "But ... " He stopped and shook his head sadly.

"But what?" Brickhill pressed him, intrigued.

Bushell searched for the right, precise words, but in the end he settled for a maddeningly mysterious generality. "Peter Finch lacks that indefinable *something*," he said.

This "lack of something indefinable", when clarified, seemed to mean that Peter Finch was, at last, and to his detriment, *definable* and *describable*. He was no longer "exciting". He was no longer "promising". He was just another known quantity.

If any of this got back to Peter, if he heard or overheard that he was being weighed in the balance and found "lacking", it did not seem to worry him. For the first time, since his arrival in England four years ago, he and Tamara were going to France to have a holiday! Moreover, George Devine had arranged for him to play Mercutio in the Old Vic's new season starting in September.

If it was solely luck (that most capricious of ministering angels) that was responsible for Peter's career, one has to ask oneself if it is possible for a man to be so freakishly lucky over and over again. Harry Watt ... Olivier ... Edith Evans ... George Devine ... the list of people in the right position to help Peter and who *did* help him runs through the rest of his life. Perhaps it only seemed like luck from the outside. The simple truth was that people who worked with Peter once wanted to work with him again.

Tamara and Peter crossed over to France on the channel ferry. England still had its post-war travel currency restrictions and the Finches had to travel as cheaply as they could. Anita was staying with Tamara's mother who had arrived from Australia and bought a guest-house in Sloane Avenue.

In Brittany and in Normandy the Finches stayed happily in shabby little hotels. Inspired by the beauty of the countryside, Peter, who had always had an aptitude for drawing, now began painting with wild enthusiasm, spending long hours with his easel propped up in fields and in front of cafés.

They travelled on to Paris. It was a sentimental journey for both of them to be in this city where they had been — unknown to each other — so happy as children. Paris in springtime was as beautiful as they remembered it. They walked all over: down the streets where Tamara had played as a child, out to the suburb of Vaucresson where Peter's grandmother had declared solemnly to the young boy, "Peter George Frederick Ingle Finch is your name", and finally to the exact spot that had been his grandmother's house, the Villa La Fleurette.

It was there no longer, but Pidgifif's memories were still bright with pleasure of those faraway times as he thought of his dog, his bicycle, the little girl from across the road he had loved and of his extraordinary and unforgettable grandmother.

The Finches stayed at a small hotel in Montmartre. One day, when Peter was out completing his picture of the Place de la Terne, an American tourist looked over his shoulder, swiftly became enamoured with his painting and insisted on paying two hundred dollars for it. Gladly Peter parted with the picture. He packed up his painting gear, rushed to the nearest parfumerie and bought Tamara a large expensive bottle of scent. The money left over gave them a few more days in the enchanted city.

"Well, well," thought Peter that night, extremely pleased with himself. "Painting's easy. When I get tired of being an actor I'll become a painter."

Back in London, Peter went into rehearsal at the Old Vic. His roles were Mercutio in *Romeo and Juliet* and Monsieur Beaujolais in Labiche's *The Italian Straw Hat* which turned out to be one of those self-consciously stylized "romps" that are far more fun for the players than the audience.

For Mercutio, Peter did his homework in his usual sane and sensible way. He went to an eminent doctor taking with him the text of Mercutio's death scene. "If I'm dying with a sword in my gut," said Peter, "how shall I deliver this speech?" The doctor asked him to read it. "Well," he said, "Shakespeare got it exactly right! You would have enough time and breath to get it straight out and without gasping."

When *Romeo and Juliet* opened in Edinburgh it was a triumph for all, especially for Claire Bloom as Juliet. This did not stop Finch-watchers from noticing, perhaps for the first time, a curious thing about Peter's performance: whenever he had a long speech he was always able to create a "listening hush" in the audience. The quality of his voice has already been discussed, as well as its timing, phrasing and intimacy. But now he was able to convey something else, simple but often uncommon in an actor: that he understood what he was talking about.

On the less serious side, Peter was determined to climb Arthur's Seat in Edinburgh. "My father is a mountaineer and so am I," he boasted as he scrambled up to the top only to have to slide ignominiously down on his butt.

Romeo and Juliet opened in London in September 1952, and continued its enormous success, running through Christmas to the beginning of January 1953. With the excitement of its popularity the performances steadily improved, Peter's beyond all recognition. The clusters of young people standing outside the stage door waiting for Mercutio marked the beginning of Peter's fan club.

CHAPTER 9

Enter Vivien

On one cold night at the end of January 1953, destiny tolled again for Peter Finch. This time it caught him sleeping. It was two o'clock in the morning and the doorbell was ringing insistently. Tamara woke up, faintly alarmed at the sound, threw on a robe and opened the front door a crack. She was confronted by the vision of Vivien Leigh in a diaphanous white evening dress and a floor-length mink coat. She was carrying a script. Tamara let in her guest. She noticed that Vivien seemed in a strange state of elation; everything about her, her speech, her movements, her gestures, seemed to be speeded up. Vivien explained that she must talk to Peter. She had seen him playing Mercutio at the Old Vic several nights before and she was full of high praise for his performance. Tamara went to awaken Peter and the three of them sat in the living-room while Vivien continued talking of his Mercutio in laudatory, even adulatory terms. Then she got down to business. She had decided that Peter was to co-star with her in a new major film Paramount was making called *Elephant Walk*. It was about an English tea-planter and his wife in Ceylon, and the principals were to fly out there in a week's time. The original choice for the role had been Olivier but he was exhausted after filming *The Beggar's Opera* and needed a rest. All ready to start shooting but desperately needing a leading man (the services of Ralph Richardson, Clark Gable, Claude Rains and Marlon Brando had been unsuccessfully solicited), the producer, Irving Asher, had sought Vivien Leigh's advice. After seeing his Mercutio, Vivien insisted on Peter. Coupled with the whole-hearted approval of Olivier and a flying visit by Asher to the Old Vic, it seemed that Vivien — not for the first time — was going to get her own way. Paramount agreed that though Peter Finch ranked internationally as a complete unknown, he should be offered the star part of the tea-planter.

As Vivien presented it to Peter, it was an emergency situation and it was also an order. He was to read the script at once. He was to fly with her to Ceylon in a week's time where they would begin shooting immediately. Then, as an afterthought, she asked if he had any conflicting commitments. Peter's mind was working almost as fast as Vivien's. There was nothing he liked better than emergency situations to rise to. The Old Vic season in which he was playing Mercutio had ended three nights ago. He quickly ran down the parts he had been offered by them for their next season — *The Merchant of Venice, Love's Labour's Lost* and *All's Well That Ends Well*. None of them was interesting; there was nothing to stop him. He would be ready to go to Ceylon with Vivien in a week, and with pleasure.

In less than an hour it was all settled, but Vivien stayed on talking with the Finches till dawn. Then she became hungry. To Tamara's embarrassment there was nothing to eat.

The last words spoken by Olivier to Peter at the airport before he and Vivien flew off together early in February for Ceylon were, "Take care of her." Peter, knowing that Vivien had been very nervous about flying ever since 1946 when she was in a plane forced to crash-land in Connecticut, protectively put his arm around her and assured Olivier "Don't worry, I will."

When their plane landed in Ceylon, Vivien and Peter stepped instantly into another universe as the hot, humid, tropic-scented air struck against their winter-acclimatized bodies. They rallied to discover an island of incredible beauty right out of an Arabian Night's tale with its rich tropical vegetation of palm groves, flowering shrubs and green forests topped by austere mountains, all surrounded by yellow sands and sapphire seas. But though Vivien and Peter were stepping forward into the future at that moment, they were also stepping back into the past. Into a time long past, but important to each in different ways.

Vivien had been born in India and had left there at the age of six. Though she had only the vaguest recollections of that time, buried within her there must have been some terrifying memories. Soon after they began shooting *Elephant Walk*, while she was being made-up one day, a young Singhalese native employed to call the actors on to the set when needed, came in to see if Vivien was ready. As he stared at her in admiration of her beauty she suddenly began trembling. When he left, the make-up man asked her what was the matter.

"I'm sorry," said Vivien, relaxing a little. "I'm ... I'm so *frightened* of black eyes. I've always been frightened of black eyes.''

"But *my* eyes are black and you're not frightened of me," said the make-up man reassuringly.

"No. Your eyes are *not* black," said Vivien firmly. "They're dark brown. I mean black — Indian black."

Peter's memories of that part of the world were not frightened ones but spiritual ones, drawn from the time when, as a questing nine-year-old, he had accompanied his grandmother on her pilgrimage to India, stopping off first in Ceylon. There Peter had seen children of his own age becoming apprentice Buddhist priests and had been so profoundly affected that later in Adyar he emulated them. When he talked about this to Vivien, he had a rapt audience for she, though convent-bred, was religiously what might be called a "far-seeker". Later in life, she was to describe herself as a "Zen-Buddhist-Catholic".

Elephant Walk was being made by Paramount, an American company. But because at the time Technicolor United Kingdom had an agreement with Technicolor Hollywood that any film made in the British Commonwealth (as Ceylon was then) would use British technicians, it became an Anglo-American project. And as often happens in such joint projects, nationalities tended to stick together. Vivien Leigh, Peter Finch and the British technicians formed one group, and the Americans, Dana Andrews (playing the foreman of the tea plantation with whom Vivien has an affair) and the director Dieterle etc., the other.

John von Kotze, an Englishman, was the main Technicolor technician on *Elephant Walk*. He had been looking forward excitedly to working with the stars well known to him, Vivien Leigh and Dana Andrews. But it was Peter Finch he took to immediately and whom he liked the best.

"Finchie", says von Kotze, "was an attractive person who didn't seem to be like other actors. He actually heard what you said. And even though after a couple of days' work it was obvious to me that he was extremely talented he was also extremely modest — with the bonus of having an unbelievably marvellous sense of humour. Also, we thought alike. In those days if you were white and European, you were taught to look down on people that weren't white and I have always found that illogical and so did Finchie. That was immediately apparent by the way he talked to the servants and the bearers. It was so different from the way many of the company did.

He was a superb horseman. I suppose from his days in Australia as a drover. I remember once riding with him and Dana Andrews, also an excellent horseman, and Andrews saying to Finchie admiringly 'By Christ, you ride like the man in the Marlboro ad!'"

Von Kotze took to Vivien also. At the beginning of the shooting he noticed that she seemed very highly strung but he put it down to high spirits because after work she was so full of gaiety and energy, bursting with plans for the enjoyment of the English contingent. Some of these plans, however, von Kotze found decidedly eccentric: "She would get us — about six of us together — to come into the jungle, build a campfire and sing songs around it. On the equator that is not what you enjoy doing. Peter always went along with her schemes. There was an old hotel in Colombo built by the Raj. It had a dining-room with a cupola for a ceiling — we used to joke that it was a miniature St Paul's. Lots and lots of very pompous English people used to eat there in white dinner jackets Friday and Saturday nights; second-generation planters who themselves had never done any work and were incredibly rude to the people of the country. Vivien thought they were dreary. She thought the women were stuffy and dressed badly and so on. So she said, 'Let's get those ice-cream bombes they have for dessert and let's take them up to the cupola and at a signal we'll drop them down on those enormous fans that are spinning around and let's see what happens.' Peter was absolutely delighted with the idea and it was only at the last minute we were able to persuade him to dissuade Vivien from this outrageous scheme."

If, at the beginning of the filming, Vivien's behaviour struck the English contingent as somewhat overwrought and unconventional, it did not trouble them for they knew her to be immensely kind and considerate of everyone, no matter how tired she was. But one night von Kotze heard something about her that troubled him gravely.

His assistant, George, arrived late in the hotel room they were sharing. He was shaking like a leaf. He was sixty-four, bald, a cockney and, says von Kotze, "utterly truthful". "He said", remembered von Kotze, "that Vivien had stopped him in the passage of the hotel and tried to *vamp* him — that's what he called it — 'vamp'. George adored Vivien and he was *shocked*! He wasn't pleased! He ran away from her. The next morning when we saw Vivien it was clear she did not remember the incident."

Soon after, von Kotze, on the set behind the camera, began noticing how increasingly pale and haggard-looking Vivien was becoming. A few days later an additional shooting schedule was quietly announced to the cameramen and crew: all dialogue scenes with Vivien in them were to be shot twice, once with her and once again without her but with just the sets and backgrounds. Von Kotze inquired of Dieterle the reason for this and the director answered casually that it was merely a safety precaution. Now, watching Vivien's rapidly changing moods — swinging from being tense and overbright to tears and black depression, von Kotze sorrowfully put two and two together. Paramount did not expect Vivien to last out the film.

Suddenly Sir Laurence Olivier arrived in Ceylon. It was hoped that his visit might relax and hearten Vivien but everyone could see that it was a strained time for them both. Olivier, feeling helpless, departed after a week.

One night during Olivier's stay, Peter and von Kotze, by now good friends, went for a walk. Peter had been silent for a long time yet there seemed to be something on his mind. He would stop occasionally as if he wished to say something and then, shaking his head, go on walking. All at once he turned to von Kotze and blurted out that his conscience was torturing him but that he was having an affair with Vivien. He was well aware that he owed more to Larry than anyone in the world but ... For a moment Peter lapsed back into silence and a load of misery seemed to settle upon him. "But ..." he continued painfully, "I find Vivien *totally fascinating.*"

The gods themselves could not have designed a more diabolic trap for Peter than this *carte blanche* opportunity for finding the wife of his benefactor — his idol — his boss — "totally fascinating". And — totally irresistible.

The triangle of Olivier, Vivien and Peter could be made into a rich mine for psychological excavation. There would be the Oedipal aspect to consider in which Olivier would be seen as Peter's surrogate father, the protector Peter found to take his own father's place. Then, it must follow in strict Freudian terms that Peter would be blindly impelled to destroy his father by carrying off his father's wife — that is, his own mother — that is, Vivien. Or, perhaps, there was a deep unconscious resentment on Peter's part at never having had a proper father that could only be appeased by destroying him in whatever way he could.

Some wag even suggested that in making love to Vivien, Peter was paying Olivier back for all those rotten parts he'd had after *Daphne*

Laureola. Though Peter's contract with Olivier left the former completely free to refuse any role he did not like, Peter always admitted to being carried away by Olivier's enthusiasms.

Or is the late, great Max Adrian's aphorism, "When it's on tour or location — it's not adultery", the last word?

Peter had often been among the weekend guests of the Oliviers at their country home, Notley Abbey. There Vivien reigned over a world of exalted names both from the theatre and outside. Its main halls were dark, baronial and imposing. But upstairs were the prettiest bedrooms imaginable — light and airy, where the eye glanced with pleasure at whatever it discovered: some delicate china figure or a book that Vivien had specially placed on the bed-table knowing it would interest that particular guest. Breakfast was in bed on a tray (often served by Vivien herself) and the tray was always decorated with a single rose in an exquisite vase. The grounds, which sloped gently down to a stream, were left as nature intended except for a rose garden. And Vivien's folly.

Vivien's folly was in the English tradition of great country houses. Without rhyme or reason, but solely for the indulgence of a fantasy, their owners constructed follies somewhere on their grounds. It might be a charming summer-house of mad architectural design, or a wildly idiosyncratic garden, or a strange bower, or an arbour, or a secret hiding place.

Vivien's folly was an alley of cypress trees with a fountain in the middle. When she had first led Peter through it with some other guests, as the evening deepened and the outlines grew dim, Peter suddenly thought he saw the silhouettes of the trees turning into men in evening dress. Then, as the breeze stirred them, they became Scarlett O'Hara's southern suitors at a ball, bending and stretching towards her, imploring her for a dance. And he seemed to see Vivien whirling amongst them — flirting ... teasing ... choosing ... refusing ... accepting ... But the moment they entered the Abbey again he knew this was all nonsense, and it was clear that she was Lady Olivier, dutiful and devoted wife of Sir Laurence graciously at the disposal of her weekend guests.

Now in Ceylon, she was not just Lady Olivier. She was herself, determined, independent and rebellious. Now, for the first time alone with her, Peter was exposed to the full impact of her personality. And he found her "totally fascinating".

In talking of Vivien Leigh, one always finds oneself returning to her astonishing beauty. Except for Garbo, Vivien Leigh was the most beautiful woman of her time. The reaction to her beauty was global; it crossed all geographical bounds. It could hardly be expected that anyone as susceptible as Peter would be immune to it. Nor was he.

Nor could he ignore Vivien's highly sophisticated attitude towards life. "I am an actress," she once told a friend. "A great actress. Great actresses have lovers. Why not? I have a husband and I have lovers. Like Sarah Bernhardt."

There is overwhelming evidence that any amatory plans concerning Vivien that had begun stirring in Peter's breast had been put there by the lady herself. In order to have resisted her, Peter would have had to be cool, prudent and circumspect. And, of course, he was none of these things.

When Peter noticed Vivien behaving oddly, he would try to question her about it but she always evaded him by replying that she was perfectly well, that it was simply the heat and the humid climate and her difficulties in getting sleep that were distressing her. He knew that after a spell of tuberculosis during the war years she had subsequently been subject to occasional flare-ups, but when he suggested she see a doctor she categorically refused. Her odd behaviour accelerated when Olivier left and finally, one day, when she followed Peter around the set calling him "Larry", it was apparent to everyone in the company that she was hallucinating and that there was something very wrong with her that was not due just to exhaustion. By now her condition was so bad that she was no longer able to work and it was decided to get her off the island as quickly as possible. Since no one in the company had the slightest idea what had come over Vivien or how to treat it, it was agreed to fly her to Hollywood where presumably with a few weeks' rest, a pleasanter climate and the proximity of her friends in familiar surroundings she might get well and be able to resume work. Paramount expressed grave apprehension and concern over the situation. *Elephant Walk* was to be their biggest and most expensive film that year.

When the plane took off, Vivien suddenly unfastened her safety belt and stood up rigid — exactly as she had done seven years before when the plane she had been in crashed in 1946. She began screaming that the wing was on fire — as it had been then. Peter, the steward and the air hostess all tried to calm her but, strong in her panic, she threw them off. She became hysterical. She flew at her window like a trapped bird, beating on it with her fists, fighting to get out. Then she tore at the neckline of her dress, ripping it down the middle. She scratched and clawed at everyone trying to restrain her. Finally they managed to sedate her.

Vivien's behaviour upset all the passengers but it had its deepest and most lasting effect on Peter, who was at her side yet powerless to control her. During the remainder of the long, seemingly endless flight, as the sedation wore off and her panic rose and burst into hysteria again and again, Peter contracted her disease of fright. Henceforth, he was never to fly unless there was absolutely no way of avoiding it.

What was really the matter with Vivien? Peter didn't have the least idea, even by the time they finally landed in Los Angeles. Nor did Tamara when she arrived with Anita soon after.

One day, while the film company was still in Ceylon, Olive Harding, Peter's agent, had telephoned Tamara and, out of the blue it seemed, insisted that she go to Hollywood to join Peter when he arrived there. Tamara protested: it was so far away and Anita was only three. She couldn't leave her. Peter had told her they would only be shooting on the West Coast for two months. What was the point in going all that way for such a short time? Anyway, she didn't fancy the role of the clinging wife who always hung around the set. But Olive insisted and kept on insisting that Tamara should go. And as soon as possible. Moreover, said Olive, it was *essential* that Tamara take Anita as well.

Tamara and Anita travelled by way of the *Queen Elizabeth*, second class, and a very delayed, very slow flight from New York to Los Angeles. Tamara tried to keep her three-year-old child amused and diverted till they reached their destination where they were met by a shiny black limousine and driven to a large beautiful house with a swimming pool. At a quarter to seven in the evening, a tired, grubby Tamara and her crumpled child emerged from the car to be greeted joyfully by Vivien in a sari of scarlet and gold. Vivien told them that Peter was still working at the studio. She explained that the house was divided in half, that one side was her apartment and the other the Finches'. Then she said to Tamara: "You have got to get yourself into a sari immediately. I've laid one out for you and I'll come up with you to show you how to drape it."

"I know how to drape a sari," said Tamara. "We used to do it in ballet. But why?"

Vivien said, "Because at seven-thirty, seventy people are coming. I'm giving a party for you."

Tamara hurried upstairs to get settled in her quarters. In Anita's room, she opened the door of the closet and was overcome by the sight of twenty little children's dresses hanging neatly in rows. They were presents from Vivien.

The next hours were fairly traumatic for Tamara. Dressed in her sari, she came downstairs to be met by a distraught Vivien who said she was feeling too ill and too unhappy to attend the party and was going to bed. And so Tamara, on her first night in Hollywood, found herself entertaining seventy people — such as the David Nivens, the Stewart Grangers, George Cukor, *le tout Hollywood* — all complete strangers to her.

There was little time for Tamara and Peter to talk that night. Tamara, after this strange experience where she constantly had to fight against behaving as if she, the newcomer, were the guest and not the hostess, fell asleep immediately after they left.

The next morning just before Peter left for the studio, he turned to Tamara and said, "You must look after Vivien. She's ill and there's no one else to."

In order for Paramount to accommodate filming in *Elephant Walk* such acts of God as plague, drought and an elephant stampede in their studio, every available square inch of their enormous lot was taken over. Work on all other Paramount films was suspended. They continued shooting without Vivien who was nursed single-handedly by Tamara for ten days while Peter was at the studio.

Looking back at this time, Tamara feels that an enormous mistake had been made on the part of the people most concerned with Vivien in not telling Peter or her anything about Vivien's true condition. Tamara did not know that Vivien was very, very ill. Later — much later — she found out what it was, "But the fact remains", said Tamara, "that the manifestations of a person who is so ill in that way — if you don't know it — are completely unexpected."

What was wrong with Vivien Leigh? One half of that golden couple, the Oliviers, winner of two Academy Awards, the centre of adoring fans, flowers, famous friends and glittering all-night parties — was she not the darling of the gods, so lavishly bestowed with talent, grace, intelligence and beauty?

The truth was that Vivien was beautiful but damned.

From as early an age as twenty-six, deep cracks began appearing in her impeccable façade. She was the victim of a mental illness diagnosed as manic depression and subject to terrifying attacks that were cyclic and periodic. In the grip of hysteria, she would turn on those she loved most, screaming abuse, becoming cat-like, hissing and clawing and scratching and ripping off her clothes. When she recovered she would be a contrite and devastated and appalled at her behaviour. She would revert to her usual self, the Vivien everyone loved — affectionate, selfless and kind.

For a long time Olivier had kept her secret from everyone but her immediate family and the few doctors who had tried to help her so that even close friends witnessing these attacks could make no more out of them (since her recovery was so swift and complete) than assume she had had too much to drink. However, as the attacks grew in intensity and frequency and the doctors seemed powerless to prevent them, and Vivien firmly refused to be hospitalized, Olivier, knowing how driven and disciplined she was, felt that work was always the best solution to her "nerves". Therefore he approved of her doing *Elephant Walk*. The reason for his not exposing Vivien's "case history" to Paramount, from the Oliviers' point of view, would be obvious. Added to all this was the fact that the Oliviers at this stage were badly in need of money and Paramount was paying $150,000 for Vivien's services, $50,000 upon the signing of the contract. And so she embarked on the film convinced it was the best thing for her.

Now in Hollywood, in the large, beautiful house with a swimming pool, one can imagine the anguish of the two women, Vivien and Tamara, trapped together and alone with each other all day for ten days.

"You must look after Vivien," Peter had said. "She's ill and there's no one else to."

It was from Vivien's lips that Tamara first learned of her affair with Peter. It was Vivien who assured Tamara that she and Peter were deeply involved with each other, and it was Vivien who declared her determination to take Peter away from Tamara. At the same time, Tamara realized that Vivien's mind was doing a strange loop in time so that as she continued frenziedly to babble, it seemed that it was not Peter but Larry she was talking of — and the perfect love that had existed between them in the past.

Frightening also to Tamara were Vivien's sharp mood changes. Great moments of elation were quickly followed by great moments of despair. Tamara did not know from hour to hour which Vivien she was trying to administer to. Would it be an ashamed, contrite

Vivien who loved Tamara dearly and only wished to make up for all the pain she had caused her? Or an utterly despairing Vivien, motionless for hours with tears running down her face? Or a Vivien who endlessly quoted passages of *A Streetcar Named Desire* in a southern sing-song voice? Or a stormy Vivien, reviling everyone and everything? Tamara also knew she must not let Vivien out of her sight or she would be found — as she had been several times — at the home of another actor, both naked, sitting silent and cross-legged on the floor staring into each other's eyes to "exorcise the devil".

"In the English theatrical world," Peter had once told Tamara, "from time to time people have light affairs. And if it happens to me and we're civilized and sophisticated and talk it over, it's no more than a passing phase."

Now in the evenings when Peter came home from the studio, Tamara, in an effort to be "civilized" and "sophisticated" attempted to talk to Peter about what had happened between him and Vivien in Ceylon and find out how serious the situation was. But Peter would say nothing. His face would become stony and his eyes empty of expression. Abruptly he would go and pour himself a drink. And that drink might be the first of many.

Was this inability or refusal to discuss Vivien an expression of his deep guilt at having, he felt, precipitated Tamara's involvement in this strange crisis? — or of an attachment so deep he could not divulge it? Tamara could only register the warning signal without being able to interpret it. Nevertheless, Peter stayed away from Vivien. Very early on, the Finches saw the adverse effect his presence had on her so he removed himself from her sight and played with Anita.

For ten fearful days Tamara tried to calm Vivien, to attend to her wishes and accede to her demands. And still neither Peter nor Tamara fully understood what was the matter with her though Tamara noticed that one or two of Vivien's friends who dropped by to visit either knew something they were not going to talk about or had witnessed her in this state before. Tamara felt some sort of invisible protective circle around Vivien that she could not permeate.

Finally Sylvia Fine, Danny Kaye's wife and an old friend of the Oliviers, took Tamara aside. She explained about Vivien's illness clearly and knowledgeably. She also gave Tamara a book on psychiatric diseases to supplement their discussion. Tamara, reading about the case-book symptoms of manic depression was astonished to find how exactly they fitted Vivien's symptoms.

Now at last she understood why Olive Harding had insisted she journey out to Hollywood with their daughter — to look after Peter, to protect Peter and to save their marriage.

On the ninth day of Tamara's vigil, Vivien seemed on a somewhat more even keel and on the tenth day she was considerably better.

On the eleventh day she was due back at the studio. She assured the Finches that she felt fine and she and Peter were driven off to work. Vivien collapsed on the set and was taken to her dressing-room where she became even worse. Peter came in to see if he could help but she rounded on him calling him "Larry" and then, in one of her frighteningly mercurial transformations she became Blanche du Bois yelling "Get out of here quick before I start screaming fire!" Her friend David Niven was sent for and he drove her back to the house.

Vivien's breakdown, in the most public and humiliating way possible, had become world news.

Shortly afterwards Olivier, travelling from Ischia via London, arrived with his friend and manager Cecil Tennant. He soon heard from Vivien herself of her affair with Peter and understandably exhibited a certain chill towards him. Not so understandably he held him responsible for Vivien's breakdown.

In the ensuing drama Tamara stood apart, upset and forgotten until Cecil Tennant, whom she had hitherto regarded as cold and reserved, devoted himself to her and became her comfort and support. Once she was startled to see tears in his eyes as she confided in him.

In due course the Oliviers and Cecil Tennant flew back to England. Vivien went into a hospital for nervous diseases in Surrey for three weeks and afterwards returned home to Notley Abbey.

Smoothly the twenty-one-year-old Elizabeth Taylor slipped into Vivien's role in *Elephant Walk*. That the director William Dieterle had expected a replacement was obvious to everyone who, like von Kotze, had noticed in Ceylon the double shooting of Vivien's scenes. Elizabeth Taylor was a thoroughgoing professional as well as a lovely, sane young woman, married at the time to Michael Wilding. She and Peter immediately hit it off both on the set and off, whiling away many happy hours together at their favourite pastime — chewing popcorn at horror movies.

With Vivien's departure, the earthquake she had caused in the lives of the Finches seemed to subside. On the surface all was tranquil, yet Tamara was anxious to discover if Peter was still experiencing any tremors from the recent explosion. Several times she tried to bring up the subject of him and Vivien but with the same results as before. Eventually she gave up trying.

The filming of *Elephant Walk* progressed with neither human nor animal problems. In fact, Peter marvelled that the elephants were so well trained: "they could step on a matchbox without breaking it." As the pleasant Southern Californian days passed, Tamara sunned herself by the pool and watched Anita being given swimming lessons. The people they met were so friendly, so almost voraciously hospitable. She felt herself relaxing. It seemed as if the Vivien and Peter affair was just a "passing phase". But it was not. The rumblings and the tremors were subterranean but they were there. In fact, it was all just beginning.

Hollywood itself had been a severe disappointment to the Australian lad who had discovered his dreams of it were twenty years out of date. The Hollywood Peter had dreamt of since he was twelve was a wild, extravagant, anarchic place where blonde cuties clung to his arms and adorable chorus girls in black velvet shorts and white satin blouses seductively tap-danced around him. Where the intellectuals at the Garden of Allah — Dottie and Scotty and Benchley and Hecht and MacArthur and the like, kicked up their heels in nightly high spirits, flinging themselves or each other or their typewriters into the champagne-filled swimming pool. The Hollywood of his imagination had been not unlike the Cross in Sydney of his youth — only a thousand times more gloriously so!

The Hollywood Peter found in 1953 was rich but scared. Far from free and easy, it submitted to a pecking order more rigid than the army. The war boom years were over and Hollywood was in a slump. Both the McCarthy witch hunt and the arrival of television had seriously demoralized it. People were not flocking to films the way they used to, and to get them back, the studios knew pictures had to be bigger and better than ever. But how? Frightened and unsure, the movie colony courted conservatism, snobbery and respectability.

For Peter, there was the added annoyance of the ever-present press agents buzzing around him, instructing him on what to do and what not to do, whom to be friendly with and whom to ignore, what parties he must attend and with whom, whose swimming pool he must be seen in and on whose tennis court he must whack around tennis balls. At first Peter, in his naïveté, thought they must be joking. He soon found out they were not.

A large press party was being given presumably for the entire cast of *Elephant Walk*. But the dignified grey-haired English actor Abraham Sofaer, who was playing the key role of the native major domo on the tea plantation, remarked to Peter that he had not been invited. "It's an oversight," said Peter thinking no more of it. "You're coming along with me."

On their arrival at the party the two actors were stopped at the door and Sofaer was refused admission. Peter held his temper. He took one of the PR men aside and reasonably began explaining the situation. "Mr Sofaer has a large role in the film," he said "and he is one of England's most distinguished actors."

"Sorry," said the PR man implacably, "this party is only for the *important* members of the cast."

Peter turned heel and stormed out with Sofaer. The shock of this boorish treatment — and he knew immediately this incident was not an isolated one — opened Peter's eyes to the brutal truth. He was devastated. He knew now he might search every hill in Hollywood, comb every beach in Santa Monica or Malibu in vain. The Hollywood he had dreamt of — that wild, gay, egalitarian society of artists did not exist any more even if it ever had.

That Peter could have been so devastated by the Hollywood he found himself in, so seemingly without foreknowledge of it (for many of his London actor friends had been there and must surely have told him what to expect) is another indication of what a strong grip his early dreams still had on him.

Nevertheless, however much it may have crushed Peter's spirits to walk along his boulevards of broken dreams, his spirits lifted every day the moment he entered the gates of Paramount studios and became the English tea-planter in *Elephant Walk*.

Whatever wrenching emotional scenes he must have gone through at the time with Vivien or with Larry or with Tamara or with Hollywood and the press agents — they never impinged on his work. He had a way of sealing himself off from the outside world and creating the world of make-believe so necessary for his acting that many people found incredible. Was it callousness? Hardness? Indifference? Was it all of them together? Whatever it was, this habit of steeling himself and sealing himself from too harsh reality was of such ancient origin that it was by now a reflex. Acting had always been his escape hatch. And he kept the hinges of the trapdoor well oiled so that at any moment he could fling it open and slip through.

If, when he worked, he successfully stopped thinking and caring about the people in his life, it by no means followed that he neither thought nor cared about the people he was working with. Quite the opposite. He gave to his co-workers — actors, directors, technicians and crews — the full load of his charm. As an actor at work he was every film company's dream: so sensitively aware of each member's problems and so innately able to make things easier and pleasanter all around. Whatever confusion was going on in his life off the set, once on it, he was the thoroughgoing professional: always the first in the make-up room in the morning, always the most wide-awake, always the best prepared when he stepped before the camera. All this was compulsive to his character for he knew there was no escape hatch for him once on the set. If he felt that an actor or a director did not like him there were no resources within him to steel or seal himself off against his morbid sense of hurt. And in these cases his work suffered. When everything was fine, as it was on *Elephant Walk*, the set was a womb to Peter. He hung about, said one of the company "like a bit player". Eager and curious and enthralled by everthing going on.

The Finches stayed in Hollywood for five months until the completion of *Elephant Walk*. The Paramount Studio bosses had seen the rough cut of the film and were favourably impressed with Peter's personality, ability and star possibilities. They offered him a seven-year contract. Peter considered. The thought of being a big international star was not unpleasing and he loved working in the conditions of smooth efficiency and professionalism that were only to be found in a big Hollywood studio. But though he loved all that, he hated Hollywood.

On the other hand, Peter the escapologist was not keen to return to London and face the explosive situation that might confront him with Vivien and Olivier. So he turned down the seven-year contract but expressed himself willing and available for a one-picture deal. Paramount offered him the part of a Spanish gigolo aboard an ocean liner in a film starring Jane Russell. That simplified things. The three Finches left California on a Norwegian cargo boat that travelled via the Panama Canal.

CHAPTER 10

FATHER BROWN

In Spain they disembarked at San Sebastian where they stayed for a month's summer holiday and shortly thereafter Peter went alone to Paris to give what was to be one of his seven great film performances: the arch criminal Flambeau in *Father Brown* with Alec Guinness, directed by Robert Hamer who had already made the comic masterpiece *Kind Hearts and Coronets*.

Father Brown (*The Detective* in America) is a little gem. A work of art. Ageless and timeless, it could be made today or tomorrow. Without being the least solemn — it is in fact an exciting comedy thriller with Alec Guinness naturally supplying most of the comedy and the director Robert Hamer taking care of the thrills — it is still about something serious: the conditions of our consciences and of our souls. It was also in this film that Peter Finch, film actor, came of age.

The silhouette of Father Brown (Alec Guinness) is comedic. His black pancake hat sits square on his head, the skirts of his cassock flap around his springy walk, his spectacles glint with intelligence. He has a mania for rehabilitating criminals before the law can get them. He goes about his task with such a happy obsessiveness, indeed he relishes his success so much, that Catholic members of the audience might be forgiven for feeling he is sailing dangerously close to the great sin of pride were it not made clear that he is doing it all in the service of the Lord.

Father Brown's task is to track down a criminal who, through a series of disguises, has stolen the priceless cross of St Augustine. Father Brown cogitates. Who can it be? He says of his method: "I try to get so far inside a man that I can move his arms and legs, think his thoughts, wrestle with his passions — *but not commit his crime.* Then I can help him. By understanding people I understand myself and by understanding myself I understand other people. I judge no one.'' He arrives at the conclusion that it must be the arch criminal Flambeau who stole the cross. The daringness of the deed and the fact that the cross is only valuable to a connoisseur points to him. To lure Flambeau into the open, Father Brown arranges for a wealthy parishioner, Joan Greenwood, to auction off her valuable chess set designed by Cellini. As Lady Warren, Joan Greenwood gives a delicious performance. She is at the height of her beauty, her eyes provocatively sliding sideways as, with dainty weariness, she utters each syllable with a plummy pleasure, always remaining serenely still except for an occasional flutter of her tiny hands. Flambeau is indeed at the auction in one of his disguises and makes off with the chess set. But gazing on the delicate Lady Warren, he comes back undisguised and chivalrously returns the chess set to her. Peter as Flambeau is a ravishment to the eye. His face is fuller than before, and Hollywood has done one thing for him: it has given him a good haircut. Now his curls cluster around his brow and temples, and seem to glint as though caught by sunbeams. His eyes are set far apart and his brow and nose are strong. The modelling of the lower part of his face is exquisite. His jawline curves round to his chin, and the chin forms another gentle sphere with a straight line indicating where it ends and the mouth begins. His full lips are so amply and sweetly carved that there is a deep shadow where the upper and lower lips meet. And there is another shadow where the corners of the mouth tuck into the cheek.

He looks like a Greek god or, to be more precise, like an Etruscan head, circa 300 B. C. in the British Museum. Peter was not the only movie actor with that look. The young Brando had it, so did young Paul Newman. But the surprise here is that when Peter opens his mouth, instead of uttering the baboon yell ''Stell-ahh'' or Newman's middle-western twang, he not only speaks with the tongues of angels but unquestionably understands what he is saying.

He has two confrontations with Father Brown: one in Father Brown's study and one in the room of his château in France where he has collected all his stolen treasures.

The film critics took the film seriously: ''The confrontations of Father Brown and Flambeau will live in conscience and memory,'' said one. And they do. In the first confrontation we have Alec Guinness, his smile at half moon and his brain at full cylinder trying to get at the essence of what has made Flambeau a criminal. Peter Finch, at ease in his chair, gracefully defers to Father Brown as a man of the cloth but never as a superior intellect. Peter's characterization of an aristocrat is noble, patrician and gently bred. One does not feel him stretching for the characterization but rather letting it envelop him comfortably. Where, one wonders, did this characterization come from? Peter Finch's life seems to have as much to do with Flambeau as Emily Brontë's with Cathy in *Wuthering Heights*. We shall have to wait two years to find the answer. Flambeau is a lonely man who steals primarily so that he may enjoy these treasures by himself, and secondly for the fun of outwitting the police.

When the police as well as Father Brown are on to him, there is a chase. "I gambled the Cross for the soul of Flambeau," says Father Brown. He gets to Flambeau's château first. A stern old woman tries to prevent him from entering but Flambeau allows him into his "nursery". It is full of priceless paintings and priceless jewels and — a child's rocking horse. Father Brown seizes on it immediately. "I like your rocking horse," he says, to Flambeau's embarrassment. "It's a pity you never grew out of it. When you were a child you thought as a child but now you are a man and you still think as a child and that's *dangerous*!" At this point the police arrive, Flambeau scrambles over the roof, Father Brown comes downstairs and says to the old woman: "You were his governess, weren't you?" And in one line we have the whole orphaned history of Flambeau.

A while later, Flambeau goes to a museum where his stolen paintings have been restored. He stands in front of one of them. A little child next to him says to another. "Comme c'est beau, n'est-ce pas?" "Oui, c'est beau," says the other. Flambeau is redeemed! He realizes the truth of what Father Brown has been telling him — that works of art are for the world not just for him. He flies to London and arrives at the church during Father Brown's sermon. He genuflects in the aisle and sits in the pew next to Lady Warren. He looks at her. The actor Peter Finch had many different ways of looking at things, as many as there are feelings behind what he is looking at. The look he bestows on Joan Greenwood is one of tender conjugality but then he leans forward to listen to Father Brown and the look instantly changes to that of a passionate convert. Another soul for Father Brown. A happy ending for Flambeau. An eminently satisfactory state of things.

On 26 August 1954, an English trade paper said, "*Father Brown* is now established throughout Britain as a top grossing attraction. It already stands high among the box-office giants of 1954." Once again Peter was discovered.

CHAPTER 11

"Je suis comme je suis"

When Peter Finch completed *Father Brown* around Christmas, he did not return to England but stayed in Paris through to the beginning of 1954. An Englishman, Hugh Millais, remembers him very well sitting every day in one of those little café restaurants that apparently have no name but are identified only by their proximity to a landmark. This one was known as the café-across-the-street from-the-Tabou-Club which at night became the celebrated head-quarters of the Existentialists, who came to pay homage to Juliette Greco singing "Je suis comme je suis".

Peter Finch, seated daily at the café-across-the-street, was an intriguing romantic figure to the denizens of the *quartier*: a hand-some Australian — an actor, it was said, although he rarely referred to it — very bright but rather sad at the back of it all, who spoke beautiful if slightly ungrammatical French with an impeccable accent. Every night he joined the rest of the crowd on their inflexible route from the café to the Tabou to Le Club Jazz in St Germain where in the early hours they listened to Mezz Mezzrow and Sydney Bechet. Next day he would be back at his seat in the café.

Peter sat alone most of the day. He was thinking. He sat for several months in that café thinking. He knew he should quit this beautiful city and get back to London but he was not eager to do so. He foresaw, back home, important decisions looming up before him. He rubbed his nose and pulled it — a habit he had when he felt uneasy. He seemed to hear his old friend Mac's voice berating him over the years as he had done in Sydney, "Lily-livered poltroon! If you ever so much as smell a decision coming your way, you're under the bed quaking with fear!"

It was true. Decisions were things Peter was incapable of coping with. With his extraordinary luck, career decisions had always been made for him by others: by Tamara saving £1000 so they could go to England when the chance came; by Olivier who put him under contract; by George Devine who had arranged for him to go to the Old Vic; and by Vivien who had decided he was to co-star with her in *Elephant Walk*.

"Life has a trick of happening," Peter liked to say as if there were no point in trying to interfere with its inexorable course. What he was really saying was that he actively disliked being forced to do something so artificial as making up his mind.

At that café he enjoyed arguing the point philosophically. "*Buddhistically*," he would say, "life is flow. You flow from one thing to another. That is nature's way. It goes against nature to do anything so false as make a decision. That's dangerously like making an *in*cision. It might pierce through your heart." But all the time that he was consciously resisting making his own immediate decision which was — simply put — whether he was to remain a married man or leave Tamara and pursue a path of pleasure-loving bachelorhood, his own feelings were unconsciously at work making the decision for him.

Like life, Vivien Leigh had happened to him and he could not make her unhappen. Nor did he want to. It was fruitless to hope to change what was unchangeable and irrevocable. The passion, the excitement that he and Vivien had shared during their brief intimacy had badly shaken him, had unleashed his old wildness and desires. "After you've been to bed with Vivien," he was to say recklessly to Bridget Boland much later, "nothing else matters."

He still loved Tamara and always would, but what had happened to him was that another kind of love was supplanting his love for her — a love stronger and more seductive because it was older than his love for a wife and a child. It was his love of freedom: selfish, irresponsible, chaotic freedom. He felt he had outgrown the need for respectability, that he was being driven forwards — or was it backwards — to his true nature: the Australian Bum. He now wanted what he had held so precious in the years before his marriage: constant instability, constant adventure and constant romance.

So Peter, still consciously resisting decision, stayed on in Paris. He had several minor romantic interludes with his old friends the *filles de joies* — pleasant but unimportant. Gradually it dawned on him that he could not sit at that cafe for the rest of his life. He had been offered the leading part of an antique dealer who falls in love with a Wedgwood vase in Wolf Mankowitz's film *Make Me an Offer* which he was enthusiastic to do.

It was eventually time to go back to London. Home. Home for the past ten years had been with Tamara, strong, patient, solid, constant and inflexible in her three loyalties: Peter, Mumma and Anita. Forsake Tamara? Abandon Anita? Impossible! As for Vivien ... No! That was playing with a fire that could burn him badly. He would stay as far away as possible.

This was *not* a decision, he told himself. He was merely being borne along the natural flow of his life. But the natural flow of Peter's life was a stream where counter-currents never ceased their trick of happening. What was happening when Peter got back to London was that the Oliviers were having a great West End success in Terence Rattigan's *The Sleeping Prince*. For strict attention to the niceties, theatre etiquette is equal only to court etiquette. However fraught the situation between Peter and the Oliviers, it was unthinkable that he should not extend to them the courtesy of seeing them in their triumph and going backstage afterwards.

Together Peter and Tamara attended a performance of *The Sleeping Prince*, both filled with foreboding though for different reasons, both absorbed in their own uncomfortable and unshared thoughts. Afterwards they went backstage to pay their respects to the Oliviers.

First they went to Vivien's dressing-room. Peter kissed Vivien in quick congratulations and rushed off to visit the rest of the cast. Tamara and Vivien, alone again as they had been in Hollywood, looked at each other. What Tamara saw was a completely normal and extremely beautiful and gracious lady. What Vivien saw, she put into words. She praised Tamara's courage and tolerance! And she added, looking her straight in the eye, "I feel very sorry for you." Other people came into the dressing-room and Tamara was introduced around by Vivien as "The most courageous girl I know." These words, however, had anything but a heartening effect on Tamara, for she heard so clearly under them those that were unspoken: "It's good you have courage, my dear — because you're going to need it."

If Vivien had happened to Peter, Peter had also happened to Vivien. But Vivien was of a different philosophic cast from Peter. In brief, if she wanted something to happen, she made it happen.

Much later Tamara was to say, "I couldn't fight Vivien. It would have been like trying to fight the Queen of England."

For the rest of 1954, Vivien and Peter were busy with their respective acting assignments.

First Peter made *Make Me an Offer*, a charming film adapted from Wolf Mankowitz's book in which Peter plays a small-time antique dealer in love with a Wedgwood vase which through various machinations he finally gets to own. It was in this film that Peter successfully brought to fruition what he had been teaching his Mercury students back in Australia in the exercise where one of them looked at an imaginary painting and the others guessed what sort of a painting it was.

In *Make Me an Offer*, in an attic, Peter at last comes face to face with the vase he has so long been looking for: it is covered in dust standing on a mouldy shelf. As a long, silent sequence with a minimum of action, this might have been unbearably static; but with Peter's skill it is just the opposite. First he seems to be talking to it, his lips moving silently. Then reverently he approaches; and in some extraordinary way, he is able to project the very essence of the vase, its fragility. Peter *fragilizes* it. Tenderly he takes it off the shelf and, as he holds it, though he does not actually fumble it, one can see that this fear is uppermost in his mind. Then he smiles down on it in his arms as if saying to a child, "Oh, you darling!" and the sequence is completed. All this from a man who was totally indifferent to possessions.

It was one of Peter's favourite film scenes and he would frequently say to Olive Harding, "If they want to see what I can do, run that."

Said one critic: "Peter Finch's fine head would itself look good on a Grecian vase, his fine voice is a worthy match and this film gives ample evidence of his acting power. Peter Finch is worth every penny of that £70,000 contract." The critic was referring to Peter signing a film-a-year deal with Pinewood — for £70,000.

It had by now become clear in England, as it had in Australia way back in '38 when Peter made his début in *Dad and Dave* as a young boy, that the camera loved him.

His reward was a contract with Pinewood. On the face of it, this looked like money for jam. But being under contract to Pinewood in those days was not like being under contract to MGM, Warners or Columbia in America — to put it mildly. Nor, for that matter, to

Korda or Ealing in England. Not by a long shot.

At the head of Pinewood was J. Arthur Rank, a flour merchant. In his mixtures of stars, scripts and directors he often produced a product that came out tasting like soggy, congealed paste for all that the boys in the front office assured Rank it tasted exactly like cake. Peter made seven films for Rank. Two of them will be discussed here because they were good and one because it was interestingly bad. For the rest, Peter may be regarded as mashing through the mush.

Peter made one other film before he started his Rank contract. It was called *The Dark Avenger* and he made it in order to meet Errol Flynn.

"You would have thought," said Roddy Mann, the *Sunday Express* columnist. "I mean *I* would have thought a man like Finch who really was a poet at heart and had the kind of attitude he had ... well, it's surprising the kind of people he admired.

"I mean he loved Errol Flynn! I introduced him to Errol. Errol was staying down at a pub in the country, The Old Bell, and I took Finchie there to meet him for lunch. Well, Finchie, always very articulate, was struck absolutely dumb when he met Flynn and he just looked at him like a boy looking at the old man on the end of the boat, listening to tales from the sea. I never saw Finch like that. He was knocked out by this man. Flynn loved it because here was an audience at last. He patronized Finch. They got along well of course but it was strange to see ... well, other people thought Flynn over the hill but ... I just never thought I'd see Peter like that."

To Peter, Errol Flynn was an original. More specifically, Flynn to Peter was the original "Up yours!" man ("Up yours!" being that coarse expression, accompanied sometimes by an even coarser gesture, that is the truculent response to someone who is trying to straitjacket you into some mould of convention or conformity you have no use for). Peter admired people who held that attitude not only towards other people but towards the world, people who said "Up yours!" to life. And this admiration was intensified by the fact that he himself, always afraid of confrontation, was never able to carry it off quite as he would like. Thus Flynn, fellow Australian and a glorious performer in his time, was to Peter an object of worship and emulation.

The Dark Avenger was one of those costume dramas, all doublets and singlets and swords and fearful rows breaking out in the banqueting hall and ladies fleeing on white chargers — the sort of thing Flynn used to do magnificiently in the past. But as this film was made by Monogram (the lowest rung on the ladder), Flynn, far from taking it seriously did not take it at all. So neither did Peter in his desire to copy his idol.

Early on Flynn came up to Peter after a take and gave him a piece of advice. "You're *acting*," he said. "Don't act! I don't act, that's why I'm a star." It was rotten advice to give an actor like Peter but he immediately followed it — and went dead. Whatever the two of them were doing in the film they were living it up a great deal after hours which earned them the *nom de guerre* "Hellraisers" for many years after in the British Press.

Then Peter made *Passage Home,* his first Rank film, a saga of the sea mixed with generous portions of Pinewood paste.

His next film *Josephine and Men* in which he plays a writer, is notable only for the fact that it was the debonair Jack Buchanan's last film.

Following that, in the spring of 1955, Peter made *Simon and Laura*, the film in which he was so interestingly bad. Simon and Laura are a husband-and-wife theatrical team who quarrel constantly in life and go on a weekly TV show and quarrel constantly there too. The comedy situations evolving therefrom are not very strong and easily slip the mind. Peter's part as Simon (which, for some reason, he played wearing a small glued-on moustache) needed a John Barrymore doing his tremendous take-off of the theatrical temperament in *Twentieth Century* to pull the thing off — a thought that seemed to occur occasionally to Peter's raised eyebrow. But Peter could not "take off" in either sense. He could not take off an actor (what could be easier than an actor taking off an actor?) and he could not take off in the Olive Harding sense; his feet could not leave the ground. And his failure is even more mysterious because he was matched with the comedienne Kay Kendall who, had she lived, would have rivalled Carole Lombard.

Peter had one happy day during the filming, however: a scene with Gilbert Harding, then the *monstre sacré* of British TV. He was very much an "Up yours!" man, always in trouble on the air for being drunk or almost drunk, arrogant, rude and outspoken. But he was also always forgiven by the British public because of his rich, cultivated wit. Peter and Harding shared a studio car going to work one morning. As they drove through the dreary suburbs along their way, Gilbert glancing out the car window murmured, "Crickle-wood! Are we to be spared nothing?" Peter laughed and cherished Gilbert long after for that remark and for many others made during that day. In fact his affection and admiration for Harding went deeper than that and was to surface curiously many years later.

That Easter, April 1955, a local newspaper in Cambridgeshire ran this item: "Well Known Actor Opens Church Fête. Mr Peter Finch at Little Shelford." Several lines later it went on to say: "The chairman then called on his church warden to introduce the visiting opener: Mr Peter Ingle Finch. Mr Finch, he said, had already visited the parish on Good Friday and had been a generous donor to the funds. Through his forebears he had close associations with the village. His great-great-grandfather was rector from 1806 to 1849.

"In a short but encouraging speech Mr Finch expressed his delight at being invited to open the fête. He also found it a moving experience to come to a place so closely associated with his ancestors ... "

This pilgrimage to Little Shelford from Good Friday to Easter Monday to pay tribute to his forebears is oddly at variance with the "Up yours!" man he so longed to be. There is in it the feeling of someone desperately needing to make contact with his roots.

It was a little after that episode, in May, just before the Oliviers embarked on their great Stratford season of *Twelfth Night*, *Macbeth* and *Titus Andronicus*, that Vivien opened fire and began waging all-out war for Peter. Telephone calls from Vivien to Peter began to happen with increasing frequency at the Finches' flat. If Tamara answered and Peter was not in, boldly but sweetly Vivien would leave a message. The Olivier car and chauffeur began appearing outside Dolphin Square waiting to bear Peter off for weekends at Notley Abbey where, apparently, he was *persona grata* again. Once or twice, late at night in their flat, the Finches would awaken to the sound of the door bell ringing. And ringing. "Don't answer," Peter would say. "It's Vivien." "She'll wake up Anita," Tamara would worry. "Go back to sleep," he would reply. They would hear Vivien shouting for Peter for a while. Then silence.

Peter was drinking again. Heavily. Every quarrel Peter and Tamara had over Vivien ended in the same way. Peter stormed out of the door — vanished. Sometimes he stayed away for a night, sometimes for two nights, sometimes for two weeks. He avoided all explanations, all discussions including even those of the most pressing sort such as Anita's school fees; whether or not they should move to a bigger flat or buy a house; and the urgent necessity of paying bills, bills, bills. Money meant nothing to Peter, he gave it away without being asked, so the Finches' joint account was always in the red. Faced with these realities, he would vanish again.

More and more he was staying at his mother's house in Bury Walk in Chelsea. He slept on the sofa. Vivien and his mother had become friends and confidantes so she and Peter could meet there. By now Vivien and Peter's romance had become almost the sole topic of gossip and speculation in the theatrical profession. Everyone had their own theories, beliefs and opinions. "Everyone was saying 'Poor Larry' or 'Poor Vivien' — or even 'Poor Peter' — but no one was saying poor me," Tamara recalled wryly.

But though the acting profession never stopped talking about Vivien and Peter, incredibly the Press never started! It was the best kept romantic secret in England since Edward and Mrs Simpson. Was it because of the respect the Press felt for the Oliviers, the Golden Couple? It seems doubtful. Things had changed since King Edward's day and, to get back down to earth, this was just too good a story. One is forced to conclude that they did not know. And they did not know for the very good reason that it was *all kept in the family*. The Vivien-Peter romance was played out at Notley and Stratford always under Olivier's nose.

A romance! According to *Brewer's Dictionary of Phrase and Fable*, "The modern application of the word 'romance' pertains to a story containing incidents more or less removed from the ordinary events of life." And that is precisely what Vivien and Peter were absorbed in that spring, summer, autumn and winter of 1955.

"More or less removed from the events of ordinary life", the lovers were never removed from the God-like presence of Olivier. The best you could say about them was probably the worst you could say about them; they did nothing behind Olivier's back. It was never a case of the mice playing while the cat was away. The cat watched the mice, and the mice watched the cat. And the Stratford company watched too. And the weekend guests at Notley Abbey. These watchers of the "triangle" in fact became slightly dizzy trying to work out the equation.

First: what did Olivier feel about all this? From his behaviour, it looked as though he did not care — as though he scarcely noticed Vivien and Peter together. Had the actor taken over the man? Or was he temporarily putting first things first to do on stage what Kenneth Tynan was to call "shaking hands with greatness", that glorious Stratford season? Or, as an actor-manager, was it his main concern also to see that everyone else in the company gave of their best and if Peter made Vivien happy, got her to rehearsals, got her through performances, he would make the best of it? He was not pleased, he was not complaisant. All he could do was to try to contain the scandal; to keep it in the family.

And what about Vivien? Some said what she wanted was Olivier *and* Peter; that she was trying to have the best of both worlds. Yet, divided in her affections, and torn within by simultaneously opposing forces, she often became ill again.

Peter was cast as the snake in the Garden of Eden. Perhaps he was miscast. For however often the spectators witnessed Vivien going from difficult to arbitrary and then into an attack (for which they condemned her with such crisp English expletives as "starkers", "round the bend" and "barking"), they never stopped to wonder how much more harrowing it might be for Peter at much closer quarters.

Life with Vivien at that point could be harrowing but Peter stayed close to her. To understand why, one must look into his past.

Though Peter never talked about the long hard period he endured in his youth, he had never forgotten what it felt like to be a victim: to be orphaned, to be unwanted and unloved; to be ill-treated and hungry; frightened; subjected, crushed — to be in short, a victim.

People surviving this sort of childhood grow up either identifying with the oppressor — and treating the underdog as harshly as they themselves were treated — or they identify with the underdog, even endowing him with special merits. The one thing they cannot ever do is be indifferent to those they see as victims.

Clearly, Peter identified intensely with those he saw as victims, giving them his full concern and sympathy. It was Charlie the wino who was his special friend at his twenty-first birthday party. That Tamara and her mother were poor when he met them was of special attraction to Peter. And so was the fact that Vivien was ill. With women, a strong sexual desire always accompanied Peter's sympathy for their victimization, and throughout his life, these were the women that were most important to him. It was a reason for — rather than against — loving Vivien — that he saw her as a victim of her illness.

So all through the summer and autumn Vivien and Peter held hands at Notley Abbey and at Stratford. They walked around Stratford holding hands. They held hands at dinner parties. Together they cavorted on the grounds of Notley Abbey. To onlookers, they seemed like two naughty children, misbehaving, teasing, tormenting, testing the benevolence of their Deity — The Great God Olivier — trying to see how far they could go before his patience was exhausted. When the Stratford season was over, they even ran off together.

It was Christmas time and they ran off to the South of France to a gorgeous villa in Le Lavandou. Their whereabouts were no secret to Olivier. He knew exactly where to find them and find them he did.

With many astringent comments, Olivier instructed Vivien to bethink herself that she was *Lady* Olivier and that it ill-became *Lady* Olivier to behave in such an unseemly fashion, running with her lover for all the world and the Press to note! He ordered her to cease all this nonsense instantly, to pack her things and to return with him to England at once. The Reverend Gerald Kerr Olivier's son Larry was laying down the law to his disciple wife. And convent-trained Vivien, like a good child, meekly obeyed.

The Oliviers returned to Notley Abbey but by now, Sir Laurence had had enough. He brooded for a fortnight and then decided things could not be allowed to continue. Peter was summoned by royal command to the Abbey. The stated purpose of the meeting was for all three of them to talk things over seriously and come to a clear understanding, and that Vivien was to choose between them. The discussion was to be conducted in a calm, quiet and — above all — dignified manner.

In the baronial dining hall at Notley Abbey, Olivier, Vivien and Peter sat down together to a resplendent dinner which they interlaced with fine vintage wines. Conversation was general and genial. When the meal was over, Olivier tossed his napkin on the table and said, "Let us now all retire to the library and thrash this thing out."

Vivien rose. "This has nothing to do with me," she announced pertly. "This is between you two. *You* must decide who is to have me." And with that, she left.

So Peter and Olivier retired to the Abbey's imposing book-lined library. Olivier poured out a whisky for each of them and seated himself behind his large mahogany desk. Peter sat in an armchair. They looked at each other...

Years later, when the centre of Peter's life shifted from London to Rome, he stayed up late one night over many potations with his friend B.R. "Bertie" Whiting, the Australian poet, and related the strange events that ensued that night at the Abbey — events so novel that many years later Whiting still recalled them in vivid and exact detail.

... In the library, Peter and Olivier looked at each other. Then they looked down at their glasses. Neither of them said a word. There was a long pause. Uneasily attempting a dignity he was far from feeling, Peter drew himself up and looked at Olivier again.

He gave a gasp as he caught Olivier's returning leer of frank and toothless senility. It look Peter a split second to respond. Raising his eyebrows superciliously he slid gracefully down into his chair, delicately sipping his whisky. As Peter contemplated the rich hangings in the room, his expression became more and more petulant and discontented and his weariness deepened into a fretful aristocratic distaste of what he saw. Thoughtfully he fingered his cigarette lighter, judicially staring at the heavy curtains draping the windows. He flicked his lighter suggestively once or twice.

Olivier staggered up from his desk with a mighty groan, toppling his chair. Rolling his eyes crazily in alarm, he creaked and wobbled crab-like across the room to Peter, limping badly on his gammy leg.

"No, no, little father!" he toothlessly implored, bringing to each syllable a remarkable variety of speech defects. "Not the *fire* again! No, no, I beseech thee, little pumpkin. Only listen to your humble serf who has loved you since he dandled you on his knee and you a wee bairn, lo these ... Ohhh — A-A-Ah, if the old master, the guv'ner were here ... " He broke down, sobbing inconsolably, his turkey gobbler neck trembling with emotion. Olivier was superb as he stood there swaying on his feet, flushed of skin, gnarled of hand and batty of mind. The world's oldest and craziest family retainer.

The young Duke — or was it Prince? — golden, wilful and spoiled, moodily flicked his lighter again. With a strangled cry, the loyal family retainer hurled himself at his young master to snatch it away but Peter extended an aristocratic leg and tripped up Olivier, sending him sprawling on the carpet.

Peter and Olivier began laughing. They laughed so hard that tears began coursing down their cheeks and they were gasping for breath. But they could not stop laughing. Every time they looked at each other they started up all over again.

These two great actors who had never appeared on stage together now settled down to giving the performances of their lives. Availing themselves freely of the whisky from which they drew inspiration, they went on to wilder and wilder flights of imagination as they improvised scene after scene featuring the young Duke and his imbecilic retainer, breaking off only to congratulate themselves on their technical brilliance, wit and inspiration and — like the great and conscientious artists they were — to go back over certain parts of a scene, polishing the bits that did not quite "come off". Needless to say, during all this there was a goodish amount of immoderate laughter.

At three a.m. the great double doors of the library were flung open. There in a nightdress stood Vivien, like Lady Macbeth, magnificent, proud, threatening. "Well?" she said, viewing with some bitterness the shambles of the library and the two dishevelled actors gaping foolishly at her. "Which one of you is coming to bed with me?"

Her words were greeted with shrieks of laughter. "Eh? Eh? Milady ... " quivered the drunken deaf old family retainer while the young Duke had found a letter opener and was capriciously trying to saw one of the buttons off his jacket.

An unwilling smile tugged at the corner of Vivien's mouth and before she knew it, she was laughing as hard as they were. Sitting in the library the three of them laughed till dawn.

"And so that was how it ended — you and Vivien?" asked Bertie Whiting in Rome when Peter had finished his tale.

"I suppose so ... Yes, ... I suppose so. Vivien stayed with Larry." Peter was silent for a while, thinking. "But you know," he said suddenly, "there was really never any question that Vivien would give up being Lady Olivier to become Mrs Fink." He pronounced the "chi" of Finch with a hard "k" in the Italian style.

It was indeed a novel scene that was enacted that night at Notley Abbey between Olivier and Peter. Novel — but for Peter, not unprecedented. Long ago as a Boy Scout, Peter had written and cast himself in just such a part as he played that night: the aristocratic *jeunesse dorée* with the House of Romanoff tumbling on his head and Paul Brickhill in the role of the aimless shuffling retainer.

Later, as a swaggie, Peter repeated the impersonation with the variation that he was an aristocratic polo player and Donald Friend his devoted serf.

Peter, in his dealings with other people, is universally talked of as a modest man, even a humble man; but Peter was also an orphan. Of what does a young orphan dream but that he is a prince? And for what other reason was it so easy for him to slip into the skin of Flambeau than that he had played him already so many hundreds of times as a child in his dreams?

But that night at Notley Abbey it must have come as a shock to Peter that, for the first time since his playing out of this charade, it was the demented old retainer who *stole the show*.

CHAPTER 12

A Town like Alice and an Agent like Olive

To go back a few months to the autumn of '55 when Vivien's and Peter's affair was at its most all-consuming, when Tamara was at her most upset and bewildered, and when Peter's mother and sister were at their most delighted at having their famous son and brother spending nights on their sofa in their little house in Bury Walk and their most thrilled with the excitement of meeting all his glamorous friends — while all this was going on in his real life, so to speak, Peter managed to find time to make two films as well. And to make them so close together that there was hardly a day between them.

First he played the "good" German Captain Langsdorff in *The Battle of the River Plate* (*The Pursuit of the Graf Spee* in America) which, as the title suggests, gives us some more of dat ole debbil sea. Pinewood had an absolute mania for doing sea stories under the impression that to the British, the myth of the sea was as potent and abiding as the myth of the Western to Americans. It wasn't.

The other film Peter made at the time was an important one for him and he almost did not do it. He read the script, went to Olive Harding's office, dropped it on her desk and said, "I'm not doing it."

Olive gave him one of those looks for which she is famous: straight in the eye through her owl-like glasses. After one or two of these looks, the most temperamental actor in the world begins to feel that perhaps he is being a leetle bit unreasonable. Then she can deal with him.

"You are not going to tell me it's a bad script," said Olive to Peter.

"No," he said. "It's a good script but it's the girl's film."

Another Olive look. "Peter, stop being childish and counting your lines. It's a wonderful script and a wonderful part for you. And it'll do you more good than anything you've done recently. Do I have to go down on my knees and *beg* you to do it?''

"No," said Peter quickly, "you don't have to do that. I'll do it."

Peter did *A Town Like Alice*, playing a happy-go-lucky Australian soldier, a prisoner of the Japs in Malaya, and he won the British Film Academy Award for it — his first important award in England.

At this point Olive Harding, his agent since *Daphne Laureola*, began to play a bigger and bigger part in his life. She became the one constant in his perpetually changing world. She remained his agent until she retired in 1971.

In 1949 when Olive took charge of Peter's affairs, there was not much she didn't know about actors: their needs, their strengths, their failings and their talent.

"Peter was to me — as were all my artists — one of my children," she says, "because very early on I realized that artists were not adult on the whole; they were unable to cope with finance and other things and therefore they had to be mothered and protected. And of them all, Peter was the most insecure. He was so insecure sometimes you could cry for him. When I realized that Peter had no idea of money, none at all, that he thought cheques were just pieces of paper you wrote on, I knew the only way to protect him from all those people who spun him hard-luck stories would be to insist on countersigning all his cheques. The queues around my office every morning with people who had been holding Peter Finch cheques in their hands since the night before! I started the countersigning very early in his career and the one time we dropped it for four months he was overdrawn like a shot so we had to start again."

Olive, crisp, upright and tweedy even in first-night evening dresses, was Auntie Olive to all her charges. She met them at the airport when they arrived, kissed them goodbye when they left. She bullied them and pleaded with them. She scolded them and praised them. Whatever they asked for, she got it. Their demands on her were great, but of all the needy artists — perhaps even including Edith Evans — Peter's demands on her were the greatest. With him it was always "Send for Olive!" whenever there was some kind of crisis. And as the years went by, his changing families found themselves depending on her almost as much as he did.

Virginia McKenna, who starred with Peter in *A Town Like Alice* only knew Peter on the set.

"I'm sure", says Virginia, "that this has been said hundreds of times, but everyone adored Peter so much that he would just come on the set and everyone would start smiling. He would have that sort of a way that everyone enjoyed being with him. I never saw him lose his temper. He was always good-humoured. He never got impatient. There was an unspoken feeling that he was a sort of leader. He was so lovely with women. He was so warm and so friendly and so sweet. He used to tease people and they would do anything for him. He never brought his troubles on the set. He left all that behind him. I had expected him, probably because of the newspapers — that hellraiser thing — to be flamboyant and noisy and he wasn't. He was a quiet person.''

A Town Like Alice was Virginia's first big film. She was nerve-racked at the beginning to have such a large role. But she found the other members of the cast wonderful, so that in spite of its being a harrowing film — the story of a group of women during World War II force-marched by the Japs across Malaya — Virgina felt it one of the happiest films she ever worked on. ''Above everyone else,'' she says, ''Peter helped me most to be relaxed and at ease. He actually read my mind!''

One day, Virginia and Peter had a special, private scene coming up where they meet in the bushes in the dark and talk. Virginia was very nervous about this scene. She was dying to rehearse it before they got in front of the camera but did not dare say to Peter, ''Do you think we should rehearse?'' And almost at that very moment when the thought was uppermost in her mind, he came up to her and said, ''Hey, would you like to come and go over this together?'' So Virginia said ''Oh, yes! I'd love to.'' ''And that'', said Virginia, ''started something which he always continued for the rest of our scenes which was to say to me 'Let's go over the words.' ''

That started something, but far more than Virginia ever knew. For Peter, as he had explained to Cyril Frankel, the director of *Make Me an Offer*, hated rehearsing in films. In fact he preferred not to look at his lines till the very last minute to preserve the immediacy of his acting.

''He was *so* lovely to be with,'' Virginia goes on. ''I mean it was so lovely to be with *that* sort of person. It made everything good. It was just that your mouth turned up when you were with him. It was as simple as that!''

In *Alice*, the little scenes showing them falling in love and then responding to that love are enormously moving, as is the scene with Virginia alone in the prison quarters thinking about him. Tender, radiant and jubilant in her love, she makes everyone in the audience see what she saw: that her Australian soldier is the most endearing, light-hearted yet courageous man in the world. Peter with Virginia had the same glorious chemistry that he had with Dame Edith Evans. The chemistry where one plus one does not equal two, but one *times* one equals *one*.

"After Peter died," says Virginia, "I went to his memorial service. I suppose that says more for what I think about Peter than anything else I could say. I only did one film with him twenty-two years ago and never saw him again, but I wanted to go to his memorial service. That shows you how deeply I regarded him as an actor. I wanted to pay my personal tribute to him. I felt that strongly. There are people I've worked with millions of times that I wouldn't feel strongly enough to go to their memorial services."

Whatever transgressions Peter may rightly be accused of committing during his lifetime, he cannot be properly weighed in the balance without adding these seven words to each accusation ... "except when he was on the set".

He was selfish and self-absorbed — except when he was on the set. He was evasive and irresponsible — except when he was on the set. He drank excessively, he was a liar, he was weak, undecided, undisciplined — except when he was on the set. He was uncaring and callous — except when he was on the set, and then he truly cared for everyone there and made sure they knew it.

Why did he keep his two sides so separate? His ideal situation was a carefully constructed, carefully constricted safe make-believe world. And in this ideal world he behaved ideally; he *wished* to. Nor did he need to drink to do it. But to face the confusion of his real world and to be always open to the endless possibilities of the encounters caused by his looks, personality and status as a movie star sex-object, he had to drink. If no one gave in to temptation more, few men have had more; a fact which less successful, less talented and less attractive people always seem to overlook. In fact one wonders if the initial, unconscious impulse that sets these tongues clucking with disapproval at Peter's "boozing" and "womanizing" is not envy.

He was an artist, a very great one as can be seen on the screen, whose art was acting and who needed as positive a creative atmosphere around him as do painters and writers and which, in his work, was far harder to achieve. But after hours of discipline on the set, he had to break out. He was a man with a childhood of deprivation he could never bury. At a very basic level, it left him with an over-developed sense of play. The child rarely takes good care of its toys.

Moving forward again, past Larry and Vivien, past Notley, or rather post-Notley, for Vivien's decision had been made and she had chosen Larry, Peter looked at the New Year, 1956, took a deep breath and did something which for him, since the age of seventeen, had been and would always be a great source of pleasure and regeneration.

He went on walkabout. Together with his old Australian mate, Alan White, he walked all over Devon. Then he returned to his mother's sofa and set out to mend his Vivien-broken heart with dozens and dozens of girls, with louder music and of course, stronger wine. Peter's mother looks back to that time, her eyes dim with nostalgia. "This small house was bending with people. Simply bending. And the mixture. Peter was able to mix all sorts of people together. Simply amazing! He never seemed to need any sleep at all. After a party, just a shower in the morning and off he'd go. And the women, the women, the women! It was a marvellous time."

For Tamara, however, this was not a marvellous time. Among her worries was a house in the Little Boltons that she had bought early in '55 when Peter was around and with his approval. Should she move in? Or what? He was impossible to get hold of. She moved in. Peter came around. "Ah," he said vaguely, "you've put up curtains." Then he went out to the garden in the back, planted a tree and left.

Their meetings became more and more rare and more and more unsatisfactory until Tamara reached a painful decision. She had always loved him and always would; she could never forget their past happiness; he was the love of her life; but she knew from the way he was behaving, roaring around town, completely neglecting her and Anita, financially as well as in every other way, that by constantly evading her he was forcing her hand. She would ask him for a divorce or a separation. Only she had to find him first to tell him. Whenever she rang his mother's house and spoke to either his mother or to Flavia, they were vague. He was out. He was lunching with this one, he had a meeting with that one, they didn't know when he'd be back. Finally she got her message across and Tamara and Peter met one morning in Bury Walk.

One of Peter's favourite subjects was how difficult it was to live with anybody, how difficult it was to come to terms with meetings and partings — lives and deaths he called them — on this planet.

How hard it was to deal with your emotions when you were about to lose somebody that you loved and how unfair it was to have emotions anyway. If someone was to leave you — if you were to leave someone — it was better to be born like an animal and have no emotions at all. Either that, or you should be given some consciousness of life after death so that emotions had a chance of being renewed later on. All this, of course, was a philosophical wish after the fact, and it did not help him in telling Tamara that his affair with Vivien had changed him, that he could not go back, that he was flowing away from his old life with Tamara ... And yet their love remained between them mortal but still-breathing — for Tamara, it refused ever to die.

A separation was agreed upon and it remained for Olive to arrange maintenance for Tamara and Anita.

CHAPTER 13

The Hero Returns

Soon after, Peter met Les Norman again, the Ealing producer of *Eureka Stockade* back in 1947, who had been so struck with Peter's talent he had argued with Harry Watt that he replace Chips Rafferty and give Finch the lead. Now he told Peter about a film he was going to direct in Australia, *The Shiralee*, adapted from the popular novel by D'Arcy Niland. Les asked Peter how he would like to play the leading role — an itinerant worker unexpectedly burdened with his small daughter. Peter read the book and the script. The character, a loner, wandering around the Australian bush from small town to small town, from ranch to ranch doing odd jobs, was so close to Peter's heart and understanding that he might have written it himself: the Australian Bum and to be filmed in Australia; the chance to return to his home and to his mates whom he had not seen for eight years! He spun a dream of himself back at the Cross. And another at the Journalists Club and another at Redleaf. Yes; he had every reason to look forward to a hero's triumphant return! His next reaction, as so often with Peter, was physical. He would sign on to a cargo boat going to Australia round the Cape (round the *Cape*!) as a member of the crew hauling and swabbing with the best. That should take three weeks or so and toughen him up. He was going to look right for this role — not like a Hollywood cowboy. Also he must write to his cousin Florrie in Queanbeyan and tell her he was going to work on her property till he got back the feel of working the Australian land. He wrote to Hal Lashwood to tell him he was coming, and would Hal get Ralph Curnow who lived off the Cross and gave wonderful parties to give him a party and invite all his old actor mates? And also, and *especially* his old friend Kate, one of the madams at the Dirty Half Mile, and his favourite prostitute, Tilly? Have it on a Saturday, Peter wrote, and then stopped, suddenly realizing that in his exhilaration he had forgotten to tell Les Norman that he was accepting the role.

Before Peter left on the cargo boat, he gave excited interviews to correspondents for all the Australian papers. He told them that he would be arriving in Sydney at the end of June and that while there, he would be staying at the Wentworth Hotel. He appealed to everyone who had ever known him to contact him there. He had never, he said, looked forward to anything so much in his life as returning to Australian soil after eight years away.

In Durban, the cargo boat lay at anchor for several days. Peter walked along the beach in a tee shirt and jeans and looked ... just like Peter Finch. A lovely young blond girl on the beach with long, perfectly shaped legs who had just seen him in *A Town Like Alice* recognized him and, vastly intrigued, asked the friend she was with to introduce herself to him and invite him for a drink. Peter, looking over at the lovely blonde the friend indicated, accepted immediately. Her name was Yolande Turnbull, she told him when they met. She was an actress from Johannesburg, and she was thinking of going to London to try her luck. Yolande was the indulged, pampered daughter of wealthy South African parents and, as Peter discovered, she was really something. Gay, carefree, adventurous and sophisticated, she was a cross between a Fitzgerald Southern Belle and Sally Bowles. In other words, a flirt. Though he still bore the scars of Vivien both in his heart and literally — his back and hands still had marks where she had clawed him during her attacks — he could be distracted by this provocative unpredictable girl.

They began their three-day romance in a holiday mood and ended it in a sentimental one. Peter reboarded ship having exacted a promise from Yolande to come to London soon and to reach him at his mother's. He sailed with her photograph tucked carefully in his wallet.

When Peter arrived in Sydney he went straight to the Wentworth. There were only two messages for him but he cheered up when he saw that they were from Hal and Mac. Anyway it was early stages, he told himself. He'd only just this minute arrived. He phoned Mac at work and Mac came right round. They had a couple of drinks and a jaw about this, that and the other, and Peter suddenly said, "It's good to be back. It's good, good, *good*! Let's go over to the Journo's and take a jar with me old mates. Mac, there's nothing like the Journo's anywhere in the world."

"Righto, Fincho," said Mac stirring himself. "The Journo's it is."

Arriving at the Journalists Club they bounded up the stairs two at a time and stood in the doorway.

"Hey, everybody," called out Mac over the noise, "Just look who's here!"

The room fell quiet. The members of the club, Peter's old mates of so many years' standing — of so many years' standing and talking and falling down — turned round from the bar and stared at the stranger with a tasteful show of indifference. Then, as though quickly remembering their manners, they made room for the guest at the bar with all the deference due to a moderately distinguished gentleman they had met briefly two years ago on some reputable occasion. After solicitously seeing that the guest was supplied with the drink of his choice, they resumed their previous conversation. A few members with even sharper memories actually recalled the guest's name. They came up to him and said, "Hello, Pete," and asked him in the friendliest way where he'd been and how he had been keeping himself.

Peter's human frailty smile was at its grisliest as he turned to Mac and remembered a sudden pressing engagement.

Mac and Peter left the Journo's.

Mac began, "Well, you know what we're like in Australia … "

"No, I don't," said Peter. "What're you like?"

"They gave you the business all right," conceded Mac. "I was afraid they might. Hell, it's just the old Australian game — don't you remember it, mate? It is called in our patois 'cutting-'em-down-to-size'. Nothing personal. If you'd achieved fame as a singer or a sportsman and come back here, you'd get the same business. We're all *equal* here in Australia, Fincho, and nobody's allowed to get above themselves."

"I'm not above myself," said Peter.

"Yes, you are. For one thing you *left* — that was bad enough. For another, you've made it. Yeah, come to think of it, maybe it was a mistake to *walk* into the Journo's. Maybe you should have crawled in."

The next day Hal Lashwood rang to say he was coming round on Saturday to take Peter to his party — Ralph was no longer available but Hal had organized it in a big hall in Oxford Street. All the other people Peter wanted were coming said Hal, except Kate and Tilly. Kate had married an American businessman and was living in Arizona and no one knew what had happened to Lily. No matter, the old gang would be there on Saturday night.

Peter was looking forward to the party. Actors and actresses, he told himself, were more sensitive than journalists. And he could not help having a moment of self-satisfaction as he thought how impressed they would be by the way he had grown in confidence, style and stature since they had last seen him.

On Saturday night Hal and Peter arrived at the hall. Peter's theatrical cronies had all assembled and they were glad to see him, really glad — there was much warmth in their greetings. Peter was overcome. It was only when he began talking about his experiences of the past eight years that he found himself in trouble.

Suddenly in his ears, those big names ... Liz Taylor ... Orson ... Larry ... Errol Flynn ... Alec Guinness — names that had been so much part of his life, fell clanging to the floor, jarring the atmosphere with hideously discordant sounds. He noticed some of his listeners actually averting their eyes from him as though pained by his crassness as each big name fell clank!

Conversation subsided. Then someone said, "How's Allan?" And someone else said "How's Thelma?" and "How's Lloyd?" and "Do you ever see Summie?" Australians abroad! At last, a safe topic because of course he knew where they all were and what they were doing — all Australians abroad did. But even that topic was not safe because eventually someone asked, "How's Tamara?"

"Well, uh, well, we've broken up," stumbled Peter. The women at the party gave him an old-fashioned look. Peter went on, "She, um, wanted me to go commercial. But I want to stick to the theatre. After all, I'm a stage actor and always will be even if there isn't any money in it." Even as he heard himself say it he began believing it — though it had no basis in fact.

Peter then proceeded to drink a great deal. Drunk and in tears, he found Hal and began sobbing to him, "What is killing me — what is really killing me about breaking up with Tamara is that I can never see my daughter again."

This also had no basis in fact, though in Peter's mind at that moment it had become a stark reality. After another drink, Peter's only thought was to go back to the Journo's and face them out. Hal protested that he was too drunk. Peter insisted. They went to the Journalists Club where they had no sooner got upstairs than Peter passed out. As in the old days, he had to be carried home.

Now, when Peter's phone rang at the Wentworth it was largely people he did not know, or knew only vaguely, or knew of. They were Sydney's high society — the despised silvertails of Peter's old days with Mac — who now formed part of the international jet set. These people, rich, gay, much travelled, loved celebrities; they doted on them, they needed them — especially one as personable and attractive as a handsome, virile, curly-haired movie star on the loose. Peter accepted their invitations with pleasure, wining and dining with them and falling into their swimming pools and into the beds of their prettiest girls. And, of course, all the hangers-on, knowing Peter was in town, hung around. Why not? Peter always had a weakness for people who liked him.

After several weeks of high-life Peter rang his cousin Florrie in Queanbeyan and told her to come and get him. He was moving to a hotel on Macleay Street off the Cross without telling anyone. He was removing himself from his silvertail life and starting to concentrate on the film.

One day two girls were walking down Macleay street arguing and giggling. "Of course it's him," stated the first one positively. "Come on, what would *he* be doing walking down Macleay street?" said the other. "I tell you it *is* him. He's wearing the same suit he wore in *Simon and Laura*. I *recognize* it!"

The man in question was behaving very strangely. Every now and then he would stop, stare at a building and then burst into laughter. Then he would walk on. The next time he stopped and stared and laughed, the bolder of the two girls following him daringly rushed up to him. "Are you Peter Finch?" she asked in a small voice. Yes, said Peter, he was.

"I thought you were," said the girl with a triumphant look at her colleague, "because I recognized your ... " She stopped. Mentioning the suit might show a want of tact. " ... Because I recognized you!" she finished the sentence. "My friend here didn't think you'd be walking down Macleay Street."

Peter laughed. "I've been walking up and down it for an hour now looking at the houses and remembering each one where I'd done a flit. I've seen four already." He laughed again.

The thrilled girls wanted his autograph of course. And they wanted to know all about films and film stars and told him that of them all he was their absolute favourite. By this time they had stopped in front of a hotel. He said he was meeting his cousin there and would they like to have tea with them? They did not hesitate. Cousin Florrie was sitting in the lounge when they appeared. He introduced the girls and left them for a minute. In his absence the girls continued gushing. Kind-hearted, bluff, no-nonsense cousin Florrie turned to them: "I'm so glad you're making a fuss over Peter," she said, "because none of his friends are and it hurts him very much."

Peter worked on his cousin Florrie's station for about a month. He rode the horses, herded the cattle, fed the stock, chopped wood, mended fences. He did, in fact, all the things the character in *The Shiralee* did to earn a living. Slowly, the knot in his stomach that had been there since his arrival in Sydney relaxed, and he was back in tune with the land.

Then Peter travelled up to the country town of Coonabarabran, about four hundred miles from Sydney in New South Wales where they would be shooting on location. The first thing he did upon arriving was to get himself a country haircut, the kind which severely lowers the ears, leaves a sunburn ring around the back of the neck, and removes the need to visit the barber for another four months.

Peter found he was thinking a great deal about his English high school teacher, the attractive Mrs Conybeare, whom all the boys had adored. He could not have said just how she happened to pop into his head, unless from some very vague word association between Coonabarabran and Conybeare. Nevertheless, once in his head, she stayed there.

One evening he picked up the phone, asked for the number from the Sydney operator and rang Mrs Conybeare. She answered the phone. She sounded just as wonderful as Peter had forgotten and now remembered. After he said, "Hello", she stopped him with — (again something else he had forgotten and now remembered) "Let me see. Now don't tell me. That must be Peter Finch."

They talked for a long time. As well as his encourager, Mrs Conybeare had been his confidante and Peter had no secrets from her.

"I owe everything to you," he said. "You always gave me the leading roles when we were studying Shakespeare, remember?"

"Peter, I gave them to you because you were the *best*."

"I'm afraid my spelling's just as bad as ever."

"Don't worry about spelling," said this remarkable English teacher. "I've always told you that. It's what's *behind* it that counts."

It was all so easy. Mrs Conybeare said all the things he wanted to hear about how proud she was of what he had made of his life, of what a fine actor he had become and how much she enjoyed his films and looked forward to seeing him on stage when she came to England.

At the end he said to her, "You took me to your heart and you gave me real affection. I love you. You know that, don't you? You know I've always loved you." And she laughed — that wonderful laugh he had forgotten and now remembered, and then they said goodbye. And afterwards he thought — but not sadly — "There is one person in Australia who understands me. And who always has.''

At London airport a young actress boarded a plane bound for Australia. In 1956 the trip took four days, stopping overnight in such exotic places as Singapore. Apart from her creamy English complexion and her dark tip-tilted eyes she seemed like any other attractive young girl until she began conversing with the other passengers, which she did with readiness and vivacity. Then one heard a voice full of delightful musical lilts and a laugh that always ended in a little squeak. Something about her face, demure and delicate and radiant, reminded one of the virgins in the Cluny tapestries who wander about in the intricate landscapes of flowers, tiny animals and unicorns.

This young actress, who was later to become the radiant centre of so many Broadway and West End productions was, as she travelled eastward on her long journey to Australia, in a state of mind made up of equal parts of excitement and apprehension. When she was not pleasantly distracting herself with the life stories of the other passengers, or sight-seeing around the exotic stopovers, she was making an anxious assessment of herself. On the plus side, she had won a gold medal at R.A.D.A. after which she had immediately been put under contract to H.M. Tennant's, the biggest and most powerful management in the West End. She had then done a season in Broadway in *Climate of Eden* and won another award. For a year she had played the girl in the English production of *The Seven-Year Itch*, after which had followed a season at the Bristol Old Vic. But the minus side — and it was a big minus — was that though she knew perfectly well how to make an effective entrance on stage, she did not have the faintest notion *how you were supposed to walk into a shot on camera.*

How could she? This was her first real part in a film. And that wasn't all she didn't know. She didn't even *know* what she didn't know. ''And anyway,'' she thought gloomily, allowing herself a moment's depression, ''I know they all really wanted Joan Greenwood.''

Her part was not a large one and it was a ''straight'' one which was a bore — always so much more difficult than a ''character'' part. She was to be Peter Finch's young girlfriend in *The Shiralee* for whom he returns for a happy ending. It was mostly being shot in Australia. That cheered her up somewhat and she had always longed to meet Peter Finch, though she was a little in awe of him because she was such an admirer of his and had seen every film and play he had been in. Then she went back to worrying. What if he found out how much she didn't know about filming?

When at last her plane arrived in Sydney and she was driven to Coonabarabran and deposited outside the inn where the company was staying, she was too exhausted to do anything but go straight upstairs to her room and sleep.

Later, up and dressed and feeling slightly better, she walked downstairs into the main room. A man came up to her whom she immediately recognized as Peter Finch.

"You're Rosemary Harris," said Peter extending his hand to her. People had just come in from the day's shooting and were shouting and milling about, but Rosemary and Peter might have been standing alone on the edge of the moon for all the attention Peter paid to the rest. Still holding Rosemary's hand and looking at her in a way that was at once shy and confident and, as Rosemary later recalled, "dear and kind and wonderful", Rosemary heard herself saying to him, quite unself-consciously, "Would you mind very much if I watched you while you're working? You see, this is really my first film."

"I'd be delighted," said Peter.

They became the best of friends for those months on location and, for Rosemary, Peter became an endless fascination as she studied him both in and out of work trying to figure out what made this complicated man tick.

On the set Rosemary observed carefully the way Peter worked. He *backed* into a shot, she noticed. He began every shot with his back to the camera, so that when the camera picked him up, it seemed as if he had come *from* somewhere, that he had had a life going on before the camera discovered him. He was always in motion she saw, his elbows out, his arms never at his sides. He was always moving, moving, lithely relaxed; but at the same time there was something inwardly driven and tense about him that set up an exciting contradiction.

Was it his eyes, Rosemary wondered, that made him such a star? Peter had talked to Rosemary about the importance of eyes in cinema and she saw that his eyes, whether in close-up or long shot, were always alert and alive. But no — perhaps it was the way all his features fitted together — his nose and his mouth and his curly hair. Or was it his voice? Well, perhaps it was *everything*.

But it was even more than that. And what Rosemary saw then at close proximity was what she was to see on the screen in all of Peter's best performances.

"Peter didn't *act* his parts," says Rosemary Harris, "he understood them. He understood their love and their pain. And it was *his* love and pain. It came from somewhere inside him. It was people's souls he was exposing. I'm glad he stayed in films; his art was too pure for the stage.''

At weekends, as the silvertail girls swam up and down from Sydney to dally with Peter, Rosemary discovered another side of him. ''I thought him very sophisticated, in fact I thought him *jaded*,'' she says. If, at only thirty-nine years of age Peter struck this perceptive actress as ''jaded'', it might be well to recall a toast given to him on his twenty-first birthday: ''To a person who at twenty-one has been through more than a man of sixty.'' Proceeding logarithmically, one could say that at thirty-nine, Peter had undoubtedly been through more than a man of one hundred and eleven. Peter now, in many ways, was jaded. About women, he was certainly jaded. But he was sated without being satisfied. And so like all jaded people he needed more and more of what — disappointingly — always turned out to be just more of the same. No woman he met now moved him to compassion any more; none of them struck that chord of sympathy that Tamara and Vivien had done previously.

On 17 August 1956, the Sydney *Daily Mirror* printed an interview with Peter headlined: PETER FINCH AND WIFE AGREE TO SEPARATE. On that very day, Peter wrote to Tamara in England, ''I miss you and the things we do.'' Had what was once real sentiment changed into sentimentality in Peter's effort to feel *something*?

''Maybe he doesn't really like women,'' thought Rosemary, ''or likes them only for sex.'' They would go to local pubs together sometimes during the week and she saw how much he loved this Australia and its folklore, loved all the people in the pubs — the shepherds, cowherders, swagmen, itinerants, bums, all getting drunk together with Peter. And then Peter did wonderful impersonations of them for the benefit of Rosemary afterwards. Watching this led Rosemary to feel that she had at last come to the essential Peter.

''I saw him now and then after the film,'' says Rosemary. ''Once at some sort of R.A.D.A. do that we were both attending. I remember him scrunched in a chair, unhappy in a dinner jacket in an agony of irritation, so out of place. If I were a painter I would paint him swaggy, brown, hard as a nut on an old cow pony, and in the background one of those huge Australian ranches, each one as big as Belgium. Or maybe Peter lying down at night under the stars, under that fantastic Southern Cross and reading a volume of Walt

Whitman — or whatever poet he liked. *That* was the essence of him.''

That was an essence of him. But it was also the essence of the part he was playing in *The Shiralee*.

In the film, Peter as Macauley comes back to his home to find his wife shacked up with another man. In a fury of revenge, he drags off his young daughter Buster only to find that when he hits the road again, he is saddled with her. She is his Shiralee — his burden. The child, however, is delighted to be with her father and on the road. As the child, Dana Wilson is a wonder: a miniature adult, all bustling efficiency when looking after her cherished possessions (a beat-up cloth animal toy and a bundle of comics), and clarity of purpose when trying both to keep up with her father and stay out of his way when his temper grows short. The film concentrates on Macauley's growing but reluctant feelings of responsibility and affection for his child which is brought to a crisis when Buster gets hit by a truck while Macauley is making love in the bush with a local girl.

Sitting outside the hospital, waiting to hear if his daughter will live, the camera closes in on Peter and he gives us a nice surprise. For instead of expressing grief, chagrin, remorse etc., all things we are expecting from him from having seen this situation many, many times before, Peter's thoughts clearly show him reconstructing the events in his mind from *Buster's* point of view; his realization of their mutual identity. As Buster, he sees himself walking down the road. Feels the sudden appearance from nowhere of the truck. Screech of brakes. Collision. Pain. Black-out. An immediate, riveting scene.

Peter's performance is excellent. Tough and irritable with humans, but gentle and easy with the nature that surrounds him and the tools of his trade.

On Rosemary's last day shooting, she announced that she was returning to London immediately to start rehearsing for Tyrone Guthrie's *Troilus and Cressida* at the Old Vic.

''I wish I could say that,'' said Peter, wistful for a moment. Then, cheering up, ''Ah, well. I'm going to Rome. You know Diana Graves?''

Rosemary nodded. ''She lives there now, doesn't she?''

''Yes. She's a great mate of mine. I'm going to visit her. I can't wait. Rome! The *history*!'' He smiled, quite happy now, ''For an Australian, you know ... '' and he went on about how he, an Australian, had been hungering and thirsting for the history and beauty of Rome all his life.

CHAPTER 14

Roman Fever and The Nun's Story

In 1956, B. R. "Bertie" Whiting and his wife, the abstract painter Lorri (sister of Australia's Prime Minister, Malcolm Fraser), had for many years been living in Rome. They were part of a group of painters, writers and just plain roisterers, who used to dine together regularly at the same friendly café. Among the English-speaking members of the group were Bridget Boland (whose friendship with Peter went back to her troublesome play *Damascus Blade*), Christopher Fry (when he was in Rome working on film scripts), Patrick and Jenny Cross and, at the centre of the group, the fragile but indomitable Diana Graves who had early given Peter such sterling support in his two crucial acting auditions. Because of a respiratory complaint, Diana had now retired from acting and was living in Rome.

One evening Diana rang Whiting. "A chum has arrived," she rasped. "And he's with a lady journalist and — you know — they're making me *nervous* darling, but he's a chum and come along and help out."

Whiting and Lorri dutifully went along to Diana's. The chum was Peter Finch and in an instant Whiting could see why Diana was nervous and why she needed helping out. Peter was displaying all the not-to-be-denied signs of an Australian sheep-shearer down on the town and determined to blow his pay cheque. He was fairly quivering in his effort to restrain himself from bustin' out, he was so rarin' to go. As for the lady journalist — a pretty young English girl sent by a national paper to do a story of Finch, she was no less avid.

"She's covering me!" said Peter of the journalist, laughing in delight.

"Every pore!" added the young girl, no less delighted.

Peter leered.

Diana coughed and exhaled a small sigh audible only to Bertie.

"We eased", recalled Whiting, "into a long evening." An evening, as it turned out, which was so long it stretched into two weeks. Peter and the girl journalist (who, inevitably, somewhere along the way became his girlfriend), both knife-keen to experience all the possible sights, sounds and tastes of Rome — sometimes all within the same hour — roared around the Eternal City dragging Diana and the Whitings, who eventually gave up their pretence of leading and simply tried to keep up.

At some point Diana gasped out the suggestion that they all go down to Positano and take a breather.

They went to Positano, wind-swept and deserted, caught their breaths and nearly lost them again along with their lives in a near-miss car accident on their way back to Rome.

Peter and Whiting had, of course, been aware from the start that they were both Australians. But, true cosmopolites that they were, they did not press the point. In fact, they barely referred to it until after their Positano trip. The Whitings, Peter and the girl journalist were all gathered together on Diana's terrace one morning for an eleven o'clock "heart starter". There sat Peter and Whiting: hung-over, unshaven, bloodshot, shaking and silent. Whiting looked at Peter and said, "Baden-Powell would be proud of us if he could see us now." Whiting pronounced this revered name in the way every Australian Boy Scout recognizes as the only *correct* way to pronounce the name of their Founder: *Barden Pool*.

Peter greeted the code words "Barden Pool" with a shout of surprise followed by howls of laughter which Whiting joined in. It was like a masonic handshake given in public; two members of a secret society declaring themselves openly. It was at that moment that Peter and Whiting's friendship blossomed, a friendship which was to last during the course of Peter's life. Whiting later became one of the executors to Peter's will though, characteristically, Peter neglected to inform Whiting of the arrangements.

Beginning with the Boy Scouts, Whiting and Peter discovered how much they had in common. They had both been at the same Scout jamborees — though they had danced around different campfires with their knobbly knees glistening. Further more, they had both attended the same school though — as Whiting was younger — at different times. And they had both passed through several camps in the war, both bored and frustrated. In fact Whiting had probably attended several army entertainments with Peter doing the entertaining without remembering either the concert or

Peter. Moreover, they had both worked as drovers over the same arid plains in the outback. They had, it seemed, missed each other by inches through the whole of their Australian youth.

Out of the complex of their experience and education and environment they became more than friends. They became brothers, blood-brothers: mates. They did not have to "explain" a joke to each other. Sometimes they did not even have to tell it; an exchanged look could set off a chain of identical associations, causing them suddenly to explode into — what was for others — incomprehensible laughter.

Whiting without his smile would be unrecognizable in a photograph. But behind the easy-going, affable, almost lazy manner, and behind the flattering readiness of a grin that engages all his features, is a mind acutely wondering and watching and reaching conclusions that are not always flattering.

Peter's friendship with Whiting was reminiscent of his friendship with Mac in the old days in Australia, though they were not remotely the same kind of people. Now Whiting, not Mac, was his "cinserest" critic and performed the same function: he told Peter the truth about himself as he saw it and without sparing his feelings. And, it must be added, he met with the same success as Mac. Peter listened. Peter thought. Peter said, "True, true." And Peter went and did what he was going to do anyway. Yet with Whiting (as with Mac) Peter both admired and needed to be near his integrity. Moreover, he knew how much both the Whitings genuinely cared about his development as an artist.

Says Whiting, "Lorri and I felt that Peter had a quality of greatness which deserved serious attention. When I talked to him about his failings — when I talk about them now — it is always from respect for a complicated man."

It was during Peter's first stay in Rome that he decided it must become his new headquarters. The city was so beautiful and so old he was dazzled by it. It was where his dear old friends Diana Graves and Bridget Boland lived. And where his dear new friends, the Whitings lived, who introduced him to all manner of exciting and *simpatico* people. For Rome at that time was not only a genuine centre for artists and writers but there really was (just like at the Cross!) an artistic *community* of such people as Alberto Moravia and the painters Gianni Novak and Gastone Novelli, who became Peter's special friends. In Rome, Peter had the comforting knowledge that if he turned up at a certain café at a certain time every day, he would be assured of seeing all these *simpatico* and amusing people; what is more, he was assured of the appreciation of his own work by people whose opinion he valued. By this time he had shed the pretty girl journalist who went tearfully back to England.

When Whiting asked what happened to her Peter said, shuddering, "She wanted to marry me and give 'important little dinners' for me. So I fled."

"Sounds pretty brutal," said Whiting.

Peter shrugged.

Soon after, Peter himself had to leave Rome for England. Pinewood was calling.

After he made *A Town Like Alice*, directed by Jack Lee and produced by Joe Janni (for Pinewood), all three men had been eager to work together again. The film decided upon was *Robbery Under Arms* from the Australian classic by Rolf Boldrewood. Peter would play Captain Starlight, the outlaw. When he returned to England, the script was ready and waiting for him in Olive Harding's office. But when Peter read it, he pronounced it vastly *un*ready and refused point blank to do it as it was. Janni and Lee agreed with Peter. Lee thought it needed months to get the script right. The Pinewood front office insisted they start immediately: the shooting schedule had been set and that was all that mattered to them. For a while it was stalemate.

To complicate matters further, Peter found to his delight that Yolande, his Girl on the Beach at Durban, had come to London as promised and had rung him at his mother's. This was the real beginning of their romance, and it was now that he realized to the fullest extent the devastating erotic effect they had upon each other. But Yolande, a true flirt, gave Peter a run for his money. She may have fallen like a ripe peach into his lap but she had no intention of rolling off and being squashed underfoot.

If he turned up late, an irritating habit he had, he might not only find her some place else but with someone else. If his eyes wandered in company (as they often did) to a pretty girl, Yolande would straightaway slap his face. Peter admired this direct approach.

Meanwhile — an unwelcome interruption to the romance — the *Robbery Under Arms* stalemate had to be broken. Peter still refused to do the script as it was. This led to Janni, Lee and Peter shutting themselves away for two weeks in a hotel, eating and sleeping there, while trying to do a rush rewrite of the script. As a co-script writer,

Jack Lee found Peter less than ideal. "If a man wakes up the first morning having decided to be a tree conservationist, the next morning a flamenco dancer, and the third, a Buddhist priest, he is not going to give of his best to a story line about nineteenth-century Australian outlaws," says Lee. This remark would be funny if there were not such tragic echoes in it of the child being forced into so many changing situations so quickly. "We were still writing the script while shooting in Australia and the script was never right," adds Lee.

Unfortunately, the anger both Peter and Lee felt against Pinewood for forcing them to shoot a bad unfinished script, spilled over on to each other, creating the kind of tension between director and actor that Peter was never able to cope with. They were on location in Australia for some months from the beginning of 1957 and it was not a pleasant experience for anyone.

In *Robbery Under Arms* Peter gallops through the Pinewood paste dressed all in black on a wonderful horse called Velox, the only creature in the film he related to. For the rest, the film rambles on incoherently.

In Sydney, before taking off to London, a big reception was held for Peter. An old actor chum of his, Chips Rafferty, rushed up to him embracing him warmly, at the same time saying, "I've got the most wonderful script, Finchie, can you give us £50,000 to do it?" This time Peter was ready, "I'll give you a fiver to be getting on with," he said, stepping back. "If I'd stayed in Australia another week they'd have had me back doing radio serials," he said to a friend later.

Back in London with Yolande, Peter, to his dismay, found himself jealous and possessive of her — as he had been earlier with Tamara. And again the discovery gave him great pain. His philosophy was supposed to shield him from that unworthy emotion. And yet ... once when he had telephoned Yolande from Australia he had been told she was in Paris. Why? Who with? And so forth.

Peter went to Corsica to film *Windom's Way* for Pinewood. Yolande went with him and their quarrels worked up to an explosion. Yolande went back to England to pursue her career and when Peter finished the film he went to Rome.

Interested spectators nodded their heads wisely. Yes, they said, the Peter-Yolande affair had been too hot not to cool down.

I wondered, when viewing *Windom's Way* recently, if it is not the most dated of all Peter's films now, sustaining, as it does, the pre-third-world myth of the White Man's Burden. Nevertheless, I not only liked it, I believed it. Peter is all gentleness and dedication. He works in his hospital for the welfare of the natives and is only able to climb into his white dinner jacket and sit exhausted on the verandah sipping gin rickeys with the rest of his white guests when he doesn't have an emergency operation to perform or an evil uprising to quell with a few well-placed words and a few deaths on his staff.

It was Peter's first role as a doctor and he was as convincing and capable in it as he was in his last doctor's role. Also times *were* changing — and for the first time Peter was to be seen in a passionate and fairly explicit love scene with Mary Ure on the beach. It was made even more effective by his particular look as he gazed at her; his eyes softening to velvet and his lips tensing to steel.

His effectiveness as a screen lover was duly noted at the box-office and when the time was ripe in the sixties, he was to land in bed on film making love many, many times.

In Rome, Peter acquired a penthouse apartment overlooking the Spanish Steps. It was during this visit that the Whitings were treated to the spectacle of Peter breaking out to his full limits — a spectacle that was to be repeated in varying degrees of intensity whenever he was in Rome. For Rome to Peter was always a holiday time, sheep-shearer-down-on-the-town-time.

Though he often touched base with the artistic community, he had built on top of it a dangerous superstructure of constant drinking, constant night-clubbing and what looked like compulsive sleeping around. The Whitings and the other artists viewed his behaviour with alarm. "Even making allowances for the artistic temperament, Peter always left us with a sense of waste — and the pity of it," says Whiting.

One facet of Peter's character that put almost as great a strain on the Whitings as his dissipation was his sentimentality, his "appalling" sentimentality as Whiting calls it. Though wincing, the Whitings were able to endure Peter asserting over and over and at mawkish length how much he loved them and how they were his only *important* friends; they could steel themselves as he proclaimed to strangers (embracing and kissing the Whitings to make his point) that "These are my dearest, my greatest friends"; and they were able to listen, though with increasing restlessness to Peter reliving his happy hours in the Boy Scouts. But one night Peter, looking "all squinny-eyed" and gently weeping, suddenly embarked on a long aria about how the most beautiful thing in the world to him was that a prostitute, for money, mind you, merely for *money*, would make love to you, would share a bed with you, would spend the whole night with you, to keep you from loneliness! This proved too much for Lorri. Grabbing the first thing handy, she bopped him over the head several times with a heavy volume of Croce's *Essays*.

Whiting considered Peter's behaviour to women, to his "monstrous regiment of women", terrible. "I want you to meet my fiancée," Peter once said, indicating a confused and reluctant girl. Then, to her, "What did you say your name was, dear?" Many of the women found their way to the Whitings' flat where they wept most bitterly about Peter. "At the flutter of an eyelash," says Whiting, "Peter would tell them he loved them. And then he would leave them." In answer to Whiting's "Why do you do it?" Peter would reply, "I just can't disappoint them. It would be rude."

Perhaps the real trouble was that Peter's code of behaviour was so odd and different and strange that he had no right to ask others to accept it.

One day Peter ran into his old friends Ken Adam, the film art director, and his wife Letitia, in Rome. Letitia looked at him and advised him to go away and have a rest. Peter agreed it was just what he needed. Letitia loaned him her house in Ischia and off he went. In Naples overnight, before embarking on the ferry to Ischia, he re-met Charles Vance, his stage-manager of *Daphne Laureola*, now a director. They decided to join up. "Peter's career seemed to be having its peculiarities for a change," said Vance. "He was fed-up especially with Pinewood — wanted to throw the whole thing in." Then, by the docks, Peter got friendly with an elderly Neapolitan character who met every boat and was known as the Philosopher of Naples. Intrigued, Peter asked him along as well. Vance remembers the next month or so in Letitia's house in Ischia. The Philosopher of Naples and Peter sat on two wooden chairs on the verandah lost in deep discussion; the former talking Italian and the latter English.

"You see!" said Peter once, turning triumphantly to Vance. "He agrees with me."

"He didn't understand a word you said," Vance pointed out.

"Of course he did," Peter insisted. "Didn't you see the light in his eye, his smile, his gestures?"

Oh well, thought Vance, it's a good way not to get into a fight.

Peter was happy in Ischia. Besides his philosophical discussions, he was painting and — as always — making friends with everyone. With the local people he adopted a habit of speaking "Italian", that is, without using a word of the actual language, his grasp of intonation, tone, rhythm and gesture was so perfect that he was often mistaken for a native.

His idyll ended when Olive found him and told him to go to Paris. Fred Zinnemann wanted to see him there for his new film with Audrey Hepburn. Peter put a knapsack on his back, caught the ferry back to Naples and walked to Paris.

The film Zinnemann wanted him for was *The Nun's Story*. He had to be in the Belgian Congo at the beginning of 1958 for shooting. Boarding Sabena, the Belgian airline, with trepidation, he had a terrible attack of flying fear as they flew to Stanleyville and a beautiful six-foot-tall air stewardess, Lucienne Van Loop, soothingly administered to him. Gratefully he proposed marriage to her and they saw a great deal of each other during the shooting of the film as she was always flying in and out of Stanleyville.

In *The Nun's Story,* after a long preparation as a novitiate, Audrey Hepburn, as Sister Luke, a young nun, goes to the Congo on her first mission. She is to work in the dispensary with Dr Fortunati (Peter Finch). Before she begins working she is warned about Fortunati by a sister nun. He is a devil, she is told. He drinks, he womanizes, he is without morals and will goad and harass her mercilessly. But, adds the nun, he is the most brilliant doctor in the Congo.

While assisting at her first operation Sister Luke closes her eyes and begins to sway. "I'd appreciate it if you didn't faint during an operation," Fortunati snaps at her. "I won't if you don't eat garlic before it," she replies.

Fortunati's startled eyebrows shoot up and his mouth flashes into his human frailty smile. Bulls-eye! he seems to be saying, but this should *not* be the reply of a submissive nun.

Contact is established, they grow to respect and care for each other — maybe even more than just care — but the more he knows her, the more he observes her, the more he sees what is tragically wrong with her. In an outstanding scene between Finch and Hepburn, he decides he must tell her the truth about herself.

Fortunati is aware that his unsavoury reputation will stand in the way of his being able to convince Sister Luke. But he also knows that the tragic misstep she has taken in becoming a nun is making her ill and could kill her. He has only one chance to succeed. His searing intelligence. His arguments must be strong and concisely arranged and he knows also that if he reveals one glimpse of his personal feelings for her, all is lost. "I've seen nuns come and go," he ends saying, "and I tell you this — you are not like them. *You have not got the vocation.*" It is like watching an operation performed without an anaesthetic. The operation is successful. The patient lives and eventually returns to secular life.

The Nun's Story made more money for Warner Brothers than any film in its history. Imagine! — the story of a nun a smash boffo at the box-office. It is the director Fred Zinnemann's opinion that the sincerity and intensity with which Audrey Hepburn and Peter Finch played their scenes together had most to do with its success. And so Peter Finch was discovered yet again.

CHAPTER 15

Yolande

While working on *The Nun's Story*, Peter had learned that Yolande Turner (as she was now calling herself) was opening in London in a play called *Roseland*. He sent her a cable of warm good wishes but he was probably too late as it closed immediately. Yolande herself, however, seemed to have made her point. She had appeared on stage wrapped only in a towel to be described enthusiastically by Milton Shulman in *The Evening Standard* as "built like a compromise between Marilyn Monroe and Joan Collins". And Kenneth Tynan felt she played her role "promisingly".

When Peter returned to London, he and Yolande got back together again and this time it looked as if they might stay together.

In the beginning of the summer of '58, Pinewood summoned Peter to Holland to make *Operation Amsterdam*. In this film the Pinewood paste proved so glutinous that Peter, apparently unable to wade through it on foot any longer, is seen mostly driving around Amsterdam in a car. Or, rather, unseen hands (and feet?) are driving him around, since Peter had never learned to drive. Three things emerged from this dreary film: a terminal row with air stewardess Van Loop in Peter's hotel room which disengaged them from each other, the beginning of a close friendship with his co-actor Tony Britton, and the much desired break between him and Pinewood, who shortly thereafter announced gruffly that they had dropped him.

Yolande and Peter settled down together in a house in Lyall Street in Belgravia. Flavia, Peter's sister, had been acting as his secretary, but Olive now wanted someone who would be a closer liaison between her and the new Finch *ménage*, so she asked Susan Coleman (already tried and tested in Olive's office) to be Peter's secretary.

"They were always in bed," says Susan of Peter and Yolande.

"No matter what time I went there, they were always in bed. And they had ripped out all the electric light wall-fixtures and put in candles for a romantic atmosphere."

She remembers Yolande as having great *savoir-faire* and a way of walking down the street that made everyone turn and stare at her. As she saw the couple in those days, Peter was utterly besotted with Yolande, while Yolande at all times remained coolly in charge. Susan felt that Yolande was also a bit too coolly in charge of her, Peter's secretary, high-handedly issuing commands that sent her out in the London rain on whatever whim of an errand she fancied at the moment. She also remembers the Lyall Street house having its share of hangers-on wandering in and out — mostly Australians down on their luck.

Because of the self-blinding quality of their physical love, Peter and Yolande ignored their very real and basic differences. Peter blinded himself to the fact that Yolande not only had serious ambitions as an actress but expensive tastes, and she liked to sparkle socially. In the same way, Yolande blinded herself to Peter's real love of vagabonding — and of farming. Farming had been on his mind as far back as his twenty-ninth birthday when he wrote to Tamara from the army hospital, "talked well into the night with the bushman in the next bed about planting seeds and vegetable gardening. I can hardly wait to get a piece of land and start experimenting."

"One side of him always longed for simple manual labour," says Whiting. "He dreamt of vegetable gardens and also of joining a road gang and digging trenches for gas pipes."

There was something else wrong with Peter and Yolande as a pair: something psychologically wrong that neither of them would have been aware of at the time, nor would they have had the power to correct. It would never be possible in any way for Peter to see this lovely, young, sophisticated, white South African girl as a victim or an underdog; that surge of sympathy so necessary and particular and peculiar to Peter could never be bestowed upon her.

Peter wanted to marry Yolande and Tamara agreed to a divorce. Though they had been seeing each other, they had now been living apart for three years and they had a quiet divorce. Peter stayed overnight in a hotel with an unnamed woman and the divorce was granted to Tamara on the grounds of adultery on 11 December 1958.

During and after the divorce and at all times in her relationship with Peter, Tamara behaved with a dignity that is, perhaps, not natural in these times. She did not tell her story to the press. She did not tell his story to the press. Nor did she tell their story to the press. She went about her own life bringing up Anita, publishing a book of Russian fairy tales called *The Little King* and becoming a Russian-English interpreter in the course of which she served as interpreter for Shirley Williams and Queen Elizabeth.

As for Peter, he would often return to see Tamara, as if looking for his former self, "when all the world and love was young". But their meetings were increasingly stormy. He would start off in the direction of Tamara's house with the best intentions and then somewhere along the way he would undergo a sea-change; by the time he arrived he would be drunk and truculent as if somehow it was Tamara who had deserted him. There would be rows that would awaken and frighten Anita, reaching their climax when he discovered that Tamara had taken a lover. Then for a time Tamara would find herself scanning the newspapers for his whereabouts, always relieved when she read that he was out of the country.

In June of '59 Peter's divorce became absolute and on 4 July, Peter and Yolande married at the Chelsea Registrar's Office, had their reception at L'Escargot, Peter's favourite Soho restaurant, and then set out for Hollywood where Peter was to film *The Sins of Rachel Cade* with Angie Dickinson.

Before this, Peter played Alan Breck Stewart in Walt Disney's (and Robert Louis Stevenson's) *Kidnapped*, a flabby script not quite counteracted by lovely shots of the Highlands, and Peter as the swash-buckling hero not quite swashing enough in his buckling.

Peter had also returned briefly to the stage. On 17 December 1958, at the Haymarket, he starred in *Two for the Seesaw*, a two-handed bittersweet comedy with Gerry Jedd about a love affair between an outgoing Jewish waif and a middle-western Wasp lawyer, that had an enormous success on Broadway with Anne Bancroft and Henry Fonda.

I, myself, found Peter as an American convincing — but — there are Americans and Americans, and for me, Peter's American was too warm. Henry Fonda's quality of Puritan reserve caught the dryness of the wind-swept prairies, throwing Anne Bancroft's Jewishness into focus for the needed contrast. And, it must also be added, Fonda possesses one of the most brilliant comedy techniques of any American actor.

Angus Wilson, reviewing for *The Observer* said, "The comic

aspects of the affair often elude Peter Finch's laboured rhythms.'' This, however, might be said to be balanced (or mitigated) by Harold Hobson calling Peter's speech in the last act on ''what love means to him'', ''the best thing in the play''. And Hobson also found it worth taking time to describe Peter delivering it ''without rhetoric, half apologetically, true to the one inescapable thing in his nature, but grievously aware that it may break the heart of the girl who hears it and whose tender but inexorable dismissal it is''. Once again a critic pays tribute to Peter's genius for handling long speeches; his inspiration flew heavenwards while at his feet the audience sat spellbound in the ''listening hush''.

Two for the Seesaw played for four months, one month too long for Peter who was feeling bored, tied down, and longing for a change.

CHAPTER 16

Hollywood Revisited; The Day

Just married and en route to Hollywood for the filming of *Rachel Cade*, Peter and Yolande stopped off in New York. Though it was Peter's first time there, only three things seemed to have impressed him: the first all-black straight Broadway play, *Raisin in the Sun*, the black jazz at *Birdland* and the size of the Radio City Music Hall, where *The Nun's Story* was playing. After these discoveries the Finches went on to Hollywood.

Hollywood: this was the second time around for Peter and he liked it no better than the first time. It brought out the very worst in him. Yolande, newly married, newly-discovered pregnant and friendless in a strange town was quickly finding out what an indifferent husband and committed bum Peter could be.

While Peter worked all day at the studio, Yolande sat in their sanitized, push-buttoned, rented apartment somewhere in that Nowhere City, with nothing to look forward to but her morning sickness every day. When invitations did come for parties and cocktails, they were abruptly turned down by Peter who preferred to do his socializing pub-crawling up and down Sunset Strip or in the rougher parts of downtown Los Angeles.

Yolande had a lively temper and a sharp tongue and she was not one to keep her impatience bottled inside. Peter was forty-three now, she was fond of reminding him, and that was eighteen years older than she was. Wasn't he just a little too old still to be playing at swagman, or whatever he thought he was playing at? And wasn't she just a little too young to start knitting? One night, driving down Sunset Strip, Yolande at the wheel wondering gloomily where all the fun was and what all the stars were doing, she glanced at her husband at her side drinking deeply from a bottle of tequila. Suddenly she saw red, opened the door on his side and threw him out of the car. Having second thoughts, she backed up to look for him but could not find him. Frantically worried for the rest of the night, she was ready to call the police when he stumbled into the flat at five in the morning and fell into bed without a word of explanation. At that moment, to Yolande, the marriage must have seemed impossible already, the honeymoon over ... and the baby still to come.

"That little piece of paper," Peter liked to say sorrowfully of the wedding certificate, "that little piece of paper, it *changes* them." But in fact it was Peter it changed — right into an old-fashioned Australian husband back-from-a-three-day-spree-and-no-questions-asked.

The film Peter was making, *The Sins of Rachel Cade*, was terrible. No doubt this coloured his attitude. It had what he was to refer to as a bad case of "script poisoning". Script poisoning, Peter explained, is what a script catches when it is initially weak, and everyone assures you it is going to get better. Invariably it gets worse, poisoned by everyone in sight who begins meddling with it. The idea of *Rachel Cade* was suspect from the start. Since *The Nun's Story* had been such a winner, went the thinking, why not make another film almost like it? A sort of *Daughter of Nun's Story*? So we are back in the Congo, only this time with Angie Dickinson instead of Audrey Hepburn. She's a missionary nurse, not a nun, and the doctor is Roger Moore (hello) not Peter Finch. And he (Moore) gets her (Angie) pregnant. Peter is a colonel in the Belgian army who ... well perhaps it is not very like *The Nun's Story*. Anyway, it was awful.

"All right," said Peter to Yolande one night. "Let's go to some bloody cocktail party." They went. Peter, looking as if reluctantly dragged by a string of wild horses, immediately headed for the Least Important Person in the Room and spent the rest of his time there with him. And again, still reluctantly, he allowed himself to be led to a dinner party Darryl Zanuck was giving for him to meet Shirley MacLaine. Peter sat through it silently, not drinking, not talking, not smiling. "Bored and boring," remembered Yolande, with exasperation.

Peter had very good manners, but his manners were the instinctive ones of the natural man; he had never cultivated the social graces. Peter had no small talk. One would not choose him as a dinner partner; he had no dinner conversation. At the table he was definitely what inveterate diners-out would label a "non-conductor". At Notley Abbey he could listen happily for hours as the great actors around him reminisced. With his mates he talked shop, spouted poetry, philosophised. He was a great story-teller, not a great conversationalist, and they are two very different things. He was shy, often tongue-tied and out of his depth with sophisticated people. His profound insecurity would surface both in what is known as "polite company" and with people who had the naked power of Zanuck.

But underneath it all, Peter had another reason for not bothering with the Hollywood élite or playing the Hollywood game. Highly sensitive to every nuance of atmosphere from childhood on, he did not have to be told what he already sensed, which was that if Hollywood had only been "scared" in his first visit in 1953, it was now "finished" (for the time being) in 1959. For Peter, at this point, Hollywood was not only unwanted but unneeded. He had been watching for some time now how the New Waves, rolling in from Europe — from France, Italy and England, especially — were beginning to pound the West Coast into an insensibility that lasted throughout the sixties.

In England, for instance, in 1957, Laurence Olivier, sniffing the winds of change, crossed the street from Stratford and the West End and bounded on to the stage at the Royal Court to join the rebels there in John Osborne's *The Entertainer*. He also married his leading lady, Joan Plowright.

Rex Harrison followed. He crossed over from Broadway, did a little known Chekhov play, *Platanov*, at the Royal Court and married *his* leading lady, Rachel Roberts. Old Wave and New Wave had joined, and the Royal Court was firmly on the map. Then the Royal Court management, George Devine, Oscar Lewenstein, Tony Richardson and John Osborne formed a film company called Woodfall Productions and began making successful New-Wave films like *A Taste of Honey* and Karel Reisz's *Saturday Night and Sunday Morning*.

It is incredible, looking back now, to realize that in the space of only five short years, from '59 to '64, the great European New Wave had exuberantly produced such notable films as Fellini's *La Dolce Vita* and *8½*; Renais' *Hiroshima, Mon Amour* and *Last Year at Marienbad*; Antonioni's *L'Avventura* and *La Notte*; Visconti's *Rocco and His Brothers*; Truffaut's *Jules et Jim, The Four Hundred Blows* and *Shoot the Pianist*; Godard's *Breathless*; De Sica's *Umberto D*; Clayton's *Room at the Top*; Tony Richardson's *Tom Jones*; and The Beatles' *A Hard Day's Night*.

It was also during those five short years that many of the brightest and the best in Hollywood were streaming across to Europe. Stanley Kubrick settled in England and made *Lolita* and *Dr Strangelove*. Carl Foreman also settled in England and proved that an American-English mixture could create giant blockbusters like *The Bridge on the River Kwai* and *The Guns of Navarone*. While Sam Spiegel, based on his yacht, proved exactly the same thing with *Lawrence of Arabia*.

It began to look as if making a film was so easy that anyone could play. The French invented the impressive word "auteur" (later translated into plain "film-maker") to describe someone who not only had the idea of a film but financed it, wrote it, cast it, directed it, cut and edited it, and also held the camera when he felt like it.

Under the circumstances, it is no wonder that Peter could not wait to leave those poor, tired, old sins of Rachel Cade and get back to the fresh waters foaming around the European shores. And in a part of his mind, he was beginning to form a plan ...

Back in London, Peter and Yolande removed themselves from Lyall Street and set up their home in a house in Sydney Street, Chelsea, which provided more adequate quarters for their coming child. One of the first things Peter did on his return was get a hold of his old friend Johnny von Kotze, the cameraman on *Elephant Walk* who had been such a mate of his in Ceylon. Peter wished to become an *auteur*. Why not? God knows, by now he had had enough experience on one side of the camera. Now was *his* chance to make a statement! Johnny was immediately infected with Peter's enthusiasm for the project and so was Yolande. The three of them embarked for Ibiza in the winter of '59. Peter and Yolande had visited this island once before and Peter felt it would be the ideal location for the story he had in mind; a story, he told Johnny, he had been thinking about ever since he was a child. And besides, Peter had bought a farm there — or rather, since this was impossible for a foreigner to do, had leased it from the Spanish government.

The Day, Peter's film which won an award in Venice the next year, was shot by Johnny von Kotze, directed and written by Peter, with Yolande acting as continuity girl. The central character and subject matter of *The Day* will come as no surprise to readers of Peter Finch's biography. It concerns a little Ibizan boy aged nine and it follows him through the day as he journeys from his father's farm to a distant town on the other side of the island, which he must reach in order to tell his relatives of the new baby that has been born. On the way, we watch him responding to the things that give him pleasure, like crawling insects and flowing water, and things that frighten him, like scarecrows and flapping laundry. Psychologically, this film is very clearly a symbolic re-working of the most important year of Peter's life when, at nine, he journeyed to India to be converted to Buddhism and then to Australia to be "reborn". And it was to those distant Australian relatives that Peter had to announce his own birth.

For Peter as a director, von Kotze had nothing but praise. "His sense of composition was beautiful. His tone values, his ability to express to his cameraman, his editor, his actors precisely what he wanted would have made him a very great director. I'd seen Carol Reed work with the little boy in *Fallen Idol*. Reed couldn't make the boy understand it. He could get the boy to mimic him, but Finchie got the boy to actually understand what it was about. He had an extraordinary sense of communication. We saw *The Day* as an exercise for bigger things. We wanted to go into production together on a feature film, with Peter directing. We kept looking for a suitable project. Finally Peter came up with Derek Monsey's book *The Hero*.

"Yolande was dragging her feet a bit at this *auteur* business in Ibiza," says von Kotze. "First of all it was winter there. I mean it was cold and there was snow. Second of all there was no big social scene." (This was an understatement. At that time the Ibizan winter population consisted almost solely of goats.) "Also," continues von Kotze, "you could say that Yolande was married to a film star and that was what she wanted to go on being married to. Directors were two-a-penny in her mind, but film stars weren't."

Nevertheless, Peter managed to prevail upon Yolande to stay in Ibiza and farm awhile. This farm has been referred to by Whiting as "the farm on which Peter grew one potato crop, and a more unlikely potato farmer I have yet to see." Olive Harding refers to it as "a fruit farm of some sort — orange trees, but then I had a cable from Peter saying that the orange trees didn't work and they were going to grow plums and so he needed some money sent over and the British Inspector of Taxes stepped in and said 'No'. So I went and faced the Inspector for several hours trying to make him see that if you can't grow oranges you *have* to grow plums, and if you're putting in plum trees you have to have a special water supply because the water was very short, so I *had* to send Peter out a pump and the pump had to be put in very far down in a sort of brick-surrounding thing, and by now it was eight-thirty in the evening and the Inspector said, 'Yes, yes, anything you say. I'm very tired and I just want to go home to my dinner.' But you see, there again, you had to do everything for Peter. Everything!''

Happily for the world, either Yolande finally put her foot down, or Peter threw his towel into the water tank. For whatever reason, the Finches left their Ibizan farm early in 1960 in the care of a rather suspect German and came back to London, where Peter faced one of the greatest challenges of his life.

CHAPTER 17

The Importance of Oscar Wilde

When the news flowed down the Buckstone pipeline and down the newer pipeline, the White Elephant, as well, it seemed as if the entire theatrical community of both clubs turned Gielgudian Inquisitor and fell to demanding of each other whether they had heard the curious rumour that "*Peter Finch* was going to play *Oscar Wilde*?" (pause) "In a *film*?" (pause) "Directed by *Ken Hughes*?" (this last given the full, mounting, incredulous delivery and allowed to fall to earth like lead).

Ken Hughes, of Liverpool, was a pro right down to his toes, known as "The man who can put six flicks in one year in the can", as he had in 1955. But they all had contemporary titles like *Timeslip*, *Joe Macbeth*, *Murder Anonymous*, *The Brain Machine*, *Night Plane to Amsterdam* and *Confession*. The guy had plenty of savvy sure, but well, what would — you know — what would his sense of *period* be like? As for Peter Finch as Oscar Wilde? That wiry, virile Australian? That was not going to make much sense either. Then came the news that Robert Morley was also going to make a film about Oscar Wilde. Now that *did* make sense. Morley was fat, experienced, accomplished and had made a huge hit on Broadway with the stage play of *Oscar Wilde*. Nevertheless, the Finch rumour was true. And both films were going to be made at the same time.

The only one who seemed completely unperturbed by all the fuss was Peter's old friend Ken Adam, the Art Director-Production Designer for the film. "Why not Peter Finch?" asked Ken Adam at the time. "He's a very fine actor and a very popular actor and he wants to do it and I don't know anyone else who could. Maybe Robert Morley looks more like Oscar Wilde, but he looks more like Oscar Wilde at a very late stage of his life. Not the period we're interested in. As for Ken Hughes, we did a film together. It was called *In the Nick*, I think. I like working with him."

"*Oscar Wilde* was a challenge," says Ken Adam today, looking back. "And we rose to it. The whole studio rose to it — carpenters, electricians, everyone. I can only compare it in spirit and feeling with some of my war-time experiences [Adam was an R.A.F. fighter pilot]. It created a comradeship amongst all of us. And on the creative side it was Ken Hughes, who had also written the script (drawing on two excellent sources: John Fernald's play *Oscar Wilde* and Montgomery Hyde's book of the Oscar Wilde trials), myself and Peter. And we worked very closely as a trio."

On the creative side also they had the services of the great cinematographer Nicolas Roeg, as well as two of the best English actors James Mason and Lionel Jeffries in the key roles of the Prosecutor for the Defence, Sir Edward Carson and the Marquess of Queensberry. It was Peter, two Kens, Nick, James and Lionel. And Oscar. That was the strength of the team. And, like the R.A.F. in the war, it proved unbeatable.

So Peter, the boy who could "become anything", was going to become Oscar Wilde. He did not have time on his side. There was going to be a very tight shooting schedule of only six weeks to try to beat the Morley *Oscar Wilde* to the post and Peter had to fling himself into a weight-gaining diet of bread, potatoes and six double-whiskies a day to put on fourteen pounds before shooting started in the beginning of April.

Peter did not have time on his side but he did have love and admiration close to worship for Oscar Wilde.

Back in 1950, while playing in *Daphne Laureola*, Peter's favourite pub was the nearby Salisbury. He and his Australian mate, Al Thomas, planned to meet there one night. When they did, "Don't sit there!" Peter suddenly cried out to Al, arresting him in mid-air. Al looked at him for an explanation. "Oscar Wilde used to sit exactly there," said Peter as one who would not let sacred ground be defiled.

Peter had loved the works of Oscar Wilde all his life. Perhaps it was not so much that three of Wilde's best plays revolve around the discovery of the hero or heroine's parents (after all, the majority of the Victorian and Edwardian novels he had read in his grandfather's study had the same theme) but in one in particular, *The Importance of Being Earnest*, Wilde could be uproariously funny about it.

Lady Bracknell: Are your parents living?
Jack: I have lost both my parents.

Lady Bracknell: To lose one parent, Mr Worthing, may be regarded as a misfortune. To lose both looks like carelessness.

The relief Peter had felt at being able to laugh at that! To be able to make someone, at last, able to laugh at his pain was surely one of the highest uses literature could be put to.

Peter became obsessed with Oscar Wilde as he drew nearer and nearer to him. An interview he gave to *Films and Filming* around that time gives us an insight on how he worked himself into a role.

"When I approach a part I have a process of unconscious absorption into the character. I do not make meticulous notes on the script or work out exterior business. But when I am thinking of a character I amuse myself by trying to think of his reactions to hypothetical situations, not only the situations in the script. It is something of a game, a bit of fun almost, that helps you feel you have created a mind for him."

This disclosure of how he worked, with its emphasis on the "fun" and the "play" aspect of it, makes it clear how much of the child was always involved in Peter's creativity.

Peter's friends were by now familiar with his habit of living his parts off-stage. Nevertheless, when Ken Adam came over to his house one night and found Peter drinking champagne (Oscar's but not Peter's drink) and directing endless witticisms into the shell-like ear of Diana Graves' fifteen-year-old son, Adam exclaimed in mock-horror, "Peter! You don't have to go that far!" And Peter actually blushed.

With his performance in *The Trials of Oscar Wilde*, Peter moved into the First Circle of the Elect. It is, perhaps, in this role more than any of his others that he justifies Rosemary Harris' dictum, "Peter Finch did not act his parts, he understood them. He understood their love and their pain ... "

"Show me a hero," said F. Scott Fitzgerald, "and I will write you a tragedy." Oscar Wilde was the hero of his day. He had held sway for nearly twenty years, first as the darling of the drawing-room, then as a star lecturer (it was Oscar who electrified the astonished Americans and brought Culture to Buffalo in the seventies), then as a poet, novelist and short-story writer and finally as a universally acclaimed playwright. The story of Oscar Wilde is not only the story of the fall of a hero. It is something of far more dread: it is the fall of a hero brought about by himself.

Discussion of Peter as Oscar Wilde must be prefaced with a

confession on this biographer's part that, although I have seen this film many times, I have never been able at any showing of it to forgo the pleasure of surrendering myself wholly to Peter's performance. Each time I have seen it, the magic of Peter's performance is evident almost from the beginning when Oscar Wilde at the height of his glory descends the St James Theatre staircase where *Lady Windemere's Fan* has just triumphantly opened, addresses a Wildean remark to a grateful Bernard Shaw, tells his disappointed wife that he will not be home for supper, steps in between Bosie and his father, the Marquess of Queensberry, and quells their over-heated quarrelling, puts on his top hat and carries off Bosie. My analytic powers cease to work, and I am simply watching Oscar step by step as he takes his terrible and pitiful journey towards his downfall.

Since Peter's Oscar Wilde defeated, or rather triumphed, over my objectivity, I cannot possibly say what Peter Finch's Oscar was like; only what Oscar was like as Peter understood him.

Oscar Wilde was naturally flamboyant in the way that many of the Irish are; but he also projected a unique, instantly recognizable silhouette which only the famous do. He was attractive, kind, good-natured, effortlessly witty and pleasantly crowd-pleasing. He wore his legend-in-a-lifetime lightly so that one rarely saw the underlying strain it caused him. His voice was extraordinarily musical. He was chubby rather than gross. His full lips and his movements were those of a deeply sensual man. His constant cigarette (gold-tipped) was a substitute for nerves.

The Great Importance of Oscar was that by his art he had success-fully kept nature under a kind of control so that he could live and function in spite of the boiling inferno of love, pain, pride, inexpressible fear, and the need to sin churning inside him. As long as Oscar, by his mode of behaviour and his epigrams and paradoxes could extract the pain from a situation and turn it into laughter, all was well and he was safe.

The film, as I have intimated, begins *in media res*. And it never lets up. It has an energy, vitality and pace rarely seen in English films that can only be compared to those television masterpieces *The Forsyte Saga* and *Upstairs, Downstairs*, both of which it resembles also in the pith and punch of its dialogue. Each scene, no matter how brief, serves a twofold purpose: to drive on the action, and to make a character point. It is edge-of-the-seat all the way and the characters establish themselves as quickly as the script does. The

Marquess of Queensberry begins in a towering rage and builds from there. Oscar's wife (Yvonne Mitchell) is passive and put-upon and goes quickly from uneasy to desperate. Ada Leverson (Maxine Audley) is not only loyal and concerned but (a nice touch) slightly meddlesome. Bosie (John Fraser) is irresponsible, selfish and tinged with his father's madness. His dependence on Wilde quickly becomes hysterically neurotic.

At Oscar's first trial, the disastrous one which begins with him prosecuting Queensberry and ends with him liable to prosecution, Oscar looks over at Sir Edward Carson, the Prosecutor for the Defence and turns to his Q.C., Sir Edward Clarke, saying, "I went to school with him, Trinity. No doubt he will perform his task with all the added bitterness of an old friend."

The first close-up of James Mason, glowering and saturnine, leaves one in no doubt that he will be performing his task with all the added viciousness of an ancient enemy.

But though Carson's tone is strident, insinuating, almost savage, his inflections rising as if trying to disassociate themselves from the disgust he feels, his first question to Oscar is merely to ask him to restate his age. "I'm thirty-nine," says Oscar. "But that cannot be," states Carson in the same tone. "Wilde was born in 1854 and is therefore 'in his forties'." Oscar is, in fact, forty-one. Only two years off. But Carson *knows* Oscar. He went to school with him. He knows his weaknesses. And indeed it is the only time in the trial that Oscar is speechless. He smiles, shrugs, shifts his weight as if he himself does not understand what made him insist on being still in his thirties. And this does not go down well in court. But he quickly recovers and his subsequent answers on the relationship between literature and morality are so brilliant that the court resounds with the sweet sound of laughter and Carson begins to look like a philistine. Carson changes tactics. Once he even joins in the general laughter. Then he moves on to soirées with stable boys, and suddenly he is talking about a young man who had been Bosie's servant at Oxford and, without a hint of bullying but simply and ingenuously, he asks Oscar, "Did you kiss him?"

Just before the trial, Oscar could say to a friend, "Don't distress yourself. The working classes are with me — to a boy", and expect this remark to be received with laughter, which it was. But Oscar could *not* say before a judge and a jury, in answer to Carson's "Did you kiss him?", "Oh dear no. He was unfortunately extremely ugly" and expect this remark to be greeted in the same fashion. It was not. That Oscar could not understand why and that Carson, knowing Oscar, knew he would not understand why, is the key to Oscar's downfall. Oscar, with these words, was damned irrevocably for mistaking a court-room for a drawing-room. As played by Morley, Oscar at this juncture breaks down completely, blubbering histrionically. Peter does not. He keeps talking. He explains perplexedly that he was making a jest because he was so astonished at Carson's insolence. Only gradually does it all dawn on him. Said the critic Alexander Walker of Peter's version of Oscar on trial, "It is a human life we have watched expand and close: not a legal set-piece." For the rest of the cross-examination there is Carson's voice striding juggernaut over and back — over and back — Oscar's liquid tones and soft padded body.

As a turn of the century piece, sets were of great importance. "I experimented in colour", says Ken Adam, "more than I ever had before. Each set had a definite colour scheme and a definite predominate colour that was an expression of what was going on on the set. I was working within a very small budget and yet it seemed that the less money I had, the better the set.

"The set most people complimented me on was the great hall in Queensberry's castle. Obviously this was my favourite set and I was delighted when the critics singled it out. They felt it had such realism. Actually, it wasn't realistic. It was completely stylized. I only had £750 for the set, so I had to use elements of other sets like the columns of the St James Theatre and the doors from some other set and so forth. I found a gigantic fireplace and the stone floor was all made out of paper and planks. And then I decided by careful colour control I could achieve a very interesting effect. It was just after the funeral of one of the Queensberry sons so I treated all the walls in a terracotta colour and the doors, fireplace, columns and everything else in black. Those were the only two colours, terracotta and black. And I insisted that all the costumes be in black. And when Ken Hughes came on the set, he was very impressed with it and he said, 'Fantastic! I'm going to stylize the acting in this scene too.' "

The result is that these rigid figures in black, the Marquess of Queensberry, the Marchioness and Bosie — father, mother and son — become Euripidean characters hurling dire imprecations upon each other, gouged out of their blood hatreds; while the absent Oscar is suddenly reduced to a mere pawn in their deadly game.

Up till then, of all the characters Peter had played, Oscar Wilde was the closest to him. He found a great resemblance to himself in

Macauley in *The Shiralee* but it was a superficial one. It is true that Macauley is outside the bourgeois society, but the character does not take into account either Peter's intelligence or his artistry, or his love or his pain. Oscar Wilde was a genius and Peter was sometimes brushed with genius. Like Oscar, Peter's sensuality and temperament would not allow him to live within the limits of the bourgeois civilization. He was in fact a man who was so much at odds with it that he had to invent his own country: the film set. For Peter, as for Oscar, reality was filled with a threatening hostility.

Ten days after completing *Oscar Wilde*, Peter gave an interview to the *Sunday Dispatch*, describing the experience. "I worked for six days a week. My wife was to have the baby just as we got to the trial scene [their daughter Samantha, who was born in April] and she was two days in labour. There were eight Peters on that set and every time the phone went we all rushed to it. I got into a terrible state. One morning I drove to work and found I had checked into the wrong studio. I went home one night and began to read some of Wilde's poetry. And as I began to read, quite suddenly and involuntarily, I began to cry. It was terrifying. In the end I was sobbing. I could hear my own wracking noises and there was nothing I could do about it. Playing the part of a man who has destroyed himself isn't easy."

Robert Morley's *Oscar Wilde* won the race. It reached the cinemas before Peter's. But though it won the race, it lost the glory, for it was Peter's performance that won the critics and the prizes. In 1960 Peter won his second British Film Academy Award for his Oscar Wilde. And in 1961, he won the Moscow Festival Award for the same. As Alexander Walker said in the *Evening Standard*, "Believe me, Robert Morley's version looks like a pigmy production beside Peter Finch's. Here is a tragedy laid bare to the heart, given heroic stature."

After Peter's brilliant success in *The Trials of Oscar Wilde*, knowing the "peculiarities" of his career, one was tensed for his next film to be a resounding flop. Strangely, it was not. In the middle of that summer Peter was at work again shooting *No Love for Johnnie*, the story of a careerist Labour M.P. based on the novel by William Fienburgh. Johnnie Byrne (Peter Finch), though a member of the people's party, is not in it for the people-in-the-street, nor even for the people in his constituency. He is in it to escape from the wrong side of the tracks which happens to be his home in a depressed area up North.

"I liked the man better as Peter played him than I would have if I had met him," said Paddy Chayefsky. And although this might imply that Peter had softened the character, in fact he achieves our sympathy by doing just the opposite. He plays Johnnie full out, revealing rather than concealing, with the result that there is something ingenuous, even sympathetic about the transparent but strenuous conniving Johnnie goes in for to keep on the right side of the power factions in Parliament, regardless of what the issues are. We are not always on the side of the angels, but we are on the side of the strivers. When Johnnie, found out, is called back to face the fierce and angry members of his constituency, he narrowly escapes a vote of no confidence. With ineffable relief he rushes to the lavatory and we hear him throwing up. It is not just that he wants to stay in Parliament, it is that he hates and fears, and is so deeply ashamed of where he comes from.

Back in London, he lets his wife walk out on him, holds the eager girl upstairs in abeyance, falls seriously in love with a very young, very innocent, very beautiful girl. Peter, as usual, works so beautifully with his leading lady (Mary Peach) that their love story — that of a middle-aged man rediscovering himself through the love of a twenty-year-old girl — with its passionate bed scenes (three years more explicit than *Windom's Way* — 1960 was the dawn of the permissive age) was so lyrical that as one critic said, "It hardly mattered what Johnnie's career was."

In 1961, for his role in *No Love for Johnnie*, Peter won his third British Film Academy Award and also, in the same year, the Berlin Film Festival award.

CHAPTER 18

Peter Breaks Down

One evening in autumn found Peter sitting at his kitchen table in Sydney Street. He had been sitting there for two hours, along with three other people: two on his left and one on his right. The two on his left were his old friend George Devine of the Royal Court, and a poet Christopher Logue. On his right was also an old friend, Liz Taylor. For two hours now each had been pressing Peter to decide in their favour. Or rather Devine and Liz had. Logue was sitting quietly wishing his director Lindsay Anderson was there in his place. Devine and Logue wanted Peter to play Creon in Logue's verse adaptation of *Antigone*, to open at the Royal Court in November. And Liz wanted him to play Caesar in her film *Cleopatra*. Peter was much attracted to the Logue play. He knew no one could speak verse better than he could. As for Devine, of all the people in the theatre besides Larry, Peter revered him most. Here was the New Wave nibbling enticingly at his toes. Why not join in as Larry had? On the other hand, there was Liz, a *very* old friend, and who knew? Maybe her wave was a great deal higher, would make a much bigger splash and get him that international status he so needed and desired, and then he could do what he really wanted to. Or not do anything and go back to being a bum again. David Selznick had wanted Peter, had offered him Dick Diver in *Tender is the Night*, but the catch was that Selznick wanted to sign him up for seven years. Not after Pinewood, said Peter. But *Cleopatra* was a one-picture deal. Better take it. What could he lose? He chose it. "I think the formidable and inhibitory presence of Liz Taylor was a contributing factor," says Logue.

Peter began shooting *Cleopatra*. Liz Taylor fell dangerously ill and was rushed to the London Clinic for a tracheotomy. In order to collect the insurance for Liz's absence, the shooting schedule now had a lunatic requirement: it could not go forward, but it had to keep *going*. So Peter was collected by the studio car every morning and driven down to the studio, where all day he was made to walk down a gangplank, put his foot on the ship, and then take it off and turn around ready for the repeat shot. Every night when Peter got home he called Olive. "What do I do?" he asked. "I can't go on like this." And Olive always said the same thing, "I don't know how long Liz's going to be ill."

How many times must Peter have thought of that scene in the kitchen, and wondered if this was retribution.

On the fourteenth day, Peter was driven to the studio as usual. As he started down the gangplank he felt very queer. In the lunch-break he changed his clothes and went off by himself to a nearby pub. He happened to glance at a newspaper there and read the headline: Gilbert Harding Dead. Gilbert Harding dead! Another "Up yours!" man dead. Last year at just this time, Errol Flynn had died in Vancouver. Glorious Flynn! How he missed him. What a gorgeous row he would have kicked up on the very first day of this Caesar fiasco. And Harding too. He wouldn't have taken it. "Cricklewood! Are we to be spared nothing?" But Peter had spent fourteen days on that crazy set meekly obeying. Why? Why couldn't he "Up yours!"? Why? He felt disorientated. What was he going to do? They were all dying off! He found his driver and told him to get him home quickly.

It happened that Diana Graves was staying in London at the time. She rang Tony Britton sounding worried. "Did you by any chance get a call from Peter?" she asked.

"Christ, yes!" said Tony.

"Oh. What did he say?"

"He said, 'Oh mate, Gilbert's dead! Dear old Gilbert died.' And then he began crying and saying over and over again 'What are we going to do? What are we going to do?' He was going on something alarming about Gilbert Harding dying and I thought, what in hell has it got to do with you? You scarcely knew him. But I don't think he was pissed. Did he call you?"

"Several times," said Diana. "He's calling everyone and going on about Harding. I think he's having a nervous breakdown. I think I'd better go over there and see."

Olive received a phone call too. It was Yolande. "Come quickly," she said in a frightened voice. "Peter's ill."

Olive and Diana arrived, one on the heels of the other and a white-faced Yolande showed them into the sitting-room. The room was bare. Peter had removed all the carpeting and the furniture, except for a large armchair in which he sat stiff and upright, like Caesar. Frozen. Not speaking and not doing anything. Olive tried to speak to him but got no answer. Nor did Yolande or Diana. "It was a terrifying sight," says Olive. "His eyes had gone. Everything about him looked absolutely gone." They called a doctor who arranged for Peter to go into a nursing home where he stayed two weeks.

Tony Britton went to visit him there. "He was put in a large, dark, quiet room and they gave him lots of books and magazines and things, and he was sort of sedated. They just kept him quiet for a while. But what the basic cause was, I don't know."

Now — only *now* did Peter break down! Never mind all the other things that had happened to him since he'd been in England: mother, father, sister, brother, Vivien, Larry, wives, children, too much drinking and too many women — he had taken them in his stride and kept going. But the *set* was his Preserve. And when the enemy invaded it, then he broke down. When his fantasy world broke down, Peter broke down.

CHAPTER 19

Jamaica

Peter used to confide in his sister Flavia about his recurring fear of madness. Far more than fearing death, he told her, he feared that he might go mad; that the cells in his brain would die one by one until he could remember nothing. He also feared that someday he might disappear into a role he was acting and not be able to come back. After his breakdown he no longer talked about these fears, but they stayed inside troubling him.

At this time, his paintings had changed from representational to abstract. He took some of his canvases to show Diana Graves. She was going to invite the well-known painter David Boyd to come round to discuss them with Peter. Boyd found the abstracts "excruciatingly traumatic and tormented. They were fascinating mainly because they seemed to be the work of a deranged mind, and I certainly never thought of Peter Finch in that light." But Boyd did not say this to Peter as at the last moment Peter was too shy to come.

Almost all of 1961 was a restless, frustrating, floating, travelling and recuperating time for Peter.

At the beginning of January he flew to Rome for a while, and upon his return he went to the Isle of Man. In February the Finches went to Jamaica on holiday, Peter having talked a reluctant Yolande into going on a cargo boat with their ten-month-old daughter and nurse. It was a rough trip with few passengers and many storms, with Peter saying "This is the life!" and Yolande murmuring seditiously, "Yes, and it's cheap too."

Peter fell in love with Jamaica immediately. How could he not? It looked like Queensland, it had the same climate, foliage and vegetation. But the blacks were not the appallingly oppressed Aborigines of Queensland, they were happy, free ones. "It's a multi-racial society that really works!" he raved to all his friends when he returned to England. And he remembered that Errol Flynn had found a paradise there, too. He promptly bought some land in Jamaica, a small property called ''Bamboo'' after the nearby village of that name. It would be something to build on and to farm in the future.

Returning to England, he went to Rome again, always his favourite city. And then he went to Moscow to receive his award, for his performance as Oscar Wilde, at the Moscow Film Festival, where he was discovered by Liz Taylor dancing in Red Square and singing *Waltzing Matilda*.

The filming of *Cleopatra* had stopped after Peter's breakdown, but Olive was seeing to it that he still got paid. As the months went by — eight of them — Peter became less and less keen on the project and more and more frustrated. Because of his two big successes, *Oscar Wilde* and *No Love for Johnnie* now being shown in the cinemas, offers were pouring in and producers were clamouring for him but he still considered himself tied to his *Cleopatra* contract. When the film started up again however, it was with a change of directors and two changes in the cast. Richard Burton replaced Steven Boyd as Antony and Rex Harrison replaced Peter Finch as Caesar. Peter was relieved. *Cleopatra* did not do Peter's career any good, but it was nothing to what it did not do for Burton's.

But now came a bitter blow. Ken Hughes had written a script about Oliver Cromwell and was planning to direct it with Peter playing Cromwell. It was to be a big picture, but they could not raise the money on Peter Finch's name. He was not ''bankable''. After the Hughes-Finch winning combination in *Oscar Wilde*, this seems hard to understand unless one steps back and views the whole film situation at that time. New-Wave films were concerned with making stars not just using them. They used minimum budgets with maximum effects. The only way Hollywood or Hollywood-type productions could hit back was with epics and spectacles which required huge budgets and therefore ''bankable'' stars. But who was bankable? Or — bankable today, unbankable tomorrow. Even the Oliviers, in spite of their enormous success in *Macbeth* at Stratford, were declared unbankable and could not therefore raise the money to film it.

And the New Wave kept gathering strength, rising higher and making more noise with each smash. By the summer of '61 Peter was getting frantic to work, but in that feast or famine fashion that is the lot of show business — by then the offers had thinned down to a very few.

In his eagerness to work Peter made one of his choices that led Alan Bates to say years later, "I consider Peter Finch and James Mason the two best English actors of the '60s. But I never understood Finch. How could he do something as beautiful as *Sunday, Bloody Sunday*, but also make all that other shit? I mean, he could read, couldn't he?"

Undoubtedly, Peter could read. And the fact that he could made some of his choices even more mysterious. And perhaps equally mysterious is that in each one of the numerous stinkers or *sinkers* Peter made, there were always some other sane, intelligent, talented people involved, going down in the same leaky boat.

In *I Thank a Fool*, there was Susan Hayward who can be an excellent actress, Cyril Cusack, a most distinguished actor, and John "Rumpole" Mortimer, a notable playwright, television-and-screen-writer. The director was Robert Stevens, a young American fresh from television. It was his first film. Peter almost always got along with his directors, but sometimes he went too far. During the shooting of the film on location in Ireland, Peter said of Stevens, "He is one of the most extraordinary directors with whom I have ever worked. He is what I call a 'visionary' director, someone who has no time for the conventional or commonplace in motion picture directing." These strong words would lead one to expect a film reminiscent of the young Buñuel or at least the middle-aged Cocteau, but *I Thank a Fool* was just plain conventionally no good.

While making this film, Stevens and Peter decided they must do another together. It was called *In the Cool of the Day*, and some of it was to be shot in Greece. As always, the lure of travel and Elsewhere weighed strongly with Peter.

In London the Finches were on the move again. In June they had purchased a £30,000 neo-Georgian house on Totteridge Lane, just outside London, called Boundary House, but always referred to as Mill Hill because of the district. It had ten rooms, five acres, a vegetable garden, one hundred and twenty chickens (courtesy Peter and called "chooks" in Australianese) and eventually a swimming pool which no one used. They moved in, in October, and moved out again in November. Installed with his family in the Carlton Towers, Peter said, "We just couldn't stand it any longer. The water tank in the roof sprang a leak. The kitchen boiler broke down. The

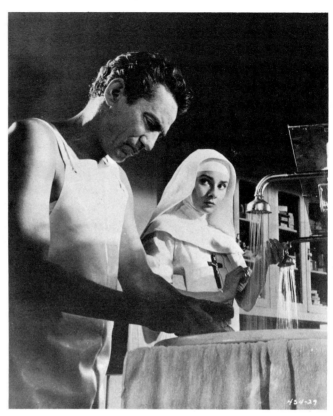

37 *The Nun's Story*, 1959: the weight of Peter's imagined experience turns him into a first-rate doctor

38 *The Abdication*, 1974: Peter making with the holy look

The Trials of Oscar Wilde, "a human life we have seen expand and close"

39 . . . the toast of the Café Royal

40 . . . Reading gaol

41 *The Pumpkin Eater*
and . . .

42 . . . *The Girl with Green
Eyes:* superb portraits of men
who have peaked, yet who
expected so much more of
themselves

43 *The Flight of the Phoenix*, 1965: Peter as the aristocratic, thick-skinned British captain

44 *Judith*, 1965: the spectacular-looking Sophia sabotages the film

45 *England Made Me*, 1972: Peter as the munitions king plans to outwit the Nazis with his English protégés

46 *Far From the Madding Crowd*, 1967: his middle-aged love oppresses her

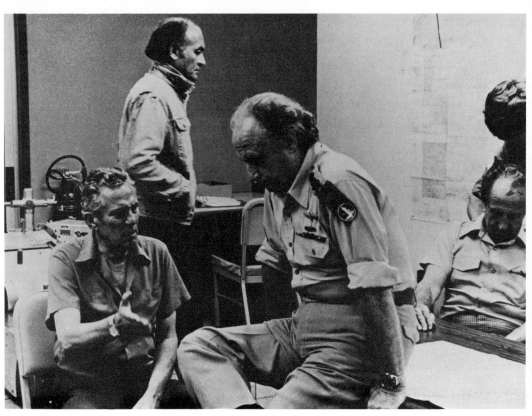

47 *Raid on Entebbe*, 1976: his Yitzhak Rabin portrayal was "as good as the real thing"
48 *Network*, 1976: Bill Holden thinks Peter is nuts, but Peter knows he's enlightened

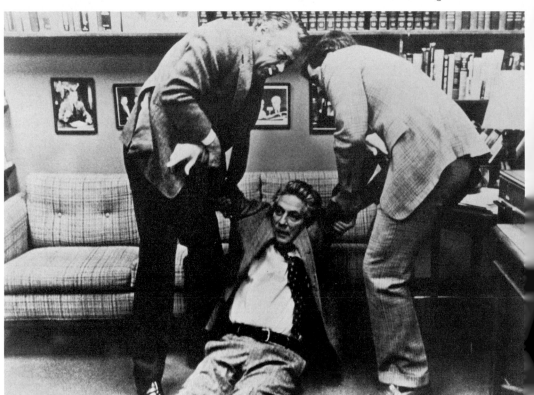

49 *Sunday, Bloody Sunday*, 1971: Hirsch in the synagogue

50 *Network*, 1976: Peter plays newscaster Howard Beale in his
"once in a lifetime" role

electricity stopped working. The telephone went dead. And our eighteen-month-old daughter Samantha caught cold.'' When the house was cured of all its ailments, and Samantha of her cold, they moved back.

In the Cool of the Day was filmed in 1962. It was one step up from no good. It was not bad. It had some of the ingredients — but not enough — of a superior soap. A superior soap, I would define as a movie in which a lot of very melodramatic, exciting and unexpected things happen to a lot of stereotyped characters, played by actors of the highest calibre, against a lot of stunning, authentic and quickly changing backgrounds.

In the Cool of the Day had a top flight cast of actors: Peter Finch, Jane Fonda, Angela Lansbury, Arthur Hill and Constance Cummings. But there were too few of them. The main story, the young girl with a limited amount of time to live who wants a final fling (Jane Fonda) and the middle-aged, unhappily married man (Peter) who together find Love for the First Time was good basic soap. But it needed a lot more interweaving stories and a lot more roller-coaster action. Ken Adam was the Art Director and the sets were impeccable. Peter's house and sitting-room as he comes in to his wife (Angela Lansbury at her shrewish best) *looked* unhappy even before either of them opened their mouths. Jane Fonda, after she sheds her ill-advised baby vampire outfits and make-up, is charming and touching, and Peter superbly displays joy, sadness and poignance at their tragic plight. Of visionary direction from Stevens, I could detect no sign.

CHAPTER 20

Burlington Bertie Campbell

In the spring or summer of 1962, something quite astonishing happened — astonishing even for Peter's astonishing life. It was an event that was to colour the rest of it. One day as he was pottering around the house, the door bell rang ...

He told Whiting about it soon after. Peter, says Whiting, put on his special "sophisticated" smile. Then, attempting to be very man-of-the-world, very Noël Coward *dégagé* — except that every now and then emotion got the upper hand and caused him to stumble over his words — he said, "D'you know my father? I mean my *real* father? I *met* my father, Jock Campbell, the other day at Mill Hill! Just rang the bell. Came up to the house and rang. I·went to the door and there was this nice old boy sort of smiling ..." Peter paused and then began stammering. "He s-s-said, 'It's an odd thing to say but I'm your father.' 'Oh!' I said, sort of smiling too. 'Won't you come in?' It was an odd kind of moment. We didn't have much to say. I mean, what was there to say? Yes ... we looked very much alike. I think. He just came in and had a drink and went off again. We kept looking at one another. I think we were quite pleased with what we saw, in a funny way."

Father and son. Lt. Col. Campbell, now a stalwart seventy-five years of age and Peter aged forty-five, saw each other and kept looking at one another and were quite pleased with what they saw, in a funny way.

It is difficult to pinpoint exactly when Peter's mother told him who his real father was. Going forward in time to 22 September 1968, there is a long interview with Peter in *The New York Sunday Times* by Enid Nemy, in which she says, "Peter Finch describes himself as 'the illegitimate son of a Scotsman named Campbell whom my mother married after her divorce from Finch'. His mother told him of the circumstances of his paternity when he was fourteen. 'I was rather thrilled,' he said, 'because I liked the feeling of being a Highlander.' "

Now for the facts. Certainly we know that Peter's mother could not have told him "when he was fourteen". Nor did she tell him for a while after they met, or why in 1953 do we find Peter in Edinburgh with the Old Vic company struggling up King Arthur's Seat "because my father is a mountaineer"? Even more to the point is his appearance at Little Shelford in 1955 when he opened its church bazaar at Easter, and made the speech about how moving an experience it was to come to a place so closely associated with his Finch ancestors. And Tamara swears that all the time she was married to Peter, until 1958, Peter accepted George Ingle Finch as his real father. One could look upon the number fourteen that Peter apparently selected at random in his *New York Times* interview as if it were, in fact, used symbolically and Peter was counting the years from his arrival in England to when his mother told him. In which case, fourteen years would add up to 1962, also the year of his meeting with Campbell. Whenever it was, Peter was then able to account for the indifference, to say nothing of the *froideur*, of George Ingle Finch upon meeting him.

But then if George *knew* Peter was not his, is it possible that he would go to such extremes to take the child away from his mother?

It is possible. And the answer lay in George himself, as he expressed his feelings in the letter he wrote to the woman who was to become his second wife. Their son, Bryan Ingle Finch, has saved these letters between George and his mother Gladys May, then a V.A.D. in Salonica.

On 10 October 1918, George wrote to Gladys, whom he called "Eve, the first woman in the world" saying:

"Listen, you shall know all that matters now. I could tell you nothing of this before, simply because I did not feel sure of you ... Darling, for years I have hidden my misery from you and all the world with the most cheerful lies I could sum up. But now when I feel you love me as I love you, you are going to be told everything.

"We must go back, far back in 1915, to just before I received my orders to go to Egypt. In those days I had a great friend Major Fred Powys Sketchley who went out to Gallipoli, leaving his wife and two children behind. My wife had naturally met Mrs P.S. and taken a strong liking to her. The long and short of it is that Fred, in response to a cable from me, was all out for the suggestion that Mrs P.S. should live with my wife while I was away on active service.

"I last saw my wife on November 28th, 1915. I went to Egypt and then to Salonica. After my recovery from malaria in October, being medically unfit, I had to stay in hospital in Salonica. Meanwhile my wife's correspondence had been none too brilliant and our marriage had not been a great success.

"Perhaps I ought to go further back and tell you how my wife and I stood in regard to one another, it will help you to understand things better. When I married my wife, I loved her as well and sincerely as was then in my power. I had settled unconditionally all the money I had on her. But within a few weeks I was speedily disillusioned when once I remonstrated with her for flirting rather heavily while we were still on our honeymoon. She flung back at me that she had merely married me for my money and the freedom and privileges my name assured her. I sank my pride and hurt completely and did everything I could do to awaken something akin to loyalty in her. But the utmost that could be attained was her assurance that, for her own sake, she would be loyal to me as my wife. Then when I had to go overseas you can imagine how glad I was that Mrs P.S. came to live at our house. Now, back to Salonica. On the 29th December, 1916, a cable arrived to say that my wife was seriously ill and would I come home quickly. I obtained special leave and arrived in England at the *end of* January, 1917. I found my wife in perfect health, *the mother of a boy of whom I am not the father for he was born on September 28th, 1916*. This is what happened. Capt. W.E.D. Campbell, Poona Horse, Mrs Powys Sketchley's brother had arrived in France from India in October 1915. Early in January he obtained leave of *ten* days which he came to spend with his sister at my house. During his stay he seduced my wife, whom he had never known before, with the result that on September 28th my wife gave birth to an illegitimate son. When my wife and I met again in January 1917 she, having no option confessed this to me. The secret of Peter's birth (for so the boy was called) is to this day known only to Mrs Powys Sketchley, myself, my wife and her seducer and now you. At first hearing of this my mind broke. My wife nursed me through and after about a week she implored my forgiveness. I still loved her after a fashion. My feelings towards Peter were none other than those of intense pity. For his innocent sake, for the sake of my own people and name I forgave my wife. I gave Peter my name as if he were my son. And in this way my 14 days of leave passed! I had a further ten days leave in France, which I employed looking for Campbell. I found him, thrashed him into unconsciousness but unfortunately (so I thought then and for a long time afterwards) did not kill him. I narrowly avoided having to face a court-martial.

"At the end of February I was back in Salonica. For three months my wife wrote regularly and her letters seemed to show her gratitude for my gift. Then her correspondence slackened off and fearing the worst I made arrangements to have her watched. What my sufferings were over all this time, I leave to your imagination. In 1917 I was more or less certain that my wife had gone off the rails again. It was then that I found out that Campbell and my wife had lived together in my house in November 1916 — that was just after Peter's birth. But as I had already condoned this by living with my wife in February, and as other proofs I had were not valid enough to stand up in court, it had to wait until I found letters of absolute proof. Before the absolute proof, my wife's object in refusing to divorce me was: to remain my wife, have a good time and do what she liked and make my life hell for me until I should slip and give her a chance to divorce me.

"Now I have procured legal proof. What I want is to be free of my wife. *I want Peter, who bears my name now. He is rather a dear little fellow. I cannot bring myself to letting his life be utterly ruined through the faults of others of which he is innocent.*"

In another letter to "Eve", dated 16 November 1918, George writes, "In all fairness to you, and the dream baby we are going to have, you and yours must come first. Peter will not live with us, for my mother, who knows nothing of the truth about him, is going to bring him up in the company of my younger brother, Antoine, who is fourteen."

Shortly after George divorced Peter's mother and married "Eve", and after Bryan was born, "Eve" divorced George and in a very short time George was married again, to Agnes Isobel Johnston (whom he called "Bubbles"), who gave him three children, and with whom he remained happily married for the rest of his life. One conclusion, swiftly reached, is that Peter's background was a hotbed of romanticism.

Quixotically, George stuck to his guns and told no one — not even Bubbles — that Peter was not his. Mrs Ann Scott Russell, one of George's daughters, said that she was told by her mother around 1950, when Peter had become a well-known actor in the West End, that "Your father was married before and Peter Finch is his son." "Yet," continued Ann, "Father never once mentioned Peter's name to me. In 1970 when my father was dying we thought he would say something about Peter. We waited for it. But he never did."

Who, then, was Major Wentworth Edward Dallas Campbell, besides the brother of Mrs Powys Sketchley, who once shared a house with Peter's mother?

"Bertie" Campbell as he was then christened by his regiment after the engaging, happy-go-lucky Burlington Bertie of music-hall fame

—later he was called "Jock"—was born in Gloucestershire in 1887. His family, army people for at least one hundred and fifty years, had fought in the Indian Mutiny. After Sandhurst, Campbell joined the Black Watch and just before the Great War he transferred to the Poona Horse, then stationed in Jhansi, India. Sometime after the war he was sent to Persia and in 1922 he came back to England to marry Peter's mother. The Campbells returned to India where from 1923 to 1926 Campbell acted as English Regent in the province of Jamkhandi to a very young maharaja. A superior horseman, Campbell was then sent to Sagar in Central India to become Chief Equitation Instructor at the cavalry school. This meant that in 1925 Peter, aged nine, was running around Adyar with his head shaved, in a saffron robe, at the same time as his mother and father were in India; an irony of fate that could hardly have been lost on him.

In 1930 Campbell left the Poona Horse to join the 18th Cavalry which he commanded, rising to the rank of Lt. Col. By then Peter's mother and Campbell were divorced, and in England she married Alexander Staveley-Hill, whom she had met in India. Around 1936 Campbell was also remarried, to a Mrs Ierne Binden-Blood who was also from an old army family. At the onset of World War II, Campbell, who had by then retired, rejoined the service and became an acting Wing Commander in the R.A.F. Afterwards he was B.O.A.C. Signal Manager in Cairo and then in Tehran. In 1950 he retired to Moffat, Scotland, and was an active golfer until he died in 1974.

One of his brother officers in the Poona Horse, Major R. F. Ruttledge, says of him, "Bertie Campbell was, I always thought, just what an Indian Cavalry Officer should be and particularly typical of the old Poona Horse — gay, good fun, smart and all the rest. He was a most likeable person at all times and the best of company."

The picture one has of Campbell is that of an easy-going, fun-loving man, who gets along well with everyone. Whether or not one believes in heredity, one would have to recognize that superficially these basic traits are those that Peter shared with him. But there is something else that father and son had in common that one would be at a loss to explain by anything other than heredity: their love of horses. Campbell lived all his life with horses, loved them and loved riding. It was for this reason he joined the Poona Horse. One would expect him to be expert, and he was an expert among experts in the regiment. But Peter had not lived among horses. He never saw them when growing up except briefly on his cousin Florrie's station. Yet he also loved them and he was also an expert horseman.

On this subject there are two interesting footnotes: first, when Peter initially arrived in London, he wrote a sort of weekly newsletter back to a magazine in Australia about the English sights, points of interest, cultural institutions. These letters are rather what one would expect — the National Gallery, the Tate, the British Museum ... But suddenly he discovered the equestrian statue of King Charles I in Trafalgar Square and we get this: "This is one of the finest equestrian statues I have ever seen. The stance of the horse is magnificent, with its rear-side left hind foot forward in most life-like position and its off-side foot pawing. It is a broad flanked horse with a strong neck and small head. I was also most impressed with the naturalness of the King's seat, in particular the position of the booted feet in the stirrups." And second, talking of acting once, Peter said, "Acting is like riding a horse never ridden before. He needs good but soft hands and alertness or else he gets away with you."

There was, however, one striking difference between father and son: Campbell always knew who he was.

Not long after Campbell's visit to Peter, a small tea party was held at Mill Hill. Probably at Peter's request, it was almost certainly arranged by Campbell's sister, Molly Poynder, who had always remained close friends with Peter's mother and who was "Aunt Molly" to Flavia and Michael. The guests at tea were Molly and Campbell and his wife Ierne. Molly remembers it taking place just before the birth of Peter and Yolande's second child — at the beginning of August 1962.

The guests arrived. They admired the house and were led into the drawing-room. A white-gloved servant brought in tea. Tea cups were passed. Yolande and Molly chattered charmingly together about this and that; Colonel Campbell and his wife occasionally joined in.

What was going through Peter's mind as he sat there listening to the clink of teaspoons against china and the fluting upper-class voices at the tea party?

A year before, that popular programme *This Is Your Life* had as its Christmas subject Peter Finch. And on came Bill Kerr, his old Australian mate ... and on came Tony Britton, his English mate ... and they had even flown over Donald Friend from Ceylon! And Bert le Blanc, the vaudeville comedian was flown in from Australia ... And directors he'd worked with, and actors he'd worked with were there ... all telling wonderful stories about him, saying wonderful and funny things about him. It was marvellous! Hilarious! And ... "Peter Finch, This Is Your Life!" said Eamonn

Andrews amidst studio cheers.

But Peter, that afternoon at tea in his drawing-room, finally recognized that his life was also his mother and Campbell, that his life was about not being wanted, that neither his mother nor Campbell when they were married had tried to find him. Because he was illegitimate. A bastard. There are no illegitimate mothers and fathers in European civilization, only illegitimate children. It was this stigma that had cast them out.

Peter would often improvise very funny parodies for his mates on the Victorian novels he used to devour at his grandfather's which went something like this:

" 'Observe, dear Fanny, that ragged little urchin standing by the fountain in the piazza. Has he not such a look in his blue eyes of poor Cicely? Do you not think so? And surely on that brow there is a strain of the Danbys! Oh, do let's ask him.' And sure enough the mother turns out to have bolted with that scallywag Pisano who deserted her when she was bearing his child, leaving her to struggle as best she could selling artificial flowers until she died of poverty right there on that very spot where the little urchin stands so forlornly. And the little fellow is forthwith swept back to his rightful home in England where his perfect manners and quaint tussles with the English language captivate everyone ... "

But this Victorian tale was not ending happily with tea at the vicarage in Little Shelford but traumatically with a forty-five-year-old man having tea for the first time with his seventy-five-year-old father at Mill Hill.

"How much more of civilization can I take!" thought Peter with sudden rage.

The clink of tea cups. The gentility of the conversation. Gentility. Refinement. What did it remind him of? Of course. It was like being back with the Zombs. Civilization! Such gentility. Such good breeding. Such strangers. *How much more of civilization could he take*?

Is it possible in this day and age to have these feelings about illegitimacy? In Peter's very special case, though his illegitimacy was the basic cause, it went far beyond that into traumatic crises of identity. Thirty-three when he finally met his mother and forty-five when he finally met his real father — the readjustment he had to make was gigantic. All those Australian relations were no longer his. His beloved grandmother, his beloved grandfather — they were now taken away from him, not only by death but by blood.

One is aware how incomprehensible Peter's suffering may seem to many people who have always known only too well who their real parents are and who spent so many fruitless hours of their childhood fantasizing about having been mixed up in the hospital and given to the wrong mother, or stolen by gypsies and deposited into the ghastly homes of those dreadful people they were forced to call their parents. Yet for better or worse they knew — and finally accepted that they knew — who they were and where they came from. They knew who were really their parents.

In anger, Peter blamed civilization entirely for his anguish, and that included every manifestation of it. He had only been in his new house for eight months, but already he was beginning to detest it. The way Yolande had furnished it — the fluttering curtains, the soft carpets, the neatness, the exquisite bandbox femininity, the possessions, possessions, possessions, wherever he looked, oppressed and overwhelmed him and rubbed against his nerves till they were raw. He hated Mill Hill. It was symbolic of everything he hated.

One day, a few months after the tea party, Peter went to Olive's office and asked her for money because, he said, he was going to Scotland to see his father. When he next came in, she asked him if he had a nice time. "Oh yes," said Peter enthusiastically. "I like him and he likes me. And do you know what?" Peter paused looking very pleased. "He says I can wear the Campbell tartan!"

But Mrs Irene Campbell, Campbell's wife for forty years and the mother of his three children says something different. "My husband never acknowledged Peter Finch as his son nor did Peter Finch *ever come* to Moffat. My husband and I and Mrs Poynder once had tea with his second wife Yolande when they were living outside London. Otherwise he never saw him or had any correspondence with him. As for wearing the Campbell tartan, anyone can wear it if they want to — or any other clan."

Poor Pidgifif! It begins to look as if he lost one father without gaining another. Was he making believe again as he had done as a child? "My mother is a French opera star ... my father is a sea captain ... "

Or did he and Campbell meet all the same, unbeknownst to anyone, in some pleasant, secluded, shady glen in Scotland? And did they sit there and talk over many things? Did they talk it all out?

One thing Peter had gained: a country, Scotland. And from then on bagpipes and pipers, imported by Peter and at his own expense, turned up at celebrations in the most unlikely places: in Dorset, in Rome, and in Yuma, Arizona.

CHAPTER 21

Anger, Drink and the New Wave

On 15 August Yolande gave birth to a boy. They named him Charles after Peter's grandfather Charles Finch, the only adult family member Peter could remember being nice to him as an adolescent. And though Peter seemed pleased with the new baby, the next six months saw a radical change in him.

Edna O'Brien, meeting him for the first time, focused on the one thing that had never seemed manifest before: Peter's anger. Or what she calls more forcefully, his "mad anger". "He had a streak of mad anger", she says, "that one was always fearing would rear up. Although I found him warm and sexual, I found him very tormented. He was made very nervous at any signs of aggression around him and I think this is because, having had a great deal of aggression inside himself, he was nervous of it in others. He tried to cover up his anger like a Celt does, with bravado and drink, but it was there just the same and it made me uneasy. It was as if some tension inside him was just waiting to snap."

At this time Lord Aberdare owned a record company for which Peter had recorded *Antony and Cleopatra*, and he and his wife became frequent visitors at Mill Hill. Both Lord and Lady Aberdare felt that Peter had a chip on his shoulder and an inferiority complex caused by being illegitimate — which he referred to often in their company.

Peter's sister Flavia had noticed that in the past sometimes some chance remark one might make — one never knew what — would set him off and Peter's reaction of hurt would be so strong he would have to leave the room or leave the house — though he would return the next day as if nothing had happened. Now Peter's anger was far more overt.

Peter and John von Kotze had resumed production plans on *The*

Hero and had commissioned Ralph Peterson to do the script. Ralph remembers that during script conferences Peter would work himself into terrible rages which would end with his smashing things in his house. When the first draft of the script was completed and to their exact specifications, Peter rang John von Kotze at three in the morning drunk and fuming. "The script's terrible," he said without preamble. "I'm not doing it." "Look," said von Kotze, "I can't talk to you now. I'm asleep. And you can't talk to me. You're drunk. It's a first draft and it can be fixed so call me in the morning." "No," said Peter. "It's hopeless. I've dropped it." Peter hung up the receiver. Those were to be his very last words on the subject and on the project.

Peter and Yolande's marriage was becoming badly unstuck. They had each tried hard in their individual ways but had become increasingly aware that they were very different people with very different goals. Yet it had not always been so. Tony Britton, recalling the couple's early days, says: "We all had a bloody good time at the beginning, you know, just after we did *Operation Amsterdam* and for two or three years after that. We had a wonderful time because I had met my wife and Peter had met Yolande and we roared around a bit and dashed about and it was very good, it was a very good time. We were totally blameless individuals, all of us in love, and our careers were fine. It was tremendous fun of the best possible kind." Peter and Yolande, possibly sharing those memories, tried even harder, but it was no good.

In all unhappy marriages one finds the same psychological stresses at work. The protagonists, instead of blending together, become more and more rigidly their own separate and distinct selves: their real selves, if you like. They become, so to speak, representatives of their own country. Put simply, Yolande came to represent Establishment country and Peter anti-Establishment. Now the lines of battle were clearly drawn. Yolande skilfully organized elegant dinner parties with candlelight, gleaming silver and fresh flowers. The Portuguese servants wore white gloves as they served succulent meals. But the only thing Peter really enjoyed about these polished dinners was when one of the servants' gloves accidentally fell into someone's soup. The more Yolande insisted they attend black-tie dinners, the more likely Peter would be to rise suddenly in the middle of one and walk out. First they employed the services of just one chauffeur-driven car but, since it was always busy taking

Peter to and from the studio, Yolande hired a second one for herself as central London was too far to reach without this convenience.

They took to scoring off each other. When Peter caught sight of Yolande's weekly bill for facials at Elizabeth Arden he hit the roof and forbade her to go there. Yolande obeyed. Instead she had the beautician come all the way out to their house once a week which cost twice as much. Peter grumbled about Yolande's hairdressing bills as well. She then came up with the bright idea of buying two wigs which, she assured him, would cut down coiffeuring costs. But the wigs apparently became very easily tousled and tangled in night club wear-and-tear and required regular if not daily re-styling. Peter, aghast at the huge car-hire bills, discovered that Yolande was simply popping the wigs into the car and sending them off to Wig Creations where they were re-dressed and sent back by car that very day. "They are the only chauffeur-driven wigs in London," groaned Peter.

Yolande was not the only one who spent money. She spent money but Peter splurged it. He would blow £300 a night in a night club and managed to give away much more to hard-luck hangers-on (in spite of his financial arrangements with Olive), yet would begrudge Yolande a new dress. If Yolande spent money, Peter drank it. Peter had become your standard movie-star drunk.

What one must never lose sight of is that the standard is very high. It is not necessary to list other famous actors — the "brightest and the best" who have tragically succumbed to alcohol in their time, nor ponder upon why it happened to them and not to equally gifted famous actors who have escaped this scourge. One can only conclude that, together with a chemical imbalance, there is always the strong psychological necessity for some actors between the ages of forty and fifty (presumably when they are at the height of their powers and should be at their most committed), to have a glorious time trying to destroy themselves; or to destroy themselves trying to have a glorious time. It is the eternal question of concentration versus dissipation.

"Peter was a romantic," says Tony Britton, "and I think, like all of us who are tinged with romanticism, had an awareness that one isn't just in a material world. There is something else to be read about, examined, looked at and talked about. And I think he needed the release of alcohol and women. Most men of that kind do. They feel that they are living most when they are using all their emotions and their feelings and are released in this way. It's romanticism — well it's also drawing a veil over one's mind really. It's self-delusion, but it's none the less a happy thing while it's going on.''

Peter was at that time spending many nights on the town and many early dawns on various sofas: his mother's, Tamara's, Olive's, and Tony Britton's in particular, while Yolande, for her part, was finding her own friends and admirers.

Tony remembers: "Peter would suddenly turn up at two in the morning swaying in the breeze saying, 'Hello, mate. Can I come in, mate?' And my wife and I would look at each other and say, 'We've got a Finch for the night.' And there he would be in the morning all curled up like a foetus. That always amazed me — the great Finch curled up like a foetus. It seemed to be a defensive position. I think he was a man who needed to defend himself all the time from something. He had his defences up all the time but they were never evident unless you sort of bumped into them accidentally.''

The pressure both in films and on the stage is tremendous. A role must be created and then telescoped to simulate life which requires minute-to-minute, second-to-second concentration. It cannot assault you with sudden rushes of colour, as in a painting. It must have its greys, its gradations and its culminations.

It now becomes necessary to praise all actors the world over because they are never going to do it themselves. The tradition of humility towards their art is too ingrained in them.

The best example of this is John Barrymore whose life and genius for self-caricature and self-ruination made him the quintessential actor of the twentieth century, and in whom can be found elements of all great actors — for that matter, of all actors. After his first great triumph in *Richard III*, he said, "I rather believe it was the first genuine acting I ever managed to achieve. I mean I thought I *was* the character and in my dreams I *knew* I was he. As to comparing myself with other Gloucesters, I'd be afraid to have an opinion. What would it prove? Probably that I was bad, and that's one reason why I could never see myself in the mirror of another man's performance. Either I would crack the mirror, or the mirror would crack my own ego. I am inclined to agree with Mr Jo Jefferson who held that 'All good actors are dead.' Perhaps we living actors should be allowed to say only this: 'We're all hams. Only some of us don't know it.' ''

It is hard to imagine a writer, a painter, poet, politician or lawyer saying casually of his profession: "We're all hacks. Only some of us don't know it." Yet it seems perfectly natural for an actor to adopt this stance.

After Barrymore's *Hamlet*, still judged by some as the greatest of this century, he said, "It is not nearly so important who plays Hamlet as it is who operates the lights." What is more, he really meant it for he goes on to say, "This virtuoso, half-Edison half-Aladdin, hidden at his amazing console should receive the loudest applause, command the largest salary and merit the posthumous statue reared in the park."

It could only be a matter of time before the New Wave would catch up with so special an actor as Peter Finch, and in April 1963 when it began foaming enticingly around him once again and he had been out of work for more than a year, he gratefully and enthusiastically leaped in.

It had all begun one day during the making of *Tom Jones* when director Tony Richardson, in the approved grand manner of a full-blown impresario, tossed a book in the direction of his second cameraman, Desmond Davis, saying, "Catch! You said you wanted to be a director? O.K. Here's your film." Davis caught. He looked at the book. It was the new writer Edna O'Brien's first novel called *The Country Girl*, renamed *The Girl with Green Eyes* for the film.

"What luck that was," says Davis looking back. "What incredible luck! Mind you, I'd been in the business eighteen years beginning as a clapper boy so I was fairly experienced, but I'd certainly never directed. And I thought I was still a long way from directing. Anyhow, I read the book and I loved it. There was no script, there was only Edna O'Brien who was very young and had never had anything to do with films before. Richardson decided Edna and I should do the script together. Edna and I took to each other wonderfully. But she was at that stage where her marriage was just breaking up and she was living with friends and would disappear for days so I found myself chasing all over London for her. Also she dissolved into tears quite often. She was, as she called herself then, a Festival of Tears. So the script did not proceed very quickly but it did proceed well. Rita Tushingham as the young girl we had always thought of from the very beginning, but we were having trouble thinking of an actor in his forties with the right charisma for the man. From the start I wanted Peter to do it but I was a tiny bit shy of approaching him because the film might be thought of as a 'woman's picture', if you want to use that sort of tired expression. Eventually, however, we did send off a script to him and he was delighted with it.

"So we met. Talked. He agreed. And there we were.

"We had about two weeks' rehearsal with Peter and Rita before we went into production in Dublin where it was to be shot. It was interesting that Peter, in rehearsal, always used the text itself as his jumping-off point. 'How would I do this line?' he would ask. And would discuss it. He was always very quick to find a line that wasn't true to the character and say, 'Well, can I perhaps say it this way?' And something else that I realized in rehearsals that surprised me was that you would have expected Rita to be nervous of Peter, but in fact it was the other way around! She was at the height of her career, the Princess of the New Wave, she was so very much in fashion and it was as if he were wondering, 'Am I doing this right? Is this the way they do it now?' But as soon as he and Rita started getting along, which they did very quickly because they are both natural clowns, the nervousness vanished. Whatever he did from then on he did whole-heartedly. There was nothing after that in his character that I saw that was in the least hesitant."

In May *The Girl with Green Eyes* company moved to Dublin, put up at the Hibernian Hotel and began shooting.

Says Davis, "Peter never drank when he was working but my God as soon as he stopped! He had ferocious energy. He had a car and a driver and the driver complained after about a week that because of Peter he was never getting home at all, and in the end we had to have two drivers for his car; one for the day and one for the night. God knows where Peter went around Dublin all night and God knows what he did but he was never late for his seven o'clock morning call, and he always knew his lines, absolutely. I think the answer is he had a completely photographic memory and could just look at a page and fairly well know it. Every day after work we would watch the rushes and then go over to the Hibernian Hotel for a drink. If Peter got drunk you would see a tremendous change come over him. We all got quite used to the Jekyll and Hyde type thing. One minute he would be smiling and joking with everybody and the next his lower lip would come out and he would be abruptly changed. Sometimes, even in the middle of a sentence or in the middle of a word, he would turn on someone and attack them, going unerringly for their weak spot. I remember one night he said to me, 'Listen, I could really fuck you up on that set, man. You wouldn't know what I was doing but I could really fuck you up.' This was my first film so he was hitting below the belt. I watched him like a hawk on the set after that but he never followed through with these threats. I don't think he even remembered them.''

In the past Peter had been a sloppy drunk, a soppy drunk, a sentimental and irresponsible one, but now he was becoming a mean drunk. But that was only at night. During the day Peter was, as usual, his ideal professional self.

Davis remembers trying to shoot a scene in which Peter was involved, which included eight of the distinguished actors of the Abbey Theatre. ''These actors,'' says Davis, ''while they were the sweetest people on earth, were utterly uncontrollable as far as I was concerned. They would shout and talk amongst each other and occasionally cries of 'Listen to the director!' would go up but nobody would listen. I mean it was sheer chaos, it was anarchy on the floor. It was the one time I totally lost control. And then Peter came up quietly behind me and said, 'It's like trying to play chess with coloured mice, isn't it?' And when I stopped laughing I'd got my grip back and was able to carry on.''

Peter's next film after *The Girl with Green Eyes* was *The Pumpkin Eater* with Anne Bancroft which he began making that autumn. Both films may be discussed together because the characters Peter portrayed are not dissimilar. Both men are writers with an abundance of charm, intelligence, talent and sensibility. But they are both men in their forties who had expected much more of themselves; men who suspect they have peaked when they thought they were climbing; who feel they are not going to get any better and that whether they remain on a plateau or descend, they must cover their disappointment with what shreds of resilience and comfort they can find. Eugene Gaillard in *The Girl with Green Eyes* finds solace in brooding isolation from which he is only temporarily distracted by the young girl Kate, while Jake Armitage in *The Pumpkin Eater* turns to womanizing and churning out slick film scripts.

Both films were exquisitely made and exquisitely acted. They are tone poems of contemporary anguish. But what gives them their added interest historically is that, for the first time in the cinema, they are expressed through the woman's point of view. Riding on the New Wave was the resurgence of the woman's movement that had lain dormant for a long time. In these films we are made aware of the plight of a woman in love with a man who is dissatisfied with himself and whom she is unable either to help or to resist. We also see her on the brink of the dawning discovery that, in spite of her anguished attempts to blame herself for the situation, it is not entirely her fault.

Peter brought to his portrayal of both these men a devastating honesty so that they emerge not as likeable men but, due to Peter's empathy with them, as human and fascinating because they are real.

"It was very odd about Peter during these films," mused Olive. "He did not once pop into my office 'in character' as he had always done when he was Captain Starlight or Oscar Wilde or Johnnie Byrne or Caesar and so forth."

Peter did not have to. He was not "in character" for these roles. He was exactly who they were and where they were at that point of time; even to the extent of worrying about whether he had peaked at *Oscar Wilde* and was now set on a downhill course.

Talking with Peter during the making of *The Pumpkin Eater*, Edna O'Brien was amused to hear him say excitedly, "Mr Pinter is coming on the set tomorrow!" Not "Harold", or "Harold Pinter", but "*Mr* Pinter". Peter had his hierarchy. And always at the top was the writer.

CHAPTER 22

The Seagull

The late George Johnston was an Australian writer. A foreign correspondent during World War II and afterwards a journalist in London on Peter's old paper the *Sun*, he was a good friend of Peter's and had written several articles about him. He then lived on the Greek island of Hydra with his family and went on to become a prize-winning novelist, though later, at a low point financially, he sought to get back his old job as a newspaperman. He was told he was too old, too ill (he had contracted T.B. while on Hydra), and too out of touch for the grind. Desperate, Johnston went to discuss his predicament with Peter. Said Peter, "If you were given another year on the island what would you do? Have a go at another book?" "Yes," said Johnston. "Listen," said Peter. "I'll shout you to another chunk of time. I'll kick in the fares back to Greece for the four of you. And I'll give you a thousand quid."

"Aggressively, almost as though he hated both of us for the situation forced on us," said Johnston, "Peter came to the rescue."

Peter next saw Johnston when making *In the Cool of the Day* in Athens. Johnston at the time was working on a novel called *Clean Straw for Nothing*, and in this novel Peter becomes the Australian actor, Archie Calverton, whose following words spoken to the main character on an Aegean beach, are based on Peter's own words to Johnston:

"I don't reach any longer. Sure I used to. I used to play Molière in factories with a bob's worth of props ... the dedicated young actor who takes Molière around the factories ... Now I just get pushed around and pushed along ... There's nothing for me anymore. There never was except being young and cocky and wanting to have a go. When you get rid of that there's nothing left. There's no provision for later when that cocky phase has worn out.

"It's funny you know ... there are probably blokes out there in Australia who envy the three of us, the three of us bloody expatriates. Kiernan with his shows in Paris and London and New York. Pictures in the Tate. You living on your Greek Island and writing your books. Me getting leads in Hollywood films. Having Sunday-newspaper affairs with glamorous floosies. Jesus, if the bastards only knew! Me drinking myself fatuous and keeping one jump ahead of the funny farm.

"Success is all bullshit. You know that ... you do envy me don't you? Because I'm what you think is successful ... I did it the hard way. And then settled for the easy way ... I should have stuck with the people I used to believe in, Shakespeare and Molière and Shaw and Chekhov and that bunch; I could have been a bloody good classical actor, you know, and not just another glossy prick in the sixpenny magazines ... "

Peter did not talk in this manner only to George Johnston. He would say much the same thing to Olive from time to time. And then he would implore her, "I *must* find a play. I must go back to the stage. Find one for me *please!*" Olive's response was always the same. She would pick up the phone and ring Binkie Beaumont whose production company, H. M. Tennant's, was at that time ruling the commercial West End theatre. And then another film offer would come up for Peter and he would dump his stage dreams.

But after *The Girl with Green Eyes* and *The Pumpkin Eater*, with the confidence he had gained from the quality of these films and their success, when Peter went to Olive and again talked about going on stage and she began to ring Binkie, he shook his head. "No," he said, "Call the Royal Court and speak to George Devine."

When it was announced in the Press that Peter Finch was to play Trigorin in the all-star cast of Chekhov's *The Seagull* to be directed by Tony Richardson with Peggy Ashcroft, Vanessa Redgrave, Peter McEnery and George Devine, and produced by the Royal Court's English Stage Company, it caused a great stir of pleasurable excitement among theatre-goers. Their appetite for Chekhov had recently been whetted by certainly the most perfect English production of *Uncle Vanya* with Laurence Olivier, Michael Redgrave, Rosemary Harris, Joan Plowright and Sybil Thorndike among others, at Chichester.

The Seagull opened on 12 March 1964 at the Queen's theatre. For Harold Hobson it was pure Chekhovian magic. Putting the last first, he begins with the play's final words: "The fact is, Konstantin Gavrilovich has shot himself." "They are a verdict," says Hobson, "a closing of an account; the last stroke of the pattern has been

drawn. That is why they give a feeling of such extraordinary fulfil-
ment; the untidiness of life has been removed and in its place we see
a whole perfect accomplishment. I have never felt this so strongly at
any previous production of *The Seagull*.

"On Thursday, George Devine spoke the words with such
accurate timing, the curtain came down so perfectly on cue that one
realised with an almost physical shock that anything that might
happen afterwards was of no importance. Relationships had been
brought to a supreme point of significance and then broken. Here
we have one entire and perfect chrysolite. Nothing we could give
would suffice to buy it. It is beyond price."

Hobson, placing Peter's "riveting" performance "on the same
high level and exact achievement" as Peggy Ashcroft's, adds, "Mr
Finch can remain beautifully still; and when he speaks in the superb
scene with the love-stricken Nina of his obsession with turning every
trivial accident of life into a story, one can really believe that he has
written thoughtful and admirable books, and that he is troubled by
what their cost has been, not to him, but to his friends." He then
sums up by bestowing upon Peter this heady accolade: *"His is one
of the finest Chekhovian performances I have ever seen."*

In 1949, Peggy Ashcroft, after seeing the young newcomer in
Daphne Laureola, had written him a letter which had moved him
mightily: "I expected to have eyes only for our matchless Edith —
but suddenly to see an actor new to me, giving such a beautiful and
movingly true performance was an unexpected excitement." Now
on equal footing, Peter was playing Peggy Ashcroft's lover in *The
Seagull*.

With his Trigorin in *The Seagull*, Peter was accepted not as in the
past as a phenomenon, or a discovery, or as a film star having a
fling, but as a serious stage actor able to work on the same stage at
the same level in the classics as all the great and serious stage actors
of the day of which England was so justly proud. Theatre audiences
could now look forward to his seasons at Stratford or at the
National Theatre — to his lovesick Colonel Vershinin in *The Three
Sisters* perhaps, or his world-well-lost-for-love Antony in *Antony
and Cleopatra*. To his gentle, introspective, intensely complex
Richard II and — who knew? — maybe after a while even to his
silver-tongued, silver-haired mad and raging Moor in *Othello*? And
finally his *Lear*.

But *The Seagull* was Peter's best performance on stage; and his
last.

CHAPTER 23

Shirley Bassey and Judith

During the run of *The Seagull* Peter fell in love with a young coloured singer in her early twenties, Shirley Bassey. Born in the dock area of Cardiff, one of seven children of a Nigerian father and a Welsh mother, she was the first black singer of note to arrive on the scene in England and her rise was meteoric.

At sixteen, a factory worker, she was singing at social gatherings for pleasure, but the sound of her voice belting out love songs in her own inimitable manner soon reached the ear of a London agent. She found herself touring in a revue billed as England's answer to Lena Horne. Singing at the Astor Club in London, the impresario Jack Hylton spotted her and placed her in a variety bill at the Hippodrome with a storm of advance publicity. She lived up to it. Peter seeing her, and meeting her, was mesmerized.

He was off again on his indefatigable pursuit of love.

While Peter was filming *The Pumpkin Eater*, Yolande, deeply unhappy with the chaotic situation at home, took up her acting career with an engagement in a play called *Early One Morning* (directed by Charles Vance), which was tried out in Chelmsford, Essex, for possible transfer to London — though nothing came of it. The try-out over, she returned to Mill Hill and after *The Seagull* opened she took herself and her children for a holiday to Porto Ercole — a fashionable little sea port town.

Yolande has described how the English scavenger press arrived there at her doorstep one day without warning, eager to know what she had to say about "her husband's close friendship with Shirley Bassey".

One wonders how these "reporters" are able to continue earning their living in this grotesque way after having once faced a stunned wife who has no idea what they are talking about and her small children's traumatic reactions as they, listening to the conversation uncomprehendingly except for hearing their father's name and noting their mother's drained face, naturally assume that something terrible has happened to him.

Peter did not know that news of his affair with Shirley Bassey had preceded him when he arrived in Italy to join Yolande at the end of June after *The Seagull* had closed. When Yolande confronted him he confessed to the affair, pleading with her to "let him get it out of his system". A near tragedy resulted that night when Yolande, in an effort to still her racing thoughts, lost track of the sleeping pills she had swallowed and narrowly escaped death. When she woke up in the hospital with Peter anxiously leaning over her, she looked at him and around her at the room lit by sunlight and everything became clear to her. "I was prepared to live for you," she said to Peter. "But I'm *not* prepared to die for you." She was going to divorce him.

Did Peter, at that moment, realize that this hitherto spirited young woman could be a victim too? And that it was he himself who had made her into one?

Peter moved out of Mill Hill and went back to stay at his mother's. The sofa had now become a divan, and from this base he journeyed in and out of England sometimes alone, sometimes with Shirley Bassey, to Jamaica, Rome, etc. At one point he moved into the Carlton Towers with Shirley from where he made one of his late-night calls to Laurie Evans, the head of Olive's theatrical agency. "I'm with Shirley Bassey," he said to Evans, waking him up at 3 a.m. "We want to do a play together. Can you think of one?" "*Othello*," said the sleepy Evans. "No — wait a minute, I've got it the wrong way round. Let's see — there was a good American play that had some success a while back called *Deep Are the Roots*. No — that's the black man and the white girl too. What about *Antony and Cleopatra*? I'm going back to sleep." And, when he did — so did the project.

In August, Peter went to Israel to make a film called *Judith* which co-starred Sophia Loren. Based loosely on the story of the biblical heroine of that name (and positively slackly on a story by Lawrence Durrell), it unfortunately fell into the by now too familiar category of many of Peter's films: the wine of High Purpose slipping twixt cup and lip and dribbling down the chin of Hilarity.

The poor film never had a chance. It was sabotaged early on by the famous sequence which introduces the spectacular Sophia (as the Jewish wife of a war criminal smuggled into Israel by the Haganah) to the story. A huge packing-case is unloaded from the cargo boat and broken into to reveal the breathtaking sight of Sophia, fresh and dewy as ever, rising like some magnificent Venus on the half shell in spite of her long and hazardous journey which apparently killed her less fortunate companion.

No sooner had the cat-calls and wolf-whistles which exploded at every showing subsided, than the audience was treated to the sight of Sophia prancing crossly around the kibbutz in the briefest of shorts. From there on the laughter became general and sustained. As the leader of the kibbutz, Peter, grim and gritty, tried to instil a little dignity into the hilarious proceedings but to no avail.

Shirley Bassey had promised Peter she would join him in Israel and arrived there during the shooting. But she had come, so to speak, only to say goodbye. Peter was now forty-eight and although his Buddhist motto had always been "Change!", within his own self he was set in many ways. Drinking would always be a problem with him. So would his inclination towards promiscuity. And so would his constant struggle to make the woman he loved devote and adapt herself exclusively to him, to his interests, and to his way of life. Shirley, even during the short, whirlwind months she had known him, was perceptive enough to realize that, interested as she was in Peter, she was not interested in him to the exclusion of other men, of her independence, or of her talent. Yet the very qualities that made her draw away from him were the qualities that drew him on. He had wanted to marry her and she turned him down. Before she left, she also told Peter that her estranged husband, Kenneth Hume, was citing him in their divorce case. Peter already knew that Yolande was starting divorce proceedings citing Shirley.

After Shirley's departure, Peter went wild. In Nahariya, a northern coastal town where *Judith* was being shot, he got roaring drunk every night and gave the cast and the visiting journalists an earful. In the daytime when not filming he would be furiously painting. At night he would shove his artwork under people's noses saying, "Look at that. It's the saddest and cruellest picture I've ever painted in my whole life. That's how I feel tonight. A clown's face in savage torment."

One night in a restaurant he was shouting over and over, "I've been in too many traps in my life! Emotional traps! Traps set by women! That's all they want to do. Take everything and give nothing. But not any more. *Not any more!* I want to be free!'' he roared, not seeming to realize that was precisely what he was at the moment — and what he could no longer bear to be.

Another night he stood up at a dinner party and announced, ''South Africa has disowned me. I'm not wanted in the southern states of America. And why? I'm an outcast because I've had an affair with a coloured girl. They've given me up because of my affair with Shirley Bassey!'' Then switching quickly into his statement-to-the-Press voice: ''Shirley doesn't want any personal entanglements but we are still the best of mates.'' Then defiantly, ''I'm on my own — I'm on my own, do you hear me?'' Then he broke down sobbing, ''My children ... my children ... they are so *young* ...'' Embarrassed, the dinner party filed out of the restaurant leaving Peter alone with his bottle of wine.

For Peter, February 1965 was a month of litigation. He had sown the wind and he was reaping the whirlwind.

On the 12 February, Yolande's divorce petition was heard naming Shirley Bassey. And on the 25th, Kenneth Hume's petition against Shirley was heard. The two co-respondents named were Peter and another Australian. Everyone admitted adultery all the way round: the sixties were beginning to swing.

Peter spent the last day of February at Tickerage, the country house of his much beloved Vivien Leigh, now divorced from Olivier and living with actor Jack Merivale. Says Merivale, ''The highest commendation Vivien bestowed upon people or things was that very English adjective 'proper'. Looking at a custom-built Rolls she would say, 'That's a *proper* car.' About Peter Finch she always said, 'That's a *proper* man.' ''

No doubt the very proper Jane Austen's Marianne in *Sense and Sensibility* would agree, for she means much the same when she says of Willoughby: ''That is what I like; that is what a man ought to be. Whatever his pursuits, his eagerness in them should know no moderation and leave him no sense of fatigue.''

CHAPTER 24

The Flight of the Phoenix and Hepatitis

"From now on," pledged Peter solemnly to producer Joe Janni after the *Judith* fiasco, "I no longer care about the size of a part. I'm only interested in the quality of the script. I think this has finally taught me the lesson that if the film is stupid, I'm going to look twice as stupid if I have a big part in it."

Good as his word, the next role Peter undertook was a small one in a film called *The Flight of the Phoenix*, shot on location in Yuma, Arizona, with an all-star male cast, directed by Robert Aldrich. It was one of the most engrossing and entertaining films Peter ever made.

Aldrich has always been known for his perceptive casting and, in casting Peter as the British Army Captain Harris, he would seem to have been extremely perceptive; there was certainly nothing in Peter's recent films or widely publicized private life to indicate that he could play this particular kind of officer and gentleman, a sort of Crimean War throwback to whom adherence to the military code is more important than having any sense. Perhaps Aldrich, scion of the famous banking Aldriches, whose grandfather Nelson was a Senator and whose uncle Winthrop an Ambassador, had intuited that through Peter's veins also flowed the blood of the ruling class.

The situation in *The Flight of the Phoenix* is simple but impressive. A cargo plane carrying passengers from their jobs in the Middle East crashes in the Libyan desert leaving twelve survivors. When we see that among these are James Stewart, Richard Attenborough, Peter Finch, Hardy Kruger, Ronald Fraser, Ian Bannen and George Kennedy, we loosen our safety belts to relax and enjoy it. We are not allowed to relax for long. The situation immediately becomes critical. Water and food supplies are low. The radio has been wrecked along with the plane and the navigator, having been too busy drinking to check their course, doesn't know where they are.

The intensity of the film lies in its straightforward realism. Days go by without hope of rescue but there are no melodramatics, no philosophical speeches; drink-crazed men do not hurl themselves about hallucinating nor do food-crazed men plan to eat each other. In a cast that includes many actors who can carry a film on their own, Aldrich is able to get each to retain his edge while subduing his own personality to the predicament thus achieving immediacy, unity, and above all believability. The film has no message save, perhaps, the most heartening of all: man is fallible — but by God, he is also ingenious.

An unlikeable little German among the survivors claims to be an aircraft designer and finally, under his bullying, prodding and tutelage, they attempt to rebuild the aircraft. Not till the plane is almost ready do they discover that the German is only a designer of aircraft models. Still they go on, complete it, strap themselves on to the wings and finally, after several abortive attempts, Jimmy Stewart gets the plane aloft and the Phoenix, risen from its ashes, flies safely to the nearest oasis.

Peter's delicately drawn, carefully built portrait of the aristocratic thick-skinned Captain — innocently antagonizing everyone with his "survival routines" and "surveillances of the terrain", gradually winning the grudging admiration of all but his sergeant who loathes his privileged nineteenth-century guts — is extraordinarily fine, especially in the scene where, unable to understand his sergeant's refusal to accompany him on another hair-brained sortie, he takes a tentative step towards him and says with gentle encouragement, "Don't be frightened."

In Yuma, Esther Gravett, a cosmopolite of Russian birth was engaged in doing foreign publicity for the film. She had met Peter several times in London at the home of their mutual friends, Ken and Letitia Adam. Now, meeting again, they quickly developed a sentimental friendship.

There had grown up in post-war times a breed of international actors whom Esther dubbed the élite gypsies. A new version of strolling players, they flew around the world making films and lived like kings for the duration of each job. These leading actors of all nationalities had learned to get along with each other in the freemasonry of their craft. Now in this small town in Arizona with few outside distractions, Peter oddly remembered that 24 May was Queen Victoria's birthday. He and the English contingent quickly decided that nothing would do but that they should honour their

Queen with a birthday celebration to which they graciously invited the foreign emissaries. The festivities opened with everyone dressed in their best, with the British flag flying and General James Stewart of the American Air Corps firing a twenty-one gun salute into a barrel. It continued with many a loyal toast to the Queen and Empress followed by a sumptuous dinner and finished with Peter turning to the stragglers with the cry, "Come on! We've got to march on Yuma!" Through the deserted main street of this desert town marched the revellers singing the *Marseillaise* backed by the skirl of bagpipes Peter had had flown in from Scotland. The few natives still awake, hearing the noisy band approaching, assumed that the Revolution had come and joined in.

After completing their studio work in Yuma, the company flew to Hollywood for further work. Esther and Peter continued to see each other. But though Shirley Bassey had made it clear to Peter that she was not considering him seriously, he still yearned for her and begged her via the telephone to join him in Hollywood. First she said yes. Then she said maybe. And finally she wired him, no.

Says Esther, "Peter wept for two days. Really crying." Watching him like this had stirred her Russian blood and on the second day she fell into sympathetic melancholy and got drunk with him. The two of them worked themselves up into a splendid Russian drama, their senses pleasantly awash with all the sadness they had encountered in life. Finally exhausted and refreshed Peter said to her, "You know, maybe it's just as well Shirley's not coming because she's a fabulous person and I'm mad about her, but she's really not the sort of person I could marry. She's too ambitious and in any case she's gone back to her husband who is her manager."

Shortly thereafter, dining with Esther and friends, Peter met Florrie Christmas, a young black ex-schoolteacher from the South who worked in the script department of a studio. Immediately Esther saw that he was attracted. And indeed this was borne out when Peter came to Esther a few days later saying guiltily, "Do you mind if I don't take you to the opening of the *Pickwick* film as we planned? I'm taking Florrie Christmas."

As a matter of fact Esther did mind. She minded very much. She had been looking forward to it. "You know what you are, Peter?" she said. "You're an inverted snob. Yes! And a reverse racist. That's why you chase after black women."

Peter was indignant. "No, that is not the reason I like black women," he retorted. "I like them because they are so frightfully relaxed. They relax you and they are relaxing. They're not all wound-up like white women are.''

Esther took exception to this statement as, although she happened to be white, she did not feel she was particularly wound-up. ''Oh, Peter, Peter,'' she sighed. ''You always see people as *categories* never as *individuals*.''

Esther was right. Peter had come to see people as categories. They were ''oppressors'' or ''victims'', they were ''fun'' or ''pompous'', they were ''Establishment'' or ''anti-Establishment''. In short, they were black or white. And black was good and white was bad, and marriage was bad, and wife was bad, bourgeois was bad, middle class, conventional and so forth. Above all, ''Finch'' was bad. In an angry quarrel with his daughter, Anita, several years later he was suddenly to turn on her saying, ''You're a typical Finch — you're a viper! You're like all of them — vipers, all of them!''

But Peter was also right in claiming that he was attracted to black women not for their race alone but for their special quality of relaxation because by and large it is a truth. It would be absurd to think that only Peter's background could have produced his inclinations — one has merely to notice how many different types of non-Jewish women are attracted to Jewish men because they find them ''more interesting'', or for that matter Jewish women to black men because they ''treat them better''.

Florrie Christmas was now the main romantic interest in Peter's life and she accompanied him on his orbit as it spun from America to Jamaica to England and to Spain. There he began working on his next film, *10.30 p.m. Summer*. Written by Jules Dassin and Marguerite Duras, with Melina Mercouri, Romy Schneider, and Peter at the head of the cast it was a murky *nouveau roman* drama of infidelity that did not add up to much. Even murkier was the way Peter was feeling. His behaviour was very uncharacteristic: lethargic, unhappy, depressed. Physically he felt sicker than he ever had in his life though he could not pinpoint his malaise. He had lost his appetite. After even the lightest meal he was filled with nausea and drinking made him sickest of all. He alternately felt chilled and feverish. He dragged himself to work every day and found it hard to concentrate. He refused to see a doctor because he ''didn't believe in them''.

He did not see a doctor until many weeks later in Paris when he was dining with Melina Mercouri and Jules Dassin in their flat. In the middle of the meal he was seized with excruciating pains in his abdomen and collapsed. By the time the doctor came, Peter's face and body had turned bright yellow. The doctor gave it to him straight. He had a very bad case of hepatitis, and had had it for some time. He must remain absolutely quiet in bed for a month. Drinking during the next six months would prove fatal — the liver would not absorb the alcohol, and he was strongly advised not to drink for a year.

Peter stayed where he was in the Dassins' flat for a month with Melina nursing him. When he felt better he went back to London and did a lot of thinking about himself and what had happened to him.

CHAPTER 25

Peter's Long Farewell and Eletha

On 3 April 1966 Roderick Mann, who had been Finch-watching for
some thirteen years, caught his butterfly poised in an extraordinary
moment in flight and perfectly pinned down in his *Sunday Express*
column Peter's wander-thoughts — full of childlike, romantic
yearnings and carefully caught regrets about the past, quickly
balanced by a hopeful peek into the future. It sounded a sad, sweet
melancholy note that we were never to hear from Peter's lips again.
It was Peter's farewell — his long farewell to England. His
"Goodbye to All That". And, unlike so many of his predictions
about his life, it turned out to be true.

Six months from his fiftieth birthday Peter, stepping back from
the emotional debris of his life, had decided to leave England for
good and live in Jamaica.

"I've had a complete clear-out," he tells Roddy Mann. "I threw
all my clothes away save a couple of sports jackets and told my
mother to give my bicycle to some deserving boy. So now I haven't
got a possession in the world. It's a good feeling.

"I don't have to be frightened any more by that unwritten pop
chart of our business. I don't have to give a damn whether I'm on it
or not. Nobody can take away my car or my home or my swimming
pool because I haven't got them. And I've just enough money so
that if I want to stay up in the hills by myself for the rest of my life I
can ... It's been a year of introspection for me. I hate introspection
but it was necessary. Now I think I finally know what sort of a
person I am. Now I realize the degree of selfishness in any artist. It
makes marriage difficult. Emotionally, anyway, I'm not cut out for
it ... I'm too romantic ...!"

He is silent for a moment, searching to illustrate this point with an
example from his peripatetic past. "Let me tell you something. Not
long ago I was on a train going to Rome and I met a girl. At first we

spoke in Italian because she didn't know I was English and I didn't realize she was Irish. After we'd found out and laughed about it we had dinner in the restaurant car. Rather romantic ... Next morning, when we arrived in Florence where she was getting off, I helped her with her bags. I said goodbye and then, just as we were drawing out she came tearing up the platform holding a red rose in her hand which she gave me. And I thought standing there: that's how romance ought to be ... Fifteen years ago I'd have jumped off that train. Today I know better to leave it at that ..."

His thoughts suddenly stumble painfully on to his not so distant past. "It's awful, isn't it, how often unmoved we are by other people's emotions ...?" he asks more to himself.

And then Peter's wander-thoughts suddenly plunge back, way back, to his first little girlfriend in Vaucresson:

"When I was a kid living outside Paris there was this little girl opposite who had a tree house. I was terribly jealous of her. I wanted one too. Deep down, you know, I still want one. And the fact that I can't have it depresses me. It's a pity that people have to be judged by the way they live. If a lawyer lived up a tree for instance, you'd automatically suspect his ability to plead a good case for you ... Sad, that, I think ..."

At the end of the evening Roddy Mann gently helped Peter into a taxi at the corner, and waved him goodbye.

On this note Peter went off to Jamaica to settle down there, as he thought, forever. But he did not quite go into the hills and off into the blue all by himself. There was a girl there, of course, and her name was Mavis, though she disliked it and changed it first to "Jackie" and then to "Eletha".

According to Peter, he first met Eletha on the beach in St Anne's Bay where he used to swim. Possibly this gave him a feeling of continuity as he had met his former wives on beaches. He subsequently told Liv Ullman he had met Eletha in her teens when she was "running wild" around the island. In any case, by 1965 they were acquainted and by 1966, when Eletha was twenty-two and Peter was living in his three-room hut he'd constructed on his Bamboo property (and was the pleased owner of a peacock and peahen he had christened Love and Kisses), they were well acquainted.

Born in Falmouth, Jamaica, Eletha at twenty-two was short, dark-skinned, not pretty but with an impish, expressive face and a neat, sweetly curved body. She had been variously a hairdresser's assistant, a telephone operator and had worked in real estate. She made up in pep what she lacked in poise. She was a bundle of energy with an explosive voice and conversed as someone remarked, " at the top of her lungs", in a sing-song Jamaican accent. Said Peter of her approvingly, "She's a true primitive."

Eletha was also very much an "Up yours!" person. "She was rough-cut," recalls the Jamaican journalist Doug Campbell who had known her for many years, "Eletha was always rough-cut." As a child and an adolescent Eletha was what is known in Jamaican patois as a "ginnel" meaning smart-aleck, a cheeky little monkey always up to tricks and mischief.

Eletha was illegitimate and proud of it.

"I'm illegitimate, my mother is illegitimate, my father is illegitimate and my son is illegitimate," she was to say later to Peter's friends and family, with seeming defiance. In actuality this was not quite the defiant declaration of heterodoxy it seemed: quite the opposite — it was, one might say, the defiant declaration of conformity.

Unlike the upper classes, who are *plus anglais que les Anglais*, Jamaican working classes very often do not get legally married. Nor is there any stigma whatever attached to not being married, nor to having children out of wedlock, nor to being born out of wedlock. Eletha's mother and father both came from the working class (her father, Benjamin, was a boat builder) and therefore for them not to be married would be the rule rather than the exception.

Says Edith Clarke, the eminent anthropologist in her standard text book on Jamaica, *My Mother Who Fathered Me*: "Among the working classes, even promiscuous or casual affairs are carried on openly ... Illegitimacy has no social significance ... Sexual activity is natural and it is unnatural not to have a child and no woman who has not proved she can bear one is likely to find a man to be responsible for her. Maternity is a normal and desirable state and the childless woman is an object of pity, contempt or derision." Abortion is virtually unknown "as a woman is not 'really' a woman until after she has had a child. Motherhood is a hallmark of adult normal living."

Moreover, Edith Clarke continues, "Children derive nothing of any importance from their fathers who are marginal and ineffective members of their families except for procreation even when in residence. It is indeed indifferent whether the children know them personally. The households are matrifocal and dominated by women. The child is accepted as the woman's responsibility and there is no public censure if the men do not accept obligations and responsibilities of parenthood."

Peter and Edith Evans: two famous profiles who admired each other throughout the years

51 *Right: Daphne Laureola*, 1949

52 On the set of *Sunday, Bloody Sunday* with Olive Harding

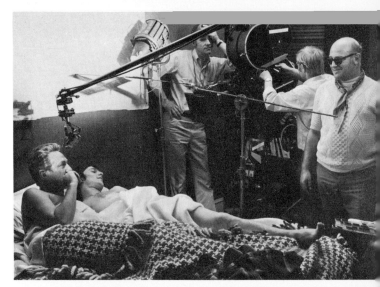

Peter as a screen
lover—

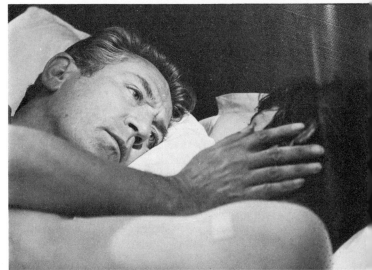

53 and 54 with Murray
Head in *Sunday,*
Bloody Sunday

55 with Anne Bancroft
in *The Pumpkin Eater*

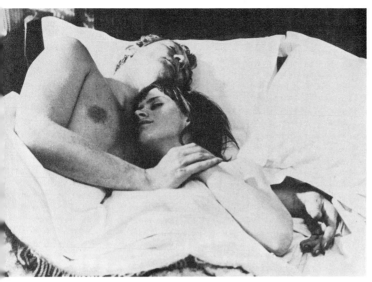

56 with Rita Tushingham in *The Girl with Green Eyes*

57 with Mary Ure in *Windom's Way*

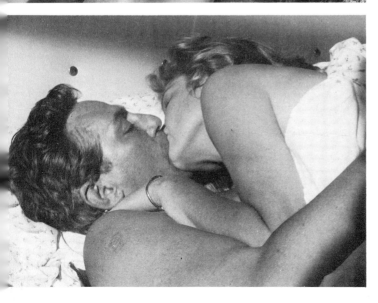

58 and with Mary Peach in *No Love for Johnnie*

Professions of Adolescent Love *and undaunted devotion are exchanged by Romeo (Alan Badel) and Juliet (Claire Bloom) while Mercutio (Peter Finch) and Tybalt (Laurence Payne) continue to battle for the honour of their respective families*

59

60 A Ronald Searle cartoon, used to illustrate the review of a production of *Othello*, which appeared in *Punch* in October 1951

Othello—MR. ORSON WELLES   *Iago*—MR. PETER FINCH

[*Otheli*

61 Peter in *The Seagull* (1964) with Peggy Ashcroft: "One of the finest Chekhovian performances I have ever seen"—Harold Hobson

62 Peter and Montgomery Clift encounter a cow on Laurence Evans' farm, 1964

63 *Top:* Major Wentworth
Edward Dallas Campbell
with the Poona Horse
Regiment in Jhansi, India
64 *Middle:* Peter with
Yolande and their three-
month-old daughter
Samantha, 1960
65 *Right:* Peter with Diana
Quiseekay

66 and 67   Peter's wedding to
Eletha Barrett in Rome,
November 1973—"Reader, she
married him!"

68 Peter with Eletha and their daughter Diana, 1970

Yet to this, Edith Clarke adds an important emotional rider. Over and over again in the interviews she conducted with working-class women, the majority expressed themselves "in some such phrase as 'I must seek a man to be responsible for me', so that", concludes Clarke, "the woman is never without hope that even the most casual relationship may lead to a 'concubinage' or marriage."

Like a Jew who has suffered from persecution all his life and comes to Israel for the first time, Peter, feeling that he had been made to pay all his life for his illegitimacy, must have seen in Jamaica a moral as well as a scenic paradise, a Promised Land where Eletha and her four-year-old child could live uncensured. It was only after he had settled down with Eletha in 1968 that he felt liberated enough to announce in *The New York Times* that he was illegitimate.

That Peter would have the greatest difficulties in assuming the role of a father could be foreseen, and there are abundant indications of this from his past. As far back as Australia, there is evidence of the emotional storms and ambivalences that would be released when he became a father. In 1944, after visiting his friends Syd and Bea Nicholls and seeing their new-born baby, he wrote to Tamara: "Saw their baby and had acute pangs of fatherhood realizing that after all it was an adult in the *prosses* of *groath* to be *protectid* and loved because it was so *helpliss* and *presious* but not to be *regardid* as a *plything* sent for the especial *benifit* of entertaining and amusing the *parints*." (Biographer's italics). Peter's attempts at correct spelling were weak but never had they so completely evaded his grasp. As previously mentioned, Peter's misspellings were strictly phonetic so we must assume with "plything" that he had even slipped into an Australian accent. A similar ambivalence was characteristic of his letters and postcards to his first-born Anita when she was only five or six, when he invariably signed himself "Peter" — never "Daddy".

After his divorce from Tamara, Peter's interest in his daughter Anita was sporadic although he supported her financially all his life which he was not legally required to do after her eighteenth year — and after his divorce from Yolande, his interest in his daughter and son, Samantha and Charles, seemed to cease abruptly.

In her late teens, Eletha had borne a child called Christopher and given him her surname, Barrett. In the manner of Jamaicans, she had kept the child, and cared for him. One can imagine the significance of this to Peter, for in the skinny little black boy, solemn faced and round-eyed, fatherless and unstigmatized, he saw himself: "if only". If only he had been born black and in Jamaica. Peter's heart went out to Christopher, and they quickly formed a bond. Olive Harding remembers the first time she laid eyes on the child in London, Peter leading the boy by the hand into her office and proudly introducing him saying, "This is Christopher and he is to have *anything* he wants." Olive also remembers Peter and Christopher sprawled on the floor in Peter's mews flat in London happily playing together with toy trains and trucks all day long.

And yet Peter insisted in preserving the honesty of the situation. When he legally adopted Christopher in the early '70s and the boy started calling him "Daddy", Peter said to him firmly, "Look mate, I'm *not* your Daddy. You call me Finchie, and we'll be great friends. Right?"

"Yes, Finchie," said the child.

With Eletha looking after him, seeing to it that he did not drink, with the simple basic life on the island, walking barefoot, exploring the hills, swimming in the Caribbean and sleeping on the beaches Peter, almost fifty, slowly recovered from the debilitating physical and mental effects of hepatitis and regained his unquenchable optimism and appetite for life. Says Doug Campbell, "Eletha always let Peter know loud and clear that she was different from all the other women, those bad women chasing after him who just wanted jewels and pretty clothes and money and photographs taken of them together to further their careers, and that *she* wanted nothing of him but himself and that he owed her nothing. In many ways she was a real star-struck kid. She just wanted to be able to tell her girlfriends that she was sleeping with a movie star." Eletha recalled for journalist Helen Lawrenson an unforgettable moment early in her relationship with Peter. "I was at a party and there was drinking and dancing and a Jamaican singer sang 'Blue Moon' and there was a big blue moon in the sky and I was with Finchie. Christ! Here were all my romantic fantasies come true." He was her key to fairyland in which she devoutly believed as she believed in all the primitive island lore and magic. She proclaimed she would weave a powerful spell around him and keep him with her always and always keep him safe.

Yet by late summer Peter was well enough to accept John Schlesinger's offer to play the tragic Boldwood in Hardy's *Far From the Madding Crowd*; he left Jamaica and left Eletha behind.

He arrived in London for pre-production discussions and costume fittings for his role and was quickly catapulted into a new romance.

Gerry had left the Buckstone and opened another theatrical club in Shaftesbury Avenue called, appropriately, Gerry's. There Peter repaired one day for lunch and there he first set eyes on Diana Quiseekay. He had said goodbye to all that — but once more — oh, just once more!

CHAPTER 26

Diana Quiseekay and Far From the Madding Crowd

Diana Quiseekay was a young singer and actress. Born and bred in Liverpool, her father was an African chieftain and her mother was Irish. She was tall, elegant, vivid as a tiger lily, and very unsure. So was Peter. She had recently made a hit in Lionel Bart's musical *Maggie May* and had been in a few television plays by Alun Owen. For the moment she was a part-time waitress at Gerry's.

"They had this new set-up at Gerry's", says Diana, "whereby you get the name of the customer and what they had at the bar before you take their lunch orders and everybody was getting very annoyed at me because I kept forgetting about it and I was getting very annoyed back. So I said to this man, writing down what he had at the bar, 'What's your name, sir?' And somebody said, 'What's his name? Don't you know who he is?' So I snapped back, 'Well, if I did I wouldn't be asking would I?' 'It's Peter Finch,' the guy said and I said, 'How nice for him.' Then I saw that Peter had heard and I thought, 'Oh-oh, I guess I lost a customer.' But then he started coming in for lunch every day and staying afterwards helping me re-set the tables. Then he invited me here and there. At first I thought he was just another uppity actor — I knew the name of course, but I'd never seen any of his films, but he did a special showing for me of *The Trials of Oscar Wilde* and I thought, my God, he's brilliant. I've seen a lot of his films now but I think he should have done some comedy because he was a very funny man. Hysterically funny."

Peter and Diana's tempestuous romance seems to have followed closely along the lines prescribed by *Private Lives*; the two contestants battling their way through bewildering lightning-struck mood changes from tenderness to assault, generosity to selfishness, passionate love to violent hatred and the underlying heartache of Noël Coward's Elyot and Amanda.

Says Amanda in *Private Lives*: "I think very few people are completely normal really, deep down in their private lives. It all depends on a combination of circumstances. If all the various thingummys fuse at the same moment, and the right spark is struck, there is no knowing what one might do. That was the trouble with Elyot and me, we were like two violent acids bubbling in the same bottle.''

Says Diana Quiseekay, the *café au lait* Amanda, ''What you have to understand is that I was dotty at the time. Completely dotty. I guess you might say I wasn't good for Peter at all — he was far too mature and clever for me. But of course, he was dotty too. It was the blind leading the blind. Only we didn't lead, we banged into each other all the time. We just did this thing to each other. We lived at the Mayfair Hotel for a long time. How they never kicked us out, I'll never know ...

''First of all there were the fights about drink. He was told he mustn't drink, he'd had hepatitis and they said that if he ever gets it again — that's *it*. He wasn't supposed to smoke either so he didn't want to see me smoking or drinking which was natural, I suppose. But I wasn't going to stop because nobody had told *me* not to, so we fought about it. Oh and petty, *petty* things! For instance, if we were sitting at the Pickwick Club where we used to go and a coloured girl walked in that neither of us knew, he'd say, 'Do you think she's good-looking?' Now, if I'd say '*yes*', he'd say 'You don't love me,' and if I said 'No, put her in a cage,' he'd say, 'You're jealous.'

''And don't forget Peter was a very possessive man, extremely, so at the least little thing — if I wasn't in when he phoned or something — he'd start a row and the worst of it was he never raised his voice, *never*, it was me who was screeching, but he would go on all night saying tu tee tu tee tu. That's what it sounded like, tu tee tu tee tu. Someone going on at you like that all night in a low voice can drive you crazy.

''At the time when we were living in the Mayfair Hotel, he had to go to court. His ex-wife, Yolande, was suing him for a lot of money, something like £65,000 and at the time he was having difficulty with money and the night before he had to go, we had a row and — he didn't know about it — but I kept my own flat on all this time, so, when we used to have rows tum-ti-tum I'd pack my luggage and I'd say right I'm off — going, going, gone. But before I'd even get into the elevator, he'd phone downstairs to the desk and say, 'There's a tall, lovely coloured girl about to go out the front door, do stop her because all the luggage she's got belongs to me. Please bring it back up.' Ha ha ha — and I would get out the elevator with the elevator man helping me and another fellow would be there putting my luggage back in again saying, 'What *are* you doing? These belong to Mr. Finch!' Well this might go on for quite a while until in the end we'd make up, order a bottle of champagne and blast the bill and fini! But that particular night before the morning he had to be in court, it was about five o'clock by then and it got so bad I hit him. I punched him really hard in the eye because I was really annoyed, he'd gone too far but of course never raising his voice. You could only hear my voice screeching through the hotel walls, never his. So I punched him in the eye and then we went to sleep and Peter's mother rang waking me about noon next day and said, 'How did the court case go?' Well of course I didn't know, he wasn't in the room and I had no idea where he was or when he'd left. I went downstairs in the lobby and started with tea and then went on to Guinness and it was about four-thirty and no Peter and I started getting worried.

"Finally he came through the swinging door and he had a great big smile on his face and he said, 'Hello darling, everything went marvellously.' And I thought thank God for that, at least he's not angry with me. Apparently he had to pay something, not as much as he expected. He said, 'I had to rush out of the hotel this morning to get there, didn't have time to shave but you hit me pretty hard last night and I wanted to find out whether I had a black eye. When I got to court I covered it with my hand and I was looking for a mirror all over the place, in the gents, none in the gents, I looked in the ladies, no mirrors.

" 'So I sat in court holding my eye and looking at the judge and everyone in white wigs and they were talking about "Now how much money" and blah, blah, blah, and suddenly I couldn't hold still any longer because I was laughing so hard because not only did I think I had a black eye but I suddenly realised that when I couldn't find my underpants this morning I'd put on your frilly yellow panties which I found on the floor. And I thought if these people should ask me to strip for some reason or other, they're going to think I'm a right lunatic. I just burst out laughing and one of the officials who was sitting opposite said, "Glad you find this amusing, Mr Finch." ' "

Around this time Diana started doing quite a lot of television shows, but whenever she asked Peter how she should say a particular line he would answer, "Oh well, do it your own way!" She realized that as far as his woman was concerned he did not want her to have a career.

"He didn't want me to work at *all*. 'I'll give you everything you want,' he'd say, which he did, but he did not want me in the lime-light. He used to buy me the most marvellous clothes, especially earrings. He was the kindest man, he was the kindest man ever — but I wasn't after his money. I didn't want to bask in his glory and this is where everything went wrong because he wanted to keep me like a china doll and I didn't want that.

"It's funny, he was a gentleman, but I think he liked me to screech my head off although he would never raise his own voice. I don't think he had much time for someone who is desperately trying to be a lady. He didn't want the tea-pot lady who is sitting there talking about, 'Eau, I was in Harrod's today, and what do you think I've bought?' He hated them, he seemed to hate those kind of people. He liked original people, he liked down-to-earth people, *well* down-to-earth, who said what they thought. Yet in a situation where I'd have lost my temper, he would just laugh."

When they started filming *Far From the Madding Crowd* in Dorset Peter rented a house in Weymouth on top of the cliffs. "A very strange house," says Diana. "The bedrooms were downstairs and the kitchen and living-room upstairs and we had mice as well. Because he had this habit, he used to get up in the middle of the night, like three or four o'clock in the morning and eat. Usually there was a huge bowl of fruit on his side of the bed so you would hear crunch, crunch, crunch and I would think, wish he'd hurry up and finish so I can get back to sleep. And sometimes he'd also go upstairs to the kitchen and eat, and in the morning I'd see bread and breadcrumbs all over the place and I said to him, 'Look Peter, if you keep this up, we will surely have mice, you are inviting them, as a matter of fact.' And he said, 'Oh don't be silly.' So one Sunday morning I was making the beds. Singing gaily and making the beds and Peter was upstairs doing his Russian borge. He imagined himself as a great cook, but it was tasteless. Russian *borge*, he called it. Ha! It was leeks, leeks, and more leeks, practically no meat at all and red wine and it was bloody tasteless. While he wasn't looking I would throw in the old Oxo cubes or something to give it some kind of body. Anyway I was downstairs doing the beds and suddenly I saw this mouse trying to struggle out of the suitcase, yes! and I took the stairs up to the kitchen six at a time. I couldn't even scream, I let out a choking sound and turned green and he said, 'What on earth is wrong with you?' and I said, 'I told you, I *told* you we'd get them, the mice!' Anyway, he had to send for the exterminator."

One thing Diana felt Peter was worried about was his looks. "For instance, it used to amaze me that in the morning the first thing he did — well, when I get out of bed in the morning I go straight to the bathroom — but he would go straight to the *mirror*. I didn't let him know I saw that. And whenever we were ready to go out wherever we were going he'd say, 'Do you think I look good today?' 'You look marvellous,' I'd say. He got more beautiful with age and I never stopped telling him that. He had the most marvellous eyes, beautiful, beautiful, he didn't have to worry but he did, you know.

"All the while he was filming in Dorset, I could never figure out when he studied his part. It must have been his fantastic brain because when I'm working, rehearsals are not enough for me, I go back home and rehearse by myself so I'm ready the next morning. But there was this little restaurant where we used to go with Alan Bates and Julie Christie and a few other people and we would all stay there very late and the next morning the chauffeur would arrive at six o'clock, Peter would be ready with the script in one hand and a cup of tea in the other and he would learn his lines in the car. Now to do that, you've got to be brilliant.

"At Christmas time and over New Year, Peter's mother came down to stay. I found her very attractive; I saw Peter when I looked at her, and I got the impression that she liked me. I was worried before she came down, I thought, let's see, what do mothers complain about when their sons invite them to stay with their girl-friends? They knock the girl's cooking, of course. But she was great. She didn't get up until two in the afternoon and I'd say, 'Would you like something to eat?' And she'd say, 'Oh lovely, that would be charming. What are you cooking today?' At first I thought, she's *got* to be knocking me, but after we'd finished eating something she especially liked she'd say, 'Diana, would you give me the recipe?' And that was really rather sweet because I suspect she couldn't boil two eggs. She gave me some really lovely earrings for Christmas and a photograph of Peter I fancied. And afterwards in London she would invite me over to her house and I always enjoyed being with her. An absolutely charming lady.

"Oh, Peter liked life, he loved life! He couldn't dance but he insisted on dancing. He used to stand still, glued to the floor, making a hole in it. The Jamaican bit. But I'm not Jamaican, I'm African, I like to move when I dance. He couldn't dance to save his life. Well, we can't have everything, can we?

"And another thing — I was terribly beauty conscious and all the rest of it then. I'd got a thing about limbs. And Peter did *not* have good legs. There was going to be a party for the company and Peter wanted to send to London for a kilt because he's half Scottish. And I said, 'Your legs aren't good enough. In order to wear a kilt you've got to have tremendous calves like a football player. And if you're going to wear a kilt, I'm leaving.' And he was very annoyed with me for the rest of the day, very hurt, wouldn't speak. But he ended up wearing tartan trousers and a dark green velvet jacket and he looked magnificent; absolutely splendid. Actually, crazy as I was then, my taste was still on. And another thing, he had bad elbows, he had just not got beautiful arms, put it that way, and when he used to push his sweater sleeves up I used to pull them down when he was busy talking and he never knew why I was doing it.''

After the film Peter and Diana wanted to go to Rome. But it was the time of money restrictions in England so instead they went to Ireland. ''We went over by ferry which left from Liverpool and somehow we got involved in a lot of drunken Irishmen as usual on the way across. When we got ready to go to bed we found we had adjoining cabins because they were all singles and when you're used to sleeping with somebody, you don't want to sleep alone and I said, 'I'm not sleeping in here by myself' and Peter said, 'Well, it's too small for two people.' But I made him sleep with me. I woke up in the middle of the night and I had forgotten all about being on a boat, and I thought, what the hell, he's too bloody close for comfort, so I thumped him and told him to move and there was no place for him to move other than the floor and then we had a row and there were people knocking on the door, saying you've woken up the entire ship, everybody's complaining about you. So he went to his cabin and I went to sleep in mine.

''Next morning I could smell kippers cooking. I opened his door and said, 'I smell kippers cooking, must be from the dining-room, breakfast don't you think?'

''He said, 'O.K. get dressed and let's go,' and I said, 'Definitely not after last night's performance because everybody on this ship knows where all the noise came from.' But I was getting hungrier and hungrier so I said, 'I tell you what, you're the big star, you go up first and see what happens and if it's O.K. come down and get me.' About ten minutes later he came back and said, 'It's O.K., everybody rushed at me for autographs.' So I walked into the dining-room like a lady, nobody said a word. And we'd upset that boat like you've never heard.

''In Dublin, Peter went on a health kick and he didn't want to go out and be tempted to smoke or drink. We had a nice flat and I used to go out to do the shopping and then I started noticing that when I walked down a ·street people used to make the sign of the cross — looking at me and making the sign of the cross.

''Now I'm Roman Catholic, and it bothered me, because I used to think, what do these people think I am, some kind of black witch? And I thought I can't tell Peter because he'll surely say, 'Oh, you've got another chip', or something. I didn't tell him for a long time until it really got on my nerves and I'd had a few drinks. I said, 'Why do these people in this bloody country make the sign of the cross every time they look at me?' He got out of his chair and said, 'Silly bitch, come on I'm taking you out because I know you won't believe it till I've proved it to you.'

"We walked down the street and he said, 'Now if you just take time to look around you, you'll notice that people who are making the sign of the cross happen to be passing a church and they can be looking at you and still know where the church is!' And I saw that was what was happening and it was perfectly true. Oh yes. Oh dear, yes.

"It got to be quite a funny set-up. Peter wouldn't go out. He was getting depressed and morose and he stayed indoors all the time. He said all I wanted was to be seen. And I said, 'Well, you buy me all these lovely things of course I want to go and show them off.' What irritated me was that everybody in Dublin knew Peter and hardly anybody knew me. Whereas in London, everybody knew me and everybody knew him. Great. I was working, he's a big star, I didn't feel ... But there we were in Ireland. He wouldn't go out, wouldn't have friends in. I started the secret drinking bit which is fatal and then he'd find out and the fight was on. And one thing led to another. I started seeing the few people I did know and he'd stay indoors all day painting. He fancied himself a painter. I know the man's a genius as an actor, right, but he claimed to be a painter and I only ever saw one painting that I really and truly liked. First of all, I'm allergic to paint and he used to wake me up in the middle of the night to show me what he'd been painting and I'd go Achoo! But the painting I liked was really lovely. It was of a cathedral near where we lived. And the sky was violet. He was always going on about how the skies in Ireland are violet around seven in the evening. And do you know, the last time I went to Ireland I noticed that they are. So he wasn't wrong. He'd painted this thing he saw through the window and that was the only one I ever liked ... He was writing a lot of poems. I never read them but I heard them all the time. They were mostly about clowns. Sad, sad, sad.

"I wasn't ready for him, you understand? I'm not saying that I was too young for him or he was too old for me, it was this: I wanted to be in the spotlight. I was the wrong kind of girl for him. He needed to marry a girl who just wanted to bask in his glory. I did not want to do that. That was the difference.

"One day I said, 'Look I'm leaving.' He said, 'I don't know why because in a couple of weeks I'll be going to New York about a film and then to Jamaica and we'll have a wonderful time there.'

"I said, 'Well, we happen to be in the funniest country in the world, called Ireland, and if I am not laughing here I can't see myself laughing in Jamaica either.'

"I got up one morning, took a bath, made myself some coffee, gave him some, got dressed and got packed. He said, 'Where are you going?' I said, 'I'm going to buy myself a plane ticket and then I'm going as far away from you as I can possibly get.' In the taxi to the airport I thought, what an awful way to leave someone. I never saw him again.

"I was writing a letter when the first bulletin of his death came on television and I was shocked. I'm not saying it brought tears to my eyes, no, but I was shocked and sorry because for many reasons, as I said, I left him bad. I would have liked to have seen him again and at least told him I'm sorry because I was wrong, yes, I was wrong, very wrong, I mean I was a raving bloody lunatic when he knew me, when I think about it now."

Peter's performance as Boldwood in *Far From the Madding Crowd*, for which he won another British Film Academy Award, ranks among his best; and the key to it is the way he answers the question in the audience's mind — why the heroine, Bathsheba, is not able to love this rich, handsome eligible man to whom she sent the provocative valentine.

It is because he bears down on her too heavily. He so oppresses her with the weight of his middle-aged love that the pressure of it becomes intolerable and repellent to her.

In one of his scenes Peter is shown playing what we always think of as the "female" role: it is the night of the ball he is holding in his house at which Bathsheba is to give him her answer. He roams around his rooms nervously checking the preparations, overbearing and irritable with the servants. Everything must be perfect for the occasion. He goes to his bedroom. From the bottom drawer of his dresser, he extracts his hopeful engagement present for Bathsheba. As he straightens up, the looking-glass on the bureau catches him by surprise and in it he sees the dread reality of his age. It is an extraordinary moment that begins with hope as he fondles the present and ends in wisdom as he sees the reflection of his face.

Was it for this remarkable scene that Diana had caught him peering anxiously into his mirror every morning? Or was it the perfect fusion of the man and the actor in his role?

CHAPTER 27

A New Life with Eletha

After Diana Quiseekay's departure, Peter went on walkabout. He walked from Dublin to Cork and back. Then he went to New York to discuss plans for his next film, *The Legend of Lylah Clare*, to be directed by Robert Aldrich and made in Hollywood.

On 7 July 1967, Vivien Leigh died. She had been ill for a year with tuberculosis and one evening, alone in her flat in Eaton Square, her lungs filled with blood and she drowned in her own fluid. In her will she left Peter a painting he had done of her. Vivien had changed Peter's life when they fell in love during *Elephant Walk*. Since that time they had become true friends and, in his mind, far more for he often confessed to intimates that he dreamed of them spending their last days together. Now he grieved for her bitterly. Was he only fifty? "*To a person who at twenty-one has been through more than a man of sixty*", had been Peter's twenty-first birthday toast. Was he now by that token really a hundred and forty years old? He felt it. One after another, in one way or another, all the women he had loved had abandoned him.

He went to Jamaica. Eletha was waiting for him, unshakeable in her loyalty. He asked her if she would go with him to Hollywood. She told him she would go with him anytime, any place, anywhere in the world. She left her child with her mother, Miss Bertha, and together she and Peter took off for California. All through the shooting of *The Legend of Lylah Clare* Eletha remained with Peter, a seeming shadow in the background, yet, in fact, always by his side.

A symbiosis had begun, marvelled at by all who witnessed it.

Peter found Eletha's view of himself and the world refreshingly different from his own. For one thing, she was not hampered by humility — spiritual or otherwise. She would have dismissed such a quality in herself contemptuously as servile and abasing, as arse-licking.

"Arse-licker" was her favourite epithet for such folk she decided belonged in this category; nor was Peter spared this epithet when from time to time she felt it necessary to warn him of the traps into which his good manners and good nature might propel him. Much given to hyperbole, she declared: "He is a prince to live with. Beside him I am a pauper." For this reason she made sure that he behaved like her idea of a prince. That it would not be everyone's idea of a prince did not disturb her in the least. Eletha was blessedly free from self-questioning or self-doubt. Dogmatic and opinionated, she was very sure. Sure enough for both of them. Never for a moment did she doubt that she was Peter's salvation. And by degrees, neither did he.

Although in the past Peter had never underrated his talents, he had been constantly tormented by self-doubt, plagued by indecisions and by the clear recognition of his faults and shortcomings. It was this lack of arrogance and aggression, he knew, that had made it impossible for him to be a successful "Up yours!" man. How could he help but be lost in wonder and admiration at the way Eletha always ended her pronouncements with, "Am I right." It was not a question; it was a flinging down of the gauntlet. Peter found her view of the world simple but exhilarating: the World was the Adversary. Under Eletha's tutelage he became less insecure and more content. He also became less easy-going, less outgoing, far less open-handed and less trustful and in his cups his streak of coarseness re-emerged.

Spotting a young English honeymoon couple in the foreign luxe hotel while on film location, he would enunciate clearly across the crowded cocktail lounge, "Going up to fuck?" whenever he saw them leave. He no longer bothered to mask his competitiveness, swearing to all and sundry that he would deal with the up-and-coming young actor who chanced to share his surname by stamping on his hands at his every attempt to scale the ladder of success.

The film *Lylah Clare* was a disaster. It was Robert Aldrich in his Gothic vein. But whereas *Whatever Happened to Baby Jane?* was great ghoulish nonsense, *The Legend of Lylah Clare*, with Peter Finch as the old-time director obsessively trying to svengali Kim Novak into the replica of an old-time movie star, was just nonsense.

Peter's next film *The Red Tent* which off and on was to take up roughly two years of his life, 1968 and 1969, and to keep him in Russia for months and months on end, was a well-intentioned bore.

This hours-long tale of the Italian explorer General Nobile's expedition to the North Pole and the subsequent court trial in which he is accused of leaving his men behind to die to facilitate his own escape, mostly takes place up North in the snow. I don't know what it is about snow blowing all over the Arctic, but somehow it is not very photogenic. For some reason snow, even when real, tends to look faked. The inside of an airship also gets a lot of footage and is not very photogenic either. Nor, I am afraid, was Peter Finch's acting. While I was trying to justify it on the grounds that an Italo-Russian production with a Russian-Italian-English-German cast etc., shot over a long period of time cannot help but diffuse and confuse the actors' portrayals, Sean Connery bounded on to the screen with his tight, riveting performance of Amundsen.

From *The Red Tent* on, when Eletha worked on the picture in Russia as a third assistant "rustling up tea and a wonderful sight in her fur boots", according to Peter, she became more and more directly involved in his work. In fact, so deep became their symbiosis that they talked of "we" in the context of his work as well as in their private lives.

Most wives or girlfriends rarely show up on a set while their husbands or boyfriends are working, preferring not to subject themselves to the immense boredom of sitting around doing nothing and feeling in the way. But Eletha on a set was not just sitting around. She was there because she had a special task to perform, and it was one that Peter wished her to perform. She was there to protect him. Says Anthony Harvey, who directed him in 1973 in *The Abdication,* "Peter would come up to me and say, 'Is it all right if Eletha comes on the set tomorrow?' and although I very much dislike having anyone not directly concerned around while I'm shooting, I always said yes, because it made him so happy."

From what was Eletha protecting Peter, one might ask, a man in his fifties with thirty years' acting experience under his belt?

Says a thoughtful co-worker on one of Peter's sorrier and later films, "Peter was fuelled by Eletha's suspicions. If Eletha saw a plot somewhere, Peter saw the plot and it could come from anywhere. Eletha's function was to keep Peter alerted to the great conspiracy surrounding him in terms of his career and its ultimate destruction and the people who were out to get him."

Says another close observer, "I think it was Peter who initially aroused Eletha's suspicions. I once heard him go into a ten-minute rather irrational diatribe about the greed, stupidity, arrogance and lack of sensitivity of people who run movie studios. He ranted on and on about how these people didn't understand the films that they produced or distributed and that they were the evil of the industry. 'The cancer of the industry', were his actual words, and that they 'must be cut out'. As I say, it lasted a good ten minutes. At the end of it, he suddenly turned to me and smiled and said, 'I'm insane. You've just seen something very few people see, but it gets me crazy.' "

Perhaps not many people had heard Peter hold forth in this vein, but enough had done so to make his feelings common knowledge. Olive had listened to this jeremiad many times as had the Whitings, Roddy Mann and Douglas Keay, and all of Peter's wives. Eletha was also very familiar with it.

The point was that Peter *had* a point, though it is arguable that "the people who run movie studios" were personally out to destroy him, however much he felt his theory justified when contemplating the majority of his films. The point also was that all his frustrated railings against the system could only lead to more frustration as the main way out of it was for him to go into production himself as many other top stars had done. Unfortunately, Peter was temperamentally incapable of doing this. Olive describes his sitting quietly through business meetings about his tax problems, bank loans, alimony settlements etc., and turning to her the minute the meeting was over, saying, "I didn't understand a word."

He might, with profit, have sought the advice of such stars as Alan Bates, Dirk Bogarde, James Mason, or the older ones like Henry Fonda and James Stewart, any of whose presence in a film has by now become almost a guarantee of its merit.

Peter's fulminations against the money men and the system fell on particularly fertile soil as Eletha listened to him. At the time she was growing up in Jamaica, a bright, energetic working-class girl, no matter how determined to get ahead, would find it well-nigh impossible to cross the class lines as an equal. The Jamaican working class was definitely kept down and "in its place" by both the middle and upper classes. There was also another curious fact that contributed specifically to Eletha's difficulty. In Jamaica at that time, black and white often mixed more equally than black and black, for the colour line was really drawn between black and tan, even subtle shadings between dark and pale being caste signs. This was what Peter had discovered when he looked more closely at the multi-racial society in Jamaica he had once exulted "really works".

For these reasons Eletha had always felt unfairly discriminated against. And when she began travelling abroad with Peter it would be natural for her to assume that this discrimination would continue on these issues. However, with her spunk and pugnacity, she was not only ready for it, she was ready and waiting. And, as Peter was always the first in her thoughts, she was prepared not merely to protect and defend herself but far more important, to protect and defend Peter.

If her protection campaign seemed at times to others to take an aggressive form, there is no reason whatsoever to suppose that Eletha, by her behaviour, was not doing exactly and precisely what Peter wished her to do even though he did not seem to take into account how other people might react to Eletha's outspokenness, lack of inhibitions, and — it must be stated — downright rudeness.

One evening in London, while they were drinking in the crush at the bar of the White Elephant, an actor came in, ordered a drink, and spotting Peter called out "Hello, Finchie." Eletha was standing near the actor and turned to him. "You a good friend of his?" she demanded.

A good friend of Finch's? Who at The White Elephant was not? Put off by her manner, the actor replied facetiously, "Never met him in my life."

"Then you don't call him Finchie," said Eletha.

The actor put down his drink and walked away in a marked manner. Eletha did not care. She was not entering a popularity contest, she was protecting her man. And one cannot blind oneself to the fact that it must also have given her a great deal of satisfaction to do it.

In pubs, Eletha liked to get up and sing and Peter liked her to do it. "Isn't she wonderful?" he would say to everyone there. In Russia, during the making of *The Red Tent*, they were dining at a large crowded restaurant in the company of a rather correct Englishman, when Eletha, feeling the urge come over her, got up and sang.

"Isn't she wonderful?" Peter asked the Englishman as they watched her. "What white person would do that?"

"I would," the Englishman surprised Peter by answering, carefully adding, "*if* I thought they wanted me to. But they *don't,* old boy, don't you see?"

But Peter did not. He marked off the Englishman's remark as just another racial snub. For Peter was as intent on defending Eletha from racial snubs as she was on defending him against the world. Standing together, they saw themselves embattled, courageously facing down The Enemy wherever it was to be found.

Alone, however, and by their own proud admission, they quarrelled a great deal. "We shout at each other and throw plates," said Eletha, "but then we begin to laugh and it's all over and we're still friends. When we are apart it is terrible. All the time we say, 'Come back — I can't live without you.' "

In the beginning, if Eletha had a fault in Peter's eyes, it was that she perhaps did not distinguish too nicely between hangers-on, which he agreed were a bad thing, and old mates and family, which were not. Eletha tended to lump them all together, especially the women, as part of his destructive, exploited former life and consequently wished to remove him from their dangerous influence. However, in cleaving through the shark-infested waters of his English and Roman past, her vessel hit a few rocks.

On one occasion in London, Letitia, Ken Adam's wife, easily as candid as Eletha, reproved her sharply. At an Adam party filled with film technicians with whom Peter dearly loved talking shop, Letitia, perturbed by Eletha sitting apart from the others looking obviously bored, finally went over to her and asked if there was something the matter. When Eletha replied that there wasn't, she just wanted to go home, Letitia pointed out that Peter was enjoying himself tremendously and that this was the second time at one of their gatherings that Eletha had behaved this way. "Can't you see that Peter's having fun and you're spoiling it for him?" said Letitia as she walked away.

In Rome, the Whitings were to see a good deal of Eletha's "Letitia" face. Says Whiting, "In an evening together the weight of entertaining her and talking to her fell on me because Peter expected me to take to Eletha and appreciate her. I tried very hard to find a subject of common interest with her but I was not able to do so. It must be said that a number of Peter's old friends in Rome drifted away from him. This was due to the fact that he himself was unfortunately more self-centered than before — but we all grow older — and was less willing to like people, perhaps less *able* to take pains over people. The arrogance of professional status and success and fame is not necessarily lovable or entertaining. It was arrogant rubbish for him to attribute the Roman reaction to Eletha to colour. The question of colour did not arise. What did arise was a reaction to Eletha's aggressiveness and Peter's defensiveness. Eletha had a side of domestic pure gold and I credited it to her. She lived for Peter and looked after him and for the first time in his life he had some money because they lived frugally and she attended to it. She boasted of her skill in bed and I have no reason to doubt it. Peter at this stage was rude to people not in a rebellious way but with the self-righteous pride of the Underdog ... ''

And yet Eletha off-guard, disarmed, relaxed, alone with Peter and her children or with new people neither she nor he had met before, could reveal a strong sense of humour and become a captivating comic.

To Roddy Mann, Peter ricochetting from what he felt were racist snubs and slights meted out to him and Eletha by his old friends, explained himself thus: ''Just because others have lost their zest for life doesn't mean I've lost mine. I've even had to dump most of my chums because they finally gave up — which is unforgivable. It's funny coming back here to London for a visit. Nobody knows me any more. Only the waiters. It's always that way. If I'm in New York, it's the coloured construction workers who yell, 'Hello' at me. The most unsympathetic characters I know are grown-up men with pipes. People keep on at me about settling down. Fortunately, I'm not afraid of packing up and getting out. It's fear of change that destroys a man. Anyway, I'm convinced that the best is yet to be.''

It is apparent that it was the fear of settling down — *physical* as well as *psychological* — that caused Peter in the last ten years of his life — always taking Eletha with him — to seem obsessively intent on recreating the conditions of his first ten years. It was as if, having got his sea-legs so early, he was unable ever to get land-legs; as if, in fact, he became literally *sea-sick* on terra firma if he remained in one place for too long.

CHAPTER 28

Sunday, Bloody Sunday

Not till the end of January 1970 did Destiny ring again for Peter — and then not a moment too soon.

The last part of '68 had been spent in Rome dubbing *The Red Tent*. And the first, middle, and last parts of '69, still in Rome, had been spent anxiously doing ... nothing. "I've got that old show-business feeling that the phone is never going to ring again," he said as he hovered over its stubborn silence, willing it to come to life as passionately as he had done at the Regent Palace Hotel during his first days in London.

Ironically, '69 was to have been a great year. It was to have been the year that Peter would make the film version of Malraux's *Man's Fate*, directed by Fred Zinnemann and surrounded by a distinguished cast. At least a year's work had been put in to the preparation of the script, contracts were signed and everyone was ready to go when internal strife at MGM caused the cancellation of the project. For Peter this was a bad blow in every possible way. Eletha was pregnant and funds were low. Money was going out to meet his alimony obligations and nothing was coming in. Yet that December, when Eletha gave birth to a baby who — although a girl whom they named Diana — was and still is the exact replica of Peter, he was ecstatic!

A black Finch! Peter had had a black Finch! He crowed his triumph all over Rome. And he particularly savoured the effect this news would have on his former "bodyguard", his aunt in the bad old days of his boyhood in Australia, who was still alive.

When Destiny did ring for him at the beginning of '70, it was Olive Harding on the phone. A month into the shooting of *Sunday, Bloody Sunday,* Ian Bannen, who had been playing the role of Dr Daniel Hirsch, was in hospital with viral pneumonia and its director John Schlesinger wanted Peter to take over the part. Olive said *immediately*! — Peter must catch the first plane to London!

At this point it is worth repeating word for word the favourite fantasy of Peter and Paul Brickhill as they ferried across Sydney Harbour in their copy-boy days:

Peter unexpectedly receives a cable from London! An emergency! He must replace the actor in the leading role of a new play about to open! It is a role that Peter is the only actor in the world able to fill! He must arrive immediately! He will have to fly! And Paul, of course, is the only pilot in the world able to fly him!

However, no doubt because Paul did not happen to be on hand in Rome at the time, Peter refused the role. Or rather, he told Olive that although the part might be all she said it was, if getting it was contingent upon entering an aeroplane and flying, then he would have to turn it down. He was sorry, but that was the way it was.

But Olive was not taking that. Crisply she pointed out that most of Peter's recent conversations with her had been taken up with him extolling the virtues of the younger generation in contrast with the shortcomings of the old fuddy-duddies of his own age. If he wished to be identified with the young, she pointed out, he must do what the young people did. They flew. And here one imagines Olive fixing him over the telephone wires with her special look.

Peter flew to London the next day. He met with Schlesinger, read the script of *Sunday, Bloody Sunday* that night and was ready to work the following week.

"There wasn't time to do a wardrobe for Peter," says Jocelyn Rickards, the costume designer. "Most of the clothes he wore in the film were his own."

"*Sunday, Bloody Sunday*", says John Schlesinger, "is probably the best film I've ever made. And I probably won't make a better one."

Certainly it is the most personal film Schlesinger ever made. Its very contemporary story is that of a triangle involving a career woman, a Jewish homosexual doctor, and a young man who designs contemporary sculpture with whom the two protagonists, each aware of the other, are having love affairs. Another person the career woman and the doctor share (and only discover they do half-way through the film), is the same woman on the same answering service.

Schlesinger had had this story on his mind as far back as '67 when he and Penelope Gilliatt, who wrote the script, first discussed it in Dorset while he was filming *Far From the Madding Crowd.*

Schlesinger also discussed it at length with his father, an ebullient eighty-one-year-old pediatrician with whom he was very close. On one of their country walks, Schlesinger *père* asked the question that had been uppermost in his mind. "Is it absolutely necessary on top of everything else, John," he said "that the doctor be Jewish?"

"Absolutely necessary," replied Schlesinger *fils*, and went on to talk of the enormous dichotomy between being homosexual and Jewish. Socially, Judaism, with its emphasis on family life, makes demands which are incompatible with a homosexual's natural inclinations, and religiously, Judaism is rooted in the Old Testament's fierce anti-homosexual stand. It was important to the conflict in the doctor's character, said Schlesinger *fils*, that he have a deep affection for his family as well as a trailing connection with his religous upbringing.

Schlesinger *père* thought it over and when they returned from their walk, he said to Schlesinger *mère*, "You know, it's going to make an awfully interesting film."

Says Schlesinger, "I had terrible opposition to get this film on in the beginning, but finally at United Artists they said, 'We don't know where you're quite going with it, but if you want to make it and it's not too high a cost for us to do it, fine. Go ahead.' Everything was thrown into our court. We made it at Bray, where they make the Hammer horror films. We had the studio completely to ourselves. And no interference from the front office. Away from everybody and shooting for about six months, we became like one big family. It was nice. Peter plunged right into his part and there was no time to talk it over with him. He knew the character in some way without, I think, ever having experienced any of it. After the very first day of watching Peter as Dr Daniel Hirsch, I sat back and said to myself with immense satisfaction, 'That's exactly what I wanted for the part: a pair of open arms.' "

Says Murray Head, who played the apex of the triangle, the young designer Bob Elkin, "I didn't have an easy time in *Sunday, Bloody Sunday*. I was working on two things at once; I was recording *Jesus Christ Superstar* in the role of Judas which I'd played in the original as well. I know they had a lot of trouble with me on the *Bloody Sunday* set because they felt I wasn't sufficiently concentrated on the film. But I think I would have gone out of my brain if I'd been stuck purely in it because it was heavy psychological stuff and my role was really getting to me. I was twenty at the time, fresh with Flower Power and embarking on a relationship with a girl and having all sorts of conflicting feelings about responsibility on the one hand and doing my own thing on the other, and I was beginning to hate the character I was playing. Things that were being pulled out of me that were like him, I didn't like a bit. It was getting very claustrophobic.

"That kiss thing — Bob Elkin and Daniel Hirsch kissing each other the first time you see them together was what finally let the outside world in for me. It was like opening a window and letting in reality.

"How can I put it? By that I mean that here was something for *everybody* to chew over, to worry about or think about. The Kiss! To me it was an infinitely simple gesture which caused ruptions right, left and centre. Suddenly one day on the set, first thing in the morning, people were coming up to me saying, 'It's *the scene!*' — that's what they called it, '*The scene*'. And I looked at my script and said, 'Well, I can't find the dialogue, what scene?' And they said, 'Ah — you know — the *kiss*.' And I said, 'Oh yeah, yeah, it is. I looked around and there were four or five photographers instead of the usual two. And a tenseness on the set. Everybody getting jumpy and I started to pick up the vibes of uneasiness. I thought, Sod them! This is ridiculous to get into this pitch over such a simple gesture of affection! So we began shooting and Peter was the easiest person in the world to get on with and do that sort of thing without any fuss.

"But there came a point in the shooting — I've never heard of it happening before — when the cameraman turned round and said to Schlesinger, 'John, is this really necessary?' and John snapped, 'Yes, of course it is!'

"And from there on in ...! At the rushes for instance, atmosphere in the viewing-room was fantastic. Everybody smoking four cigarettes at a time, crossing and re-crossing their knees, coughing and spluttering. This went on for a long time because there were quite a few rushes, different takes of the scene. I mean, the more it went on, the more they were embarrassed. I started to worry about it. And then, as I said, it let the world in for me because it helped me to get myself into perspective. I thought: Well, at least as a young person I don't find any trouble accepting this kiss at all. It consolidated my own feelings and the feelings that I knew people my age would have about the scene and the film as opposed to the older generation that was sitting all around me in the viewing-room.

"After that, for two or three weeks, members of the crew, you know, the grips, the sparks, who were men mainly in the thirty-five to fifty-year-old age group would come up to me and launch into sort of generalized discussions about the whole business of this film and homosexuality, and after about five minutes of this they'd zero in with, 'Of course, you being an actor, I suppose ... I mean, I don't know, but it's the sort of thing that would worry *me*. I mean, when you kissed Peter Finch, didn't you feel, well ... disgusted?' They'd finally got it out.

"I'd say, 'Well, you know, I really can't help you. I can see it's bugged you but no, it didn't feel any different from anything else I have to do in the film. I don't feel any problem about it.'

"So I started to think about the older generation, the war generation, where the roles had to be clearly defined: the men fought, the women stayed home or worked in munitions factories, and for these people after the war there was a continuation of this role-playing, and education was similarly structured — boys and girls separated and in somehow opposing roles, and then somewhere, sometime, they were supposed to meet and get together and everything was going to be O.K. And then came my generation in the sixties with our emotional explosion, young men with long hair and — to them — effeminate views and gestures. I wondered, was it that these forty-five/fifty-year-olds were brought up so differently from us, that they suppressed things in themselves so much, that when confronted with a symbolic gesture like the kiss, what really disturbed them about it was that it could happen with such *ease*?"

Has Murray Head illuminated for us the reasons behind the shock waves set off by this kiss? Undoubtedly it is its very casualness, the fact that it takes place while Murray and Peter stand together fully clothed, that gave the scene its shock value to audiences in the early seventies and was still doing it — I may add — to audiences in the late seventies.

"The unit was pretty tight," says Murray. "It was like a large family where if they're thinking one way and you're thinking differently — it starts up! It was the time of a general election and over lunch one day they asked me who I was going to vote for. I said, 'Well, to be honest, I'm not partisan at the moment because I still can't get it into my head what I feel is necessary.' Then it started up! 'That's typical! That is typical of your generation! It's people like you who are responsible for the downfall of this country, etc. No morals, no interests, no political commitments.' In the end I just sat there, potent with Flower Power and its vast and vague faith in peace, love and understanding. Peter wasn't there that day but it was to Peter that I increasingly looked as an ally because I was a Flower Child, but as I got to know him and saw how he lived — this mature man with his black girlfriend and no possessions — I thought of him as a Flower *Man*, and that's a lot harder to be!''

Interesting. While Schlesinger, Penelope Gilliatt and their seasoned actors were waging one war — the battle for sexual tolerance — Murray was deep in another one — the battle of Youth.

Peter's performance in *Sunday, Bloody Sunday* seems to be his most effortless. He was, after all, portraying a recognizable contemporary man in recognizable contemporary dilemmas. It seemed to me when I first saw it that I was quick in accepting the factors which formed Hirsch's character simply because the script had told me to. But I was deceived. Dr Daniel Hirsch is, in fact, Peter's most skilful performance. For nothing about Hirsch must seem in any way unusual. Neither his commitment to the medical profession, nor his commitment to homosexuality, nor his Jewish roots must ever "show". Yet at all times they must clearly be revealed.

Peter reveals Hirsch's Jewishness in a thousand different ways. He munches chocolate cookies and *marrons glacés* like a Jew. He loses his temper with the answering service like a Jew. He is respectful of his mother and father like a Jew. He enters the synagogue and slips off his yamulka and shawl like a Jew. And he shrugs like a Jew: that racial, self-incriminating shrug that says, "It's terrible — but it's funny too,'' instead of, for example, the Gallic shrug, which says, "*Imbéciles*! *Rien à faire*.''

As a homosexual, when he is with his beloved, Hirsch relaxes. He stretches and, ever so slightly, but positively — he *flirts*.

And, as a dedicated doctor Peter again brings to the role the full weight of his imagined experience.

His two most telling scenes in *Sunday, Bloody Sunday* are sharply contrasting ones:

Slowly driving through the night traffic in Piccadilly, Hirsch is suddenly accosted by a rather sinister young tough he once picked up when drunk, who jumps into his car and proceeds maliciously to needle him. Mortified and angry, Hirsch's only impulse is to throw him out. But the boy has hurt his hand in slamming the car door. That problem is easily solved for a doctor. He pulls up in front of Boots, the all-night chemists in Piccadilly to get something to relieve the pain in the boy's hand. But what Hirsch sees inside, the lost teenage addicts waiting for their drug prescriptions, is a pain beyond solving and in Peter's face we see their despair hitting at the heart of the doctor and his profession full force.

The other scene is in the synagogue where Hirsch has gone to watch his thirteen-year-old nephew's Bar Mitzvah. As he is watching the ceremony the camera shows us, in close-ups and in quick flashbacks, Hirsch's awed remembrance of his own Bar Mitzvah. And then, with a prickling of the spine, we seem to *hear* Hirsch's very thoughts (and they are complicated ones) as clearly as if uttered: as we watch him considering his life, we seem to feel first the doctor, then the homosexual and then the Jew gain ascendancy.

In conveying thoughts so powerfully, Peter was able to strike chords in whole audiences' group subconscious about their own early religious training whether it was in Judaism, Catholicism or Protestantism. It was, at bottom, the grown Peter reacting kinetically to an important experience, much as he had done when a child in Greenwich Point. Then, as he had watched the Australian Prime Minister "Billy" Hughes, his expression, we are told, changed in tune with that of Hughes', while his childish hand waved, now gently pleading, now clenched and unclenching, now pointing and drawing circles in the air, in unconscious emulation of Hughes' gestures. And, just as Muriel Farr so vividly remembered these reactions of Peter's after so many years, so Hirsch in the synagogue will haunt us for a long time.

We do not know whether *Sunday, Bloody Sunday* is to be Schlesinger's finest film but it is certainly his finest document, reminding us that in the late fifties, he was one of Britain's foremost documentary film-makers.

Some works of art are so precisely and accurately set in a certain country, in a certain city, in a certain year that their reality radiates in all direction — into the past that led up to them and into the future which they will shape. And by this token, paradoxically, they become dateless, because they become history. Such a work of art is Schlesinger's *Sunday, Bloody Sunday*, specifically about people in London in the specific year of 1970.

After *Sunday, Bloody Sunday*, in which, needless to say, Peter was discovered yet again and nominated for the Academy Award, he was out of work for over eight months. Murray Head, who was out of work for a year and a half, wonders if the film was possibly premature. People in the film industry viewing Murray's performance thought, well, O.K. he was all right in that film but I don't see him doing anything else. John Hurt later suffered the same predicament after his brilliant TV portrayal of the outspoken homosexual, Quentin Crisp. The only roles he was offered for the next year were homosexual ones. In print, discussing the situation, Hurt referred to the kiss in *Sunday, Bloody Sunday* as the Kiss of Death.

Sunday, Bloody Sunday was the last film Peter was to do with Olive Harding as his agent. By then, Olive had more than earned her right to retire from the triumphs and despairs she had shared for so many years with such originals as Edith Evans, Ralph Richardson and Peter Finch. From her cottage in Dorset and her house in Corfu, she looks back with pleasure at a career that started early in 1936 at the A. D. Peters Agency when, so green a girl from Devon she was nicknamed "Little Olive", she unwittingly committed a heinous breach of etiquette by re-sending an already rejected playscript to three leading producers at once, simply because she'd enjoyed reading it so much. When they all accepted it, she sorted out their outraged feelings by suggesting that since she had behaved in such an unorthodox way, why didn't they do the same and all three produce it? Forced to agree, they acceded to her proposal and the play opened at the Criterion on 6 November 1936. That was *French Without Tears*. And that was "Little Olive".

Jill Saint Amant, a close friend of Peter and Eletha's in both London and Rome, was working in the Barry Krost agency at the time and introduced the latter to Peter. From 1970 until his death, Peter was managed by Barry Krost.

CHAPTER 29

The Hard Way Down

The next film Peter made began shooting in May 1971 and was called *Something to Hide* based on the novel of Nicholas Monserrat. Having everything to hide, it disappeared from the cinemas very quickly.

In December, he went to Belgrade to work on the film of Graham Greene's novel, *England Made Me*. In spite of the good script and the excellent performances of Michael York and Hildegard Neil as incestuous brother and sister and Peter as the Krupp-type munitions tycoon, *England Made Me* was, maddeningly, a just-miss due to the incredibly fussy and overwrought performance of Michael Hordern who managed to give the whole plot away in his first frame.

In the spring of 1972 Peter went to Hollywood to begin filming *Lost Horizon*, an attempt to remake the Ronald Colman original by Hall-of-Faming it up with Charles Boyer, Sir John Gielgud, Liv Ullman and Michael York, as well as odd (very odd) bits of singing and dancing. In this "musical version", Shangri-La consists of an outdoor school room, a bridge over a couple of fish ponds, some pretty but unexceptional scenery, a dining hall where the survivors of the plane crash can all sit around and jaw about Life, and a dark room someplace off-stage where Charles Boyer as the Grand Lama has been in residence for about a thousand years.

After that Peter and Eletha returned to London to make *Bequest to the Nation* (in America *The Nelson Affair*), Terence Rattigan's screen adaptation of his stage play, with Peter playing Lord Nelson and Glenda Jackson as the now boozy and blousy Lady Hamilton. This film need not be dwelt upon as it was of no artistic importance whatever. It was, however, of grim importance to Peter's life as, during the shooting of it, at fifty-six, he suffered his first heart attack, albeit a mild one.

On the other hand Peter's next film must be dwelt upon because it is, I think, one of the funniest he was ever connected with, although — as in the case of *The Power and Glory* with the Australian Nazi thugs, and *Judith* with the spectacular Sophia — unconsciously so.

The Abdication was directed by Anthony Harvey in 1973 and starred Liv Ullman as Queen Christina and Peter as Cardinal Azzolino. Queen Christina arrives in Rome announcing her abdication from the Swedish throne, her conversion to Catholicism, and her desire to receive communion from the dying Pope. The college of Cardinals is sceptical and elects Azzolino to interrogate her closely over a period of time to assess whether or not her motives are sincere. The parallels of this seventeenth-century inquisition and today's popular psychoanalysis were unfortunately not lost on scriptwriter Ruth Wolff and in a thrice, as Liv and Peter begin their dialogue, we seem to be transported, fancy clothes and all, into a pricey New York analyst's office. I said "dialogue", but actually, like all good analysts, Peter allows Queen Christina to take up most of the footage and talkage flashing back and forth, dredging up details of her sensationally busy, but not (as presented) very interesting past, while Peter, static, supplies the feed lines on the order of "Yes, and then what happened?" between her gusts of highfalutin' language. Then, as in all successful analyses, we have the "transference": Christina falls in love with Azzolino. And then the "counter transference": Azzolino returns the compliment, though he gives her up in the end as the Pope is by now dead and he is to become, I *think*, Pope.

Richard Burton's début in Hollywood was in the religious epic *The Robe* in which he played the cynical Roman Centurion to Victor Mature's Noble Slave. At the foot of the Cross during the Crucifixion, in the wait between camera set-ups, Burton noticed Mature's face doing the most extraordinary things: his eyes bulged and his lips trembled. "Are you all right? What's the matter?" asked Burton in some alarm. "I'm making with the Holy Look," said Mature. Peter's Holy Look, as Azzolino, that of the frowning concentration of a man desperately trying to stifle a burp, was not as effective as Mature's. In fact it seemed to me as if Peter, uncomfortably trapped in his Cardinal's robes and the whole proceedings, was looking as silly as he dared without actually getting kicked off the film.

Noel Trevarthan, playing one of the ecclesiastics, says that Peter seemed very tired and unwell during the film. He took it very easy when not working, and his stand-in even went up and down the huge staircase at the Palazzo Farnese, outside Rome, before actual camera shooting. Peter told Trevarthan that he had a tricky heart, that it missed one beat out of every ten and that it had always done so. His contract stipulated that he neither smoke nor drink during the filming, and, adds Trevarthan, he did neither.

Says Anthony Harvey, "My strong feeling is that Peter was very glad to wake up in the morning and find himself still alive."

Eletha struck Harvey as "loud, animated, with a mad, childlike quality and a bubbling sense of humour. On location she would often have lunch with us and by the way, you could hear her coming all over the ravines, and Peter's face would light up." Says Liv Ullman, "The endearing thing about Eletha was that she was so loved by Peter." Said another member of the company who shared these lunch hours, "Eletha would start talking and out would come a non-stop stream-of-consciousness monologue that sounded like a James Joyce character let loose in the room. Then she would sail off somewhere and Peter would smile and say, 'Isn't she wonderful?' "

Shortly after *The Abdication* was finished, Peter decided upon his own abdication. He abdicated from the strong anti-marriage, anti-nesting position he had been so articulately vehement about for the past seven years; "that strange alchemy that happens when you marry and get that piece of paper that spoils everything" and so forth.

Reader, she married him! as Charlotte Brontë might have put it.

Eletha, having lived with Peter for six years and borne him a daughter who was now aged four, got her dearest wish and was married to him in November 1973 at the Methodist Church in the Piazza di Sant Angelo in Rome in a full white wedding. She wore a white satin bridal gown and veil and her two bridesmaids wore pink. Bertie Whiting was best man and afterwards, Prince Borghese, the one friend, said Peter, who had remained loyal to him, gave the reception.

Peter and Eletha had been living in the Italian sector of Switzerland in a little village surrounded by mountains near Lake Como called Ruvigliama. Their small apartment, without curtains, and with only the barest necessities in the way of furniture had been their home base since 1971.

About six months before this seemingly odd move to Switzerland ("All that tax-dodging and those actors reading *The Financial Times* and dining with their accountants would depress me," Peter had once said), George Ingle Finch, M.B.E., F.R.S., the distinguished Alpine climber and scientist died at his daughter Ann's house outside Oxford. In certain circles, being an F.R.S., a Fellow of the Royal Society, is of more significance than winning an Oscar, consequently George's obituary in *The Times* is inches longer than Peter's. In his last hours, George harkened back to his happy university days in Zürich and spoke only in his beloved Schweitzer Deutsch. It would be interesting to discover whether Peter knew of his official father's death and whether or not, in a strange way, it prompted his move to Switzerland, though this was perhaps for health reasons — or tax-dodging. What is a matter of record is that the difficulty of establishing residency in Switzerland was facilitated for Peter by the Swiss government's knowledge that he was the son of the great Alpine climber.

After his marriage Peter and his family, Eletha, Christopher and Diana, packed up, Finch-fashion, and got out of Switzerland. Although *The Abdication* had not yet been released, Peter did not need to be gifted with prescience to predict how it would be received by the majority of the critics and all of the public. The new Finch family camped in one of London's de luxe hotels while trying to decide what their next move would be.

If the film industry still did not know how to use Peter's extraordinary talents properly after all the clues he had given it over three decades, he might be excused for turning his back on it. Noting the films that swept the board at the Academy Awards from 1971 to 1974 — *The French Connection, The Godfather, The Sting* and *Godfather II* — he might also be excused for coming to the conclusion that since films could not use him, he had better use his other talents to do other things. There was a world Elsewhere.

At this point he could quite easily have returned to the stage. For all that the film people seemed to have ganged together for the sole purpose of misusing him, the stage still wanted him. It always had done. Not a year had gone by since *Daphne Laureola* without Peter receiving offers to act at Stratford, the Old Vic, and the National Theatre, to say nothing of the West End.

But the pluses — first, that securing the good parts in the English theatre could easily be accomplished and second, that a painful nostalgia and a strong desire gripped him now whenever he walked into a West End theatre — had to be weighed against such minuses as money (he was now supporting three families), his problem of tying himself down to one place and one artistic venture for any length of time and, above all, the consideration that Eletha was no happier in London than she had been in Rome — and if she were not happy, Peter could not be. These factors finally convinced him to return to Jamaica where, having already sold the small property Bamboo, he could buy another bigger estate and begin farming in earnest.

But some strange call of blood, some ancestral voice, seems to have been powerful enough to divert Peter, if only for the moment, from his appointed course.

On 2 February 1974, Peter's real father, Jock Campbell, died in Moffat, Scotland, aged eighty-seven. Peter and Eletha were in London at the time and his sister Flavia says, "I want to emphasize that this is all second-hand, but my mother told me that Campbell wanted to see Peter before he died and — and this is also second-hand — that Eletha did not want Peter to go up there."

It is a definite fact that, although Peter did not go to Scotland then to see his father, he nevertheless did go soon after his death. "I took Eletha up to Scotland just before deciding on Jamaica," he told Roddy Mann. "I thought I might buy a place there. I had visions of myself as a laird. But the weather was dreadful. I saw some poor shepherd huddling on the mountainside trying to shield himself from the scudding rain and I don't mind telling you that my Scottish dream evaporated. Without even getting out of the car, I just turned round and headed back."

CHAPTER 30

The Ungentlemanly Farmer

Upon the Finches' return to Jamaica, Peter purchased a property called Brighton, near Oracabessa and not too far from St Ann's Bay. The land consisted of about a hundred acres of bananas, allspice, citrus and timber.

Peter, in his fifty-eighth year, and having had only very sporadic spells of actual farming in his past, now took on the immense challenge of becoming not merely a plantation owner but a plantation worker. He had that "old Tolstoy thing" as he put it, "of believing that you must share the sweat and tears of the workers. No good sitting and sunning yourself on the verandah."

At first and as always, he flung himself into his new and arduous existence with characteristically wild enthusiasm, with that extra dose of life he always seemed to possess. It was a common sight to see him taking a short break stretched out in his fields with a handkerchief over his face to keep off the flies. Neither Eletha nor the children, however, shared his wild enthusiasm. In fact it was a clear case of How're-you-going-to-keep-them-down-on-the-farm-now-they've-seen-the-world, the beautiful little chocolate-coloured Europeanized Diana constantly wanting to know, "Daddy, when are you going to take me away from this Africa place?" And soon other problems surfaced.

Bananas were Peter's main crop and a tricky one. They are not seasonal. They require constant attention and expense. They bruise easily and require special packers and special packing. Many of the bananas that Peter offered for sale were rejected because of bruising and swamp spots. There was also the local custom of "sugar money" which, by tradition, allowed the workers to "keep" rather than "steal" bunches of bananas regularly. Moreover, Peter himself stank so badly of banana fertilizer that his children begged him not to come to their school for them. Added to these setbacks were political upheavals and increasing anti-white feelings in Jamaica.

After a year of persevering, of fighting and losing battles, Peter sold Brighton and in the spring of 1975 he bought a splendid eighteenth-century manor-house called Cardiff Hall on a plantation with a more manageable seven acres. He was not to remain there long.

Shortly after the Finches were settled, Destiny was on the phone again, this time in the stocky guise of Paddy Chayefsky calling to tell Peter he was sending him the script of his upcoming film, *Network*. This time Destiny was ringing for Peter for the last time.

Network from its very inception was one of those rare films blessed to proceed smoothly, steadily and surely towards its final triumph. "When things go so right it seems so easy you don't see how they ever went wrong before," says Susan Landau, one of the production assistants. Paddy Chayefsky, still in a euphoric daze months after its completion, was telling people, "As writer-producer always on the set every day, I'm a pain in the ass and I know it. I'm a worrier. I'm used to panic and hysteria in a production. It's always there. So I waited for it all through making *Network,* waiting for something to go wrong, something to snap, for cracks to appear ... and ... *it never happened!*"

It all seemed to come about like a fairy-tale: one morning the director Sidney Lumet received the completed script from Chayefsky. He read it that day, thought about it that night, and the next morning rang Paddy to say, "It's magnificent! Let's do it." Wheels were promptly set in motion with Chayefsky and Howard Gottfried as producers in conjuction with MGM and United Artists. So far so good.

Now for the business of casting, which turned out to be a very serious business indeed. Chayefsky is one of those scriptwriters who has grasped the revolutionary principle that "talkies" should talk. *Network* had what is known as a "literate" script, the sort in which only highly experienced actors, hopefully actors with stage experience, could succeed. "In looking for those kind of actors," says Chayefsky, "with a few obvious exceptions, you have to get out of America fast."

The casting sessions, however, were not without their lighter side. Lumet, one of the most popular and sought-after directors, tended to say of everyone suggested, "Oh yah. Yah, I hear he wants to work with me," until silenced by the remark, "What about Edward Arnold? He's dead, but I hear he wants to work with you."

Chayefsky and Lumet arrived at Peter Finch by a roundabout way. Says Paddy, "First we thought of him for the part of Max Schumacher, the head of the network News Division and we thought of William Holden as the anchorman newscaster, Howard Beale, who becomes the mad prophet. Then suddenly we realised we'd got it wrong way round. It was Holden as Schumacher and Finch as Beale — *if*. The big 'if' was: if Finch could do the American accent."

In Jamaica Peter waited impatiently for the *Network* script to arrive. He had long been a staunch admirer of Chayefsky, having said as far back as 1964, "We English don't have anyone like Paddy Chayefsky, any really outstanding screenwriters who come blazing up with original screenplays the way he does." When he read the script, when he studied the astonishing role they wanted him to play he was over the moon with joy. Immediately he got in touch with Lumet through his agent Barry Krost and told him to send tapes of the top American anchormen. Tapes of Walter Cronkite, Howard K. Smith, and John Chancellor were sent. It was Chancellor's voice and personality Peter felt closest to as he studied these tapes and worked on his voice for two months.

Says Lumet, "When Peter came over to America to see me and began reading to me from the script, what I heard was all the British quality of his speech marked out. But more than that, I heard that he had been clever enough to understand that our best news commentators speak *un*-accented English, mid-Atlantic if you like, so he didn't try to reproduce some travesty of a regional American accent as many English actors do. The part was Peter's."

Lumet continues: "Paddy and I always had a very clear picture of what we wanted in the character of Howard Beale. We needed first someone with a great understanding of language: the rhythm of language, the use of language, and its *sense*. It is unusual to say the least for a film to have four- or five-page-long speeches in it and Beale had five of them over the body of the film. So language was very important. But we needed equally someone who could convey the fact that although Beale is a madman, he makes the most sense of all the characters in *Network*. So it is vital that we see Beale's underlying humanity at all times. Because he is such an outrageous character, there is always the danger that at some point the audience might switch off and say, 'Oh, God, it's just too bloody much! He's crazy, why listen?' But the essential quality in all Peter's work was tenderness, an extraordinary vulnerability and a deep humanity. And it was that humanity that enabled the character Beale never to lose his connection with the audience. Peter was a director's dream to work with because he had everything he needed to help a director: an incredible instinct and a back-up of formidable technique so that he did not have to stay on simply an instinctive level, but could reach higher and higher in performance.''

And so it came to pass that the Finch caravan of élite gypsies—Peter, Eletha, Christopher and Diana—again packed up and left home. March 1976 found them encamped at the Hotel Pierre in New York.

CHAPTER 31

Network

There were to be two weeks of rehearsals for the *Network* cast before the actual shooting of the film. Every morning Peter left the millionaire spaciousness and splendour of his Fifth Avenue suite to walk eighteen blocks south and one long cross-town block west to attend rehearsals in the ballroom of a hotel named, with unaffected fastidiousness, the Diplomat, located on 43rd Street and Sixth Avenue, not far from the most sordid red-light district in the world. Although it was March, it was cold and snowy and the ballroom was unheated.

The only one who caught cold, however, was Chayefsky sitting on the sidelines.

It was make-believe-ballroom time and any layman who has watched actors recreating whole sets and circumstances and situations out of their imaginations in these unpromising surroundings will agree that it is an awe-inspiring sight.

Ail the members of the *Network* company vividly remember the first meeting between the veteran actors William Holden and Peter Finch. It boded well for the film.

Susan Landau, a production assistant, says: "Bill and Peter took to each other instantly. I have never seen such love and recognition like that between two people; such mutual respect. Both men had been there and back in their lives, you might say, and both had been away from films for a long time. They shared so much together. Anger, and respect for acting, and pride in acting. And they loved swapping stories about the old days. Then Paddy joined them and the three were as thick as thieves."

Paddy: "When we went up to Toronto to shoot the TV sequences, Bill and Peter and I had lunch every day and dinner every evening together and we so looked forward to these meals we almost couldn't wait for the day's shooting to be over. The three of us talked about everything under the sun. Peter was a great story-teller and also entertained us vastly with on-the-spot improvisations. He improvised scenes by Chekhov, scenes by Shakespeare, scenes by contemporary American playwrights. They were brilliant! He read a lot and gave me books to read — anything from Chekhov's letters to scientific articles.

"However, one thing we did *not* talk about was his role. I started to once, adding, 'Actors tell me all I end up doing is frightening them' — and after half an hour, Peter agreed. But like George Scott, Peter didn't have to be talked to about his part. He didn't have to be directed. He had already done his work. But, unlike Scott, he loved acting. Loved everything about it. Hung around the set all day whether he was working or not. And God, he was handsome. He looked like a Roman senator."

Susan Landau: "The physical transformation of Peter on the set was remarkable. He *was* Howard Beale. But slumped on a chair in the hotel lobby waiting for Eletha who was always late, he looked ... well ... he looked a lot older. We all became good friends and saw a lot of each other and I could see pain behind a lot of things he did; pain behind his drinking and his travelling and running around. By the time we were shooting in Toronto, Peter and Eletha had rented an apartment in that old Art Deco building, the Sunset Towers on Sunset Boulevard where Edith Sitwell had once stayed and wrote about in her memoirs, and Eletha was flying up and down between the two places. Peter seemed lost when she wasn't there. Only with Eletha was he really happy."

On the set, Peter was the Ultimate Professional. In Toronto, working every day for three weeks from eight in the morning till six in the evening creating his long and difficult part, he was always letter perfect. Says one of the company, "For Peter, there wasn't any other way to do it except perfectly."

If Peter was the ultimate professional, Eletha was the ultimate amateur. An unflagging film fan — she sometimes took in three films a day with pleasure — she enjoyed overseeing the work on a film set. One day, after viewing some of the rushes, she went up to Sidney Lumet and explained to him that Peter needed two more close-ups in a certain scene. "Yah, pussycat, yah," said Lumet hugging her affectionately. Peter did not get them. Undeterred, Eletha went back into the arena again and fought Lumet hard for the close-ups. She did not win. In the making of a film the director is the ultimate boss. A film editor once told me of Liz Taylor in tears in the cutting-room, begging the director to allow the image of Burton's face to linger on the screen for five seconds more. The answer was no. There can be no doubt that the "two more close-ups" scheme was one of Peter's wishes, and there is something wonderfully innocent about the two of them thinking that Eletha was going to obtain them.

In the character of Howard Beale, the magisterial middle-aged news anchorman recently fired from the UBS-TV network because of his plunging ratings (one is reminded of Peter's remark to Roddy Mann in '66 of his fears about "that unwritten pop chart of our business"), Peter, at last, had found that once in a lifetime role in which his weight of *imagined* experience was no longer required. He no longer had to imagine himself a Jew, a homosexual, a cardinal, a doctor, a millionaire munitions tycoon or an Admiral of the Fleet. He no longer had to imagine anything. The reality of Peter's life experiences matched those of Howard Beale both in a general way and in strikingly similar details. Peter's long experience of broadcasting studios were those of Beale. Peter's close ties of male mateship were those of Beale with his long-standing friend Max Schumacher (the very sight of Beale asleep in a rumpled ball on Schumacher's sofa was to be unbearably poignant for Peter's old mates, many of whom did not see *Network* until after his death); and Peter's tirades against the monster film industry matched Beale's tirades against the monster television. For not only had Peter lived through Beale's experiences, but he also shared Beale's beliefs, thus proving Einstein's theory that parallel lines do meet at some point in time.

Actors will tell you they can take no greater risk than to attempt to play themselves; for if one no longer has to imagine anything, one can no longer hide behind the protection of one's imagination. To play oneself honestly, one must be willing to strip one's soul bare in public. Dame Edith Evans said she had to reach her fifty-seventh year to find the courage to do so. Peter was lucky in that when his time came to accept this challenge with all its attendant dangers, his technical skills had perfected themselves enough to permit him this kind of naked self-expression.

Network is Paddy Chayefsky's searing, savage, satirical look at the misuses and abuses to which the power of television can be put when those in command become crazed with greed and starved for profit. Specifically, the question he poses is: how far is an ailing network prepared to go in the exploitation of the public's "tastes" and "trends" to regain and hold its vast audience?

Diana Christensen (Faye Dunaway) and Frank Hackett (Robert Duvall), both television executives schooled in the glories of ruthlessness and cut-throat competition, are prepared to initiate a popular weekly series of blood-bath celebrations of man's inhumanity to man, featuring terrorists kidnapping heiresses, robbing banks, hijacking aeroplanes, blowing up bridges and assassinating ambassadors executed by — as Diana cutely puts it — "a bunch of hobgoblin radicals" called the Ecumenical Liberation Army. Diana is secure in her knowledge gleaned from mountains of market research reports, polls and surveys, that that is what the public wants. So why shouldn't UBS-TV serve it up to them?

The American people, she announces in sprightly tones to her staff, have been clobbered on all sides by Vietnam, Watergate, inflation and depression. They are turning sullen. They've turned off, shot up and fucked themselves limp, and nothing helps. So, she concludes, what the American people now want to see on television is *angry* shows, someone to articulate their rage for them.

Although the theme is treated satirically, Hackett and Diana are instantly recognizable as the types of people who often hold down important positions in mass media. The sort of people who, in President Truman's memorable phrase about the Kennedys, "keep their ears so close to the ground they've got grasshoppers in them".

Therefore when the magisterial anchorman Howard Beale cracks up and announces on his news show that he is going to "blow his brains out right on the air a week from today ... (pausing to give Peter's famous "human frailty" smile) next Tuesday", and Diana sees that one of the results of the ensuing uproar and publicity is that Beale's ratings have shot up, she begins to take a personal interest in him.

The next day, repentant, Beale pleads with Schumacher to let him go back on his show that evening just to make some brief farewell statement. "I have eleven years at this network, Max," he says. "I have some standing in this industry. I don't want to go out like a clown."

(At these words of Beale's, Peter's old mates felt another knife-like stab, for if *The Abdication* had been Peter's last film he would indeed have "gone out like a clown".)

Out of regard for their old friendship, Schumacher agrees to give Beale two minutes on television to bow out with dignity. That evening Beale reappears on his show and begins, "Good evening. Yesterday I announced on this programme that I would commit public suicide, admittedly an act of madness. Well, I'll tell you what happened. I just ran out of bullshit ... " Chaos in the studio again. Telephones jangling. But Schumacher, who has just been informed by Hackett that his news division is being drastically reduced in status from that of an independent division to that of a department accountable to Hackett himself, refuses to cut Beale off the air.

"I'm leaving him on," he shouts into one of the telephones. "He's saying life is bullshit and it is. So what are you screaming about?" And Beale continues on the air explaining exactly why he feels life is bullshit, ending with "I don't have any bullshit left. I just ran out you see ... "

For saying that life is bullshit on TV, Beale becomes something of a folk hero. Quickly cashing in on his notoriety, Diana and Hackett take over Beale and his news programme, advertising him as The Mad Prophet "inveighing against the hypocrisies of our time" and urge him on to continue doing "his angry man thing".

One night in bed Beale is awakened by an invisible Voice talking to him. Imbued with the Voice he goes on television the next night telling the public he has agreed from now on to allow the Voice to put words into his mouth about the truth. Not Eternal Truth, Absolute Truth or Ultimate Truth, but impermanent, transient, human truth. "I don't expect you people to be capable of Truth," said the Voice to Beale, "but goddammit, you're at least capable of self-preservation! That's good enough! Right now you've got forty million people in America listening to you and after tonight's show you'll have fifty million. So I want you to tell these people how to preserve themselves." "So I thought about it for a moment," finishes Beale, "and then I said: O.K."

Then comes a sequence that is certainly the most irresistibly moving — the most breathtakingly *bearably* moving sequence ever filmed of Peter. Asleep on Schumacher's sofa, he wakes to the sound of the Voice. Putting on a coat over his pyjamas he walks out into the rain and tramps around New York all day. That evening just before his broadcast, still in pyjamas and drenched from the slashing torrents of rain, his grey hair plastered in streaks across his forehead, Beale enters the UBS-TV building. "How do you do, Mr Beale," beams a black security guard respectfully. Beale stares at him. "I must make my witness!" he exclaims. "Sure thing, Mr Beale!" says the guard enthusiastically springing forward to open the studio door for him. (And at the roar of laughter from the audience that this short exchange is always greeted with, Peter's old mates smiled with delight. At last — if only for a moment — Peter was playing comedy!)

Now on the air, still soaking wet, Beale delivers his first exhortation towards the self-preservation of humanity.

"We all know things are bad," he begins. "Worse than that. They're crazy." And he proceeds to list some of them: shopkeepers forced to keep guns under a counter, punks running wild in the streets, the dollar that doesn't buy a nickel's worth, the air not fit to breathe and the food not fit to eat while we, the people, sit in front of our TV sets listening to a newscaster telling us that today we had fifteen homicides and sixty-three violent crimes as if that's the way things are supposed to be. "All I know," says Beale, "is first you've got to get mad. You've got to say, 'I'm a human being, goddammit. *My life has value.*' I want you to get out of your chairs and go to the window," he exhorts his unseen audience. "Right now. I want you to open it and stick your head out and yell. I want you to yell: '*I'm mad as hell and I'm not going to take it anymore!*' "

The glorious and exhilarating scenes that follow in the accompanying thunderstorm — when inspirited by Beale's message, window after window goes up all over New York and people call out from their hearts, "I'm mad as hell and I'm not going to take it any more!" — have been compared by some critics to the mass hysteria at the Nuremberg rallies. To compare these pain-filled, heart-lifting cries, united in the common understanding of human frustration, with the demagogic rantings of Hitler's gang at Nuremberg, is like comparing a reprieve to a death sentence. And the ringing tones of Beale's sad brave voice make this abundantly clear.

Just so must the voice of Krishnamurti at the Theosophy Golden Jubilee in 1925 have inspired the nine-year-old child, Peter Finch, as he sat at his feet in Adyar and heard him proclaim: "I come to those who want sympathy, who want happiness, who are longing to be released. I come to reform, not to tear down, not to destroy but to build ... " And as Beale was imbued by his Voice to go on television and preach self-preservation, so Peter was imbued by Krishnamurti's voice to run off to a Buddhist priest, to take his Buddhist vows in search of enlightenment.

The Howard Beale hour, now the number one show on television, gets a new format. The star is Beale. In a huge, packed television studio, the curtain parts. As Beale, silver-haired and impressive, walks on to the dais a golden spotlight lights up his figure while above him, a shimmering stained-glass window pulses waves of exquisite colour.

The parallel with Peter's own spiritual experience is perfect! One recalls Annie Besant saying of Krishnamurti in 1925 in Adyar: "Pulsing with waves of exquisite colour, a pillar of golden mist vested Krishnamurti's body. Overhead shone great globes of light too dazzling to look upon. He stood on a dais under the banyan tree. An audience of three thousand delegates sat on the ground at his feet."

Once a week Howard Beale goes on television to inveigh against the dangers of our time. With facts, revelations, and reasoned if impassioned arguments, what he is preaching, basically, is common sense. As Sidney Lumet said, although Beale is supposed to be a madman, he makes the most sense of all the characters in *Network*.

Meanwhile, Diana as "Television Incarnate", backed up by Hackett, goes about her merry way, busily corrupting everything she touches: Schumacher with their love affair; Laureen Hobbs a sincere young black Communist and The Great Ahmed Khan, the chicken-bone-munching leader of the Ecumenical Liberation Army, by turning them both into showbiz for her three-ring TV circus where the media is the message and the message for the performers is money.

This takes us into the wild landscape of a farmhouse hide-out, the perfect setting for a conspiracy. Inside, Laureen Hobbs, a kidnapped heiress, Ahmed Khan, a clutch of corporation lawyers and agents from I.C.M. and the William Morris Offices, each flipping through their eighty-page contracts, engage in acrimonious hassles over gross proceeds, sub-licencings, subsidiary rights, overheads, residuals and distribution costs, while hurling bits of political dogma at one another. In its stinging hilarity, it is reminiscent of the famous Big Board scene in *Dr Strangelove*.

Twists and turns of the plot finally lead to Beale telling the people the final truth: that the world today is a vast corporate cosmology expressly designed for the consumption of useless things. It is a truth too unpalatable for the public.

His ratings plunge again because he refuses to let up on what Diana disgustedly calls "all that corporate shit" and the network board of directors finally has to silence him. Permanently.

The casting of *Network*, down to the last non-speaking earphoned studio engineer, is impeccable. Lumet's well-known preference for working primarily with stage actors pays off in brilliant vignettes by William Prince, Wesley Addy, Ned Beatty and Beatrice Straight. As for the stars, Dunaway, Holden, Finch and Duvall, they are all at their best. Students of fine acting will be well rewarded by seeing this film four times, allowing themselves each time to savour one of these four brilliant performances.

Peter's performance was unique and underivative. It owed nothing to anything or anyone but himself and the unique way he saw and felt and did things. But as I watched *Network*, listening to him and responding to his rhythms, some strangely matching rhythms, some strangely matching words, matching harmonies, some distant echoes of *something* ... something quite separate and distinct from the film seemed striving to make itself heard in my consciousness. What? I only found out after he was dead.

CHAPTER 32

Running for the Oscar

When the Finches returned from Toronto to their apartment in the Sunset Towers so that Peter could complete *Network* at M.G.M. studios, he found much to his surprise that he *loved* life in Southern California!

This new love was based on Eletha's joy and excitement at living in the film capital as well as Peter's enormous new satisfaction in his work. It was a love, one might say, based on both his and Eletha's final all-round acceptance of the reality that Peter was an actor before anything else and that as Hollywood had again become the centre of the film industry, it was the place to be. But Peter — being Peter — was also glorying in the Southern Californian desert scenery which reminded him of his Australian outback. He was painting constantly now, every chance he got, and his paintings were almost exclusively hard-edged abstracts of desert landscapes.

Now the Finches wished to become Americans. To this end Peter immersed himself in Americana, interesting himself in recent Indian excavations in California and reading huge amounts of books on American history such as volumes of the *Adams Chronicles* while, more practically, Eletha saw to it that their lawyer set the wheels in motion so that they would be eligible for citizenship when the time came. Peter, of course, already had his H-2 visa granting him special permission to enter the United States for the purposes of work, and it would be a matter of months before he got his Green Card, that card of magical colour, that changes one's status from visitor to immigrant and gives one special permission to work in the States *without* having to get special permission.

All that was left for the Finches was to find a house for them and the children to settle down in. The one they chose as their hearts' desire was a modest one in Beverly Hills off Benedict Canyon on Ysidro Drive on the other side of that street where the grander residences of Fred Astaire and Danny Kaye flourish with their rolling lawns, tennis courts, swimming pools and private cinemas. By Hollywood standards, the Finch house was a tiny house with a tiny garden and no swimming pool. By English standards, it might, with perfect justice, have been described as a *cottage*, that dreaded word that had been so associated in Peter's past with stifling domesticity, that had evoked in him nightmare visions of women sighting these abodes and, "instantly displaying all the alarming characteristics of mother-birds" as they laid plans to trap him in "these rose-covered nests while they brought back refrigerators and carpets in their beaks". Peter bought the house and paid the entire amount at once in a lump sum. Not for him those mortgages with their consuming interest rates.

As we have seen, Peter had never had a normal relationship with money. In his Australian youth it had slipped through his open fingers with abnormal speed. Now in his Hollywood middle age, it stayed abnormally tight within his closed fists. He was, in fact, well-known in the movie colony for being a close man with a buck; a man who counted every dime; a man who had never been known to pick up a cheque that could not be charged to the studio he was working for. His good friend Radie Harris, the columnist, had learned to say, "Is this on you or on MGM?" before ordering a glass of champagne. Nor did he like to see his friends being too free with their dollars. Money had become something of a mania with him and even Eletha teased him about it.

Yet: "In the matter of getting their new home fixed up," says Mike Maslansky, who was to be Peter's publicist for the next six months, "Peter gave Eletha full rein. But Eletha never told any of the workmen concerned with the renovations that she was Mrs Peter Finch, and Peter was fond of saying that all of them probably thought she was the maid coming around to oversee the work."

This "maid" motif was a theme that ran throughout Peter's and Eletha's life together. Remarks about Eletha being mistaken for the maid were a common topic of conversation both with their friends and in the press.

"I bought Eletha a mink coat," Peter said in London, "so that when she goes flat-hunting they don't think she's the maid." "I bought Eletha a Mercedes," he said in Jamaica, "so that the neighbours won't think she's the maid."

The interesting thing about Peter coming out with these statements is that whatever initial hurt it may have caused them — if indeed it ever did — was quickly replaced by their satisfaction in exposing the world's snobbishness and bigotry and at the same time turning it to their own advantage. For, they reasoned, if the workmen on the house found out that Eletha was the wife of a movie star and not the maid, their prices would have doubled.

The film Peter chose to do after *Network* was *Raid on Entebbe* for American TV starring Charles Bronson, Martin Balsam, Sylvia Sydney and Horst Buchholz as well as himself, and he went into it the day after he finished *Network*. It was the "factional" recreation of the thrilling Israeli rescue of aeroplane hostages from terrorists in Uganda. In something of a repetition of the Oscar Wilde situation the film had to be made fast and the actors had to work long and hard as there were at least two other Entebbes hot on their trail. So although Peter was only employed for three weeks, he was working as much as fourteen hours a day. And though the circumstances were somewhat reminiscent of the Oscar Wilde race, Peter was fifteen years older and fifteen years less resilient. He was nevertheless so excellent as the Israeli Prime Minister Rabin, who must make the final decision as to whether it is worth chancing the raid, that his performance elicited the highest praise from political correspondent Daniel Schorr in *The New York Times*, who said that forever thereafter Yitzak Rabin would be confused in his mind with Peter Finch.

Very soon after the completion of *Network*, at the beginning of August to be precise, the possibility of all four of its stars winning Academy Awards began to present itself strongly in their thoughts as well as in the thoughts of everyone connected with the film.

Peter had always taken awards in his stride — perhaps, one might say, because they had always been showered upon him. Liv Ullman remembers the first day of shooting on *Lost Horizon* which was also the day of the Academy Awards for 1972 with Peter one of the two strongest contenders for his performance in *Sunday, Bloody Sunday*. She remembers it particularly well because she observed Peter going about his business as usual: the best prepared and hardest working actor of them all. And when asked whether he did not want to be let off early, he merely said, "Why? No one else is getting off."

Peter's stand on doing film publicity and going on publicity junkets was well-known. He despised it. He had never had a press agent in his life. During *Network*, however, MGM and Barry Krost strongly urged him to get one. He agreed reluctantly because they suggested Mike Maslansky whom Peter and Eletha liked personally.

In keeping with his new thriftiness, however, Peter would only consent to paying Mike an absolute minimum for his services. "I didn't care about that," said Mike. "It was a great honour to work with Peter. It really was! I'd just started a new firm and he was our first really important client. I'd met Peter and Eletha in Rome through my brother Paul and I thought they were terrific. After that we'd had a couple of lunches and a couple of dinners and we certainly enjoyed one another and I thought she was particularly terrific with him."

But let us return to August. What had happened around that time to reverse Peter's casual, off-hand stand about the awards? What had changed him overnight from reluctant to keen, from keen to determined, and from determined to obsessed with the desire — as Eletha was — to win for that year?

Eletha and Peter had learned through the grapevine that MGM was planning to enter Peter not in the Best Actor category, but in the Best *Supporting* Actor category.

Peter's blood was up. Howard Beale a supporting part? In a word, *no*. Not for that had he experienced the thrill of his genius which had lain idle for so many years, springing forth exultant and victorious! Not for that had he, for once in his life, exceeded his expectations in performance! Not for that! Not to be fobbed off as a *supporting* player! He wanted that Oscar and he wanted it for Best Actor. He wanted it not only for the recognition of his acting ability from his peers but for the recognition of himself. It was to be a vindication of his whole life and of his beliefs.

MGM must be made to put him in his rightful category and Peter must show them that he was prepared to fight for Best Actor. More — that he was determined to win.

Says Mike Maslansky, "Peter wanted to win that Oscar. It was an obsession with him. And we went to all lengths, let me tell you, during the period I was engaged. Between August and January, Peter must have done three hundred interviews with foreign and domestic media — radio, television, the works. Nobody, but *nobody* was missed. And there was no one Peter refused to talk to. He was a wonderful interviewee. Funny and frank with all these people and always with lots of good stories."

Mike had become infected with Peter's Academy Award fever

and spent every possible moment with him. "On the few occasions that I did pass on an interview that was less important than another to someone who worked for me, I detected a note of querulousness in Peter's voice when I heard from him the next day, so I made pretty sure that at least in all the key things that had to be done, I was on hand," he said.

Though no one has yet been able to figure out whether Academy Awards are based on merit, money or the popularity of a particular actor at the time — there are just too many variables — the short answer a film studio would give you is: popularity based on publicity.

And so Peter was off: not, as might be thought from the time, care and effort spent on the campaign in dogged pursuit of some high political office, but for a gold-plated thirteen-inch statuette of a faceless man holding a sword and standing on a reel of film which was christened by a film librarian who had exclaimed upon seeing it, "My God, it looks just like my Uncle Oscar!" He found himself committed to a mad schedule of three hundred interviews in six months. This included two promotional trips to New York for which he refused to take aeroplanes and instead travelled across country and back by train while Mike and Eletha flew.

Peter was mostly in high spirits during these trips. There was, however, one upsetting incident that occurred in October in New York in the Finches' suite at the Pierre that caught Mike completely off-guard and perturbed him for a very long time. He says, "Peter and I were sitting there and I can't honestly say what brought it on — whether something had made him angry, or he was exhausted, or he wasn't feeling well, but suddenly out of nowhere it seemed to me, he turned white with rage and then launched into this overwrought speech about the evils of the business world and how the business people in the movies corrupt the artists. Then it was all over and never referred to again."

But these publicity junkets to New York also had their compensations for Peter. One compensation was seeing old theatre friends; another was seeing new theatre productions on Broadway. He was able to enjoy these pleasures to the maximum degree when he visited the smash-hit revival of Kaufman and Ferber's *The Royal Family* starring his old film-mate, Rosemary Harris, whom he had helped and encouraged through *The Shiralee*.

Mike Maslansky, in the early days of his friendship with Peter, had been struck by how untypical a movie star he was — how he lacked *that* kind of an ego and *that* kind of concern for his image — and he was amused to find that as Peter progressed in his campaign, he was beginning to remind Mike not a little of the other movie stars he had dealt with. Especially in the matter of the Actor's Vanity.

Bursting with enthusiasm the day after he saw *The Royal Family,* Peter told Mike he intended to do it on the stage in London. "But what part will you play?" Mike made the mistake of asking.

Peter just looked at him. "Tony Cavendish, of course," he replied a trifle coldly.

"Oh, of course," said Mike quickly, thinking to himself: but Peter's sixty and Tony Cavendish is at *most* thirty-five.

"Yes," Peter went on happily lost in his dream, "I'll do it! I'll do it with Maggie ... or with Glenda ... "

And then Mike had another thought: Peter Finch and Maggie Smith in *The Royal Family*? Or, Peter Finch and Glenda Jackson in *The Royal Family* in the West End? Hmm ... Well, why not! Certainly Peter had never stopped getting stage offers from England.

What did Peter Finch have to say three hundred times over in interviews? He talked about his early days in the Buddhist monastery, his middle years in the Australian outback and his not-too-distant days Hellraising and how those had never really existed — except in the eyes of the Press. He was, after all, and always had been, a one-woman man. He talked domestically about Eletha and the children and occasionally he mentioned remembered remarks of Vivien Leigh's or reminiscences of his grandmother. But there were no more *New York Times* revelations about his origins. His father was George Ingle Finch, the mountaineer.

Mainly, of course, he talked about *Network*. He talked of how much he approved of its anti-violence, anti-materialism message. He did not talk about its anti-the-big-publicity-hype message.

That summer, before launching himself on his campaign to win his Oscar, Peter lunched at Barry Krost's house with Eletha, John Osborne and Jill Bennett. As they sat in the sun on the patio, Jill studied him. Peter and Jill's long friendship had begun during her West End début playing the maid in *Captain Carvello* ("Larry was the director and he played the maid so much better than I did I was sure he was going to sack me.")

It had been three years now since she had seen Peter, since he and Eletha had come to her dressing-room after seeing her in *Private*

Lives. Jill says of that occasion, "He stood in the doorway, welling. He was awfully good at welling and so am I. In fact, I don't think I've ever been with Peter in my life for any length of time without the two of us bursting into tears at some point going down memory lane. So there he stood in the door of my dressing-room that evening, just welling for a moment. And it communicated itself to me! I felt, this is The Great Love of My Life. He wasn't, of course. Not even one of them.

"It's difficult for me to stay in a dressing-room after a show for half an hour, but the three of us sat there talking for three and a half hours; Peter and I talking and crying about old times, and how he wanted to come back to London and act again on the stage, and all the plays we wanted to do together, and 'Do you remember when ... ?' A couple of times he got me mixed up with some other actress, but I didn't like to say ... "

Looking at Peter now, sitting on the patio of Barry Krost's house, Jill thought of the first time she'd met Peter and the impact he had made on her, "with his extraordinary lolloping walk, his pigeon chest, his beautiful hands — like a girl's, so delicate and narrow, and his face like that of some elegant animal."

Then she saw him as he was now. "He looked outrageously beautiful as only he could — that beautiful liquid face — but he just didn't look himself. He was very quiet and we didn't talk much. And then I noticed that *his clothes didn't seem to fit him.*" And all at once Jill's skin began to crawl and the horrifying thought lurched into her mind and took root, *this man is going to die!*

Soon after she and John Osborne left, she had to say it out loud, "Peter is going to *die!*"

"Rubbish," said Osborne. "What makes you think that?"

"I don't think it, I *know* it," answered Jill. "He looks just like Godfrey Tearle looked before he died ... His clothes ... they seemed to be falling away from him."

The Finches' good friend Jill Saint Amant had been away from California most of that autumn and had not seen Peter until she dined with them in November. Afterwards she left puzzled and troubled. Peter was not looking well. It was not anything she could exactly put her finger on because they'd all spent a happy evening together, but he looked somehow ... frail. And it seemed to her that his skin had a sort of pearly blue tinge.

This bluish tint to the complexion is, perhaps, a symptom only recognizable to people familiar with heart conditions.

Mike Maslansky: "How much was Peter aware, as he must have been, that he had a bad heart? I don't know. He never mentioned it to me. I do know that one of the things one does to exercise a bad heart is to walk all the time. And Peter walked constantly. He walked everywhere. When he was doing *Entebbe* he walked for miles every day from Sunset Towers to Twentieth Century. But he looked — I thought he had looked for the six months I was working for him — *awful*. His colour was bad, his skin was pasty looking. He wasn't drinking. He only fell off the wagon a couple of times. One time was the night of the first preview of *Network* at MGM and he got pissed. Mostly he drank Perrier or Club Soda and Lime. I have no idea whether he had any intimation of his imminent death. I don't know if he refused to see a doctor but I do know that he did not believe in them.

"Eletha's obsession at the time was to get the house all fixed up by New Year's Eve ready to move into and she accomplished it. The Finches moved in on New Year's Eve. She's done the house up beautifully. It's in various shades of white and beige with some of Peter's paintings hung on the walls.

"The evening before Peter died he was in terrific spirits. He had just taped his guest appearance on Johnny Carson's *Tonight* show and he was marvellous in it. He talked about his eccentric grandmother in Paris and her harp. And there was some comedian on the show who did a long monologue about death which Peter and I talked about that night when we were driving back to his home after the show. And Peter talked about death, saying how fitting and funny a subject it could be for a comic monologue because death was, in the ceremonies and incidents surrounding it, 'a hilarious thing'. That is what he said. 'A hilarious thing'. That's a direct quote."

CHAPTER 33

Winning the Oscar

The next day, Peter was to appear on the *Good Morning, America* TV hour. He rose early, dressed, spoke on the phone to Mike Maslansky, kissed Eletha and walked down to the Beverly Hills Hotel to meet Sidney Lumet who was to be on the show with him.

It was under a mile from his house to the hotel, a short walkabout for Peter and one he had often undertaken. Down the hill went Pidgifif for the last time.

To his death.

For a man who loved life so much, who so much enjoyed the present moment, it may be thought odd that he had often speculated on how he would spend his last days. Or perhaps that was also part of his ability to enjoy.

We have seen that he once wished to spend those days with Vivien Leigh, and before that it had been with Tamara, "bound and entwined by our mutual love of Chopin waltzes, the surge of feeling at an encounter with some historic spot, the vital words of a poet, the wisdom of philosophies ... till time withers us as gently as old autumn leaves and blows us gaily into the dark pathways of after-life." When married to Yolande, he told Douglas Keay he foresaw himself ending his days on his own plot of land in Italy. "By then the rebelliousness in my heart will have sunk below the rim. I see myself sitting in the sun, a straw hat on my head and a donkey grazing nearby to remind me of my foolishness ... an old man seeking the shade ... "

He should have known better. He should have known he was an actor born and would die an actor's death, in the thick of it with his boots on, at the right place at the right time. He was to die in the lobby of the Beverly Hills Hotel before going on television to get votes for himself for his finest performance!

At nine a.m. that morning Peter collapsed in a chair in the lobby. He was rushed in an ambulance to the University of California Hospital and at 10.19 declared dead of a heart attack.

As he knew he would, Peter Finch won his Oscar although he was not there to receive it. In his place, Eletha stood in front of the Academy Award audience and gave a graceful speech and everyone wept.

But I was following the awards on a television set and had begun weeping before that, had begun weeping when the film clip of Peter as the mad prophet came on the screen. Watching him, listening to the beautiful voice weave its magic of cadence and phrasing and rhythm, shimmering with colour but water-clear in meaning, and connected, as Beale put it, "to all living things, to flowers, birds, to all the animals of the world, and even to some great unseen living force", I found myself crying. And those other strangely matching words and harmonies I had been searching for finally spun upwards in snatches surfacing to my consciousness mixing with Peter's own "... a savage place! as holy and enchanted ... and from this chasm, with ceaseless turmoil seething ... huge fragments vaulted like rebounding hail ... through wood and dale the sacred river ran, then reached the caverns measureless to man and sank in tumult to a lifeless ocean ...

And now! The mingled measure from the fountains and the cave! A miracle of rare device!

And all who heard should see them there,
And all should cry, Beware! Beware!
His flashing eyes, his floating hair!
Weave a circle round him thrice,
And close your eyes with holy dread,
For he on honey-dew hath fed,
And drunk the milk of Paradise.

Those other words were the words of Kubla Khan! Words? *Feelings!* Those seething rhapsodic risings and fallings of feelings that Peter Finch was matching with his own suddenly burst forth.

I watched in tears as Peter stood at the brink of greatness and death and triumphantly crossed the threshold.

Epilogue

So Peter did not go out like a clown.

Or did he?

The night before he died he had talked to Mike of the comedian's monologue about death on the *Tonight* show. He had approved of it. He had said how funny and fitting a subject for comedy death was with all its attendant ceremonies and incidents. He had said that death was "a hilarious thing".

As always with Peter Finch, tears mingle with laughter and laughter mingles with tears.

A few years before Peter's death, Eletha had been converted to Catholicism and so Peter Finch, the lifelong Buddhist, Peter Finch, who had said, "I find the symbol of a man dying on a cross a ghastly symbol for a religion and that of a man sitting under a bo tree becoming enlightened, a beautiful one," was given a Catholic funeral service at the Church of The Good Shepherd in Los Angeles and then buried in Hollywood Memorial Cemetery, a non-denominational cemetery off Santa Monica Boulevard. The internment was conducted by a Catholic priest. Peter's grave was in a pretty plot near a kind of man-made lake or moat, facing Tyrone Power's grave. Mourners noticed that his adopted son, Christopher, was the most outwardly broken up of the family.

In the shocking suddenness of Peter's death, Eletha's grief, as the ineffable reality of it awakened hourly in her consciousness, was pitiful to see; and friends worried that it might prove too much for her to bear.

Ever since she had known Peter, she had loved him. He had always been her first thought and now that he was gone he was her only thought. Like many another sorrow-blinded widow, she yearned to follow him and both comforted and tormented herself with fantasies of ways to do it soon.

But not for her the cowardly passivity of the overdose. She

imagined herself sitting on his grave and allowing a poisoned snake to bite her, or of getting on the next aeroplane and willing it to crash by her magic powers. But life was too strong in her and instead she visited his grave daily and read aloud to him from the *Hollywood Reporter*.

The puzzle of Peter's identity which had so persistently confused and haunted him for so much of his life — indeed all of it — seemed to pursue him impiously beyond the grave.

Over the breakfast table on 15 January 1977, his many fans and acquaintances were startled to read in the august London *Times* the following obituary: "Peter Finch, whose real name was William Mitchell ... "

And, though still recovering from the sad shock of Peter's death, his multitudes of mates must have involuntarily let out groans of despair as their eyes fell on those words.

William Mitchell? *William Mitchell*, indeed! Really, this was too bloody much! And how like bloody Finch! Really how could anyone have ever been so simple as to have believed one *single* word that bloody monster, that bloody angel, had ever said?

Who then was "William Mitchell"?

William Mitchell is a Canadian actor whose low, growly voice is one of the best known voices on English TV commercials. This burly actor, one night on the town in Rome with his mate Peter Finch, found that his fists had been too fast for his good sense and that before he knew it he was in the midst of a barroom brawl. Not many minutes after, along with his peace-loving mate Finchie, he was being hauled off by the Roman carabinieri to the police station. "I hope you've got your passport, mate — " said Peter as they were being dragged along, "they always ask for it." Unfortunately, Mitchell did not, though Peter had his. So William Mitchell appeared in front of the Roman law as Peter Finch and that made Peter Finch, William Mitchell. The whole incident could not have taken an hour and the real mystery is how it ever insinuated itself into the files of *The Times* in the first place.

There was no headstone on Peter's grave. It had all happened so quickly that there had not been time. And then afterwards, Eletha began worrying about him out in the rain and the cold all the time.

So in 1979, on the second anniversary of his death, Eletha had Peter dug up and reburied in one of the huge rococo mausoleums in the same cemetery. This time he faces Rudolph Valentino.

Oh, poor Pidgifif! Will he never Rest In Peace?

Would he ever want to?

List of Films made by Peter Finch

EUREKA STOCKADE (US title *Massacre Hill*)
UK 1949
Director: Harry Watt
Cast: Chips Rafferty, Jane Barrett, Peter Finch, Ralph Truman, Gordon Jackson
Played: John Humffray

TRAIN OF EVENTS
UK 1949
Director: Basil Dearden (of Finch's episode)
Cast: Valerie Hobson, Mary Morris, Peter Finch, John Clements
Played: Philip Mason

THE WOODEN HORSE
UK 1950
Director: Jack Lee
Cast: Leo Genn, David Tomlinson, Peter Finch
Played: RAAF officer

THE MINIVER STORY
UK 1950
Director: H. C. Potter
Cast: Greer Garson, Walter Pidgeon, Peter Finch
Played: Polish officer

THE STORY OF ROBIN HOOD AND HIS MERRIE MEN
UK 1952
Director: Ken Annakin
Cast: Richard Todd, Peter Finch, Joan Rice, Hubert Gregg
Played: The Sheriff of Nottingham

THE STORY OF GILBERT AND SULLI-VAN (US title *The Great Gilbert and Sullivan*)
UK 1953
Director: Sidney Gilliat
Cast: Robert Morley, Maurice Evans, Peter Finch, Eileen Herlie, Dinah Sheridan, Isabel Dean
Played: Rupert D'Oyly Carte

THE HEART OF THE MATTER
UK 1953
Director: George More O'Ferrall
Cast: Trevor Howard, Elizabeth Allan, Maria Schell
Played: Father Rank

ELEPHANT WALK
USA 1953/4
Director: William Dieterle
Cast: Elizabeth Taylor, Peter Finch, Dana Andrews
Played: John Wiley

FATHER BROWN (US title *The Detective*)
UK 1954
Director: Robert Hamer
Cast: Alec Guinness, Peter Finch, Joan Greenwood
Played: Flambeau

MAKE ME AN OFFER
UK 1954
Director: Cyril Frankel
Cast: Peter Finch, Adrienne Corri, Rosalie Crutchley
Played: Charlie

THE DARK AVENGER (US title *The Warriors*)
Director: Henry Levin
Cast: Errol Flynn, Joanne Dru, Peter Finch
Played: Count De Ville

PASSAGE HOME
UK 1955
Director: Roy Baker
Cast: Peter Finch, Diane Cilento, Anthony Steel, Bryan Forbes, Gordon Jackson
Played: Captain "Lucky" Ryland

JOSEPHINE AND MEN
UK 1955
Director: Roy Boulting, Frank Harvey, Nigel Balchin

Cast: Peter Finch, Glynis Johns, Jack Buchanan, Donald Sinden
Played: David Hewer

SIMON AND LAURA
UK 1955
Director: Muriel Box
Cast: Peter Finch, Kay Kendall, Ian Carmichael
Played: Simon Foster

A TOWN LIKE ALICE
UK 1956
Director: Jack Lee
Cast: Peter Finch, Virginia McKenna
Played: Joe Harman
British Film Academy Award for the Best Actor, 1957

THE BATTLE OF THE RIVER PLATE
(US title *The Pursuit of the Graf Spee*)
Director: Michael Powell and Emric Pressburger
Cast: Peter Finch, Anthony Quayle
Played: Captain Langsdorff
Royal Film Performance, 1956

THE SHIRALEE
UK 1957
Director: Leslie Norman
Cast: Peter Finch, Dana Wilson, Elizabeth Sellars, Rosemary Harris
Played: Jim Macauley

ROBBERY UNDER ARMS
UK 1957
Director: Jack Lee
Cast: Peter Finch, Maureen Swanson, Ronald Lewis, David McCallum, Jill Ireland
Played: Captain Starlight

WINDOM'S WAY
UK 1957
Director: Ronald Neame
Cast: Peter Finch, Mary Ure, Michael Hordern
Played: Alec Windom

THE NUN'S STORY
USA 1959

Director: Fred Zinnemann
Cast: Audrey Hepburn, Edith Evans, Peter Finch, Peggy Ashcroft
Played: Dr Fortunati

OPERATION AMSTERDAM
UK 1958
Director: Michael McCarthy
Cast: Peter Finch, Eva Bartok, Tony Britton, Alexander Knox
Played: Jan Smit

KIDNAPPED
UK 1959/60
Director: Robert Stevenson
Cast: Peter Finch, James MacArthur
Played: Alan Breck Stewart

THE SINS OF RACHEL CADE
USA 1960
Director: Gordon Douglas
Cast: Angie Dickinson, Peter Finch, Roger Moore
Played: Colonel Henry Derode

THE TRIALS OF OSCAR WILDE (US title *The Man with the Green Carnation*)
UK 1960
Directed and written by: Ken Hughes
Cast: Peter Finch, Yvonne Mitchell, John Fraser, James Mason
Played: Oscar Wilde
British Film Academy Award for the Best Actor, 1961
Moscow Festival, Award for the Best Actor, 1961

NO LOVE FOR JOHNNIE
UK 1961
Director: Ralph Thomas
Cast: Peter Finch, Billie Whitelaw, Mary Peach, Stanley Holloway, Donald Pleasence
Played: Johnnie Byrne
British Film Academy Award for the Best Actor, 1962
Berlin Festival, Silver Bear Award for the Best Actor, 1962

I THANK A FOOL
UK 1962
Director: Robert Stevens

Cast: Susan Hayward, Diane Cilento, Peter Finch
Played: Stephen Dane

IN THE COOL OF THE DAY
UK 1962
Director: Robert Stevens
Cast: Peter Finch, Jane Fonda, Angela Lansbury
Played: Murray Logan

GIRL WITH GREEN EYES
UK 1963
Director: Desmond Davis
Cast: Peter Finch, Rita Tushingham, Lynn Redgrave
Played: Eugene Gaillard

THE PUMPKIN EATER
UK 1963
Director: Jack Clayton
Cast: Anne Bancroft, Peter Finch, James Mason
Played: Jake Armitage
British Film Academy Award for the best screenplay, 1964

JUDITH
USA 1965
Director: Daniel Mann
Cast: Peter Finch, Sophia Loren
Played: Aaron Stein

THE FLIGHT OF THE PHOENIX
USA 1965
Director: Robert Aldrich
Cast: James Stewart, Richard Attenborough, Peter Finch, Ronald Fraser, Hardy Kruger
Played: Captain Harris

10.30 P.M. SUMMER
USA/Spain 1966
Director: Jules Dassin
Cast: Melina Mercouri, Peter Finch, Romy Schneider
Played: Paul

FAR FROM THE MADDING CROWD
UK 1967
Director: John Schlesinger

Cast: Julie Christie, Peter Finch, Terence Stamp, Alan Bates
Played: William Boldwood
British Film Academy Award for the Best Actor, 1968

THE LEGEND OF LYLAH CLARE
USA 1967
Director: Robert Aldrich
Cast: Kim Novak, Peter Finch, Ernest Borgnine
Played: Lewis Zarkin

THE RED TENT
USSR/Italy 1969
Director: Mikhail Kalatozov
Cast: Peter Finch, Sean Connery, Claudia Cardinale, Hardy Kruger
Played: General Umberto Nobile

SUNDAY, BLOODY SUNDAY
UK 1970
Director: John Schlesinger
Cast: Peter Finch, Glenda Jackson, Murray Head
Played: Dr Daniel Hirsch
Society of Film and Television Awards for the Best Actor, 1971
Voted Best Actor by the National Society of Film Critics USA, 1971
Runner-up for American Academy Award, 1971

SOMETHING TO HIDE
UK 1971
Director: Alastair Reid
Cast: Peter Finch, Linda Hayden, Shelley Winters, Colin Blakeley
Played: Harry

ENGLAND MADE ME
UK 1972
Director: Peter Duffell
Cast: Peter Finch, Michael York, Hildegard Neil, Michael Hordern
Played: Erich Krogh

LOST HORIZON
USA 1972
Director: Charles Jarrott
Cast: Peter Finch, Liv Ullmann, Sir John

Gielgud, Charles Boyer, Michael York
Played: Robert Conway
Royal Film Performance, 1973

BEQUEST TO THE NATION (US title *The Nelson Affair*)
UK 1973
Director: James Celland Jones
Cast: Peter Finch, Glenda Jackson, Anthony Quayie
Played: Lord Nelson

THE ABDICATION
UK 1974
Director: Anthony Harvey
Cast: Liv Ullman, Peter Finch and Cyril Cusack
Played: Cardinal Azzolino

NETWORK
USA 1976
Director: Sidney Lumet
Cast: Faye Dunaway, Peter Finch, William Holden, Robert Duvall, Beatrice Straight
Played: Howard Beale
American Academy Award for the Best Actor, 1977
Hollywood's Golden Globe Award for the Best Actor, 1977
British Academy of Film and Television Arts Award for the Best Actor, 1977

RAID ON ENTEBBE
USA 1976 (Television in the USA, Cinema abroad)
Director: Irvin Kirshner
Cast: Charles Bronson, Peter Finch, Horst Buchholz, Martin Balsam, Sylvia Sidney
Played: Yitzhak Rabin

Peter Finch's Australian Films
THE MAGIC SHOES
Australia 1935
Director: Claude Fleming

DAD AND DAVE COME TO TOWN (UK title *The Rudd Family Goes To Town*)
Australia 1938
Director: Ken G. Hall

MR CHEDWORTH STEPS OUT
Australia 1939
Director: Ken G. Hall

THE POWER AND THE GLORY
Australia 1941
Director: Noel Monkman

RATS OF TOBRUK
Australia 1944
Director: Charles Chauvel

RED SKY AT MORNING (Re-titled *Escape At Dawn,* 1950)
Australia 1945
Director: J. Hartney Arthur

A SON IS BORN
Australia 1946
Director: Eric Porter

List of Plays

Daphne Laureola, 1949
Damascus Blade, 1950
Captain Carvello, 1950
Point of Departure, 1951
Othello, 1951
The Happy Time, 1952
Romeo and Juliet, 1952
Two for the Seesaw, 1958
The Seagull, 1964

Index